FLORIDA

Real Estate Exam Manual for Sales Associates and Brokers

41st Edition | Linda L. Crawford

Dearborn™
Real Estate Education

This publication is designed to provide accurate and authoritative information in regard to the subject matter covered. It is sold with the understanding that the publisher is not engaged in rendering legal, accounting, or other professional advice. If legal advice or other expert assistance is required, the services of a competent professional should be sought.

President: Dr. Andrew Temte
Executive Director, Real Estate Education: Melissa Kleeman-Moy
Development Editor: Rosita Hernandez

FLORIDA REAL ESTATE EXAM MANUAL FOR SALES ASSOCIATES AND BROKERS 41ST EDITION

Published by DF Institute, Inc., d/b/a Dearborn Real Estate Education
332 Front St. S., Suite 501
La Crosse, WI 54601

Printed in the United States of America

First revision, March 2018

ISBN: 978-1-4754-5837-4

CONTENTS

How to Use This Manual vii
Successful Exam-Taking Strategies xi

KEY POINT REVIEW 1

Real Estate Law, Florida Real Estate License Law 1

SECTION 1 Real Estate License Law and Qualifications for Licensure 1
(See Unit 2 in *Florida Real Estate Principles, Practices & Law* and Unit 1 in *Florida Real Estate Broker's Guide*) 1

SECTION 2 Real Estate License Law and Commission Rules 9
(See Unit 3 in *Florida Real Estate Principles, Practices & Law* and Unit 1 in *Florida Real Estate Broker's Guide*) 9

SECTION 3 Authorized Relationships, Duties, and Disclosure 15
(See Unit 4 in *Florida Principles, Practices & Law* and Unit 10 in *Florida Real Estate Broker's Guide*) 15

SECTION 4 Real Estate Brokerage Activities and Procedures 21
(See Unit 5 in *Florida Real Estate Principles, Practices & Law* and Units 2 and 4 in *Florida Real Estate Broker's Guide*) 21

SECTION 5 Violations of License Law, Penalties, and Procedures 33
(See Unit 6 in *Florida Real Estate Principles, Practices & Law* and Unit 5 in *Florida Real Estate Broker's Guide*) 33

KEY POINT REVIEW 39

General Real Estate Law 39

SECTION 6 Federal and State Laws Pertaining to Real Estate 39
(See Unit 7 in *Florida Real Estate Principles, Practices & Law* and Units 2, 12, 17, and 18 in *Florida Real Estate Broker's Guide*) 39

SECTION 7 Property Rights: Estates and Tenancies, Condominiums, Cooperatives, and Time-Sharing 45
(See Unit 8 in *Florida Real Estate Principles, Practices & Law* and Units 11, 12, and 18 in *Florida Real Estate Broker's Guide*) 45

SECTION 8 Title, Deeds, and Ownership Restrictions 51
(See Unit 9 in *Florida Real Estate Principles, Practices & Law* and Units 15 and 18 in *Florida Real Estate Broker's Guide*) 51

SECTION 9 Real Estate Contracts 59

(See Unit 11 in *Florida Real Estate Principles, Practices & Law* and Unit 11 in *Florida Real Estate Broker's Guide*) 59

SECTION 10 Planning, Zoning, and Environmental Hazards 65

(See Unit 19 in *Florida Real Estate Principles, Practices & Law* and Unit 16 in *Florida Real Estate Broker's Guide*) 65

KEY POINT REVIEW 71

Real Estate Principles and Practices 71

SECTION 11 The Real Estate Business 71

(See Unit 1 in *Florida Real Estate Principles, Practices & Law*) 71

SECTION 12 Legal Descriptions 75

(See Unit 10 in *Florida Real Estate Principles, Practices & Law*) 75

SECTION 13 Residential Mortgages 79

(See Unit 12 in *Florida Real Estate Principles, Practices & Law* and Unit 12 in *Florida Real Estate Broker's Guide*) 79

SECTION 14 Types of Mortgages and Sources of Financing 85

(See Unit 13 in *Florida Real Estate Principles, Practices & Law*) 85

SECTION 15 Real Estate Appraisal 95

(See Unit 16 in *Florida Real Estate Principles, Practices & Law* and Units 6–8 in *Florida Real Estate Broker's Guide*) 95

SECTION 16 Real Estate Investments and Business Opportunity Brokerage 103

(See Unit 17 in *Florida Real Estate Principles, Practices & Law* and Units 9 and 15 in *Florida Real Estate Broker's Guide*) 103

SECTION 17 Taxes Affecting Real Estate 109

(See Unit 18 in *Florida Real Estate Principles, Practices & Law* and Unit 14 in *Florida Real Estate Broker's Guide*) 109

SECTION 18 Real Estate Markets and Analysis 115

(See Unit 15 in *Florida Real Estate Principles, Practices & Law*) 115

SECTION 19 Real Estate–Related Computations and Closing of Transactions 117

(See Unit 14 in *Florida Real Estate Principles, Practices & Law* and Unit 13 in *Florida Real Estate Broker's Guide*) 117

SAMPLE EXAM QUESTIONS 123

Real Estate Law, Florida Real Estate License Law Sections 123

General Real Estate Law Sections 135

Real Estate Principles and Practices Sections 149

Math Problems 165

Broker Investment Problems 175

Closing Disclosure Questions for Broker Candidates 177

PRACTICE EXAM 1 179

100 Multiple-Choice Question Exam 1 179

PRACTICE EXAM 2 197

100 Multiple-Choice Question Exam 2 197

ANSWER SHEETS

Practice Exam 1 Answer Sheet 215

Practice Exam 2 Answer Sheet 217

ANSWER KEY WITH EXPLANATIONS 219

Sample Exam Questions 221

Real Estate Law, Florida Real Estate License Law Sections 219

General Real Estate Law Sections 224

Real Estate Principles and Practices Sections 231

Math Problems 239

Broker Investment Problems 244

Closing Disclosure Questions for Broker Candidates 245

Math Cross-Reference Key 247

Practice Exam 1 249

Practice Exam 2 255

Index 261

Glossary Flashcards 263

HOW TO USE THIS MANUAL

The *Florida Real Estate Exam Manual for Sales Associates and Brokers* (*Exam Manual*) provides a concise, focused approach to preparing for the Florida real estate license exams, and is designed to aid both sales associate students and broker students. You can review key concepts in a relatively short span of time and work through a variety of practice questions. The State of Florida does *not* use national real estate exams. The license exams are developed by the Bureau of Education and Testing within the Florida Department of Business and Professional Regulation (DBPR). The material in this book is specifically designed to prepare you for Florida's license exams.

The Key Point Reviews contain the most important concepts explained in the textbook, *Florida Real Estate Principles, Practices & Law (PP&L)*, and will reinforce the information learned in the sales associate course. Sales associate *and* broker candidates are tested on material from the sales associate prelicense course, so it is important to study this material to prepare for the license exam.

It may seem a little odd that the Key Point Reviews are not in numerical order. Instead, we have grouped the reviews by topics: real estate law, Florida real estate license law, general real estate law, and real estate principles and practices. The units listed in the Contents refer to the units of *PP&L*. Because a good portion of the state exam concerns Florida license law, we have grouped these units together to make exam preparation easier.

This edition has been revised to further assist broker candidates with preparing for the broker license exam. The sample exam questions (starting on page 123) indicate the unit in the sales associate textbook, *PP&L*, that corresponds to the sample questions. We have also included the corresponding units in the broker textbook, *Florida Real Estate Broker's Guide*. If there is a set of questions that are particularly troubling for you, refer to the corresponding units in *PP&L* and the units in *Broker's Guide* for additional study. This edition also features math problems exclusively designed for broker candidates. Broker candidates should be proficient in solving *all* of these math problems, including the investment problems that follow the general math problems.

SUCCESSFUL EXAM-TAKING STRATEGIES

This section of the book lays out a strategy for answering multiple-choice questions. You need a proven strategy (or plan) for taking and passing the exam on the first try. Part of a successful strategy is learning how to become "test wise." It also involves understanding a test writer's objectives. If you understand how questions are constructed and are familiar with the subjects that are tested, you are well on your way to reaching your goal on exam day.

KEY POINT REVIEWS

The key point reviews are a no-nonsense approach to reviewing the most important concepts in *PP&L*. The key point reviews are organized into three parts. The first two parts cover Florida real estate license law and general real estate law (units 2–9, 11, and 19). Sales associate candidates *and* broker candidates need to study these units carefully to prepare for the state license exams! Part three covers real estate principles and practices (units 1, 10, and 12–18). The principles and practices units cover primarily sales associate material. However, broker candidates are tested on sales associate material. Broker candidates should study all of the material in this manual to properly prepare for their state license exam.

Each section in this manual begins with a Key Term Review. Each key term features a straightforward definition. Terminology is a big part of testing! Study each of the terms carefully. The glossary in the back of the book provides the key terms in one handy location for review.

Key Concepts follows Key Terms. Key Concepts lists the most important concepts found in each unit. The background material and explanations have been omitted and just the highlights are presented here. If a concept seems foreign to you, go back to *PP&L* for a complete explanation. The purpose here is to help you focus on the exam and bring the most important concepts in each unit together in a simple, straightforward review.

At the end of some of the sections in this book you will find Important Dates and Time Periods to Remember. Some of the license exam questions require you to recall a certain number of days (for example, a licensee has just 10 days to notify the DBPR of a change in mailing address). The most important dates and time periods are featured at the end of each section (if applicable). These time periods should be memorized as part of the exam preparation process.

Important Formulas to Remember appears at the end of the real estate principles and practices sections described earlier. Many of the types of math calculations that may appear on your exam are featured. The formula and a sample problem have been worked for you. Be sure to master the various types of math calculations. If math is not your "bag," so to speak, consider purchasing a copy of the author's *Real Estate Math: What You Need to Know*, published by Dearborn™ Real Estate Education. It provides numerous practice problems with the solutions so that you can study step-by-step how to perform each type of math problem.

PRACTICE QUESTIONS

This section of the manual is composed of sample exam questions and practice exams totaling 711 practice questions. The first part consists of multiple-choice questions on license law followed by general real estate law. Sales associate candidates *and* broker candidates will benefit from studying the law questions. The practice questions use the same type of item format that is used on the license exam. Many of the practice questions are difficult. Do not let that deter you. You want to be prepared for whatever you find on the license exam. The purpose here is to help you stretch. Just can't figure out the answer to a tough practice question? No worries—an explanation to every practice question is in the back of this manual. Reading the explanation to each practice question after you have taken the practice quiz is part of test preparation.

The next part of the practice questions section contains real estate principles and practices multiple-choice questions. The principles and practices questions (as well as the law and math questions) are presented in the same unit sequence as is used in the Key Point Reviews section of the manual.

The last part of this section is made up of math problems. Each math area is represented. A step-by-step math solution is provided for every math calculation. This edition also features math problems exclusively designed for broker candidates. Broker candidates should be proficient in solving all of these math problems, including the broker investment problems on page 177 and closing disclosure questions on page 179.

Practice Exam 1 and Practice Exam 2 are found after the sample question section. These are 100-question practice exams. The exams have been carefully constructed to match the proportion of principles and practices, license law, and math questions on the state license exam. Every effort has been made to ensure that the practice exams are approximately as difficult as the typical Florida state license exam. Use the answer sheets to fill in your answers to the practice exams.

ANSWER KEYS

Answer keys to all the questions appear at the end of this book. The answer keys to the two practice exams are cross-referenced to the appropriate unit in *PP&L*. This will help you focus on those areas where you need additional review. The answer key explanations and solutions provide immediate feedback on what you answered right and wrong on all test items. In addition, a Math Cross-Reference Key lists the math testing areas by name and unit number.

I want to extend a special thank you to Howard Stevens, Instructor, Bob Hogue School of Real Estate, and Michael Stoufer for their valuable contributions to this edition of *Florida Real Estate Exam Manual*.

Every effort has been made to provide you with a great study tool. But success doesn't come easy. It takes hard work and determination. So pull up a chair and get a cup of coffee or your favorite beverage and get to work. I know you can accomplish your goal!

Best of luck,

Linda L. Crawford

November 2017

PURPOSE

The main purpose of this section of the *Exam Manual* is to help you master a strategy for success. A *strategy* is a plan or method for achieving a specific goal. An effective strategy is what successful persons develop and use. This section of the book is designed to show you proven strategies to help you succeed on the Florida real estate license exam.

STATE LICENSE EXAM PROCESS

If you have not already done so, you will need to submit a license application to the Department of Business and Professional Regulation. The application form and information concerning application fees are posted at the real estate page of the DBPR's website at www.myfloridalicense.com/dbpr/re/forms.html. Once your application has been approved by the DBPR, a file of authorized candidates is electronically submitted to the test vendor, Pearson VUE. The test vendor loads the candidate authorization file into its reservation system and then mails authorization letters to each eligible candidate. Upon receipt of the authorization letter, candidates are eligible to reserve an exam date and location through Pearson VUE.

SCHEDULING YOUR TEST DATE

Exam reservations may be made by calling Pearson VUE Customer Care at 888-204-6230 Monday through Friday from 8:00 am to 11:00 pm, Saturday 8:00 am to 5:00 pm, and Sunday from 10:00 am to 4:00 pm (ET). It is recommended that you call Pearson VUE at least five business days before the desired examination date. Reservations are made on a first-come, first-served basis. Candidates will receive a confirmation number at the time of the call. (Jot down the confirmation number because you will need it when you go to the test center.)

Internet reservations may be made at Pearson VUE's website, www.pearsonvue.com. You will need to include a valid email address and a credit card number or electronic check. A reservation confirmation will be returned via email. Examination reservations may be canceled or changed via the Pearson VUE website.

When making your exam reservation, you will be asked to indicate a desired test center location. Test centers are located throughout the state. The license exam may also be taken in any state where the test vendor has a test center. To find the location nearest to you, visit Pearson VUE's website. Addresses, days and hours of operation, and directions to each test site are posted on the website.

Candidates are charged an examination fee payable directly to Pearson VUE. You will be instructed to pay the fee with a major credit card or electronic check at the time you make your test reservation. Examination fees are posted on Pearson VUE's website. Payments are not accepted at the test center. Choose your test date and location carefully. Candidates who wish to cancel or change an examination reservation may do so without penalty up to four business days before the examination. Candidates who are absent from or late for an examination, or who change or cancel their reservations without proper notice, will be charged the full examination fee. For additional information, refer to the Candidate Information Booklet for Real Estate at www.myfloridalicense.com/dbpr. Select "Bureau of Education & Testing" in the column on the left side of the page and then "Candidate Information Booklets."

What to Bring on Exam Day

Allow sufficient time to arrive at the test center 30 minutes prior to your exam time. You will be required to show the test administrator two forms of signature identification, one of which must be a photo ID. You must take your original course completion slip (Certificate of Prelicensing Education Completion). You will also be asked for the confirmation number that was given to you when you made your test reservation Although it is not required, it is recommended that you bring with you the official authorization notice that Pearson VUE mailed to you.

You are allowed to bring a silent, hand-held, battery-operated, nonprinting calculator. The calculator cannot have an alphabetic keypad. Standard (nonprinting) four-function electronic calculators are recommended for the Sales Associate examination. However, financial calculators with an alpha button are allowed. Put fresh batteries in your calculator on exam day and run a few simple calculations on your calculator to verify that it is working properly. Avoid using a solar-powered calculator because the light may be insufficient for sustained use. Cell phones and pagers are *not* allowed in the testing center.

You are allowed to bring and use one foreign language translation dictionary to the exam. Translation dictionaries must contain only word-for-word or phrase translations. Dictionaries that contain definitions of words, explanations of words, or handwritten notes may not be used. For information regarding acceptable translation dictionaries, contact the Bureau of Education and Testing, Examination Administration Unit, at 850-488-5952.

COMPUTER-BASED EXAM

You will take your exam on a computer. Each test question will be displayed on the computer screen. You will record your answer to each question by clicking the answer choice (A, B, C, or D) with your mouse. Your answer choice will be highlighted so that you immediately know the answer choice that is recorded electronically. Read every answer choice before choosing the answer!

You can go forward or backward through the test, mark test questions for review, and change answers. A summary screen, which can be accessed at any time during the exam, informs the candidate of the number of test questions answered, the number unanswered, and/or the number of questions skipped. The time remaining is displayed on the computer screen.

The PC (computer) you will be using is easy to operate. However, it is *strongly recommended* that you take the tutorial provided before the exam starts to familiarize yourself with the equipment. The tutorial takes about 15 minutes. It provides sample test questions so that you can familiarize yourself with how to indicate your answer choice and how to navigate through the exam. The tutorial explains all the test features, such as how to turn the exam clock on and off and how to access the summary screen.

A Strategy for a Paperless Exam

The computer will automatically keep track of any questions you skip. For this reason, it is recommended that you plan on going through the entire exam at least twice. On the first time through, answer the easy questions first. These are the test questions that you are familiar with and are confident that you know the correct answer. There are three types of test questions for which you should press "next screen," skipping them until the second time through. They are

- unfamiliar questions for which the correct answer is not obvious;
- lengthy questions that fill up much of the computer screen; and
- math questions (it is most efficient to do all of the math questions at one time when you have your calculator and scratch paper ready).

Your strategy is to use your time efficiently and to get every point possible. Therefore, answering the questions that are easiest for you first is a strategic way of maximizing your score. Once you have finished the first pass, it is time to take a second pass through the exam. Go to the summary page on your testing device. Press "Review Unanswered," and the test questions left unanswered will appear, one after the other. Now it is time to finish the examination and add to your total score.

ORDER OF TEST QUESTIONS

Your exam is made up of three broad categories (law, principles and practices, and math). Math questions are sprinkled throughout the exam. The questions have no particular order, and they are *not* arranged from "easy" to "difficult" (or vice versa). This is why the strategy of answering the easy questions first is so important. In addition to law, principles and practices, and math questions, broker candidates must answer eight questions regarding the closing disclosure. The closing disclosure questions require broker candidates to calculate closing entries and know what information is entered on the pages of the closing disclosure without access to the form.

PREPARING FOR SUCCESS

Knowing how to study increases your knowledge of the subject. Knowing how to take exams helps raise your score when you are tested on that subject. Now it's time to prove to yourself and to the Florida Real Estate Commission (FREC) that you have mastered the subject areas of real estate law, principles and practices, and math. The strategies described in the following paragraphs will help build your test taking skills. You *can* raise your score. Here is how to do it!

DEVELOP A POSITIVE ATTITUDE

Research shows that optimists do much better than pessimists in classes, on exams, and at work. Pessimism and optimism are *not* fixed at birth. Attitude is learned, so pessimism can be unlearned. The night before and the day of the exam, put yourself in a positive frame of mind. Reject any negative thoughts, such as "I'm not sure I'm ready" or "I don't think I'll pass," because they are self-defeating and can contribute to failure. Too much test anxiety can seriously interfere with your ability to succeed on the exam. On the other hand, a little anxiety can increase your mental processes. Adopt a positive attitude toward the exam. The exam is based on information you have already studied and been tested on in class. Use the many memory aids from your course to help you recall important facts, terms, and concepts. Maintain a confident outlook. Put yourself in the exam driver's seat. Acknowledge that there are easy *and* difficult questions to answer. Don't panic if you draw a blank on a question. Visualize yourself as relaxed and in control of the situation. See yourself as working all the way through the exam with good concentration and energy. Stay in control to maximize your exam results. The power of positive thinking applies in the test-taking arena just as it does throughout life's activities. Picture yourself leaving the test center with your passing notice!

CONTROL ANXIETY

Again, some pre-exam anxiety is natural and helpful. It "psychs" you up, sharpens your senses, and gets the adrenaline flowing. But too much worrying gets in the way of your timing, as will anger, resentment, disgust, and a lot of other counterproductive emotions. Prepare an antipanic strategy!

If you become uptight or tense, use relaxation techniques to reduce the effect. Move your muscles (for example, briefly let your arms hang at your sides or shake or rotate your arms and hands). Relax with a sigh. Take a deep breath and hold it for a second or two. Close your eyes, clear your mind, relax your body (but don't fall off your chair). Practice this five-second "exam-jitters eliminator" *before* exam day so that you can personally experience the benefits should you need the technique on exam day.

BUDGET YOUR TIME

Allotted exam time (currently three and one-half hours) is at a premium for most examinees and must be used wisely. Although everyone feels the pressure of time, not every examinee makes good use of it. Too many start right off answering questions, acting like a motorist with the gas pedal to the floor and no trip itinerary! The goal is to pass the exam, so you cannot afford to rush blindly. Successful carpenters "measure twice, cut once." The following suggestions will help you improve your exam score by using time more efficiently.

One useful technique for planning your test-taking time is to set a mental *halfway point* on the exam as well as on your watch. Think in terms of three hours for taking and one-half hour for reviewing your exam. Because you are taking a 100-question exam with each question counting as one point, be sure that you have finished about 50 questions midway through the three-hour period. Continue to work at the remaining questions in the next hour and a half and use the remaining one-half hour for review. Keep track of the passing time, but don't panic if you get slightly off schedule. Work swiftly but intelligently. Don't linger too long over difficult questions—skip and return to them. Do not get uptight or rush if you see other examinees finishing early or before you. Studies prove that students who turn in their exams early include high *and* low scorers. To stay on your preplanned time schedule, be emotionally as well as academically prepared.

Toward the end, you may feel you are running out of time, that if you only had more time you could answer all the questions. As mentioned earlier, everyone feels pressured by time. Try to keep that thought from hurting your exam-taking schedule. You have allowed time for going back to questions you couldn't answer or were unsure of on the first pass. Go over difficult questions you marked for review. Do *not* leave any questions unanswered (we can't say this enough) because then your chances of getting the correct answer are zero!

Your Personal Strategy

Because different exam-taking strategies work for different people, some of the strategies in this section may not work for you. Follow those techniques that seem best for *you*. Do not consider the ideas set forth here to be a lock-step guide to follow—take the ones that make sense to you. Using *your common sense* throughout is the single best guide. Why? Because some of the situations described in exam questions are simply facts of everyday life and experience.

For example:

1. An acre consists of
   a. 208 cubic feet.
   b. 360 degrees.
   c. 5,280 feet.
   d. 43,560 square feet.

Stop and answer the question. Using common sense as well as common knowledge, you know answer A is a measure of volume, answer B is a circular measure, and answer C is a linear measure. An acre is a *surface* measure of area, so answer D is correct. You didn't even have to know the numbers, although as familiar "traps," each side of an acre is approximately 208 feet, a circle has 360 degrees, and a mile is 5,280 feet in length. When answering a multiple-choice question, your common sense, sound reasoning, personal experience, and known information all come into play.

QUESTION TERMINOLOGY

If you do not know the parts and functions of an exam question, you begin with one strike against you. Because only multiple-choice formats are used on the exam, you need to understand that the first part of a question is called the *stem* or *lead-in*. It may come in the form of a question ("Which statement best defines a title search?"), an incomplete sentence ("A title search is defined as:"), or a direction ("Select the definition that best describes a title search."). The stem provides the information needed to determine the correct answer. The four possible answers are called *choices*, *alternatives*, *options*, or *responses*. One of the four choices will be the correct (or best) answer; the other three will be incorrect answers called *distractors* or *throwaways*. They are called distractors because their purpose is to distract (divert) your attention away from the correct option.

Occasionally, distracting or irrelevant information may also appear in the stem of a question to test your knowledge of the key point or formula being examined. Distractors in the lead-in may appear to you to be tricky or unfair, but if you know the course material and read carefully, you will not be misled by such distractors.

For example:

2. An efficiency condo unit sold for $45,000. The new owner applied for and was granted a $25,000 homestead tax exemption. The property was assessed for $40,500, which is 90% of its selling price. If the tax rate is 28.8 mills, how much will the property taxes be?
   a. $1,049.76
   b. $576.00
   c. $446.40
   d. $401.76

Stop now and work the problem. To solve this property tax problem, subtract allowable tax exemptions from the assessed value and multiply the result by the tax rate: [($40,500 – $25,000) × .0288]. The price the property sold for is a distractor, as is the phrase, "which is 90% of its selling price." Both are irrelevant to solving this problem. Answers A, B, and D are also distractors—wrong answers in this case. Math questions are often designed so that each wrong answer can be arrived at if you fail to read the question carefully or do not know the correct way to solve the problem. Answer A [($40,500 × .90) × .0288], answer B [($45,000 – $25,000) × .0288], and answer D [$446.40 × .90] above demonstrate this. Like life, an exam is full of "red herrings." Now you see how important it is to know the component parts and structure of a question and, in the case of a math problem, to also know how to solve it.

MORE ABOUT MATH QUESTIONS

Another important strategy is to read the math exam question and then make a mental estimate of the answer. So often, teachers are amazed at how students calculate a number that is not plausible. *Estimating* the answer first before *calculating* the answer will raise a red flag if the number you calculate isn't in the estimated ballpark. An important word of caution—the incorrect answer choices typically are the results of common mistakes, such as reversing dividend and divisor, failing to carry the math calculation to the final step, failing to convert inches to feet or feet to yards, misplacing the decimal point, and so forth. So if you mentally estimate how big a number should be *before* you calculate the answer, you are less likely to fall for one of those red herrings!

RESTATE THE STEM

If you have difficulty understanding the meaning of a question, mentally restate the stem from its present form into another form. If the stem is in the form of an incomplete statement, recast it into a question if that helps you. *For example*, if the stem reads "A deed is defined as," then put the stem in question form: "How is a deed defined?" Or, "How do you define the term 'deed'?" If the stem is in the form of a question, rephrase it in the form of a complete or an incomplete statement. *For example*, if the lead-in is "Which condition may result from a change of zoning?" reword it mentally to "A change in zoning may result in ...". By rephrasing a sentence that has a confusing or complex word order, you can analyze the stem more easily and determine the correct answer more readily.

Caution: When changing the form of a stem, be certain *not* to change the meaning!

FOREIGN QUESTIONS

You may also come across one or two questions that might just as well have been written in a foreign language you've never seen or heard! It may be a genuinely difficult question. It may represent a blind spot in your learning. It may be a point never covered in class. In a 63-hour course (in fact, 60 "classroom hours" plus exam translates into 50 hours of class time, given the "50-minute hour"), thousands of facts and hundreds of concepts are covered in a short time. Therefore, not everything can be taught or learned in that period, realistically speaking. Keep in mind that a "foreign" question represents only 1 out of 100 points. Choose the correct answer using a process of elimination (common sense plus sound reasoning and your own knowledge). Don't panic and bog down. Minimize the effect this one question has on your overall positive approach to the exam.

THE BEST ANSWER

On the state license exam, the three basic approaches to structuring the stem are: find the correct answer, find the incorrect answer, and find the best answer. When you are asked to select the "best" (or "most accurate") answer or description of the situation (as opposed to the "correct" answer), you are being alerted to the strong possibility that more than one answer is correct. Your strategy, as with all questions, is to read the lead-in carefully, think of the correct answer, and read the four choices given. Because only one of the choices is the "best" answer, you must systematically eliminate the other three.

For example:

3. Checks, townships, and sections are
   a. units of measurement.
   b. measurements of areas.
   c. measured by surveyors' tapes.
   d. metric measurements.

Stop and answer this question. You look at A above and it seems to be correct. The same holds true for B. Answer C is too limiting. Answer D seems ridiculous. So you reexamine A and B and determine that, whereas A is a "correct" answer, it is not as specific a description of the lead-in as is B. Thus answer B is the best choice.

THE INCORRECT ANSWER

Whenever you come across an exam instruction that requires you to find the incorrect answer among the choices, apply the lead-in to each listed answer, one at a time, and determine if each choice is T or F.

For example:

4. Select the incorrect answer. A broker retains a buyer's deposit in an escrow account until the
   a. transaction is concluded.
   b. deposit is forfeited by the buyer.
   c. FREC issues an escrow disbursement order (EDO).
   d. buyer changes his/her mind after the seller's acceptance of the offer.

Answer the question by choosing T or F for each choice. If necessary, keep track of this on the scrap paper provided at the test center. For answer A, you should have written a T because this is the typical time at which a deposit is released. For answer B, you know that when a buyer forfeits a deposit for whatever the reason, this too constitutes a "correct" time to release a deposit. So, you should have put down a T. For answer C, an "escape procedure" has been used due to conflicting demands on escrowed funds, and the broker is therefore required to release the deposit. You should have marked T for answer C. Finally, for answer D, the buyer is bound by acceptance of his/her offer, and because the seller accepted it, answer D is the choice you were looking for—the incorrect answer (the broker should not release a buyer's deposit under the conditions specified).

GUESSING

It is important to understand that there is *no* penalty for guessing on the state license exam. This means that wrong answers are *not* subtracted from right answers to arrive at your exam score. However, not answering a question is counted as a wrong answer! Therefore, make certain that all 100 questions have been answered. Now, let's see what intelligent guessing—not wild haphazard guessing—can do to raise your score.

With careful reading, rereading, common sense, and logic, you will find you are able to eliminate one, perhaps two, of the wrong answers in almost every case. Educated guessing on the remaining possible answers increases your chances of correctly handling a difficult question and scoring an overall 75 or higher. You have 25 chances to be wrong and still pass the state license examination and receive your license. An illustration of guessing at the correct answer, but doing so using common sense and solid reasoning, might help you understand this strategy.

For example:

5. Inflation by itself
   a. makes it possible for more people to buy homes.
   b. is good for the overall economy.
   c. has no effect on buying power.
   d. decreases buying power.

Stop and answer this question. In thinking about the concept of inflation and analyzing your four choices, answer A makes no sense; B is silly; C can't be right; and D makes sense, and it is correct.

Another guessing strategy arises with an answer that contains an *unfamiliar* word or words. This may be a distractor. In other words, do *not* assume that a word or term that is foreign to you is probably the correct answer. More often, the unfamiliar is a deliberate distractor—an incorrect answer.

IMPROVING YOUR ODDS

When you haven't a clue as to the correct answer, don't mentally flip a coin or throw a dart! Instead, remember that *the correct answer to every question is right in front of you* on the exam! You don't have to cope with fill-in-the-blank or essay-type questions. Sure, the right answer is carefully hidden among the group of wrong answers (distractors), but you have a one-in-four, or 25%, chance of choosing the correct answer. If you can eliminate just one choice for whatever the reason, you increase your odds of getting credit for a correct answer to one in three, or 33⅓%. If you can eliminate two choices, you raise your odds to 50%. Theoretically, if you know the answers to only 72 questions (failing) but make educated guesses at the remaining 28, you could end up with a score ranging from 79 to 86, which would be passing! Making the odds work in *your* favor is using your head.

IGNORING THE ANSWERS

Most test takers read a question stem and immediately look at all four answers. For some, this approach causes no problems. For others, it causes unnecessary tension and confusion over every question. Common errors are often used as incorrect choices (distractors), so to prevent individual question anxiety, try not reading the four choices while reading the stem. After you have read the stem one or more times, think about (or calculate) the correct answer. Then read the four choices and see if your thought-out answer is there. The result of using this approach could be to reduce your nervousness, heighten your confidence, and raise your score.

HANDLING NEGATIVES

The shock of encountering questions that are worded in unexpected and awkward ways can scare and frustrate anyone. On the state license exam, *negatives* in the stem or in a choice (for example, "not" or "un-" or "except") are typically in uppercase letters for emphasis. A negative in a stem is asking you to respond in the opposite manner from an affirmative statement. Whereas usually you eliminate incorrect answers to a question, in the case of a negative in a stem, you *discard the correct answers*. Therefore, be alert for a negative, particularly one found in the stem of a multiple-choice question.

For example:

6. Escape procedures available to a licensee for resolving conflicting demands on escrowed funds do NOT include
   a. mediation.
   b. arbitration.
   c. subpoena.
   d. lawsuit.

Stop and answer this question. Because of the word "NOT" in the stem, you need to rule out the correct answers (A, B, and D), and thus C is the answer to this negatively worded question.

The form of a negative question may be shaped by the word "except," which is usually in uppercase letters. Use the same strategy by ruling out the correct answers, or put another way, choose the one answer that is different from the other three.

For example:

7. These features affect the size of the monthly payments for adjustable-rate mortgages EXCEPT
   a. index rate used by the lender.
   b. margin used by the lender.
   c. principal borrowed by the mortgagor.
   d. assumability of the loan.

Stop and answer the question. From your knowledge of the components of adjustable-rate mortgages, you know that the index, margin, and principal affect the monthly payment amount. So you reject the correct answers and are left with D as your answer choice.

CLUES IN STEMS AND CHOICES

A clue may come from the use of "general qualifiers" or "absolute words" in the choices.

For example:

8. When reconciling value, an appraiser
   a. usually weighs the quantity and quality of the relevant data/information.
   b. must select the highest price in terms of cash equivalency.
   c. gives the most weight to the median indicator of value.
   d. always chooses the mean of the three indicators of value.

Stop and answer the question. Because qualifiers, such as "usually" (as well as "generally," "tends to," "most," and "some") *lessen* the strength of a statement or answer, they are often clues to a correct response. Because absolutes such as "always" (as well as "all," "entirely," and "never") *tighten* a statement or answer, they are often hints to an incorrect response (distractor). In the example, "usually" is a clue to the right answer (A), whereas clues to wrong answers are "must" (B) and "always" (D). You know answer C is incorrect as a result of your knowledge of the subject area being tested.

Other strategies could be lumped under the heading "clues in stems and choices," but it is unnecessary to cover them in light of the higher quality of questions now appearing on real estate license examinations.

DESPERATION STRATEGIES

Originators of exam questions generally find it easier to create the wrong answers than the right (or best) answers. Consequently, test-writers sometimes have a tendency to qualify the correct answer with extra words to ensure its preciseness. Therefore, the correct choice is sometimes the longest answer among the four choices because it is more detailed. However, recognize this as a desperation strategy, one that should be used only if you "draw a blank."

By this same reasoning, you may be able to increase your odds by dismissing the shortest answer. But again, this is very nearly "blind guessing," as is the tactic of throwing out answers A and D on the grounds that test-writers tend to "hide correct answers in the pack." A similar but equally blind approach is to eliminate the highest and lowest answers to a math problem. These three strategies are in the same league as the longest-answer approach—rash moves indeed!

EXAM RESULTS

Exams are graded at the test site and candidates are given a grade notice at that time. The grade notice includes pass/fail information, and failure notices include a breakdown of the points scored in each major subject area. An initial inactive license is mailed directly to licensees following notification of a passing score. Sales associate applicants may legally begin to operate as licensees once they notify the DBPR of their employer's name and address by filing the appropriate DBPR form.

EXAM-TAKING REMINDERS

Start your review several weeks, or at least several days, before the exam. Get plenty of rest the night before the exam. Be careful of "cramming" to the point that you are drained and unable to think clearly on exam day. Study smart, not necessarily more. Wear comfortable clothing and shoes to the test center. Remember to bring whatever materials are required. Don't arrive hungry or too full—eat "appropriately" beforehand. Be at the test center a little ahead of the start time. Make a "pit stop" before you go into the exam room. Be mentally and physically prepared; listen to, understand, and follow all verbal and written instructions. Budget your exam time by preparing a preplanned approach. Read every word of every question (stem as well as choices). Think before you answer. Answer the question asked—not the one you expected or hoped would be on the exam. Check and recheck. Answer all 100 questions even though you don't know the answer to every question on the exam—no one knows it all. Review your work as time permits. Remember that the objective is a passing score, not necessarily a perfect score.

The preceding strategies constitute neither solutions nor substitutes for learning and knowing the required subject matter. They are offered as guides to improve your exam-taking ability and to assist you in passing the state license examination. Put these strategies to work for you by systematically progressing through the review outlines that follow, answering the math questions, and taking the two practice 100-question exams.

EXAM-TAKING REMINDERS

SECTION 1 REAL ESTATE LICENSE LAW AND QUALIFICATIONS FOR LICENSURE

(See Unit 2 in *Florida Real Estate Principles, Practices & Law* and Unit 1 in *Florida Real Estate Broker's Guide*)

KEY TERM REVIEW

Broker is a person who, for another and for compensation or other consideration (or anticipation of compensation or other consideration), performs real estate services.

Broker associate is an individual who meets the requirements of a broker but who chooses to work (operate) in real estate under the direction (employ) of another broker.

Compensation is anything of value or a valuable consideration, directly or indirectly paid, promised, or expected to be paid or received.

Expungement is a process by which the record of a criminal conviction is destroyed or sealed after expiration of time.

Florida resident, for application and licensing purposes, is a person who has resided in Florida continuously for a period of four calendar months or more within the preceding year, regardless of whether the person resided in a recreational vehicle, hotel, rental unit, or other temporary or permanent location.

License is a written document issued by the DBPR that serves as *prima facie evidence* (valid on its face) that the person is licensed on the date shown.

Mutual recognition agreement is a transactional agreement between Florida and another state that provides for the two states to recognize each other's real estate prelicense education.

Nolo contendere/no contest is a plea of no contest entered in a criminal court of law. The defendant does not admit or deny the charges, though a fine or sentence may be imposed by the court.

Owner-developer is an unlicensed entity that sells, exchanges, or leases its own property.

Prima facie evidence is a legal term used to refer to evidence that is good and sufficient on its face to establish a given fact or prove a case.

Real estate services include any real estate activities involving compensation for performing the service for another.

Reciprocity is the practice of mutual exchanges of privileges. Some states have reciprocal arrangements for recognizing and granting licenses to licensed real estate professionals from other states.

Registration is the official placement of a real estate business or individual into the DBPR's records (database).

Sales associate is a person who performs real estate services for compensation but who does so under the direction, control, and management of an active broker or owner-developer.

Sealed records cannot be examined except by order of the court or by designated officials.

Withhold adjudication occurs when the court determines that a defendant is not likely to again engage in a criminal act and that the ends of justice and the welfare of society do not require the defendant suffer the penalty imposed by law. After such determination, the court may withhold adjudication of guilt, stay (stop) the imposition of the sentence, and place the defendant on probation.

KEY CONCEPTS

- **Florida statutes and rules** important to real estate
  - Chapter 20: Organizational Structure, Executive branch of Florida government
  - Chapter 475, Part I: Real Estate License Law
  - Chapter 475, Part II: Real Estate Appraisal
  - Chapter 475, Part III: Commercial Real Estate Sales Commission Lien Act
  - Chapter 475, Part IV: Commercial Real Estate Leasing Commission Lien Act
  - Chapter 455: Department of Business and Professional Regulation (DBPR)
  - Chapter 120: Administrative Procedures Act
  - Chapter 61J2: Rules of the FREC
- **Three real estate license categories**
  - Sales associate is the introductory level; sales associates are employed by and work under the direction and control of a broker or an owner-developer; sales associates are agents of their employer
  - Broker licenses require additional education and experience and passing the broker license exam
  - Broker associate holds a broker's license but chooses to register and work in real estate under the direction of another broker
- **Owner-developer** is an unlicensed entity that sells, exchanges, or leases its own property
  - Sales staff must hold active real estate licenses to be paid commission
  - Sales staff is exempt from licensure if paid strictly on salaried basis
- **Application requirements**
  - Application fee in addition to initial biennial license fee (plus an unlicensed activity fee and a Real Estate Recovery Fund fee, if applicable)
  - Fee waiver for low-income applicants
  - Fee waiver for military personnel and their spouses (and surviving spouses)
  - Fee waiver for military veterans and their spouses who apply for a license within 60 months after honorable discharge
  - Fingerprints to determine any criminal history
  - Background information required concerning whether the applicant is currently under criminal investigation or has been convicted of a crime, pled guilty to a crime, or pled *nolo contendere*/no contest
  - Must disclose prior conviction even if court action (*adjudication*) was withheld
  - Disclose on the application any other name or alias, including a maiden name

- Applicants are not required to disclose a personal bankruptcy
- Applicants should confirm that a criminal matter has been expunged and no longer appears on the criminal history
- 30-day period to check application for errors and omissions
- 90 days to inform applicant of approval or denial
- Exam eligible, DBPR notifies test vendor
- Theft of a license exam or unauthorized copying of an exam is a third-degree felony

■ **Reciprocity for U.S. armed service members and their spouses**
- Must hold a valid license in another state or foreign jurisdiction
- Applies to spouses (or surviving spouse)
- Applies to all DBPR licenses if the member applicant holds a valid license for the corresponding profession

■ **Nonresident applicant requirements**
- Proof of U.S. citizenship is *not* required; however, applicants must possess a Social Security number
- Applicants do *not* have to be residents of Florida
- Nonresident applicants must indicate on the application that they are not residents of Florida
- Resident licensees who move out of the state (become nonresidents of Florida) must notify the Commission of the change in residency within 60 days
- Nonresident licensees must comply with all Chapter 475, F.S. requirements and FREC rules

■ **Mutual recognition agreements** recognize the education and experience that real estate licensees have acquired in another state or nation
- Applies exclusively to *nonresidents* licensed in other jurisdictions
- Requires applicants to submit a certificate of license history from the real estate commission of the state in which they are licensed
- Requires applicants to pass a 40-question, Florida-specific real estate law exam with a grade of 75% or higher
- Licensees licensed through mutual recognition must complete the Florida post-licensing requirement

■ **Florida resident**
- A person who has resided in Florida continuously for a period of four calendar months within the preceding year
- A person who currently resides in Florida with the intention to reside continuously in Florida for a period of four months or more

■ **Sales associate qualifications for licensure**
- Be 18 years of age or older
- Have earned a high school diploma (or equivalent)
- Possess a United States Social Security number
- Be honest, truthful, trustworthy, of good character, and have a reputation for fair dealing
- Be competent and qualified to make real estate transactions

- **Applicants must disclose**
  - If ever convicted, found guilty, or entered a plea of nolo contendere; or if currently under criminal investigation
  - If the applicant has done business under any name or alias (including a maiden name)
  - If disciplinary action has been taken against a license to practice a regulated profession
  - If ever denied a real estate license in any state
- **Summary of applicants**
  - Applicants with a criminal history will be placed on the FREC agenda
  - The Commission will review the applicant's criminal history records and decide whether an applicant listed on the summary of applicants (SOA) must appear in front of the FREC
  - After the appearance in front of the FREC, the Commissioners will vote to approve or deny the application
- **The license application is valid for two years from the date the complete application is received by the DBPR**
- **Sales associate education requirements**
  - Complete Course I (Commission prescribed prelicense course for sales associate candidates) with a passing score of at least 70 on the end-of-course exam
  - If applicant does not pass the state license exam within two years after the course completion date, the course completion expires and the applicant must again complete Course I
- **Exceptions to the prelicense course requirement**
  - Individuals with a four-year degree or higher in real estate from an accredited institution of higher education are exempt from Course I, but must pass the license exam
  - Attorneys who are active members of The Florida Bar are exempt from Prelicense Course I, but must pass the license exam
- **License examinations**
  - License exam is offered in English and Spanish
  - Passing score on the license exam is a grade of 75 or higher
  - New licensees must not begin working until the DBPR website indicates that the license is active status under the employing broker or brokerage entity
  - Failure notice and examinee rights to review the exam
  - Qualifications for reexamination in a foreign language, other than Spanish
- **Post-licensing education**
  - Florida sales associates *must* complete the 45-hour post-licensing course *before the expiration* of the initial sales associate license
  - Failure to complete the post-licensing requirement prior to the expiration date will cause the license to become null and void
  - Sales associates who do not complete the post-licensing requirement must requalify for licensure by again completing Course I and passing the state license exam

- Florida-licensed attorneys who are also licensed real estate sales associates must complete the post-licensing education requirement
- Individuals with a four-year degree or higher in real estate from an accredited institution of higher education are exempt from the post-license education requirement
- Hardship cases allow licensees an additional six-month period following the initial license expiration to complete the post-license education
- There is no legislative authority to extend

■ **Continuing education**

- Following the initial license period, active and inactive licensees must complete 14 hours of continuing education during every two-year license period
- Licensees must take a three-hour Ethics and Business Practices course once during each license renewal period
- Licensees must also complete a three-hour core law course once during each license renewal period
- Licensees may substitute attendance at one legal agenda session of FREC for three classroom hours of specialty continuing education (CE) (once per renewal cycle)
- Attorneys who are active members of The Florida Bar are exempt from Course I (for sales associates) and continuing education (but not post-licensing education)

■ **Broker requirements**

- Complete Course II (Commission prescribed prelicense course for broker candidates) with a passing score of at least 70 on the end-of-course exam
- Must complete at least 24 months of real estate experience during the five-year period preceding becoming licensed as a broker
- Broker applicants who hold a Florida real estate sales associate's license must complete the 45-hour post-licensing course for sales associates before the initial sales associate's license expires to be eligible for a broker's license
- Broker applicants who have received a four-year degree or higher in real estate from an accredited institution of higher education are exempt from Course II

■ **Broker experience requirements**

- Active sales associate working for a Florida or out-of-state broker for at least 24 months of the preceding five years
- Active sales associate in the employ of a government agency for at least 24 months of the preceding five years who is paid a salary and performs duties that require a real estate license
- Active broker in another state or nation for 24 months of the preceding five years

■ **Broker post-licensing education**

- Florida brokers must complete the 60-hour post-licensing course *before the first renewal* of their license
- Failure to complete the post-licensing requirement prior to the expiration date will cause the license to become null and void

- In such cases, the broker may request and receive a sales associate's license if the licensee completes 14 hours of continuing education within six months following expiration of the broker's license
- Brokers who have a four-year degree or higher in real estate are exempt from the broker post-license education requirement

- **Registration and licensure**
  - Registration is the process of submitting information to the DBPR that is entered into the Department's records
  - A real estate license indicates the licensee's name, issue date, and expiration date and serves as *prima facie evidence* that the licensee holds a current and valid license
- **Real estate services (A BAR SALE)**
  - **A** **A**dvertise real estate services
  - **B** **B**uy
  - **A** **A**ppraise
  - **R** **R**ent or provide rental information or lists
  - **S** **S**ell
  - **A** **A**uction
  - **L** **L**ease
  - **E** **E**xchange
- **A real estate license is required** if a person performs any real estate service for compensation *or the implied intent* to collect compensation, unless specifically exempt
  - Compensation includes money in the form of a salary, bonuses, commissions, and gratuities
  - Compensation is also things of value such as dinner, flowers, wine, gift certificates, and event tickets
- **Presumption of acting as a real estate broker**
  - If a person performs services of real estate for another and a disciplinary case is filed, there is a presumption that the individual acted as a real estate licensee
  - The individual may be held liable even if acting for another without being compensated for the services
- **Individuals who are exempt from a real estate license**
  - A person who performs real estate services for others must be licensed, unless specifically exempted by law
  - Five groups of exemptions
    1. Owner exemptions
    2. Exemptions based on career
    3. Salaried employee exemptions
    4. Court and legally appointed persons
    5. Miscellaneous exemptions

- **Owner exemptions**
  - Property owners may buy, sell, exchange, or lease their own property
  - Officers and directors of corporations (and owners of other business entities) may buy, sell, exchange, and lease the property of the business entity
  - Partners in a real estate partnership are exempt from licensure if selling property owned by the partnership, provided the partners receive a share of the profits in proportion to their interest in the partnership
- **Salaried employee exemptions**
  - Salaried employees of a business entity may buy, sell, exchange, and lease property for their employers, provided they are not paid on a transactional basis
  - Salaried employees of an apartment community who work in an onsite rental office in a leasing capacity and who do not receive commission (no restriction on duration of rental leases)
  - Salaried managers of condominium or cooperative apartment complexes who rent individual units for periods no longer than one year and who are not paid a commission (Salaried managers of community associations must obtain CAM licenses.)
  - Salaried employees of an owner-developer (real estate developer), provided they do not receive commission
- **Court and legally appointed persons**
  - Court-appointed individuals acting within the limitations of their duties
  - A person given a power of attorney to sign contracts on another's behalf
- **Miscellaneous exemptions**
  - Persons who sell cemetery lots (This exemption exists because Chapter 475, F.S., excludes cemetery lots from the definition of real property.)
  - Individuals who rent lots in a mobile home park or recreational travel park (Rentals in mobile home parks and recreational vehicle lot rentals are not considered real property.)
  - Dealers who are registered with the SEC selling business enterprises to accredited investors
  - Hotel and motel clerks who rent lodging accommodations on behalf of the establishment
  - Tenants of an apartment community may receive a fee up to $50 for the referral of a new tenant to the same apartment community
- See the *Florida Real Estate Principles, Practices & Law* textbook for other exemptions

IMPORTANT DATES AND TIME PERIODS TO REMEMBER

- **21 days.** Time period for DBPR to receive a request to review the state license exam or to request a hearing before an administrative law judge
- **30 days.** Time period after receipt of application to check for errors and omissions
- **60 days.** Number of days to notify the DBPR if a licensee becomes a nonresident

- **90 days.** Time period to inform applicant of approval or denial of license application
- **Six months.** Extension period for hardship case following the initial license expiration
- **Up to one year.** Salaried managers of condominium or cooperative units who prepare rental agreements with a duration of up to one year are exempt from real estate license
- **More than one year.** Managers of condominiums or cooperatives who prepare lease agreements with a duration longer than one year must be licensed
- **Two years.** Time period after which the license application expires
- **Two years.** Time period after which the prelicense course expires
- **Two years.** Experience requirement for broker applicants obtained within preceding five-year period

SECTION 2 REAL ESTATE LICENSE LAW AND COMMISSION RULES

(See Unit 3 in *Florida Real Estate Principles, Practices & Law* and Unit 1 in *Florida Real Estate Broker's Guide*)

KEY TERM REVIEW

Active license status is required to engage in real estate services. Sales associates achieve active status by finding an employer and registering with the DBPR under the employing broker or owner-developer.

Cancel means to become void without disciplinary action.

Cease to be in force (or cease to be in effect) means that when certain events occur, such as a broker changing a business address, the licensee cannot conduct business until the DBPR receives notification of the change.

Current mailing address is the current residential address a licensee uses to receive mail through the U.S. Postal Service.

Current status indicates the licensee is up to date with respect to the DBPR's licensure requirements.

Executive powers of the Florida Real Estate Commission (FREC) include the power to regulate and enforce license law.

Group license is issued to a sales associate or broker associate employed by an owner-developer (real estate developer) who owns properties in the name of various entities and entitles the licensee to work for the separate sales projects owned by the owner-developer.

Involuntary inactive status results when a license is not renewed at the end of the license period.

Ministerial duties of the Division of Real Estate (DRE) involve recordkeeping.

Multiple licenses refers to when a broker holds more than one broker's license.

Null and void means to no longer exist.

Probation allows the licensee to continue to practice real estate under the guidance of the FREC for a period of time while completing conditions specified by the FREC.

Promulgate means to enact and publish rules and regulations.

Quasi-judicial powers of the FREC include the power to grant or deny license applications, to determine license law violations, and to administer penalties.

Quasi-legislative powers of the FREC include the power to enact administrative rules and regulations and to interpret questions regarding the practice of real estate.

Voluntary inactive is the license status that results when a licensee has applied to the DBPR to be placed on inactive status.

Voluntary relinquish occurs when a person no longer wants to engage in the real estate business, provided there is no investigation or discipline pending against the licensee.

KEY CONCEPTS

- **Department of Business and Professional Regulation (DBPR)**
  - Agency charged with licensing and regulating businesses and professionals
  - Under the executive branch of the governor
  - Governed by Florida Statute 120
  - Secretary of DBPR is appointed by the governor, subject to confirmation by the state Senate
  - Has authority to investigate consumer complaints, issue subpoenas when conducting investigations, issue cease and desist orders to unlicensed individuals, and issue citations to licensed individuals
  - Initial application fee, biennial license fee, and unlicensed activity fee are waived for military veterans who apply for a DBPR license within 60 months after honorable discharge
- **Division of Professions** regulates education courses and license examinations
- **Division of Service Operations**
  - Customer Contact Center
  - Central Intake Unit
- **Division of Florida Condominiums, Timeshares, and Mobile Homes**
  - Arbitration program for HOAs
- **Division of Real Estate (DRE)**
  - **The Director of the DRE** is appointed by the Secretary of the DBPR, *subject to* FREC approval
  - Administrative duties of DRE include routine duties and clerical functions on behalf of the FREC
  - Ministerial duties involve recordkeeping
- **The Florida Real Estate Commission (FREC) consists of seven members**
- **Five Commissioners are professional (licensed) members**
  - Four must be Florida real estate brokers who have held active licenses during the five years preceding appointment
  - One must be either a Florida real estate broker or sales associate that has held an active license during the two years preceding appointment.
- **Two remaining members are consumer (unlicensed or lay) members**
  - Consumer members have never been real estate brokers or sales associates
- **Seven Florida Real Estate Commissioners**
  - Appointed by the governor, subject to confirmation by the Florida Senate
  - Appointed to four-year staggered terms
  - May *not* serve more than two consecutive terms
  - Paid $50 per day per diem for official business and meetings
  - At least one of the seven members must be 60 years or older
- **Commission powers** include three general areas
  - Executive power to regulate and enforce license law include
    a. Foster the education of applicants and licensees

   b. Adopt a seal
   c. Establish fees
- — Quasi-legislative power to enact and revise administrative rules include
   a. Create and pass (promulgate) rules and regulations
   b. Regulate professional practices
- — Quasi-judicial power to grant or deny applications and administer penalties include
   a. Grant and deny applications for licensure
   b. Suspend and revoke licenses, and impose administrative fines
   c. Make determinations of violations

- **FREC *may not* impose imprisonment as a punishment**
  - — FREC powers are limited to administrative matters and do not extend to criminal actions
  - — FREC must inform the Division of Florida Condominiums, Timeshares, and Mobile Homes when disciplinary action is taken against a licensee
- **License renewal periods**
  - — Real estate licenses are issued with an expiration date of either March 31 or September 30
  - — The expiration date that is assigned to a particular license is the date that will give the licensee as close to 24 months of licensure as possible, without exceeding 24 months
- **License renewal**
  - — Licensees submit renewal and biennial license fees
  - — Licensees must complete the applicable post-licensing or continuing education requirements before renewing license
- **Armed Forces renewal exemption**
  - — Members of U.S. Armed Forces who have licenses in good standing are exempt from license renewal while on active duty and for two years after discharge
  - — If the military duty is out of state, the exemption also applies to a licensed spouse
  - — The exemption does *not* apply if the licensee engages in real estate services for profit during that period
- **Active versus inactive status**
  - — Active status required to engage in real estate brokerage services
  - — The licensee must have an active license at the time the service of real estate was *performed*—however, the licensee may be inactive at the time payment is *received*
- **Voluntary inactive**
  - — A licensee has timely renewed but chooses not to engage in the real estate business; licensee requests to be placed in this status and the licensee may renew as voluntary inactive indefinitely
- **Involuntary inactive**
  - — A licensee failed to renew the license on time; license automatically expires (becomes null and void) after two years by operation of law

- — When a license has been involuntary inactive for 12 months or less, complete 14 hours of continuing education
- — When a license has been involuntary inactive for more than 12 months but less than 24 months, complete 28-hour reactivation education
- — FREC may reinstate a license that has become null and void if the former licensee applies for reinstatement within six months and the FREC determines that the former licensee failed to comply with the renewal requirements because of illness or economic hardship

- **Broker's license suspension or revocation**
  - — Sales associates placed in involuntary inactive status
  - — License is returned to active status when new employer is chosen and the information is filed with the DBPR
- **Null and void license** means the license no longer exists
  - — When a license is involuntary inactive for more than two years, the license becomes null and void without any further action by the DBPR or FREC
  - — A license becomes null and void when it has been revoked
  - — A person who no longer wants to engage in the real estate business can voluntarily relinquish the license; when a license is canceled, it becomes null and void
  - — Cancellation does not involve disciplinary action
- **Cease to be in force** means that the licensee cannot conduct business
  - — If a sales associate leaves one brokerage and wants to work for another, the DBPR must be informed of the new employer
  - — Until the sales associate is registered under the new employer, the sales associate cannot work
  - — The sales associate's license ceases to be in force until the sales associate has registered with the new broker
- **Change of employer**
  - — Sales associates who work for a different brokerage firm have certain responsibilities to their former employer
  - — Duplication of records from a previous employer is a breach of trust
  - — Fiduciary duties do not end with termination of employment
- **The DBPR must be notified within 10 days when**
  - — A broker or registered school changes business address
  - — A sales associate or real estate instructor changes employer
- **Current mailing address**
  - — The residential address a licensee uses to receive mail through the United States Postal Service
  - — A P.O. Box is an acceptable mailing address
- **DBPR License Portal Online Service**
  - — The DBPR maintains a database of licenses issued by the Department
  - — Primary status is the first status followed by the secondary status
  - — Primary status must state either *current* or *probation* to be eligible to operate as a licensee

- **Sales associate's license status is changed in one of two ways**
  - Broker updates the online portal service in real time by adding the sales associate to its roster of licensees
  - Status can also be updated by submitting a change of status form signed by the licensee and the broker
- **Multiple licenses**
  - Issued to a broker who qualifies as the broker for more than one brokerage entity
  - For each business that a person is a broker, a separate broker license must be obtained
  - Because sales associates and broker associates may have only one registered employer at a time, sales associates and broker associates may *not* hold multiple licenses
- **Group license** is a term that means a sales associate is registered with an owner-developer who owns properties in the name of various entities
  - Sales associates and broker associates who are employed by an unlicensed owner of real estate (a developer) are issued a group license
  - The group license entitles the licensee to work at various sales projects for the owner-developer

IMPORTANT DATES AND TIME PERIODS TO REMEMBER

- **10 days.** Number of days to notify the DBPR regarding a change of business address or a change in current mailing address
- **10 days.** Number of days a sales associate, broker associate, or an instructor has to notify the FREC of a change of employer
- **Two years.** Grace period after discharge from military duty to renew license
- **Two years.** Time period after which involuntary inactive license becomes null and void

SECTION 3 AUTHORIZED RELATIONSHIPS, DUTIES, AND DISCLOSURE

(See Unit 4 in *Florida Principles, Practices & Law* and Unit 10 in *Florida Real Estate Broker's Guide*)

KEY TERM REVIEW

Administrative law is a body of law created by administrative agencies in the form of rules, regulations, orders, and decisions.

Agent is a person entrusted with another's business; the person authorized by the principal to act on the principal's behalf.

At arm's length means that people conduct negotiations on their own behalf without trusting the other's fairness or integrity and without being subject to the other's control or influence.

Caveat emptor is a policy of let the buyer beware (buyer is responsible for own knowledge in real estate transactions).

Common law is judge-made law manifested in decrees and judgments of the courts (case law) as opposed to statutory law.

Consent to transition is a written agreement to gain the principal's written permission to a change in brokerage relationship.

Customer is a member of the public who is or may be a buyer or a seller of real property and may or may not be represented by a real estate licensee in an authorized brokerage relationship.

Designated sales associates are two real estate licensees from the same brokerage company designated to represent the buyer and the seller as single agents in *nonresidential* transactions.

Dual agency refers to a broker representing as a fiduciary both the buyer and the seller in a residential real estate transaction; dual agency is illegal in Florida.

Fiduciary occurs when a broker is in a relationship of trust and confidence with the broker as agent and the seller or the buyer as principal.

General agent is authorized by the principal to handle the affairs related to a business or trade, or to handle all the business at a certain location; for example, a property manager.

Limited representation is nonfiduciary representation to a buyer, a seller, or both in a real estate transaction.

No brokerage relationship is an arrangement where the broker does not represent either the buyer or the seller, but instead the broker works to facilitate the transaction.

Nonrepresentation is a no brokerage relationship.

Principal is the seller (or the buyer, but not both) in a single agent relationship; the principal authorizes the agent to act on the principal's behalf, while the principal is responsible for the actions of the agent.

Residential sale is defined in Florida license law to mean the sale of improved residential property of four or fewer units, the sale of unimproved residential property intended for use as four or fewer units, or the sale of agricultural property of 10 or fewer acres.

Single agent is a broker who represents either the buyer or the seller (but not both) and has a fiduciary relationship with the party represented.

Special agent is authorized by the buyer or the seller to handle only a specific business transaction or to perform a specific act; a broker who has a single agent relationship is a special agent with limited power or authority.

Statutory laws are written statutes and rules enacted by the legislature.

Subagent is a person authorized to assist and represent the agent and whose duties are delegated by the original agent.

Transaction broker is a broker who provides limited representation to a buyer, a seller, or both in a real estate transaction, but who does *not* represent either party in a fiduciary capacity or as a single agent.

KEY CONCEPTS

- **Law of agency**
  - Common law is judge-made law (case law)
  - Statutory law is enacted by the legislature
  - Administrative law consists of rules and regulations created by administrative agencies
- **Agency relationships in general business dealings**
  - A person who delegates authority to another is called the principal
  - Agent is the person entrusted with another's business
  - A fiduciary acts in a position of trust and confidence for another
  - Caveat emptor means "let the buyer beware"
  - General agent is authorized by the principal to perform acts associated with the continued operations of a particular job or a certain business of the principal
  - Special agent is authorized to perform a specific act
- **Three brokerage relationship options in Florida (1) transaction broker; (2) single agent; and (3) no brokerage relationship (nonrepresentation)**
  - The appropriate type of agency relationship is determined by the broker
  - Sales associates must consult with the employing broker regarding brokerage relationships practiced by the brokerage
- **Residential transactions**
  - Improved residential property of four or fewer units
  - Unimproved residential property intended for use as four or fewer units
  - Agricultural property of 10 or fewer acres
- **Disclosure requirements do *not* apply to**
  - Nonresidential transactions
  - Rent or lease agreements, unless there is an option to purchase property improved with four or fewer residential units
  - Business opportunities unless improved with four or fewer residential units

- Auctions
- Appraisals

- **Transaction broker relationship**
  - The broker may work as a transaction broker for the buyer and/or the seller (presumed relationship)
  - Transaction brokers provide limited representation
  - The buyer or seller is *not* responsible for the acts of the licensee
  - Parties give up their right to undivided loyalty
  - Allows licensee to facilitate the transaction by assisting both buyer and seller
  - A written disclosure notice is *not* required for residential real estate transactions when a transaction broker relationship is established
- **Duties of a transaction broker**
  - Account for all funds
  - Disclose all known facts that materially affect the value of residential real property and are not readily observable to the buyer
  - Deal honestly and fairly
  - Use skill, care, and diligence in the transaction
  - Present all offers and counteroffers in a timely manner (Note: Even if a valid contract exists)
  - Exercise limited confidentiality, unless waived in writing by a party
  - Provide any additional duties that are mutually agreed to with a party
- **Single agent relationship**
  - The broker may work as a single agent for either the buyer or the seller (but *not* for both in the same transaction)
  - Dual agency is illegal in Florida
  - Fiduciary relationship exists only in a single agent relationship
  - Broker *agent* and seller (or the buyer) *principal* or client
  - A single agent disclosure notice must be made before, or at the time of, entering into a listing agreement or an agreement for representation, or before the showing of property, whichever occurs first
- **Subagents are persons authorized to assist and represent the agent**
  - A subagent has the same duties as the agent
  - A broker's sales associates are general agents of the broker and subagents of the broker's principals
  - In a single agent relationship, the broker is an agent of the principal
  - Because a sales associate is an agent of the broker, the sales associate is a subagent of the principal
  - Sales associates and broker associates owe the same fiduciary obligations to the principal as their broker
- **Single agent relationship duties**
  - Account for all funds
  - Disclose all known facts that materially affect the value of residential real property and are not readily observable to the buyer

  - Deal honestly and fairly
  - Confidentiality
  - Obedience (must obey all *lawful* instructions of the principal)
  - Loyalty (act solely in the best interest of the principal)
  - Full disclosure
  - Use skill, care, and diligence in the transaction
  - Present all offers and counteroffers in a timely manner (*Note*: Even if a valid contract exists)
- **No brokerage relationship (nonrepresentation)**
  - The broker may act in a no brokerage relationship (the broker doesn't represent either the buyer or the seller)
  - The no brokerage relationship notice must be disclosed in writing before the showing of property
- **Dual agency**
  - Dual agency occurs when a brokerage firm represents as a fiduciary both the buyer and the seller in the same real estate transaction
- **No brokerage relationship duties**
  - Account for all funds entrusted to a licensee
  - Disclose all known facts that materially affect the value of residential real property
  - Deal honestly and fairly
- **Brokerage relationship limitations**
  - If the brokerage firm has a transaction broker relationship with the seller, the brokerage firm can also work with the buyer, in the same transaction, as a transaction broker or in no brokerage relationship. The brokerage firm *cannot* represent the buyer as a single agent if the firm has a transaction broker relationship with the seller
  - If the brokerage firm is representing the seller as a single agent, the brokerage firm can work with the buyer, in the same transaction, in no brokerage relationship. The brokerage firm *cannot* represent the buyer as a single agent or work with the buyer as a transaction broker if the firm is also representing the seller as a single agent
  - The brokerage relationship limitations apply even if the buyer and seller are working with different sales associates in the same brokerage firm
- **Written disclosure requirements for residential transactions**
  - Duties of the single agent relationship and nonrepresentation must be disclosed in writing
  - The disclosure document may be separate or incorporated into another document
  - Broker must retain all required disclosure documents for five years on residential transactions that result in a written contract to purchase
  - Under Florida law it is presumed that all licensees are operating as transaction brokers unless another brokerage relationship is established. Therefore, there is no requirement to give a written transaction broker disclosure notice to the buyer and/or the seller

- **Recordkeeping and retention of disclosure documents**
  - Brokers must retain agreements that engage the services of a broker
  - Retain brokerage relationship disclosure documents and buyer broker agreements for five years
  - Retention of documents applies to residential transactions that result in a written contract and nonresidential transactions that utilize designated sales associates
- **Transition from single agent to transaction broker**
  - Accomplished with the Consent to Transition to Transaction Broker Notice
  - Buyer's or seller's signature (or initials) required before the licensee may change from one brokerage relationship to another
  - If the principal refuses to sign or initial the consent to transition notice, the broker must continue to act as a single agent
- **Duties and obligations of the brokerage relationship law apply to *all* real estate transactions**
- **Nonresidential transactions**
  - Designated sales associates
  - Buyer and seller must each have assets of at least $1 million
  - Broker designates one sales associate to work with buyer as a single agent and another to work with seller as a single agent
  - Broker facilitates and advises designated sales associates
  - Buyer and seller must request the arrangement
  - Buyer and seller must sign disclosure notice
- **Terminating a brokerage relationship**
  - Fulfillment of brokerage relationship's purpose (performance)
  - Mutual agreement
  - Expiration of terms of the agreement
  - Broker renouncing relationship by giving notice (resignation)
  - Principal or customer revokes by giving notice
  - Death of either party
  - Destruction or condemnation of the property
  - Bankruptcy of the principal or customer

IMPORTANT DATES AND TIME PERIODS TO REMEMBER

- **Five years.** Period required to retain brokerage relationship disclosures for all transactions that result in a written contract

SECTION 4 REAL ESTATE BROKERAGE ACTIVITIES AND PROCEDURES

(See Unit 5 in *Florida Real Estate Principles, Practices & Law* and Units 2 and 4 in *Florida Real Estate Broker's Guide*)

KEY TERM REVIEW

Antitrust laws are state and federal laws designed to maintain and preserve business competition.

Arbitration is a process whereby, with the prior written consent of all parties to the dispute, the matter is submitted to a disinterested third party who makes a binding judgment.

Blind advertisement is advertising that fails to disclose the licensed name of the brokerage firm and that provides only a post office box number, telephone number, and/or street address.

Commingle is the illegal practice of mixing a buyer's, seller's, tenant's, or landlord's funds with the broker's own money or mixing escrow money with the broker's personal funds or brokerage funds.

Conflicting demands occur when the buyer and seller make demands regarding the disbursement of escrowed property that are inconsistent and cannot be resolved.

Corporation is an artificial person or legal entity created by law and consisting of one or more persons that is formed by filing articles of incorporation.

Declaratory judgment is filed with the judge in a court of law if brokers believe that they are entitled to a portion of the disputed escrow funds.

Deposit is a sum of money, or its equivalent, delivered to a real estate licensee as earnest money, payment, or partial payment in connection with a real estate transaction.

Earnest money deposit also referred to as a *good-faith deposit* or *binder deposit* is money given as good faith to accompany an offer to purchase or lease real property.

Escrow account is an account for the deposit of money held by a third party in trust for another for safekeeping.

Escrow disbursement order (EDO) is a determination by the FREC of who is entitled to disputed funds.

General partnership is an association of two or more persons for the purpose of jointly conducting a business together and each to share the profits and losses of the business.

Good faith doubt occurs when the broker questions or doubts the parties' willingness to fulfill the duties or obligations set forth in the contract and therefore the broker requests guidance as to which party should receive the escrowed property.

Immediately is how soon trust funds must be deposited into an escrow account according to Chapter 475, F.S.

Interpleader is a legal proceeding whereby the broker, having no financial interest in the disputed funds, deposits with the court the disputed escrow deposit so that the court can determine the rightful claimant.

Kickback occurs when a broker receives money from someone other than the buyer or the seller, such as for referring a buyer or seller to a particular vendor for services.

Limited liability company (LLC) is a form of business organization that offers the best features of a corporation and a partnership; members of a LLC are protected from personal liability as in a corporate form of ownership and the tax advantages of a partnership.

Limited liability partnership (LLP) features protection from personal liability in much the same way as limited partners in a limited partnership.

Limited partnership consists of one or more general partners and one or more limited partners.

Litigation is one of the settlement (escape) procedures that provides for the matter to be resolved in a court of law when there are disputing parties regarding escrow funds.

Market allocation is an agreement between brokers to split up competitive market areas among themselves and not compete in each other's areas.

Mediation is an informal, nonadversarial process intended to reach a negotiated settlement that is *not* binding.

Ostensible partnership (or quasi partnership) exists where the parties do not form a real partnership but act or do business in such a manner that the public, having no knowledge of the private relations of the parties, would reasonably be deceived into believing that a partnership exists. (Note: Brokers *may* share office space *provided* they make true status known on signs, telephone listings, advertising, and so forth.)

Personal assistants are individuals hired by a licensee to perform administrative tasks associated with real estate transactions. The tasks performed by a personal assistant determines whether the assistant must be a real estate licensee.

Point of contact information refers to any means by which to contact the brokerage firm or individual licensee including mailing address(es), physical street address(es), email address(es), telephone number(s), or facsimile (fax) telephone number(s); the brokerage firm's name must be above, below, or adjacent to the point of contact information.

Price-fixing occurs when competing brokers conspire to establish a standard commission.

Professional Association (PA) is a business corporation consisting of one or more individuals engaged in a primary business that provides a professional service.

Sole proprietorship is a business owned by one person with no legal separation between the owner and the business.

Telephone solicitation is the initiation of a telephone call for the purpose of encouraging the purchase of, or investment in, property, goods, or services.

Trade name is a business name other than the legal name of the person doing business.

Trust funds are cash, checks, money orders, or other items that can be converted to cash and that are held by a third party in connection with a real estate transaction.

Trust liability *(Study material for broker candidates only)* is the sum total of all deposits received, pending, and being held by the broker at a point in time.

KEY CONCEPTS

- **Brokerage offices**
  - Active brokers required to have an office and to register the office with the DBPR
  - Must be at least one enclosed room in a building of stationary construction

- The broker's books, records, and real estate transaction files must be kept in the office
- Brokers are not required by law to have a telephone, desk, business checking account, or an escrow account
- Office may be in broker's residence *provided* the entrance sign is displayed and local zoning permits business in residence
- Sales associates must be registered and work out of the broker's office or branch office and may *not* open their own offices

■ **Branch offices**
- Each branch office must be registered (two-year period)
- Branch office registrations are *not* transferable to another location
- A broker may reopen a branch office in the same location during the same license period by requesting a reissue of the branch office license
- A *temporary shelter* in a subdivision being sold by a broker is not a branch office if the shelter is intended only for the protection of customers and sales associates (if business records are maintained at location and sales associates are assigned to location, then it must be registered as a branch office)

■ **Active real estate brokers must display an official entrance office sign** with the following:
- Trade name (if one is used)
- Name of the broker
- Words "Licensed (or Lic.) Real Estate Broker"

■ **Entrance sign of brokerage partnerships, corporations, limited liability companies, or limited liability partnerships** must include the following:
- Name of the business (or trade name, if one is used)
- Name of at least one active broker
- Words "Licensed (or Lic.) Real Estate Broker"
- Names of sales associates (if included) must be separate from the broker's names and identified as sales associates or broker associates

■ **Advertising**
- Advertising real estate services is a broker activity
- Advertising must be in the name of the brokerage and under the supervision of the broker
- Sales associates may not advertise real estate services in their own names

■ **Team advertising**
- Teams must advertise in the name of the brokerage firm

■ **Blind advertisements**
- An ad that fails to disclose the name of the brokerage firm
- Advertising must be worded so that reasonable people will know that they are dealing with a licensee

■ **Personal information**
- If licensees include their personal name in an advertisement, they must use their last name as registered with the DBPR

  - FREC does not require that the brokerage firm's phone number or address be included in ads
  - Yard signs, classified ads, and promotional advertising must include name of real estate brokerage firm
- **False advertising**
  - False advertising is a second-degree misdemeanor
  - A broker associate cannot use the title broker because the associate is not working in a broker capacity for the brokerage
- **Internet sites**
  - Internet advertising must include point of contact information
  - Internet advertising must include the brokerage firm's name adjacent to, above, or below the point of contact information
- **Unauthorized use of association names**
  - Must be a current member in good standing to use designation
  - False advertising if not entitled to represent oneself as a member
- **Licensee selling property "by owner"**
  - A licensee who owns property and is selling the property "by owner" may place a classified ad
  - Licensees are *not* required to indicate in the ad that they are licensees
  - Licensees should disclose to prospective buyers that they are licensed prior to entering into serious negotiations
- **A telephone solicitation is the initiation of a phone call for the purpose of selling property, goods, or services**
  - Telemarketers must search the National Do Not Call Registry before making telemarketing calls
  - Violators of the federal Telephone Consumer Protection Act may be fined up to $16,000 per call
- **Prerecorded telemarketing calls**
  - Federal Communications Commission (FCC) bans text messages sent to mobile phones using an autodialer, unless the consumer gave consent to receive the message
  - Must obtain written consent before sending a prerecorded telemarketing call to a residential phone number or making an autodialed or prerecorded telemarketing call or text to a wireless number
- **Email advertising**
  - CAN-SPAM Act restricts sending unwanted commercial email messages to computers
  - Must allow the consumer to opt out of receiving future messages
- **Fax solicitations**
  - It is unlawful to send unsolicited advertisements to a residential or business fax machine without the recipient's prior express permission
- **State regulation**
  - Florida also maintains a no-sales-solicitation calls list

- — Florida Telemarketing Act allows real estate licensees to call For-Sale-by-Owner or Expired Listings (provided the number is not on the national call list)
- — Violators of Florida's Telemarketing Act may be fined $10,000 per call
- — Businesses that use telemarketing must develop and adhere to written procedures regarding the firms' calling policies

- **Escrow or trust accounts**
  - — Money associated with leasing property must be held in an escrow account
  - — Brokers are not required, but are recommended, to keep earnest money deposits separate from rental deposits
  - — Broker must be a signatory on broker's escrow account
  - — Broker must reconcile escrow account each month
  - — Broker must review, sign, and date monthly reconciliation
  - — Broker is accountable for reviewing the brokerage's escrow accounting procedures to ensure compliance with Florida law
- **Immediately defined**
  - — Sales associates must deliver earnest money deposits to their broker no later than the end of the next business day
  - — Brokers must place deposits into their escrow account no later than the end of the third business day

    EXAMPLE Sales associate receives a deposit on Wednesday (no legal holidays involved); sales associate must turn over to broker by end of business on Thursday, and broker must deposit by end of business on Monday

  - — The date the buyer gives the funds to the brokerage is *not* included in the broker's time period
  - — The broker's three-business-day time period always begins on the business day after the check is given to the brokerage company
- **Postdated checks and insufficient funds**
  - — Broker must obtain seller's approval before accepting a postdated check
  - — Broker is not held responsible for the nonpayment of an escrow check provided the broker timely deposits the check
- **Acceptable depositories**
  - — Broker's escrow accounts are maintained at Florida commercial banks, savings associations, and credit unions
  - — Alternatively attorneys and title companies with trust powers may hold the funds instead of the broker (but *not* in stock or bond brokerage house)
- **Signatory on escrow accounts**
  - — Brokers are required to be a signatory on all their brokerage escrow accounts
  - — Brokers must reconcile escrow accounts each month and review, sign, and date the monthly bank reconciliations
- **Title company and attorney escrow accounts**
  - — If an attorney or title-closing agent will hold the deposit, the broker is still required to deliver the funds to the escrow agent within the same time frame required for depositing funds into a broker's escrow account

- Licensee who prepared or presented the sale contract must indicate on the contract the title company's name (or attorney's name, if applicable), address, and telephone number
- No later than 10 business days after the deposit is due under the contract, the licensee's broker must make a written request to the escrow holder for written verification of receipt of the deposit
- If the deposit is held by a title company or by an attorney nominated in writing by the seller or the seller's agent, the verification is waived
- No later than 10 business days after the date the broker made the written request for verification of the deposit, the broker must provide the seller's broker with a copy of the written verification
- If the title company or attorney failed to provide the written verification, this information must be conveyed to the seller's broker no later than 10 business days after making the request for verification of the deposit
- The same procedure must be followed for each deposit required in the sale contract

- **Interest-bearing escrow accounts**
  - Escrow account may be an interest-bearing or a non-interest-bearing account; if interest-bearing, must secure the written permission of all interested parties and broker must get written authorization from the buyer and seller as to who is entitled to interest earned
- **Recordkeeping and retention**
  - Records must be retained for at least five years from the date of an executed agreement
  - If records are the subject of litigation, the relevant records must be preserved for two years beyond the conclusion of the litigation, but for not less than five years
- **Misappropriation of escrow funds**
  - Brokers may not commingle (mix) escrow deposits with business funds or personal funds
  - Conversion is the unauthorized control or use of another person's personal property
- **Money to maintain escrow account**
  - Broker is allowed to place up to $1,000 of personal funds in sales escrow accounts
  - Broker is allowed to place up to $5,000 of personal funds in property management escrow account
  - Brokers who maintain sales escrow funds *and* property management escrow funds in a single escrow account may place up to $5,000 of personal funds into the escrow account
- **Monthly reconciliation procedure** *(Study material for broker candidates only)*
  - Determine trust liability by adding contract deposits held
  - Begin with reported bank balance, add deposits in transit, subtract outstanding checks; result equals reconciled bank balance

- Reconciled bank balance should equal trust liability: if trust liability exceeds reconciled bank balance, broker has a shortage; if trust liability is less than reconciled bank balance, broker has an overage
- Shortages and overages must be corrected and explained

- **Interest-bearing escrow accounts** *(Study material for broker candidates only)*
  - If interest is to go to the buyer or seller, both deposit and interest earned must be deposited into non-interest-bearing escrow account before disbursing
  - Alternative method if interest is to go to the buyer or seller: open a separate interest-bearing account for each transaction
  - If interest is to go to the broker, interest must be withdrawn monthly
- **Conflicting demands and good-faith doubt**
  - Broker must notify the FREC, in writing, within 15 business days
  - Broker must institute one of four settlement procedures within 30 business days from the time the broker received the conflicting demands
- **Four settlement procedures (MALE)**
  - **M** **M**ediation (negotiated settlement)
  - **A** **A**rbitration (binding)
  - **L** **L**itigation
  - **E** **E**scrow disbursement order (EDO)
- **Litigation can involve either of two court procedures**
  - Interpleader is used when the broker does not have a financial claim to the disputed escrow funds and deposits the funds with the court registry
  - Declaratory judgment is used when brokers believe they are entitled to a portion of the disputed funds
- **Requesting an EDO**
  - FREC makes a determination as to who is entitled to the disputed funds
  - Applicable only if the funds are held in a broker's escrow account (not applicable if escrow funds are held by an attorney or a title company)
  - Broker must notify the FREC within 10 business days if the dispute is settled or the matter goes to court before the EDO is issued
- **Three exceptions to notice and settlement procedures**
  - Sale of HUD-owned property using a HUD contract
  - If buyer of a residential condominium unit gives written notice of buyer's intent to cancel the contract as authorized by the Condominium Act
  - If buyer in good faith fails to satisfy the terms specified in the financing clause of a contract
- **Title company or attorney as escrow agent**
  - Broker has no obligation to report an escrow dispute to FREC or to institute a settlement procedure
- **Monies paid in advance for performing real estate services**
  - Funds must be placed into an escrow account until the services are completed

- Once service is completed, the broker must transfer funds into the operating account
- The Timeshare Act prohibits a real estate licensee from collecting an advance fee for the listing of a time-share unit

■ **Rental information and lists**
- Rental list must include a receipt to prospective tenant concerning repayment
- If rental information is in error: 100% refund
- If unable to find a suitable rental: 75% refund
- Demand for refund must be made within 30 days following the day of purchase
- Violation is a first degree misdemeanor

■ **Sales associate's commission**
- All commissions, listings, and contracts are legal property of the broker
- Monies earned by sales associates for real estate services must be paid by their employer and not directly by buyers or sellers
- Sales associates cannot contract directly with customers or clients
- Exception for sharing commission with a party to the transaction with full disclosure in writing to all interested parties

■ **Antitrust laws**
- Price-fixing occurs when competing brokers conspire to establish a standard commission rate rather than let the rate be set by the open market
- Market allocation is an agreement between brokers to split up competitive market areas among themselves and not compete in each other's areas

■ **Liens on real property for unpaid sales commission**
- Only the broker can initiate an action for unpaid commission
- Sales associates cannot sue a customer or client for unpaid commission
- Regulations regarding unpaid sales commission are dictated by the type of real estate

■ **Residential real property**
- Broker must be authorized in the contract to place a lien on residential real property for nonpayment of commission
- Broker's license may be suspended or revoked for the unauthorized recording of a lis pendens or a lien that affects the title of residential real property

■ **Commercial real estate sales**
- The Commercial Real Estate Sales Commission Lien Act gives brokers lien rights on commercial property for nonpayment of earned commission
- Lien is against owner's net proceeds from the sale (personal property) and does not attach to the real property
- Broker must disclose at the time of executing the listing agreement that the agreement creates lien rights for commission earned and that the seller cannot waive the lien right once agreed to

- **Commercial Real Estate Leasing Commission Lien Act**
  - Part IV of Chapter 475 gives brokers lien rights for earned commission associated with a brokerage agreement to lease commercial real estate
  - If the landlord is the person obligated to pay the leasing commission, broker's lien attaches to the landlord's interest
  - If the tenant is the person obligated to pay the leasing commission, broker's lien attaches to the tenant's leasehold estate
- **Kickbacks**
  - A *kickback* is an unearned fee paid to a licensee associated with a real estate transaction for non-real estate services
  - Prior to the payment and receipt of the kickback, the buyer and seller must be fully informed of facts regarding the kickback
  - Kickbacks must not violate RESPA
  - Kickbacks are *not* allowed for title and casualty insurance transactions
  - Person receiving the kickback must be properly licensed if a license is required to perform the service (In Florida, real estate licensees must also be licensed as mortgage loan originators to be legally paid a fee for referring prospects to a mortgage lender)
  - Licensees are prohibited from sharing commission with an unlicensed person for real estate services (exception if sharing commission with a buyer or seller in a real estate transaction, provided the rebate is disclosed to all interested parties)
- **Types of business entities that may register as a brokerage entity**
  - *Sole proprietorship* (features unlimited liability and no formal requirement to create)
  - *General partnership* (each partner is responsible for all business debts)
  - *Limited partnership* (created by filing agreement with the state, and features unlimited liability for general partners and limited liability for limited partners; word "limited" or abbreviation must be used in name, and limited partners make cash or property investment but *not* managerial services)
  - *Limited liability partnership* (protection from personal liability for acts of another partner or employee)
  - *Corporation* (features separate legal entity from the owners and is formed by filing Articles of Incorporation and must include "company" or "incorporated" or abbreviation in name [*Note:* Sales associate and broker associate may *not* be officers or directors of a brokerage corporation; broker associate must change status to broker before becoming an officer or director.])
  - *Limited liability company* (protection from business debts)
- **Real estate brokerage general partnership**
  - The partnership must register with the DBPR under the partnership name
  - At least one partner must be licensed as an active broker
  - Partners who deal with the public and perform real estate services must be licensed as active brokers
  - All partners not licensed as brokers must register with the DBPR for identification purposes

- Sales associates and broker associates may *not* be general partners in a real estate brokerage partnership
- If the partnership has only one active broker who dies, resigns, or is removed from office, the broker of record must be replaced within 14 calendar days
- It is the responsibility of every active broker in the partnership to see that the partnership and all of its partners and sales associates have current and appropriate registration and licenses

- **Real estate brokerage limited partnerships**
  - The limited partnership must register with the DBPR under the limited partnership name
  - General partners who deal with the public and perform real estate services must be licensed as active brokers
  - All other general partners must register with the DBPR for identification purposes
  - Sales associates and broker associates may *not* be general partners in a real estate brokerage limited partnership
  - Sales associates and broker associates may be limited partners in a real estate brokerage limited partnership (regarded in same light as stockholders in a corporation)
  - Limited partners are not required to register with the DBPR
- **An ostensible partnership (or quasi partnership) is created when the actions of two or more persons create the appearance that a partnership exists**
  - Fraudulent and deceitful if the public is deceived into believing that a partnership exists
  - Parties may be held liable for each other's debts and torts
  - Licensees may be subject to license suspension
  - Brokers in the same office building doing business separately must each have their own office signs, use separate telephone numbers, register their own business names, and indicate the brokerage names on separate letterhead and business cards
- **Real estate brokerage corporations**
  - The corporation must register with the DBPR under the corporation name
  - At least one officer or director must be licensed as an active broker
  - Active Florida brokers, inactive Florida brokers, and unlicensed people may serve as officers and directors of a real estate brokerage
  - Officers and directors who deal with the public and perform real estate services must be licensed as active brokers
  - All officers and directors who are not licensed must be registered with the DBPR for identification purposes
  - Sales associates and broker associates may *not* be an officer or director in a real estate brokerage corporation
  - Sales associates and broker associates may be shareholders of a real estate brokerage corporation

- **Vacancies of office**
  - Vacancy of only active broker must be filled within 14 calendar days
  - Vacancy may be filled with a temporary broker registered with the DBPR for up to 60 days
  - After 60 days, must be properly registered with the Department of State
  - Failure to appoint another active or temporary broker within the 14-day deadline results in automatic cancellation of the brokerage registration
- **Business entities that may *not* register as a brokerage**
  - Corporation sole (churches)
  - Joint venture (an agreement to participate in one or a limited number of transactions)
  - If two parties form a joint venture to provide real estate services for compensation, both parties must be licensed real estate brokers
  - Business trust (for example Real Estate Investment Trust—REIT)
  - Cooperative association
  - Unincorporated association
- **A trade name is a business name other than the legal name of the person doing business**
  - Fictitious name refers to the name registered with the Department of State
  - A broker or brokerage entity may use a trade name after it is registered with the DBPR
  - DBPR will not allow a broker to register a trade name if the name is already registered with the DOS or the DBPR
  - A brokerage entity cannot be registered or operate under more than one trade name
  - Sales associates and broker associates may not use a trade (fictitious) name
  - Real Estate sales associates and broker associates may form a professional corporation, limited liability company, or professional limited liability company for income tax purposes
- **Personal assistants**
  - Unlicensed assistants may not perform any service of real estate
  - Unlicensed assistants may not be paid a commission or on a transaction basis
  - Licensed assistants may perform any service of real estate
  - Licensed assistants must be registered under the licensee's employing broker
  - The employing broker must pay licensed assistants for all activities that require a license
  - Licensees may pay licensed and unlicensed assistants for activities that do not require a license

IMPORTANT DATES AND TIME PERIODS TO REMEMBER

- **End of next business day.** Time period for sales associates to turn funds over to broker
- **End of third business day.** Time period for broker to deposit funds into escrow account
- **10 business days.** Number of days to notify the FREC if the broker requested an EDO and the escrow dispute is either settled or goes to court before the EDO is issued
- **14 calendar days.** Number of days to replace broker of record
- **15 business days.** Number of days to notify the FREC of conflicting demands or good faith doubt
- **30 business days.** Number of days to institute settlement procedure after receiving conflicting demands
- **60 days.** Number of days a temporary broker may be registered with the DBPR without being registered with the Secretary of State
- **Five years.** Time period to preserve broker's business records (two years after litigation, if longer than five years)

SECTION 5 VIOLATIONS OF LICENSE LAW, PENALTIES, AND PROCEDURES

(See Unit 6 in *Florida Real Estate Principles, Practices & Law* and Unit 5 in *Florida Real Estate Broker's Guide*)

KEY TERM REVIEW

Breach of trust is the breaking of a promise or obligation.

Citations are fines for violations that have been specified in the citation rule for which there is no substantial threat to the public health, safety, and welfare.

Commingle is to mix the money of a buyer or seller with a broker's own money.

Complaint is an alleged violation of a law or rule.

Concealment is the withholding of information.

Conversion is a licensee's personal use or misuse of client (or customer) monies.

Culpable negligence is failing to use the care a reasonable person would exercise.

Division of Administrative Hearings (DOAH) is the entity that employs administrative law judges (ALJs) to conduct formal hearings of administrative complaints against licensees.

Failure to account for and deliver is the act of failing to pay money to a person entitled to receive it.

Final orders are the Commission's final decisions as to innocence or guilt and the determination of the appropriate penalty.

Formal (administrative) complaint is an outline of charges against a licensee.

Formal hearings are used if the licensee-respondent either requests a formal hearing or if the licensee-respondent disputes the allegations.

Fraud is the intentional deceit and reliance on the deception for the purpose of inducing another person to rely on the deceitful information and as a consequence be harmed by the deceit.

Informal hearings are an expedited way of resolving disciplinary cases provided the licensee does not dispute the alleged facts stated in the complaint.

Legally sufficient means that a complaint contains facts indicating that a violation of Florida statute, DBPR rule, or FREC rule may have occurred.

Material fact is a piece of information that affects the value of the real property and is relevant to a person making a decision about the property.

Misrepresentation is an untrue statement of fact or an incorrect or false representation of the facts.

Moral turpitude is conduct contrary to honesty, good morals, justice, and accepted custom.

Notice of noncompliance may be issued for a first-time minor violation (licensee has 15 days to correct minor infraction).

Probable cause is reasonable grounds (sufficient facts and evidence) to warrant prosecution.

Recommended order contains the administrative law judge's findings, conclusions, and recommended penalty.

Stipulation is an agreement as to the penalty reached between the attorneys for the DRE and the licensee or licensee's attorney.

Subpoena is a command to appear at a certain time and place to give testimony.

Summary (emergency) suspension is an order that must be issued by the DBPR secretary or the secretary's designee.

Voluntary relinquishment for permanent revocation occurs when a licensee-respondent chooses to avoid a disciplinary hearing by relinquishing the real estate license, permanently putting the licensee out of the real estate business.

KEY CONCEPTS

- **Legal terms to know**
  - Breach of trust
  - Commingle
  - Concealment
  - Conversion
  - Culpable negligence
  - Failure to account for and deliver
  - Fraud
  - Material fact
  - Misrepresentation
  - Moral turpitude
- **Complaint process** (quasi-judicial procedure)
  - A complaint is filed
  - Investigation of the complaint
  - Probable cause determination
  - Formal complaint is issued if probable cause is found
  - Informal hearing or formal hearing is conducted
  - Final order is issued
  - Judicial review (appeal) of the final order
- **Complaint is filed with the DBPR**
  - Complaint must be legally sufficient
  - DBPR may issue a notice of noncompliance for a first-time offense of a minor violation
  - FREC rule lists violations for which a notice of noncompliance may be issued
- **Investigation** of the complaint
  - Complaint must be in writing and legally sufficient
  - Anonymous (unsigned) complaint is accepted if complaint is substantial
  - DBPR/DRE investigates (not the FREC)
  - Summary (emergency) suspension issued by DBPR Secretary in serious cases to suspend licensee immediately

- **Probable-cause panel**
  - Composed of two current members or one current and one former member of the FREC
  - Closed to the public
  - Decision as to whether probable cause exists is made by majority vote of the panel or by the DBPR, if the profession does not have a board
  - If probable cause not found, may dismiss case or dismiss with letter of guidance
- **Formal (administrative) complaint is issued if probable cause is found**
  - Outline of allegations of facts and charges against the licensee
  - Sent to address of record by certified mail and includes respondent's election of rights
- **Licensee-respondent and DRE may reach a possible settlement prior to a hearing and enter into a stipulation**
  - The agreement as to the facts of the case and the penalty reached between the attorneys for the DRE and the licensee is a *stipulation*
  - The terms of the stipulation are approved or denied by the FREC during a Commission meeting
- **Voluntary relinquishment for permanent revocation**
  - Licensee-respondent chooses to avoid a disciplinary hearing
  - Licensee voluntarily relinquishes the real estate license in lieu of discipline
  - Permanently puts the licensee out of the real estate business
- **Informal hearing**
  - Licensee signs *election of rights* and does *not* dispute allegations of material fact and requests an informal hearing before the FREC for final action of the complaint
  - Held during regular Commission meeting
  - Probable cause members do not participate in informal hearing
  - Licensee *must* agree that there is no dispute of the material fact to choose informal hearing
- **Waiver hearing**
  - Subject of complaint failed to timely respond to Election of Rights; licensee respondent has waived Election of Rights
- **Formal hearing**
  - Respondent/licensee signs *election of rights disputing* allegations of material fact and requests a formal hearing to determine the facts
  - Formal hearing is mandatory if licensee/respondent disputes the allegations
  - Administrative law judge (ALJ) hears testimony
  - ALJ has power to swear in witnesses, take testimony under oath, and issue subpoenas
  - ALJ prepares and submits a *recommended order* to the DBPR that includes judge's findings and conclusions, and the recommended penalty based on range of penalties in FREC rule

- **Final order**
  - Probable cause members do not participate
  - Commission may accept, reject, or modify the conclusions of law in the administrative law judge's recommended order
  - Effective 30 days after final order is issued
  - Licensee may operate during complaint process and during 30-day period
- **Appeal (judicial review)** must be filed within 30 days with District Court of Appeals
  - Licensee may request appeals court to stop enforcement of penalty
  - *Writ of supersedeas* stops (stays) enforcement of penalty
  - Writ supersedes the action of the FREC and allows the licensee to practice real estate until the case is heard on appeal
- **Licensee may continue to operate pending appeal provided**
  - Licensee has filed an appeal
  - An *order of stay* is requested
  - Request for stay is granted (*writ of supersedeas* is issued)
- **Three types of penalties for violations of license law**
  - Administrative
  - Civil
  - Criminal
- **Types of administrative penalties**
  - Denial of a license application and refusal to recertify a license for renewal
  - Letter of reprimand is least severe administrative penalty
  - Notice of noncompliance issued by DBPR for first-time minor violation
  - Citation issued by DBPR investigator for minor violation during investigation or audit
  - Administrative fine of up to $5,000 per count or separate offense for violating Chapter 475 and Chapter 455
  - Suspension for up to 10 years
  - Revocation with prejudice (*Revocation without prejudice* applies to license issued in error)
  - Probation
- **Civil penalties** are enforced by courts if an unlicensed person performs real estate service or a licensee commits fraud
- **Criminal violations must be reported to the state attorney**
  - FREC must inform the Division of Florida Condominiums, Timeshares, and Mobile Homes of disciplinary action taken against a real estate licensee
  - FREC cannot issue incarceration (jail sentence)
  - FREC does not have authority to order restitution

- **Unlicensed practice of real estate for compensation, theft of a license exam, and falsifying a license application are felonies of the third degree**
  - The criminal penalty is a fine of not more than $5,000 and/or up to five years in jail
  - DBPR issues cease and desist order, or it may issue an injunction or a writ of mandamus ordering unlicensed activity to stop
- **Criminal self-reporting**
  - Licensee must inform the Commission, in writing, within 30 days of being convicted or found guilty of a crime
- **First-degree misdemeanor** is a criminal penalty punishable in a court of law by a fine of not more than $1,000 and/or by imprisonment for not more than one year
  - Failing to provide accurate and current rental information for a fee
- **Second-degree misdemeanor** describes all other violations of Chapter 475
  - $500 fine and/or 60 days imprisonment
- **Real Estate Recovery Fund**
  - Separate account used to reimburse an individual judged by a Florida court to have suffered monetary damages as a result of license law violations by a licensee
  - Licensee must hold an active license at the time of the alleged act
  - To be eligible for reimbursement, the injured party must file a civil suit, a final judgment must be issued against the licensee, and an attempt must be made to collect on the judgment
  - Claims for reimbursement must be made within two years of the alleged act or within two years of the discovery of the alleged act
  - Claim limited to $50,000 per transaction (or the unsatisfied portion of a judgment claim, whichever is less) regardless of the number of claimants
  - Claims against one licensee may not exceed in total $150,000
  - Fee collected from licensees when fund drops below $500,000; collection is discontinued when the fund exceeds $1 million
  - License is automatically suspended upon payment from the fund until the fund is reimbursed (including interest)
  - A broker who complies with an escrow disbursement order (EDO) and is later sued may be reimbursed from the fund without penalty
- **Persons NOT eligible to seek reimbursement from Recovery Fund**
  - Spouse of the offending licensee
  - Licensee who acted as a single agent or a transaction broker in the transaction may not make a claim for unpaid commission
  - Anyone who bases the claim on a real estate transaction in which a licensee owned or controlled the property and was dealing for his or her own account (not acting as a licensee)
  - Anyone who makes a claim against a licensee with an inactive real estate license at the time of transaction
  - Judgment was issued against a business entity and not an individual

IMPORTANT DATES AND TIME PERIODS TO REMEMBER

- **15 days.** Number of days to correct minor infraction listed in notice of non-compliance
- **30 days.** Number of days after which a final order becomes effective
- **30 days.** Time period to file an appeal
- **30 days.** Number of days licensee has to accept or file a written objection to a citation
- **60 days and/or $500 fine.** Penalty for second-degree misdemeanor
- **One year and/or $1,000 fine.** Penalty for first-degree misdemeanor
- **Two years.** Time period allowed to file claim against recovery fund
- **10 years.** Maximum period of suspension

SECTION 6 FEDERAL AND STATE LAWS PERTAINING TO REAL ESTATE

(See Unit 7 in *Florida Real Estate Principles, Practices & Law* and Units 2, 12, 17, and 18 in *Florida Real Estate Broker's Guide*)

KEY TERM REVIEW

Blockbusting is to use entry, or rumor of entry, of a protected class into a neighborhood to persuade owners to sell.

Civil Rights Act of 1866 prohibits any type of discrimination based on *race* in *all* real estate transactions (sale or rental) without exception.

Fair Housing Act created protected classes of people and prohibits discrimination when selling or renting certain residential property.

Familial status is a protected class of people under the Fair Housing Act, consisting of families with children younger than 18 and pregnant women.

Handicap status is a protected class of people under the Fair Housing Act who have a physical or mental impairment that interferes with normal life functions.

Property reports are disclosure documents required under the federal Interstate Land Sales Full Disclosure Act.

Public accommodations are facilities open to the public, including sales and rental establishments, hotels, and shopping centers.

Redlining is to deny loans or insurance coverage by a lender or insurer or presenting different terms or conditions for homes in certain neighborhoods.

Steering is channeling protected-class homeseekers away from areas that are not mixed with that class into areas that are.

KEY CONCEPTS

- Civil Rights Act of 1866
  - Prohibits racial discrimination
  - Applies to all real estate transactions without exception
  - *Jones v. Mayer* upheld Civil Rights Act of 1866
- Civil Rights Act of 1964
  - Prohibits discrimination based on race, color, religion, or national origin
  - Applies to public accommodations
  - Applies to public facilities operated by state or municipal governments
  - Ended racial segregation

- **Civil Rights Act of 1968: The Fair Housing Act** as amended, established protected classes
  - Race
  - Color
  - Religion
  - Sex
  - National origin
- **Fair Housing Amendments Act** of 1988 expanded protections
  - Familial status
  - Handicap status
  - No protection is given to individuals based on age, occupation, marital status, or sexual orientation
  - Fair Housing Act prohibits discrimination in sales, leasing, advertising sales and rentals, financing, and brokerage services
- **Discrimination in general**
  - It is illegal to direct discrimination at a protected class
  - Laws protect specific protected classes
- **Fair Housing Act requires use of equal housing opportunity poster**
  - Poster features housing logo and statement pledging adherence to the Fair Housing Act
  - Must be displayed in real estate offices
  - Failure to display poster may be considered evidence of discrimination in the event a discrimination complaint is filed
  - Burden of proof to prove no discrimination has occurred is on a broker who fails to display the poster
- **Housing under Fair Housing Act** includes sale or rental of housing, financing of housing, and brokerage services, specifically
  - Government-owned residential property
  - All privately owned residential property if a real estate licensee is employed
  - Residential property owned by a person who owns four or more residential units
  - Residential property when the owner, during the past two years, sells two or more houses in which the owner did not reside
  - Multifamily dwellings of five or more units
  - Multifamily dwellings of four or fewer units if the owner does not reside in one of the units
- **Housing for older persons** is exempt from familial status protection under the Fair Housing Act provided one of two situations exists
  - All units must be occupied by persons 62 years of age or older
  - At least 80% of the units are occupied by one or more persons 55 years of age or older
- **Real estate transactions exempted under the Fair Housing Act**
  - Two conditions must be met: (1) real estate licensee not involved and (2) no discriminatory advertising

  - Seller owns three or fewer single-family dwellings and sells or rents the property
  - Seller was not living in the single-family house and was not the most recent resident when the property was sold or rented (one sale is exempt within a 24-month period)
  - Rentals in multifamily dwellings of four or fewer family units, and the owner lives in one of the units
  - Although these transactions are exempt under the Fair Housing Act, if racial discrimination occurs, the individual can be sued under the Civil Rights Act of 1866
- **Special exemptions under the Fair Housing Act**
  - Religious organizations may restrict dwelling units they own or operate to members of their religion provided the organization does not discriminate in accepting its membership
  - Private clubs may restrict rental or occupancy of its units to its members
- **Prohibited activities**
  - Refusing to rent to, sell to, negotiate with, or deal with a member of a protected class
  - Quoting different terms or conditions for buying or renting
  - Advertising that housing is available only to people of a certain race, color, religion, sex, national origin, handicap status, or familial status
  - Steering: channeling protected-class homeseekers away from areas that are not mixed with that class into areas that are mixed with that class
  - Blockbusting: inducing a person to sell or lease because the area is "in transition"; use of entry or rumor of entry of a protected class to persuade homeowners to sell
  - Redlining: denying loans or insurance coverage or offering loans or insurance coverage with different terms or conditions for homes in certain neighborhoods
  - Denying membership in or use of any real estate service, brokers' organization, or MLS
  - Making false statements concerning the availability of housing for inspection, rent, or sale
- **Enforcement of the Fair Housing Act**
  - Complaints filed with HUD under the Fair Housing Act
  - Action taken by the Department of Justice
  - Civil suits filed in Federal District Court
  - Responsibility and liability of real estate licensees
- **Florida Fair Housing Act**
- **Fair Housing Case**
- **Americans with Disabilities Act of 1990**
  - Protects employment and accessibility rights of individuals with mental and physical disabilities
  - Individuals with disabilities may not be denied access to public transportation, public accommodations, and commercial facilities

- Public accommodations and commercial facilities must be newly constructed or altered, if readily achievable, to meet accessibility standards
- Broker offices must comply with ADA provisions
- If the broker's office is in a private residence, the accessibility standards apply to that portion used exclusively as an office and to portions available to customers, including bathrooms

- **Florida Americans with Disabilities Accessibility Implementation Act**
- **Interstate Land Sales Full Disclosure Act (ILSA)**
  - Advertising and sale or lease of real estate in one state to buyers in another state is subject to federal regulations
  - ILSA is intended to prevent fraudulent marketing schemes when land is sold without being seen by purchasers
  - ILSA is administered by the director of the Consumer Financial Protection Bureau
  - Developers who market subdivisions of fewer than 25 lots are exempt from ILSA
  - Developers of 25 or more lots must provide each purchaser with a property report before the signing of the contract
  - Purchasers who receive the property report prior to signing the contract may cancel the contract within seven days
  - Contract must state purchaser's right to cancel contract
  - Developers must register subdivisions of 100 or more lots by filing a statement of record with the Consumer Financial Protection Bureau
- **Florida Residential Landlord and Tenant Act** applies to residential tenancies
- **Landlord must maintain security deposits and advance rent**
  - Separate non-interest-bearing escrow account
  - Separate interest-bearing account and pay tenant 5% interest or 75% of interest earned
  - Separate account is *not* required if the landlord posts a surety bond for the lesser of the amount of the funds or $50,000 (pay tenant 5% interest)
  - Landlords of five or more units must give tenants written notice of the advance rent or deposit within 30 days of receipt
- **If a real estate broker holds the funds on behalf of a landlord, the broker must abide by real estate license law concerning escrowed funds**
  - Landlords must approve or deny the rental application of an active military service member within seven days
  - Sale of a property does not terminate a lease unless the lease specifically provides for its termination when title is transferred to a new owner
- **Landlords must approve or deny the rental application of an active military service member within seven days**
- **Sale of property does not terminate a lease unless the lease** specifically provides for its termination when title is transferred to a new owner
- **Case study**
- **Landlord's obligation to maintain premises**

- **Tenant's obligations**
- **Landlord's access to premises**
- **Vacating premises**
- **Termination of rental agreements by the tenant**
- **Termination of rental agreements by the landlord**
- **Eviction requirements**

IMPORTANT DATES AND TIME PERIODS TO REMEMBER

- **24-hours.** Time period after notice is posted by sheriff that eviction will take place and landlord recovers the property
- **Seven days.** Time period allowed to cancel contract under the Interstate Land Sales Full Disclosure Act
- **Seven days.** Time period for landlord to approve or deny a rental application for an active duty military prospective tenant
- **15 days.** Number of days for landlord to return security deposit if not making a claim on deposit
- **15 days.** Time period for tenant to file a written objection to the landlord's claim on deposit
- **30 days.** Number of days for landlord to notify tenant if making a claim on the deposit
- **30 days.** Number of days landlords of five or more units have to inform tenants regarding how funds are being held
- **One year.** Time period from the day the discriminatory act occurred to file a complaint with HUD.

SECTION 7 PROPERTY RIGHTS: ESTATES AND TENANCIES, CONDOMINIUMS, COOPERATIVES, AND TIME-SHARING

(See Unit 8 in *Florida Real Estate Principles, Practices & Law* and Units 11, 12, and 18 in *Florida Real Estate Broker's Guide*)

KEY TERM REVIEW

Bundle of legal rights are real property ownership rights consisting of the rights of disposition, enjoyment, exclusion, possession, and control.

Common elements such as roofs, elevators, and recreational facilities are legally attached to condominium units and are transferred with the units when they are sold.

Concurrent ownership means ownership by two or more persons at the same time.

Condominium documents are a set of papers describing the condominium and the association.

Condominiums are multiunit projects consisting of individual ownership of a dwelling unit and undivided ownership of common areas.

Cooperative is a multiunit dwelling owned by a corporation; owners purchase shares in the corporation and receive a proprietary lease.

Declaration of Condominium is a recorded document that creates the condominium.

Estate for years is a written lease with a definite termination date.

Estate in severalty occurs when title to property is held by one person.

Fee simple estate is the most common type of ownership; it is the most comprehensive collection of property rights and may be inherited.

Fixtures are objects that were personal property but have been permanently attached to or made part of real property by attachment.

Freehold estate is an ownership interest for an indefinite period of time.

Homestead law provides certain types of protection and benefits to homeowners regarding their permanent residence.

Joint tenancy is an ownership interest between two or more persons with right of survivorship.

Land refers to the surface of the earth and to everything attached to it by nature.

Leasehold estate (tenancy) is an interest in real property that a tenant possesses (measured in calendar time).

Life estate is a freehold estate that ends with the death of a named person; ownership for an individual's natural life span.

Littoral rights are associated with land abutting tidal bodies of water, such as an ocean, sea, or lake.

Nonfreehold estates have a known duration and do not involve an ownership interest.

Personal property or chattel is any tangible item that is *not* real property and that is movable.

Proprietary lease is the document that entitles a shareholder in a cooperative to possession of a unit.

Prospectus A developer is required to provide purchasers a prospectus if the condominium consists of more than 20 residential units, or is part of a group of residential condominiums that will be served by property to be used in common by unit owners of more than 20 units. The prospectus summarizes some of the major points detailed in the condominium documents.

Real estate refers to the land and all improvements permanently attached to land.

Real property includes all real estate plus the legal bundle of rights inherent in the ownership of real estate.

Remainderman is the third party to whom a property is transferred at the end of a life estate (*vested* if named; *contingent* if not named).

Right of survivorship means that when a co-owner dies, that co-owner's share goes to the surviving co-owner(s) and not to the deceased tenant's heirs.

Riparian rights are associated with land abutting the banks of a river, stream, or other watercourse.

Separate property is nonmarital assets.

Tenancy at sufferance exists when the tenant, after rightfully being in possession of the rented property, continues possession after the tenant's right has ended; a *holdover* tenant.

Tenancy at will is a leasehold in which the tenant holds possession of the premises with the owner's permission but without a fixed term.

Tenancy by the entireties is an estate created by a married couple who take title together at the same time.

Tenants in common is the most frequently used form of co-ownership except for ownership by a married couple.

Time-share ownership involves an undivided interest in a living unit according to the number of weeks purchased.

Trade fixture is an item of personal property attached to real property that is owned by a tenant and used in a business that is legally removable by the tenant.

Undivided interest is an interest in the entire property, rather than ownership of a particular part of the property.

KEY CONCEPTS

- **Land, real estate, and real property**
  - *Land* refers to the surface of the earth and items attached by nature
  - *Real estate* includes land and all human-made improvements
  - *Real property* includes real estate plus the legal bundle of rights
- **Physical components (rights) of land**
  - Surface
  - Subsurface
  - Air
- **Surface rights** include water rights
  - Riparian—associated with land abutting a flowing water way, such as the banks of a river or stream
  - Littoral—associated with land abutting tidal bodies of water, such as an ocean and sea, and nonflowing water, such as ponds and lakes
- **Subsurface rights** consist of an owner's rights to underground minerals, petroleum, and natural gas, referred to as mineral rights

- **Definitions** associated with water rights
  - *Accretion* is the process of land build-up from water-borne rock, sand, and soil
  - *Alluvion* is the resulting new deposits of land caused by accretion
  - *Erosion* is the gradual loss of land due to natural forces
  - *Reliction* is the gradual receding of water, uncovering additional land
- **Real property versus personal property (chattel)**
  - Anything that is *not* real property is personal property
  - Real property becomes personal property by *act of severance*
  - Personal property consists of items having a limited life that are easily movable from one place to another
  - Real property is land and improvements
- **Fixtures** were originally personal property but have been permanently attached to and made part of real estate
- **Legal tests to decide if an item is a fixture (IRMA)**
  - **I** Intent of the parties
  - **R** Relationship or agreement of the parties
  - **M** Method or degree of attachment
  - **A** Adaptation of the item
- **Basic property rights (DEEP C)** (real property ownership rights) includes the right of
  - **D** Disposition (right to sell or give away)
  - **E** Enjoyment (right of quiet enjoyment)
  - **E** Exclusion (right of no trespass)
  - **P** Possession (right to occupy)
  - **C** Control (right to control)
- **Estates and tenancies**
  - *Estate* refers to the degree, quantity, nature, and extent of interest (ownership rights) a person can have in real property
  - Estates are divided into two general groups:
    - *Freehold estates* are for an indefinite length (of unknown duration)
    - *Leasehold estates (nonfreehold estates)* are for a fixed term (known duration)
- **Fee simple estate (fee, fee simple, fee simple absolute)**
  - Largest bundle of legal rights
  - Ownership interest with complete power to use, to dispose of, and to allow the property to descend to heirs
  - Highest type of real property interest recognized by law
  - Most title to property is held in fee
- **Life estate (measured by a person's lifetime)**
  - A type of freehold estate created by the person who holds the fee simple title to real property

  - Conventional life estates are created by agreement of the parties in one of two ways: (1) grantor conveys life estate to another individual; or (2) grantor reserves a life estate for own use and transfers the remainder interest to another person
  - The duration of a life estate is determined by the lifetime of a designated individual
  - At the end of the life estate, titled is conveyed back to the original grantor (estate in reversion) or to a third party (remainder estate)
  - Life estates can also be created by law (homesteaded property)
- **Homestead** benefits and protections
  - Protection of the family (if a married person dies and the family homestead was titled in the deceased person's name only, by operation of law, the surviving spouse receives a legal life estate and the children [lineal descendants] receive a remainder estate). If no children, surviving spouse receives a fee simple estate in survivor's name only (in severalty)
  - Protection of homestead from forced sale for certain debts
  - Tax exemption up to $50,000 for qualifying homesteads
  - Size restriction of one-half acre inside a city or 160 acres outside a municipality
  - Personal property of $1,000 included in homestead protections
- **Nonfreehold estates (leaseholds)** have a known duration and do not involve an ownership interest
  - Grants the right of quiet enjoyment (to use and possess, but not own) real property
  - Under a lease, the tenant possesses a leasehold estate, and the landlord (property owner) possesses a reversion estate
  - At end of a leasehold estate, the right of quiet enjoyment reverts to the property owner
  - *Estate for years* is a written lease agreement with a specific starting and ending date that establishes an interest in real property for the tenant but does not convey actual title or the right of disposition
  - *Tenancy at will* is a lease agreement that has a specific beginning date but no fixed ending date
  - *Tenancy at sufferance* occurs when the lease period has ended and the tenant is a holdover
- **Sole ownership versus concurrent ownership**
  - Sole ownership occurs when title to property is held by one person
  - Property that a spouse owns in her name only before marriage and property acquired by one spouse during the marriage by inheritance or gift is separate property
  - Property acquired during marriage, except by inheritance or gift, is referred to as marital assets
- **Co-ownership** means title to real property is shared by two or more persons (concurrent ownership)
  - Tenancy in common

- Joint tenancy
- Tenancy by the entireties

- **Features of tenancy in common**
  - Two or more people
  - Undivided possession
  - Interest equal or unequal percentage
  - Take title at same time or at different times
  - Heirs inherit (*no* right of survivorship)
- **Features of a joint tenancy (PITTS)**
  - **P** Each joint tenant has undivided **P**ossession
  - **I** Each joint tenant has equal **I**nterest
  - **T** Joint tenants take title at the same **T**ime
  - **T** Joint tenants are all named on the same **T**itle
  - **S** Must expressly state right of **S**urvivorship
- **Features of tenancy by the entireties**
  - Married couple takes title together
  - Undivided possession
  - Right of survivorship
  - Same title, same time
  - Only available to husband and wife
- **Cooperative** is a multifamily building owned by a corporation
  - Corporation holds title to the land and improvements
  - Unit owners purchase share of stock in the corporation
  - Proprietary lease entitles purchaser right to occupy the unit
  - Transfer of ownership of a cooperative unit accomplished by sale of stock
- **Condominium** consists of condo units and common elements
  - Individual owns a unit in fee simple plus an undivided fractional share of the common elements
  - Property taxes are levied on individual units
- **Condominium documents**
  - Declaration of condominium contains legal descriptions of the units and once recorded creates the condominium
  - Articles of incorporation of the association create the corporate entity responsible for operating the condominium
  - Bylaws of the association describe operational requirements and provide for the administration of the association
  - Frequently Asked Questions and Answers (FAQs) inform prospective purchasers about restrictions on the leasing of a unit, information concerning assessments, and whether the unit owners or the association are obligated to pay rent or land-use fees for recreational facilities

- **Condominium disclosures—new residential units sold by developer**
  - Prospectus for 20 or more new residential units
  - Estimated operating budget
  - Declaration of condominium
  - Articles of incorporation
  - Bylaws
  - FAQ
- **Condominium disclosures—resale units (private party sales)**
  - Most recent year-end financial report
  - Rules of the association
  - Declaration
  - Articles of incorporation
  - Bylaws
  - FAQ
  - Governance form
- **Time-sharing**
  - Property is first organized as a condominium
  - Each unit is divided into time intervals
  - Time-share disclosure allows purchasers to cancel the contract within 10 calendar days
  - Time-share resale listing agreement disclosure
- **Time-share ownership**
  - *Interval ownership* is fee simple ownership
  - *Right-to-use* is a leasehold interest

IMPORTANT DATES AND TIME PERIODS TO REMEMBER

- **Three business days.** Notice to cancel resale cooperative or condominium contract
- **Seven days.** Notice required for week-to-week tenancy at will
- **10 days.** Notice to cancel time-share contract by developer or resale
- **15 days.** Notice required to cancel month-to-month tenancy at will
- **15 days.** Notice to cancel cooperative or condominium contract with developer

SECTION 8 TITLE, DEEDS, AND OWNERSHIP RESTRICTIONS

(See Unit 9 in *Florida Real Estate Principles, Practices & Law* and Units 15 and 18 in *Florida Real Estate Broker's Guide*)

KEY TERM REVIEW

Abstract of title is summary report of what a title search found in the public record.

Acknowledgment is the formal declaration before a notary public by the grantor that the grantor's signing is a free act.

Actual notice is direct knowledge acquired in the course of a transaction, such as having actually seen the deed instrument or heard that there is a lien on the property.

Adverse possession arises when the true owner of record fails to maintain possession and the property is seized by another.

Alienation is the act of transferring ownership, title, or an interest in real property.

Appurtenance is a right or privilege associated with the property, such as a parking space in a multiunit building

Assignment of a lease occurs when a lessee (tenant) assigns to another person all of the leased property for the remainder of the lease.

Chain of title is the complete successive record of a property's ownership.

Condemnation is a judicial proceeding to exercise the power of eminent domain.

Construction lien is a statutory right of material suppliers or laborers to place a lien on property that has been improved by their supplies and/or labor.

Constructive notice is accomplished by recording the information in the public records.

Deed is a written instrument used to convey title to real property through sale or gift that must be in writing, signed by a competent grantor and two witnesses, and voluntarily accepted by the grantee.

Deed restrictions are a part of the deed and affect a particular property's future use.

Easement is the right to enter and use a portion of an owner's land for a specific use.

Easement appurtenant benefits an adjacent parcel of land.

Easement by necessity is created through a court of law if a property is landlocked.

Easement by prescription is created through a court of law after longtime uninterrupted use.

Easement in gross benefits an individual or business entity and is not related to a specific adjacent parcel, for example, utility easement.

Eminent domain gives government the power to take land for a public use from an owner through a legal process known as *condemnation*.

Encroachment is the unauthorized use of another person's property created when an improvement crosses over a boundary line.

Equitable title is the beneficial interest in real estate that implies that an individual will receive legal title at a future date.

Escheat provides for the State of Florida to take the property of an owner who dies intestate and without any known heirs.

Further assurance is a promise in a general warranty deed that guarantees the grantor will sign and deliver any legal instrument that might be required.

General lien is not restricted to one property but may affect all properties of a debtor.

General warranty deed is the most common type of deed for conveying real estate, and it contains all the covenants and warranties available to give the most complete protection.

Grantee is the person(s) receiving title to property in a deed.

Granting clause is a clause in a deed that contains the premises or the words of conveyance.

Grantor is the person(s) giving title to property in a deed.

Gross lease is an agreement for the tenant to pay a fixed (base) rent and for the landlord to pay all of the expenses associated with the property.

Ground lease is an agreement for the tenant to lease the land only and erect a building on the land.

Habendum clause describes the type of estate being conveyed and starts with the words "to have and to hold."

Intestate is to die without leaving a will.

Involuntary alienation occurs when a person dies intestate and the property either descends to the decedent's heirs or the property transfers to the state through escheat.

Junior liens are characterized by priority based on the date of recording in the public records.

Legal title is ownership of a freehold estate.

Lender's policy is title insurance issued for the amount of mortgage debt to protect the lender (mortgagee).

Lien is a written document that states that a person is owed money and establishes that the party may foreclose on the property if the debt is not satisfied; the right to have property sold to satisfy the debt.

Mechanics' liens are statutory liens created in favor of materialmen and mechanics to secure payment for materials, supplies, and services rendered in the improvement, repair, or maintenance of real property. Also known as construction liens.

Net lease is an agreement for the tenant to pay fixed rent plus property costs such as taxes, insurance, and utilities.

Opinion of title is executed by an attorney after studying the abstract of title.

Owner's policy is title insurance issued for the total purchase price of the property to protect the new owner (mortgagor).

Percentage lease is an agreement for the tenant to pay rent based on the gross sales received by doing business on the leased property.

Police power represents the broadest power of the government to limit or regulate the rights of property owners in order to protect the health, safety, and welfare of the public.

Quiet enjoyment is a promise in a general warranty deed that guarantees peaceful possession undisturbed by claim of title.

Quitclaim deed releases the grantor of any rights in the property that the grantor may have and is used to clear clouds on the title and to cure title defects.

Restrictive covenants are recorded by the developer along with the subdivision plat to maintain specific standards in the subdivision, such as requiring certain architectural specifications.

Seisin is the clause in a deed that is a promise that the grantor has the right to convey title (a statement of ownership).

Specific liens apply only to a certain specified property.

Sublease is a lease given by the lessee for a portion of the leasehold interest, while the lessee retains some reversionary interest. The sublease may be for all or part of the premises, for the whole term or part of it, as long as the lessor retains some interest in the property.

Superior liens take priority over all other liens. There are three superior liens: (1) real estate tax liens, (2) special assessment liens, and (3) federal estate tax liens.

Testate is to die with a will.

Title is a legal concept signifying ownership of a collection of rights to real property.

Title insurance is a contract that protects the policyholder from losses arising from defects in the title.

Variable lease is an agreement for the tenant to pay specified rent increases based on a predetermined index (CPI) at set future dates.

Voluntary alienation is a legal term used to indicate the transfer of title is accomplished with the owner's control and consent.

Warranty forever is a promise in a general warranty deed that guarantees the grantor will forever warrant and defend the grantee's title against all unlawful claims.

KEY CONCEPTS

- **Legal title** is ownership of a freehold estate
- **Equitable title** implies individual will receive legal title at a future date
  - The interest in real property a buyer receives upon executing a contract and prior to title closing
- **Alienation is the act of transferring ownership, title, or an interest in real property from one person to another** and may be
  - Voluntary (with the owner's control and content)
  - Involuntary by operation of law (without control and consent of the owner)
- **Types of voluntary alienation**
  - Deed
  - Will (testate)
- **Types of involuntary alienation**
  - Descent (intestate)
  - Escheat to the state
  - Adverse possession
  - Eminent domain
- **Alienation by adverse possession (HOT CAN)**
  - H Hostile possession
  - O Open possession
  - T Taxes paid by *adverse possessor*
  - C Claim of title
  - A Adverse possession continues for *seven or more years*
  - N Notorious public possession

- **Two types of notice to legal title**
  - *Actual notice* is direct knowledge acquired in the course of a transaction
  - *Constructive notice* is accomplished by recording a document in the public records
- **Title insurance protects the policyholder from title defects**
  - Real estate licensees are not qualified to render an opinion of title
  - Licensees must advise the buyer to either contact an attorney or a title insurance company to determine the condition of the seller's title
  - Municipal lien searches provide added protection in the event there are unrecorded special assessment liens, unrecorded liens existing because of local ordinances, and unpaid county waste fees
- **Owner policy**
  - Issued for the purchase price
  - Claim will pay up to the purchase price
  - Benefits owners and their heirs
  - Not transferable
  - Seller typically pays this closing expense
  - One-time premium
- **Lender (mortgagee) policy**
  - Issued for the loan amount
  - Claim will pay up to the current loan balance
  - Benefits mortgage lender
  - Transferable (assignable)
  - Buyer typically pays this closing expense
  - One-time premium
- **Parties to a deed**
  - *Grantor* (owner giving title who must be mentally competent)
  - *Grantee* (person receiving title)
- **Parts of a deed**
  - Names of grantor and grantee
  - Consideration
  - Words of conveyance
  - Interest or estate being conveyed
  - Exceptions and reservations
  - Deed restrictions
  - Appurtenances
  - Legal description
  - Voluntary delivery and acceptance
  - Signature of grantor and two witnesses
- **Requirements of a valid deed**
  - In writing (statute of frauds)

- Names of the grantor and the grantee
- Grantor must be of legal capacity (competent)
- Consideration must be described
- Habendum clause (ownership interest being conveyed)
- Legal description
- Signed by the grantor and two witnesses (names of the grantor and two witnesses must be printed immediately beneath the signature of the grantor and the witnesses)
- Voluntary delivery and acceptance

■ **Types of statutory deeds**

- General warranty deed is the most comprehensive and common type of deed used in real estate
- Special warranty deed is used by lenders for foreclosed properties where the grantor (lender) only assumes title responsibility for the period that the property was owned by the grantor (lender), thus avoiding title liability for the period prior to foreclosure
- Bargain and sale deed contains the covenant of seisin (statement of ownership where grantor states right to convey) but does not warrant to defend future title
- Quitclaim deed is issued to cure title defects (clouds on title) and grantor makes no warranties or guarantees (no covenant of seisin)

■ **General warranty deed includes**

- Covenant of seisin
- Covenant against encumbrances

■ **General warranty deed also includes three special covenants**

- Further assurance
- Quiet enjoyment
- Warranty forever

■ **Special purpose deeds**

- Personal representative deed—settle estate of deceased
- Guardian's deed—act on behalf of minor
- Committee's deed—incompetent grantor
- Tax deed—conveyance of property sold for nonpayment of taxes

■ **Government restrictions on ownership (PET)**

- **P** Police power
- **E** Eminent domain
- **T** Taxation

■ **Private restrictions on ownership (DELL)**

- **D** Deed restrictions
- **E** Easements
- **L** Leases
- **L** Liens

- **Restrictive covenants versus deed restrictions**
  - Deed restrictions refer to a single parcel of land
  - Restrictive covenants concern entire subdivisions
- **Easement is a right to use the land of another for a specific and limited purpose**
  - *Easement appurtenant* benefits an adjacent parcel of land; it allows an owner the use of a neighbor's property, such as the right to cross parcel A to reach parcel B
  - *Easement in gross* benefits an individual or a business entity and is not related to a specific adjacent parcel, such as utility easements
  - *Easement by necessity* is created through a court of law to allow property owners to enter and exit their landlocked property
  - *Easement by prescription* is created by a court of law after longtime usage
- **Encroachments**
  - Unauthorized use of another's property
  - Encroachments that continue for more than seven years may create an implied easement
- **Types of leases**
  - Gross lease (tenant pays a fixed rent; landlord pays expenses associated with the property)
  - Net lease (tenant pays fixed rent plus property costs)
  - Percentage (overage) lease (tenant pays rent based on gross sales)
  - Variable (index) lease (tenant pays specified rent increases based on a predetermined index at set future dates)
  - Ground lease (tenant leases land only and erects a building)
- **Calculate the rent owed for a percentage lease**
- **Calculate the rent owed for a variable lease**
- **Assignment and sublease**
  - Assignment of a lease occurs when a lessee assigns to another party all of the leased property for the full remaining portion of the lease
  - Sublease is used when the lessee assigns less than the entire property or assigns all of the property for less than the full remaining period
- **A lien** is a claim to have a debt or other obligation satisfied out of property belonging to another
  - Voluntary, such as a mortgage lien
  - Involuntary liens are created by law
- **General liens** are not restricted to one property but may affect all properties of a debtor
  - Judgment lien
  - Income tax (IRS) lien
  - Estate tax lien
- **Specific liens** apply only to certain specific property
  - Property tax and special assessment liens become liens as soon as assessment is made

- Mortgage lien pledges real property as collateral (priority is based on date of recording)
- Vendor's lien is created when a purchase money mortgage is recorded by seller (priority is established by date of recording)
- Construction lien must be filed within 90 days after last work is done and assumes priority over mortgage liens created after first work was done

- **Lien priority** determines the order in which the liens will be paid off if the property must be sold
  - Real estate (property) tax liens, special assessment liens, and federal estate tax liens are *superior liens*, meaning that they take priority over all other liens
  - All other liens are *junior liens*
  - Priority of junior liens is based on the recording date with the clerk of the circuit court in the county where the property is located
  - Construction liens are an exception to the priority rule regarding the recording date
  - Subordination agreement changes the priority of liens

IMPORTANT DATES AND TIME PERIODS TO REMEMBER

- **90 days.** Number of days to file a construction lien (retroactive to the date of the first delivery of material or the first day of work)
- **Seven years.** Number of years of hostile possession to claim adverse possession
- **20 years.** Minimum time period of uninterrupted use to create an easement by prescription

IMPORTANT FORMULAS TO REMEMBER

- **Calculate the rent owed for a percentage (overage) lease**
  1. Gross sales – sales threshold = gross sales subject to rent
  2. Gross sales subject to rent × percentage charge in lease = additional rent
  3. Base rent + additional rent = total rent

  EXAMPLE A store rents for $50,000 annually plus 2% of the gross sales above $1,000,000. Gross sales for the year were $2,500,000. Calculate the annual rent.
  $2,500,000 total gross sales – $1,000,000 sales threshold = $1,500,000 subject to 2% charge
  $1,500,000 × .02 = $30,000 additional annual rent
  $50,000 annual base rent + $30,000 additional rent = $80,000 total annual rent

- **Calculate the rent owed for a variable (index) lease**
  1. Divide the new index by the original index
  2. Multiply the number from step one by the original rent

  EXAMPLE An office rents for $5,000 a month in the first year based on an index of 60. The next year the index increases to 63. Calculate the new monthly rent.
  63 new index ÷ 60 original index = 1.05
  1.05 × $5,000 original rent = $5,250 new rent

SECTION 9 REAL ESTATE CONTRACTS

(See Unit 11 in *Florida Real Estate Principles, Practices & Law* and Unit 11 in *Florida Real Estate Broker's Guide*)

KEY TERM REVIEW

Assignment refers to a transfer of rights and duties under a contract.

Attorney-in-fact is a person who is authorized to perform certain acts for another under a power of attorney.

Bilateral contract obligates both parties to perform in accordance with the terms of the contract.

Buyer brokerage agreement is an employment contract with a buyer.

Community development district (CDD) is an independent special district created by law to service the long-term needs of its community.

Competent parties have the legal capacity to contract, no mental defects, and are of legal age to contract.

Contract is an agreement between two or more parties to do a legal act for a consideration, which creates certain rights and obligations.

Enforceable contract is a legally binding contract that the law will recognize.

Exclusive-agency listing is given to one broker, but the seller reserves the right to sell the property without paying a commission.

Exclusive right-of-sale listing is a listing given to one broker who is assured of a commission no matter who sells (best from broker's standpoint).

Fraud is the intent to misrepresent a material fact or to deceive in order to gain an unfair advantage or to harm another person.

Good consideration is a promise that cannot be measured in terms of money, such as love and affection.

Homeowners associations are responsible for the operation of a community in which the voting membership is made up of parcel owners, membership is a mandatory condition of parcel ownership, and the association is authorized to impose assessments that, if unpaid, may become a lien on the parcel.

Liquidated damages is the amount specified in the contract (usually the earnest money deposit) to be paid to the seller in case of default by the buyer.

Meeting of the minds is reaching an agreement on all terms in a contract.

Misrepresentation is an untrue statement of fact or the concealment of a material fact.

Net listing is created when a seller agrees to sell a property for a stated acceptable minimum amount.

Novation is the substitution of a new party for the original one.

Open listing is a listing given to any number of brokers (least preferred by brokers).

Option contract is a unilateral contract (only optionor must perform) to keep open for a specified period of time an offer to sell or lease real property.

Parol contract is an oral agreement.

Procuring cause is the chain of events that results in a sale.

Statute of frauds requires that certain contracts must be in writing and signed to be enforceable (contracts conveying an interest in real property).

Statute of limitations designates the period of time during which the terms of a contract may be enforced.

Unenforceable contract means a contract would not stand up in a court of law because it does not meet the requirements of the statute of frauds or it runs beyond the statute of limitations.

Unilateral contract obligates only one party to perform.

Valid contract is binding on both parties and legally enforceable.

Valuable consideration is the money or a promise of something that can be measured in terms of money.

Vendee is the buyer.

Vendor is the seller.

Void contract does not meet all of the required elements of a valid contract and has no legal effect.

Voidable contract allows one party to avoid contractual duties, such as when one party is a minor or a party is mentally incompetent.

KEY CONCEPTS

- **Contracts in general**
  - An agreement between two or more parties to do or not to do certain things supported by a sufficient consideration
  - Key to every contract are the promises made
- **Four types of contracts real estate licensees may prepare**
  - Listing agreement is broker's employment contract with seller
  - Buyer brokerage agreement is an employment contract with buyer
  - Sale and purchase contract may be prepared by the sales associate if the licensee acts as an agent or facilitator for contracting party
  - Option contract is an agreement to keep open for a specified period an offer to sell or lease real property
- **Licensees may *not* draw**
  - Deeds
  - Mortgages
  - Promissory notes
  - Leases
- **Licensees may fill in the blanks on Florida Supreme Court preapproved lease instruments for lease periods that do not exceed one year**
- **A valid contract complies with the provisions of contract law and has four essentials**
  - Contractual capacity of the parties (competent parties)

- Offer and acceptance (mutual assent)—meeting of the minds
- Legality of object (legal purpose)
- Consideration

- **Two types of consideration**
  - Valuable (money)
  - Good (the promises each party agrees to)
- **Statute of frauds requires that contracts *conveying an interest* in real property, and contracts that are not to be performed within one year of the date created, must be in writing and signed to be enforceable**
  - Purchase and sale contracts
  - Option contracts
  - Deeds and mortgage instruments
  - Lease agreements for a term longer than one year
  - Listing agreements for a term longer than one year
- **Statute of limitations**
  - Written contracts: five years
  - Oral (parol) contracts: four years
- **Contracts** may be written or oral
  - Contracts that involve a transfer of real property must be in writing to be legally enforceable
  - The parties to an oral real estate contract may have a valid contract (contains the four essentials) but the contract will not be enforceable in a court of law
  - Letters and telegraphic communication can be part of a valid sale contract
- **Elements of a valid and enforceable real estate sale contract (COLIC)**
  - **C** Competent parties
  - **O** Offer and acceptance (*meeting of the minds*)
  - **L** Legal purpose
  - **I** In writing and signed (statute of frauds)
  - **C** Consideration (*valuable* or *good*)
- **Void, voidable, and unenforceable contracts**
  - Void contracts lack one or more required elements of a valid contract and have no legal effect
  - Voidable contracts allow that one party be permitted to avoid any contractual duties
  - Unenforceable contracts appear to have all essential elements but cannot be enforced in court
- **Real estate contracts** are *not* required to be witnessed or notarized, nor do they require a deposit
- **Formal and informal contracts**
  - *Formal contract* is written and under seal
  - *Informal* (*parol*) contract is oral

- **Bilateral and unilateral contracts**
  - *Bilateral* obligates both parties (sale contract)
  - *Unilateral* obligates only one party (option contract)
- **Express and implied contracts**
  - *Express contract* exists when all of the terms and conditions have been spelled out and a meeting of the minds is reached
  - *Implied contract* exists when some of the conditions may be reasonably implied
- **Executory and executed contracts**
  - *Executory contracts* are not yet fully performed
  - *Executed contracts* have been completely performed
- **Contract negotiation**
  - *Offeror* (person making offer)
  - *Offeree* (person receiving offer)
  - Note: Parties switch roles when there is a *counteroffer*
- **A contract is created when three events occur**
  - Offer is made by the offeror
  - Offer is accepted by the offeree
  - Acceptance is communicated back to the offeror (if the statute of frauds is applicable, the acceptance must be communicated in writing)
- **Ways to terminate an offer (WILD CARD)**
  - **W** Withdrawal by offeror
  - **I** Insanity
  - **L** Lapse of time
  - **D** Death
  - **C** Counteroffer
  - **A** Acceptance
  - **R** Rejection
  - **D** Destruction of the property
- **Ways to terminate a contract**
  - Performance
  - Mutual rescission
  - Impossibility of performance
  - Lapse of time
  - Bankruptcy
  - Breach
- **Remedies for breach of contract**
  - Specific performance—the court orders the other party to perform according to the terms of the contract
  - Liquidated damages—amount of damages stipulated in the contract (usually the earnest money deposit)

- Rescission—cancellation of the contract and restoration of the parties to their original positions
- Compensatory damages—involves a lawsuit to recover the actual amount of the monetary loss (unliquidated damages)

■ **Assignment and novation**
- Assignment does NOT terminate a contract
- Transfer of a person's rights and duties under a contract to another person
- Contracts are assignable unless prohibited in contract
- Novation is used to substitute new party for original party

■ **Types of listings**
- Open listing
- Exclusive-agency listing
- Exclusive right-of-sale listing
- Net listing
- Multiple listing

■ **Multiple listing** refers to a service provided by brokers and not to a specific type of listing

■ **Buyer brokerage agreements**
- An employment contract with the buyer
- Broker is presumed to be employed as the buyer's transaction broker

■ **Broker's compensation** is specified in the listing or the buyer brokerage agreement
- Find a purchaser
- Effect a sale
- Procuring cause

■ **Option contracts**
- Optionor is the property owner
- Optionee is the prospective buyer
- Optionor has obligation to sell
- Optionee has a right to buy
- Unilateral contract

■ **Sale and purchase contracts**
- Parties to the contract: vendor (seller) and vendee (buyer)
- Both spouses must sign the sale contract if the property is co-owned by the couple or if the property is homesteaded

■ **Contract disclosures**
- Material defects disclosure—sellers of residential real property must disclose material defects
- Radon gas disclosure—consists of explaining what radon is
- Lead-based paint disclosure—applies to sale contracts and leases if the home was built prior to 1978

  - Energy efficient brochure—informs buyers, before signing the sale contract, of the option for an energy-efficiency rating on the building
  - Homeowners association disclosure—requires sellers of property subject to a homeowners association to provide buyers with a disclosure summary
  - Property tax disclosure—concerns ad valorem (property) taxes
  - Building code violation disclosure—applies if a seller has been cited for a building code violation and is the subject of a pending enforcement proceeding
  - Community development district disclosure
- **Misrepresentation and fraud**
  - Misstatement of fact or omission or concealment of a factual matter
  - Three elements for fraud
- **Elements for a cause of action for fraud**
  - The licensee made a misstatement or failed to disclose a material fact
  - The licensee either knew or should have known that the statement was not accurate or that the undisclosed information should have been disclosed
  - The party to whom the statement was made relied on the misstatement
  - The party to whom the statement was made was damaged as a result

IMPORTANT DATES AND TIME PERIODS TO REMEMBER

- **10 days.** Time period sellers must allow homebuyers to conduct an inspection for the presence of lead-based paint
- **Five days.** Time period after title transfer, regarding a building code violation, to forward to the code enforcement agency the name and address of the new owner and a copy of the disclosures given to the buyer
- **Four years.** Time period to enforce oral contracts under the statute of limitations
- **Five years.** Time period to enforce written contracts under the statute of limitations

SECTION 10 PLANNING, ZONING, AND ENVIRONMENTAL HAZARDS

(See Unit 19 in *Florida Real Estate Principles, Practices & Law* and Unit 16 in *Florida Real Estate Broker's Guide*)

KEY TERM REVIEW

Asbestos is a mineral fiber used until 1978 in a variety of building construction materials for insulation and as a fire retardant.

Buffer zone is a strip of land separating one land use from another (for example, a landscaped park can be used to screen a residential area from nonresidential areas).

Building codes protect the public health and safety from inferior construction practices.

Building inspections are conducted by county officials during construction to confirm that the workmanship conforms to the building code.

Building permit is a document issued after local government has review of the architectural and engineering drawings and the energy calculations.

Certificate of occupancy is an occupancy permit issued by the local government after construction is completed and the final inspection is approved.

Comprehensive plans are master plans for the future physical development of a city, county, or region.

Concurrency provision in Florida's Growth Policy Act that requires water and waste treatment facilities needed to support additional population be in place before new development is allowed.

Density is the number of homes or lots per acre.

Developments of regional impact (DRI) include any development that, because of its character, magnitude, or location, could have a substantial effect on the health, safety, and welfare of citizens of more than one county.

Environmental due diligence *(Study material for broker candidates only)* is the process by which a purchaser evaluates the likelihood of site contamination. It is normally accomplished by employing an environmental consultant to conduct an environmental site assessment.

Environmental impact statements summarize the effect that proposed development will have on the surroundings.

Health ordinances regulate maintenance and sanitation of public spaces.

Impact fees *(Study material for broker candidates only)* are charged by local governments to fund major off-site improvements.

Intensity is the concentration of pedestrian traffic and vehicular traffic used as a means of designating land for commercial zones.

Laissez-faire is a noninterference by government in trade, industry, and individual action.

Mixed land use is more than one type of zoning such as a condominium that has residential and commercial units.

Nonconforming use is continuing land use that is not in compliance with a newly enacted zoning ordinance.

Planned unit development (PUD) is a self-contained development planned under special zoning ordinances that allow maximum use of open space by reducing lot sizes and street sizes.

Potentially responsible persons (PRP) *(Study material for broker candidates only)* are liable for the cost to clean up a contaminated site, including past and present owners and operators of the site, creators of the hazardous material, and transporters of the hazardous material to the site.

R-value refers to the effectiveness of insulation and is measured by its resistance to heat flow.

Special exception is permission to build or to use property in apparent conflict with existing zoning ordinances.

Special flood hazard areas (SFHAs) are located in a 100-year flood plain.

Special purpose property refers to a combination of land and improvements with only one economically feasible use because of some special design.

Subdivision regulations *(Study material for broker candidates only)* control the size and location of streets, sidewalks, water and sewer lines, mandated drainage facilities, and the location of parks and open spaces.

Variances allow property owners to vary from strict compliance with all or part of a zoning code because to comply would force an undue hardship on the property owner.

Wetlands *(Study material for broker candidates only)* are areas with groundwater levels at or near the surface for much of the year or areas that have aquatic vegetation.

Zoning ordinances authorize the segmentation (dividing) of a community into districts or zones in keeping with the character of the land and structures and with their suitability for particular uses to protect the property owners from undesirable land uses on neighboring property.

KEY CONCEPTS

- **History of planning and zoning**
  - Laissez-faire
- **Florida's Growth Policy and Community Planning Act**
  - Concurrency
  - Comprehensive plan
- **Planning commission goals**
  - Save tax money by preventing sprawl
  - Provide adequate provision of services
  - Provide for road right-of-ways and setbacks
  - Protect against costly drainage, flooding, and environmental problems
  - Reduce problems associated with political and equity issues
- **Planning commission composition**
  - Commission is composed of laypersons who are a representative sample of the community
  - Appointed (not elected)
  - Not paid to serve on the planning commission—voluntary

- **Planning commission authority**
  - Subdivision plat approval
  - Site plan approval
  - Sign control
- **Calculate lots per acre**
- **Zoning ordinances**
  - Local laws that implement the comprehensive plan
  - Exercise of police power
  - To protect property values
  - Each zone is assigned a specific land-use classification
- **Zoning classifications**
  - Residential (regulates *density* of number of homes per acre)
  - Commercial (regulates *intensity* of use, types, and traffic volume)
  - Industrial (controls emissions and effluents)
  - Agricultural (all-inclusive)
  - Special use (includes city parks and federal buildings)
- **Building codes**
  - Protect against inferior construction practices
  - Set minimum standards for materials and quality of workmanship, R-values, and wind load requirements
  - Issue a building permit before construction begins
  - Periodic building inspections
  - Final *certificate of occupancy* is issued
- **Variance** allows a property owner to vary from strict compliance of a zoning ordinance
  - Property owner must show that a *hardship* exists or will be created
  - Property owner did nothing to create the hardship
- **Special exceptions** are used to control the location of a particular land use
  - A departure from the zoning ordinance
  - Must demonstrate that the special exception will benefit the surrounding property owners
- **Legally nonconforming uses**
  - The use is grandfathered
  - Property owner is allowed to continue a use even though zoning ordinances have changed that would no longer allow the use if being constructed today
  - The government may not use eminent domain via condemnation just because a property no longer conforms to code
- **Developments of regional impact**
  - Required for large projects that impact more than one county
  - Concerned with air quality, water quality, waste treatment, public school classroom space, and roads

- **Planned unit development (PUD)**
  - Allows a mix of land uses along with a high density of residential units
  - Clustering of residential units to allow for open spaces
  - Reduced lot sizes and street sizes to allow maximum use of open space
  - A self-contained development
- **Environmental impact statement** concerns the environmental impact on waste-disposal systems, air quality, roads, employment, and so forth as the result of large development
- **Clean Water Act of 1997** *(Study material for broker candidates only)*
  - Protects wetlands
  - Permits required prior to dredging or filling of wetlands
  - Permits issued by U.S. Corps of Engineers
- **National Flood Insurance Program (NFIP)**
  - Special flood hazard areas (SFHA)
- **Comprehensive Environmental Response, Compensation, and Liability Act (CERCLA)**
  - Identifies potentially responsible persons (PRP) who are liable for cleanup of hazardous waste sites; strict, joint and several, and retroactive liability
  - Liability under CERCLA is considered strict, joint and several, and retroactive
  - Provides for a purchaser to claim innocent landowner immunity/defense if buyer did not know of contamination before purchase; acted responsibly when contamination was discovered; and made reasonable inquiries before purchasing
  - Authorizes EPA to publish and maintain the National Priorities List (NPL) of known contaminated sites
- **Environmental hazards associated with real estate**
  - Asbestos
  - Radon
  - Lead-based paint
  - Mold
  - Water supply
  - Wood-destroying organisms

IMPORTANT FORMULAS TO REMEMBER

- **Calculate number of potential lots in a subdivision (lots per acre)**
  1. Calculate number of square feet available for development
  2. Determine the potential number of lots per acre
  3. Potential number of lots × number of acres = total number of lots in subdivision

  EXAMPLE A parcel contains 40 acres. Fifteen percent of land must be set aside for common areas plus another 600 feet by 30 feet is allocated for a street. Each lot must contain at least 10,000 square feet.
  (Note: *Memorize* 43,560 square feet in one acre.)
  43,560 square feet per acre × .85 = 37,026 square feet available after allowing for common space
  37,026 square feet available per acre × 40 acres = 1,481,040 total available square feet (before allowing for the street)
  600 × 30 = 18,000 square feet for street
  1,481,040 – 18,000 = 1,463,040 total buildable square feet in parcel
  1,463,040 ÷ 10,000 minimum square feet per lot = 146.304, rounded to 146 lots

- **Calculate cost per front foot**

  Total cost ÷ front feet = cost per front foot

  EXAMPLE A parcel's dimensions are 400' by 600'. Total cost is $260,000.
  $260,000 ÷ 400 = $650 per front foot

- **Calculate the number of acres in a parcel given the cost and price per square foot**
  1. Calculate total square feet
  2. Total square feet ÷ 43,560 = number of acres in parcel

  EXAMPLE The lot cost $10 per square foot for a total cost of $250,000. (Round to two decimal places)
  $250,000 ÷ $10 = 25,000 square feet
  25,000 ÷ 43,560 = .5739 (or approximately) .57 acres

SECTION 11 THE REAL ESTATE BUSINESS

(See Unit 1 in *Florida Real Estate Principles, Practices & Law*)

KEY TERM REVIEW

Absentee owners are owners who do not reside on the property and who usually rely on a property manager to supervise the real estate.

Appraisal is the process of estimating the value of real property; a supported, defended estimate of the value of real property as of a specific date.

Appraiser is registered, licensed, or certified by the DBPR and provides an estimate of value.

Broker's price opinion (BPO) is a written opinion of the value of real property. BPOs may not be referred to as appraisals.

Business brokers are real estate licensees who engage in the sale, purchase, or lease of businesses.

Business opportunity is real estate activity dealing in the sale, purchase, or lease of businesses (going concern operations).

Community Association Manager (CAM) holds a CAM license to manage community associations of more than 10 units or associations with an annual budget in excess of $100,000.

Comparative market analysis (CMA) refers to a marketing tool and may not be referred to or represented as an appraisal; CMAs are developed by reviewing the real estate activity in the area, including recent sales of similar properties, properties currently offered for sale, and recently expired listings to indicate what a subject property might be worth based on current market activity.

Dedication is the gift of land by an owner to a government body for a public use.

Farm area refers to a selected geographic area or a group of people from which licensees solicit real estate business and devote special attention and study.

Follow-up is what a sales associate does for buyers and sellers after the sale (closing) to promote customer loyalty.

Multiple listing service (MLS) is a database that allows real estate brokers representing sellers under a listing contract to share information about properties with real estate brokers who may represent potential buyers.

Property management is real estate activity devoted to leasing, managing, marketing, and overall maintenance of property for others.

Property manager is the local representative of the owner.

Real estate brokerage is that part of the real estate business that is concerned with bringing together buyers and sellers, owners and renters, and completing real estate transactions.

REALTORS® are real estate professionals who are members of a local board (or association) of REALTORS® and are affiliated with the Florida Realtors® and the NAR.

Rental agent typically finds a tenant for property and collects a fee.

Subdivision plat map refers to a plan of a tract of subdivided land that is submitted by the developer to the government planning agency showing the size and location of individual lots, planned amenities, streets, and utilities.

Target market is a specific group of prospects chosen because of its demographic, financial, and lifestyle characteristics.

KEY CONCEPTS

- **Real estate brokers provide specialized service for others in return for compensation**
  - The product real estate licensees market is expert information
- **Real estate professionals provide expert information in three areas**
  - Knowledge of property transfer
  - Knowledge of market conditions
  - Knowledge of how to market real estate and businesses
- **Real estate brokerage** is the business of bringing together buyers and sellers, owners and renters, and completing real estate transactions
- **Sales and leasing**
  - Real estate license–related activities performed under authority of the broker
  - Broker acts as agent or as intermediary between two or more people in the negotiation of the sale purchase, or rental of real estate
  - Sales associate works for the broker
- **Five sales specialties**
  - Residential
  - Commercial
  - Industrial
  - Agricultural
  - Businesses (business brokers)
- **Target marketing**
  - Expertise in locating prospects
  - Database of leads to send targeted advertising
  - Farm area
  - Follow up
- **Property management** is a professional service involving leasing, maintenance, managing, and marketing of real estate owned by others
  - Property manager is the local representative of property owner
  - An *absentee owner* often relies on a professional property manager to manage the owner's investment
  - Primary objective is to protect the owner's investment and to maximize the owner's return
  - Rental agents find a tenant for property and collect a fee

- Property managers continue to manage property after tenant is secured
- Compensation and licensure requirements
- Community Association Manager (CAM) required when community association consists of more than 10 units or annual budget exceeds $100,000

- **Appraisal** is the process of developing and communicating an opinion of property's value
  - Based on established valuation methods and appraiser's professional judgment
  - Appraisal reports involving a federally related transaction must be prepared by a state-certified or licensed appraiser
  - Appraisers are paid a fee; to base the fee on the appraised value is a conflict of interest (*USPAP* violation)
- **Valuation and real estate licensees**
  - Real estate licensees may prepare appraisals *except* when a federally related transaction is involved (a licensee may *not* conduct an appraisal for the purpose of procuring a listing)
  - When preparing appraisals, real estate licensees must abide by the *Uniform Standards of Professional Appraisal Practice (USPAP)*
- **Comparative market analysis and broker's price opinion**
  - A CMA is a marketing tool used by licensees to secure listings—it is *not* an appraisal
  - A CMA may *not* be referred to as an appraisal
  - Sales associates may perform broker price opinions (BPOs) only at the direction and under the control and management of the associate's employing broker
  - If a sales associate performs a BPO, the compensation must be paid to the broker and not directly to the sales associate who prepared the BPO
  - *USPAP* does not apply to brokers and sales associates who perform BPOs
- **Financing**
  - Anyone who takes residential mortgage loan application or offers to negotiate the terms of residential mortgage loan application for compensation must be a licensed mortgage loan originator
  - Real estate licensees may not accept referral fees from lenders unless licensed as a mortgage loan originator
- **Development and construction** includes three phases:
  - *Land acquisition* (developer seeks approval for the proposed project from the local municipality and incurs costs for engineering plans, attorney fees, surveys, and application fees)
  - *Subdividing and development* (subdividing is the process of converting parcels of land into smaller units; development is the process of improving raw land)
  - *Recording the subdivision plat map*
- **Subdivision plat map**
  - To protect consumers, most local governments require that developers submit a subdivision plat map of a new development

- A subdivision plat map is an engineer's plan for land use superimposed on a map of the land to be developed
- Plat maps indicate the size and location of individual lots, streets, and public utilities, including water and sewer lines
- Developer indicates on the plat map that the streets, sidewalks, and other improvements that will not be sold to private individuals will be *dedicated* to the local municipality
- Dedication of land

■ **Three types of residential construction**

- *Spec homes* involves purchasing one or more lots and constructing homes without securing a buyer in advance of construction—construction without a presale
- *Custom homes* refers to constructing homes under contract with a buyer using building plans provided by an architect or the buyer—building according to the owner's plans and specifications
- *Tract homes* is a type of speculative building involving model homes that are used to promote construction of new homes on lots in a subdivision

■ **Role of government**

- Local government—property taxation and regulatory activities including occupational licensing, building permits, and zoning
- State government—state documentary and intangible tax
- Federal government—fiscal and monetary policies

■ **National Association of REALTORS® (NAR)** is the largest real estate trade organization

- REALTORS® must subscribe to the Code of Ethics
- The term *REALTOR®* can only be used by members of the NAR
- REALTOR® is a copyrighted designation
- Multiple listing service
- Real estate licensee versus REALTOR®

SECTION 12 LEGAL DESCRIPTIONS

(See Unit 10 in *Florida Real Estate Principles, Practices & Law*)

KEY TERM REVIEW

Acre contains 43,560 square feet.

Assessor's parcel number is assigned to each parcel of land in a tax district that are used to prepare tax maps.

Base lines are imaginary lines running east and west that are used as reference lines in the government survey system; they are used to identify the numbering system townships (or tiers) north and south of the base line.

Check is formed when two guide meridians and two correction lines intersect to form a 24-by-24-mile square.

Government survey system is used in Florida and other states except the original 13 states and Kentucky, West Virginia, Tennessee, and Texas.

Legal description is a series of boundary lines on the earth's surface to identify the boundaries of a land parcel.

Lot and block method of legal description is used to identify lots within a recorded subdivision plat map.

Metes-and-bounds description is the most accurate method of land description that is used to describe both regular and irregular shaped parcels.

Monument is a fixed object (marker) used to identify the point of beginning (POB) and the corners of a parcel.

Point of beginning (POB) is the starting reference point in the metes-and-bounds method of legal description.

Principal meridians are imaginary lines running north and south that are used as reference lines in the government survey system; they are used to identify the numbering system of ranges east and west of the principal meridian.

Range is a six-mile-wide vertical (north/south) strip enclosed between two range lines.

Section is one mile square.

Survey is a drawing of a parcel of land that shows the boundary lines, including a legal description of the property.

Tier is the east/west row of townships in the government survey system.

Township (or tier) is an east/west strip of land on either side of a base line (think of a tiered wedding cake); *township* also refers to the square formed by the intersection of two range lines and two township lines.

Township lines are six miles apart, run east and west, and are parallel to the base line.

KEY CONCEPTS

- **Purpose of a legal description**
  - Describe a parcel in sufficient detail that it will be accepted by the courts
  - Based on a survey
  - Licensee's role and responsibilities
- **Methods of legal description**
  - Metes-and-bounds
  - Government survey
  - Lot and block
- **Description by metes-and-bounds**
  - Oldest method of land description
  - Used for regular and irregular shaped parcels
  - *Metes* refers to distance (think meters)
  - *Bounds* refers to direction
  - Starting reference point is the point of beginning (POB)
  - First direction (primary reference direction) is always North or South—due North and due South are both zero degrees
  - Second direction is always East or West—due East and due West are both 90 degrees
  - Maximum number of degrees one can move is 90 degrees
- **Description by government survey**
  - Grid system used in Florida and most of United States except original 13 states
  - Based on north-south lines and east-west lines
- **Principal meridian and base line**
  - Florida's *principal meridian* is a north-south line that runs through a monument located in the city of Tallahassee
  - Florida's *base line* is an east-west line that runs through a monument located in the city of Tallahassee
- **Range**
  - Range lines are north-south lines every six miles from the principal meridian
  - First range west of the principal meridian is R1W
  - First range east of the principal meridian is R1E
- **Tier or township**
  - Township lines are east-west lines every six miles parallel to the base line
  - Range lines and township lines intersect to form six mile squares called *townships*
- **Townships**
  - 6 mile square (six miles on each side)
  - 36 square miles
  - 36 sections

- Note that the term is also used to describe a six-mile-wide east-west strip of land on either side of the base line
- First township tier north of the base line is T1N
- First township tier south of the base line is T1S

■ **Sections**
- 1 mile square (one mile on each side)
- Contains 640 acres
- Sections are numbered within a township right to left, left to right, right to left

■ **Measures and terms** associated with the government survey system
- *Check* is a square 24 miles on each side created by intersecting guide meridians and correction lines; used to adjust the grid pattern of squares because of the curvature of the earth; containing 16 townships
- *Township* is a square 6 miles on each side (6 miles square) containing 36 square miles (36 sections); also an east-west strip of land north and south of a baseline (called a tier)
- *Section* is a square 1 mile on each side (1 mile square) containing 1 square mile (or 640 acres)
- *Quarter section* is 160 acres; historically, it was the area of land originally granted to a homesteader; used today to establish the limits of homesteaded property outside the boundaries of a municipality
- *Government lot* is a fractional piece of land less than a full quarter section located along the banks of lakes and streams

■ **Locating sections**

■ **Subdividing sections**

■ **Calculating size**
- "And" in a legal description

■ **Description by lot and block numbers**
- Used where plat maps of single family subdivisions have been recorded in the public records
- Platted subdivision is divided into blocks and each parcel within the block is a lot

■ **Tax maps**
- Parcel ID (PID) number or assessor's parcel number
- Parcel numbers used to prepare tax maps

IMPORTANT FORMULAS TO REMEMBER

- **Calculate the acres in a government survey legal description**

  Multiply the denominators of each fraction together and then divide 640 by the result

  EXAMPLE NW ¼ of the NE ¼
  4 × 4 = 16
  640 ÷ 16 = 40 acres

  Alternative method: Working backward or forward from the 640-acre section, divide 640 by the denominator of each fraction

  EXAMPLE N ½ of the NE ¼ of the SW ¼ of section 12
  640 ÷ 2 ÷ 4 ÷ 4 = 20 acres

  (Note: Either method will result in the same answer. *Memorize* the method that is easiest for you to calculate.)

- **Calculate the acres in a government survey legal description with *and* in the description**

  1. Multiply the denominators that immediately precede the *and*
  2. Multiply the denominators that follow the *and*
  3. Find the acreage of each
  4. Sum the two acreages

  EXAMPLE SE ¼ of the N ½ *and* the SW ¼ of the NE ¼

4 × 2	= 8
4 × 4	= 16
640 ÷ 8	= 80 acres
640 ÷ 16	= 40 acres
80 acres + 40 acres	= 120 acres
Alternative Solution:	
640 ÷ 4 ÷ 2	= 80 acres
640 ÷ 4 ÷ 4	= 40 acres
80 acres + 40 acres	= 120 acres

- **Convert acres into square feet**

  1. An acre contains 43,560 square feet

  EXAMPLE How many square feet are in 3.5 acres?
  3.5 × 43,560 = 152,460 square feet

Note to Readers

For a more complete description of math as it specifically applies to real estate, see the author's *Real Estate Math: What You Need to Know* Dearborn™ Real Estate Education. This self-study book covers the basics of math and provides practice opportunities in all areas. Step-by-step solutions to the math problems are included in *Real Estate Math: What You Need to Know*.

SECTION 13 RESIDENTIAL MORTGAGES

(See Unit 12 in *Florida Real Estate Principles, Practices & Law* and Unit 12 in *Florida Real Estate Broker's Guide*)

KEY TERM REVIEW

Acceleration clause authorizes the mortgagee to accelerate or advance the due date of the entire unpaid balance and call the entire debt due and payable if the mortgagor defaults.

Assignment of mortgage is a legal instrument that states that the mortgagee assigns (transfers) the mortgage and promissory note to the purchaser.

Assumption of an existing mortgage obligates the buyer to assume liability for the debt.

Blanket mortgages pledge a number of parcels, usually building lots as security for the loan.

Buydown is a way to temporarily lower the interest rate on a mortgage.

Contract for deed (land contract) is a financing method in which the title to the real property remains with the seller until the loan is repaid.

Deed in lieu of foreclosure is a friendly foreclosure (a nonjudicial procedure) in which the mortgagor gives title to the mortgagee.

Default occurs when a borrower fails to fulfill certain obligations agreed to in the promissory note.

Defeasance clause in title theory states, requires the lender to convey legal title to the borrower once the debt is repaid; in lien theory states, the clause requires the lender to release the mortgage lien when the debt is repaid.

Discount points are an extra up-front fee charged by lenders to increase the real yield or the APR.

Due-on-sale clause allows the mortgagee to call due the outstanding loan balance plus accrued interest thereby preventing the loan assumption; loan is due upon sale of the property.

Equity is the monetary interest the owner has in property over and above the mortgage indebtedness.

Equity of redemption allows the mortgagor to prevent foreclosure from occurring by paying the mortgagee the principal and interest due plus any expenses the lender has incurred in attempting to collect the debt.

Escrow (impound) accounts are required by most lenders to set aside funds to cover future payments for taxes, assessments, private mortgage insurance, and hazard insurance.

Estoppel certificate is signed by the borrower verifying the amount of the unpaid balance, the rate of interest, and the date to which the interest has been paid prior to assignment; also, often requested by a closing agent to verify the payoff amount for the seller prior to conveying a property.

First mortgage is the first mortgage loan to be executed and recorded.

Foreclosure is a legal procedure whereby property used as security for a debt is sold to satisfy the debt owing to default in payment of the mortgage, note, or default of other terms in the mortgage document.

Hypothecation refers to the pledging of property as security for payment of a loan without surrendering possession of the property.

Interest is the cost for the use of borrowed funds.

Junior mortgage is a mortgage that is behind (in priority) to the first mortgage.

Land development loans finance the installation of the on-site and off-site improvements.

Lien theory states treat a mortgage solely as a security interest in the secured real property with title retained by the mortgagor.

Lis pendens is a notice of pending legal action; it is filed before initiating a lawsuit.

Loan origination fee is a finance fee charged by a lender for making a mortgage.

Loan servicing is an extra source of income for lenders earned by handling the loan payment collection and recordkeeping for the mortgages it originates.

Loan-to-value (LTV) ratio is the relationship between the amount borrowed and the appraised value (or sometimes purchase price).

Mortgage is a security instrument signed by the mortgagor to voluntarily pledge the property as collateral for the debt.

Mortgagee is the lender who holds a mortgage on specific property as security for the money loaned to the borrower.

Mortgagor is the borrower who gives a mortgage on the property in order to obtain a loan from a lender.

Note is the legal instrument that represents the evidence of a debt and a promise to repay the debt.

Novation is the substitution of a new debtor (buyer) and release of a former debtor (seller) for an existing debt by mutual agreement and with approval of the mortgagee.

Partial release clauses are commonly used in blanket mortgages and provide for the release of individual parcels from the blanket mortgage upon payment of a specified amount.

PITI is the monthly principal, interest, taxes, and insurance payment charged on a mortgage loan.

Prepayment clause allows the borrower to pay off part or all of the mortgage debt, without penalty or other fees, prior to maturity.

Prepayment penalty allows an extra charge if any amount of the loan is paid off early.

Receivership clause allows a receiver to be appointed to collect income from a property and use the income to make mortgage payments.

Right to reinstate is the mortgagor's right to reinstate the original repayment terms in the note after the lender initiated the acceleration clause.

Satisfaction of mortgage, or *release of mortgage*, is a recordable instrument provided by the lender within 60 days of payoff as evidence the mortgage debt is paid in full.

Short sale involves a real estate transaction where the net proceeds at closing will not satisfy the payoff amount of mortgages and other liens on the property.

Subject to the mortgage occurs when a buyer makes regular periodic payments on the mortgage but does not assume responsibility for the mortgage note.

Subordination agreement provides that the lender voluntarily will allow a subsequent mortgage to take priority over the lender's otherwise superior mortgage (the act of yielding priority).

Takeout commitment is a commitment by a permanent lender to "take out" the interim lender by paying off the construction loan, leaving the developer with a permanent long-term loan once the project is complete.

Title theory states consider the mortgagee to have legal title to the mortgaged property, and the mortgagor has equitable title until the debt is repaid.

KEY CONCEPTS

- **Two legal theories**
  - *Lien theory* states (including Florida) protect the lender with a lien against the property but title remains with the borrower—if borrower defaults, lender will foreclose to recover money owed
  - *Title theory* requires borrower to transfer title to the property to the lender until the mortgage debt is paid in full—borrower retains equitable title
- **Promissory note**
  - Note must accompany all mortgages
  - Acknowledgment of the debt and a promise to repay (evidence of a debt)
  - Makes borrower personally liable
  - Includes terms of the agreement
- **Mortgage**
  - Pledges the property as security (collateral) for a debt
  - Provides for the lender to place a voluntary lien on real estate
  - *Hypothecation* is the pledging of property as security for the mortgage debt without surrendering possession
  - Parties to mortgage are the mortgagor (borrower) and mortgagee (lender)
- **Satisfaction of mortgage**
  - Mortgagee records the satisfaction, which releases the lien
  - Florida law requires satisfaction within 60 days of payoff
- **Mortgage lien priority**
  - Priority of mortgage liens normally determined by the recording date
  - First mortgage is first mortgage loan to be recorded
  - Second mortgage also called a junior mortgage
  - Subordination agreement used to voluntarily take a lower priority
- **Essential elements of the mortgage**
  - Promise to repay according to terms of note
  - Promise to pay property taxes, assessments, and so forth
  - Promise to pay property insurance
  - Occupy as a principal residence for at least 12 months
  - Maintenance and covenant of good repair
  - Promise not to remove any improvements pledged as security for the debt
- **Important mortgage provisions**
  - *Prepayment clause* provides conditions to repay debt in advance of due date
  - *Prepayment penalty clause* requires a borrower to pay a monetary penalty if mortgage payments are made in advance of the normal due date
  - *Acceleration clause* provides that upon default the entire debt is due

- *Right to reinstate* provides for the mortgagor's right to reinstate the original repayment terms in the note after the mortgagee has initiated the acceleration clause
- *Due-on-sale clause*, if the property is sold or transferred without the lender's prior written consent, allows the lender to immediately demand the outstanding loan balance plus accrued interest
- *Defeasance clause*, in title theory states, requires the lender to convey legal title to the borrower once the debt is repaid; in lien theory states, requires the lender to release the mortgage lien when the debt is repaid

- **Mortgage features**
  - Down payment
  - Loan-to-value ratio (LTV)
  - Equity
  - Interest
  - Loan servicing
  - Escrow (impound) account
  - PITI (Principal, interest, property taxes, hazard insurance)
  - Discount points
  - Loan origination fee
- **Loan-to-value calculation**
- **Mortgage discounting**
  - Discount points are based on loan amount
  - Charged as prepaid interest at the closing
  - Up-front charge paid at closing (prepaid interest) to increase lender's yield
  - One discount point is equal to 1% of the loan amount
  - Each discount point increases the yield by about ⅛ of 1%
- **Assignment of mortgage**
  - Occurs when ownership of a mortgage is transferred (sold) from one company (assignor) or individual to another (assignee)
  - Person or company purchasing the mortgage receives an estoppel certificate (estoppel letter) verifying the amount of the unpaid loan balance
- **Methods of purchasing property encumbered by an existing mortgage loan**
  - Subject to the mortgage
  - Assumption of an existing mortgage
  - Due-on-sale clause prevents assumption
  - Purpose of estoppel certificate
- **Contract for deed (land contract)**
  - A financing device that is used when a buyer does not have sufficient cash
  - Buyer gets possession at the time the contract is signed and makes payments to seller
  - After buyer has made the agreed-upon payments, the seller delivers the deed, conveying legal title to the buyer

- During the term of the contract for deed, while the buyer is making the payments, the buyer has equitable title
- If recorded, buyer gets equitable title, can file for homestead tax exemption, and is protected from later liens against the seller

- **Land development loans** and **construction loans**
  - Finance installation of on-site and off-site improvements
  - Draws
  - Takeout commitment
  - Buydown
  - Blanket mortgage
  - Partial release clause
- **Foreclosure**
  - Judicial process that requires a foreclosure auction after court process
  - Foreclosure is enforcement of the mortgage lien
  - Two remedies: (1) initiate a suit on the promissory note; (2) initiate a foreclosure proceeding
- **Equity of redemption**
  - Allows the borrower to prevent foreclosure by paying the lender the principal and interest due plus expenses the lender has incurred in attempting to collect the debt
- **Short sale**
- **Deed in lieu of foreclosure** is a nonjudicial procedure involving transfer of title from the defaulting borrower (mortgagor) to the lender (mortgagee)
- **Income property**
  - Receivership clause
- **Lis pendens**
  - Constructive notice of pending legal action involving real estate

IMPORTANT FORMULAS TO REMEMBER

- **Calculate equity**

  Current market value – mortgage debt = equity

  EXAMPLE Current market value is $475,000.
  Loan amount is $356,250.
  $475,000 – $356,250 = $118,750 equity

- **Calculate the loan-to-value ratio**

  Loan amount ÷ price = LTV ratio

  EXAMPLE Purchase price is $116,000. Loan amount is $92,800.
  $92,800 ÷ $116,000 = .80 or 80% LTV

- **Calculate the loan-to-value ratio when given down payment**

  1. Price – down payment = loan amount
  2. Loan amount ÷ price = LTV ratio

EXAMPLE Purchase price is \$250,000. Down payment is \$25,000.
\$250,000 – \$25,000 = \$225,000
\$225,000 ÷ \$250,000 = .90 or 90% LTV

- **Calculate the cost of points**

Loan amount × number points × .01 = cost of points

EXAMPLE Loan amount is \$95,000. Lender charges 3 points
\$95,000 × .03 = \$2,850

- **Calculate the lender's yield**

(Note: *Memorize* that each point increases the yield by ⅛ of 1%)

(Number of points × ⅛) + interest rate = lender's approximate yield (also called effective yield)

EXAMPLE The interest rate is 6% plus 2 points.
2 × ⅛ = 2⁄8 + 6 = 6 2⁄8, reduced to 6¼% yield

- **Calculate the lender's yield using decimals**

Convert a fraction to a decimal: ⅛ = 1 ÷ 8 = .125

EXAMPLE The interest rate is 5% plus 3 points.
3 × ⅛ = ⅜
3 ÷ 8 = .375 + 5 = 5.375%

(Note: If your calculator is not set to at least three decimal places, it will round up the answer internally. In such cases, your answer will vary from the solutions presented in this text.)

SECTION 14 TYPES OF MORTGAGES AND SOURCES OF FINANCING

(See Unit 13 in *Florida Real Estate Principles, Practices & Law*)

KEY TERM REVIEW

Adjustable-rate mortgage (ARM) is a financing technique in which the lender can raise or lower the interest rate according to a predetermined index.

Amortized mortgage is a financing technique in which the debt is gradually and systematically killed or extinguished by equal regular period payments; the entire loan is paid off at the end of the loan term.

Annual percentage rate (APR) includes the interest rate and other loan costs and represents the true yearly cost of credit.

Balloon payment is a single large final payment, including accrued interest and all unpaid principal due at maturity of a partially amortized mortgage.

Biweekly mortgage is a mortgage loan amortized the same way as other loans with monthly payments, except that the borrower makes a payment every two weeks.

Closing Disclosure is a form that replaced the HUD-1 Statement and must be provided to the borrower at least three business days prior to closing.

Conforming loans are loans that meet Fannie Mae guidelines regarding size and type of loan.

Conventional loan is one that is not insured or guaranteed by a government agency.

Discount rate is the interest rate charged banks for borrowing money from the Fed.

Disintermediation is the removal of intermediaries; buyers bypass the middlemen.

Entitlement is the maximum amount for an individual veteran that the government will guarantee for a VA loan.

Fannie Mae is an institution in the secondary mortgage market that buys and sells mortgages.

Freddie Mac is a secondary mortgage market institution that buys and sells conventional, FHA, and VA loans.

Ginnie Mae is a federal agency that is part of the Department of Housing and Urban Development.

Home equity loans are loans secured by the borrower's residence to finance consumer purchases, consolidate existing credit card debt, and pay for other expenses.

Index refers to the rate to which an adjustable-rate loan is tied; at set adjustment periods, the borrower's interest rate moves up or down as the index rate changes.

Intermediation financial institutions serve as intermediaries between depositors and borrowers.

Level-payment plan is a mortgage in which the monthly payments are a fixed amount (payment does not change) but the amount applied to principal increases each month and the amount applied to interest decreases each month.

Lifetime caps limit the total amount the interest rate can increase over life of the loan.

Loan estimate is a form that contains information about the lender, property, loan terms, projected payments, and total estimated cost at closing.

Margin is the percentage that is added to the index to calculate each interest rate change in an adjustable rate mortgage; it covers the lender's expenses plus profit.

Monetary policy refers to the actions undertaken by the Fed to influence the availability and cost of money and credit.

Mortgage broker is a person or business entity who conducts loan originator activities through one or more licensed mortgage loan originators.

Mortgage fraud is the intent to materially misrepresent or omit information on a mortgage loan application to obtain a loan or to obtain a larger loan than would have been obtained if the lender or the borrower had the true facts.

Mortgage insurance premium (MIP) is a premium for mortgage insurance on FHA mortgages to protect the lender from loss in the event of a default.

Mortgage lenders are business entities that originate, sell, and service mortgage loans. Mortgage lenders are not depository institutions. They originate loans and then package the loans together and sell the entire package.

Mortgage loan originator (MLO) is a person who solicits mortgage loans, accepts mortgage loan applications, negotiates the terms of new and existing mortgage loans on behalf of a borrower or lender, processes mortgage loan applications, or negotiates the sale of existing mortgage loans to noninstitutional investors for compensation.

Negative amortization occurs when the mortgage payments are not large enough to cover the interest expense.

Nonconforming loans exceed the Fannie Mae loan amount.

Open market operations involve the purchase and sale of U.S. Treasury and federal agency securities.

Package mortgage includes both real and personal property as security for the debt.

Partially amortized mortgage requires the buyer to make regular payments smaller than what is required to completely pay off the loan. On the loan's maturity date, a balloon payment is due.

Payment caps limit the amount the monthly payments can increase during any adjustment.

Periodic caps limit the amount the interest rate may increase at any one time, usually a year.

Primary market is the market where securities are created.

Principal is the unpaid balance of the debt.

Purchase money mortgage (PMM) is a new mortgage accepted by the seller as part of the purchase price.

Receivership clause allows a receiver to be appointed to collect income from the property to ensure it is used to make mortgage payments in the event of default.

Reserve requirements are the amount of funds that an institution must hold in reserve against deposit liabilities.

Reverse mortgages enable elderly homeowners to borrow against the equity in their homes so they can receive monthly payments needed to help meet living expenses.

Secondary mortgage market is an investor market that buys and sells already existing securities.

Special information booklet contains consumer information regarding closing services for which the borrower may be charged at closing.

Teaser rate is a below-market interest rate usually offered for the first year on some adjustable-rate mortgages.

Triggering terms include certain credit terms or specific financing information in an advertisement.

Truth in Lending Act (TILA) is a federal law that is part of the Consumer Credit Protection Act, and implemented by the Federal Reserve Board's Regulation Z. The act ensures that borrowers and customers of consumer credit are given information regarding the cost of credit so that consumers can compare credit terms available.

Up-front mortgage insurance premium (UFMIP) is a one-time mortgage insurance fee paid at closing on FHA mortgage loans.

KEY CONCEPTS

- **Two categories of mortgage loans**
  - Conventional loans are not insured or guaranteed by a government agency and require the lender to assume the full risk of default
  - Nonconventional loans include FHA-insured and VA-guaranteed loans and typically require a smaller down payment compared with conventional loans
  - With nonconventional loans, the government provides some risk protection to the lender
- **Conventional mortgage loan features**
  - Interest rate is negotiated between lender and borrower
  - Assumption not allowed (due-on-sale clause)
  - Prepayment clause allows borrowers to prepay principal
  - Down payment and loan-to-value ratio
- **Qualifying for a conventional mortgage loan**
  - Total obligations ratio (TOR) must not exceed 36%
  - TOR calculation
- **Amortized mortgage**
  - Constant (level) monthly payment of principal and interest
  - 30-year and 15-year terms
- **Three facts needed to calculate a mortgage amortization**
  - The outstanding amount of the debt (principal)
  - The rate of interest
  - The amount of the payment (principal and interest "PI" *only*)
- **Mortgage amortization calculation**
- **Adjustable-rate mortgage (ARM)**
  - Index is an economic indicator used to adjust interest rate
  - Margin represents lender's cost of doing business plus profit
  - Calculated interest rate is the index plus margin
  - Adjustment interval is how often interest rate adjusts
  - Interest rate caps limit how much interest rate may change per adjustment
  - Payment caps limit the amount the monthly payment may increase during an adjustment

- — Negative amortization occurs when the mortgage payments are not large enough to cover interest expense
- — Teaser rate is a below-market initial interest rate

- **Partially amortized mortgage loan**
  - — Regular payments do not completely pay off the loan at end of term
  - — Single final balloon payment for unpaid balance
- **Biweekly mortgage loan**
  - — Borrower makes a payment of one-half the normal monthly payment every two weeks
  - — Borrower makes 26 biweekly payments, which is the equivalent of an extra month's payment each year
- **Package mortgage loan** includes both real and personal property as security for the debt
- **Home equity loans** secured by borrower's primary residence
- **Purchase money mortgage (PMM)** is taken back by seller in lieu of purchase money
- **Home equity conversion mortgage (HECM)** reverse mortgage loan
- **FHA government-insured mortgage loan**
  - — Section 203(b) FHA program insures fixed-rate loans on one- to four-family residences
- **Characteristics of FHA mortgage loans**
  - — Insures mortgages made by approved lenders
  - — FHA-approved lenders make FHA loans to borrowers
  - — Lenders may charge discount points
  - — Borrowers make a down payment of at least 3.5%
  - — FHA sets loan limits on amount that can be borrowed
  - — Borrower pays up front mortgage insurance premium (UFMIP) at closing
  - — Borrower is charged an annual mortgage insurance premium (MIP) paid monthly as part of the monthly mortgage payment
  - — FHA mortgages are assumable (no due-on-sale clause)
  - — Interest rate is negotiable between lender and borrower
  - — FHA-approved appraiser must appraise home and confirm the property meets HUD's minimum property standards
- **FHA qualifying ratios**
  - — Housing expense ratio (HER) cannot exceed 31%
  - — Total obligations ratio (TOR) cannot exceed 43%
- **VA loan guarantee program**
  - — Veterans, unremarried surviving spouse of veterans, and active military are eligible to apply for a VA loan
- **VA mortgage loan characteristics**
  - — Eligibility requirements are based on period of active duty or the period of continuous service

- Eligible to purchase, refinance, or construct one- to four-unit properties provided the veteran resides in one of the units
- Maximum loan term is 30 years
- Lender sets interest rate, discount points, and closing costs
- VA establishes loan guarantee limits called the VA loan guarantee or the maximum entitlement (guarantee)
- VA partially guarantees the loan
- Veteran's entitlement is maximum amount government guarantees the lender will be paid if borrower defaults
- Certificate of eligibility states the amount of entitlement available to the veteran borrower
- VA does not set loan limits; amount veteran may borrow depends on the value of the real estate and the veteran's income
- VA allows 1% loan origination fee to be charged to veteran borrower
- Borrower pays a funding fee or user's fee to VA
- Down payments are not required on loans of $417,000 or less
- Veteran may not be charged for termite report (unless refinance), nor commission (broker fees)
- No due-on-sale clause; they are assumable (even by nonveterans)
- No prepayment penalty clause

- **VA qualifying ratio**
  - Total obligations ratio (TOR) cannot exceed 41%
- **Loan application process**
  - Credit evaluation and credit scoring
  - Qualifying ratios
  - Qualifying the property
  - Preapproval and prequalification
- **Primary mortgage market consists of lenders who originate new mortgages**
  - Three major depository lenders that originate mortgage loans (1) savings associations; (2) commercial banks; and (3) credit unions
- **Savings associations**
  - Savings associations (formerly called savings and loan associations) are also referred to as savings banks
  - Chartered by state or federal government
  - Federal SAs are members of Federal Home Loan Mortgage Bank System (FHLBS)
  - Primarily make conventional loans
- **Commercial banks**
  - Make conventional, FHA, VA mortgage loans, construction loans, home equity loans
  - Chartered by either a state or the federal government
  - *National* or NA in name if federally chartered
  - Deposits insured by FDIC up to $250,000

- **Credit unions**
  - Nonprofit cooperative organizations that maintain savings and demand deposit accounts for members
  - Deposits insured to $250,000
  - Makes conventional, FHA, and VA loans
- **Mortgage lenders**
  - Full-service mortgage companies that make mortgage loans or services mortgage loans for others
  - Sells mortgage loans in secondary mortgage markets
  - Not a depository institution
  - Originates loans, packages loans together, and then sells the package
  - Primarily makes FHA and VA loans and sells them on the secondary mortgage market
  - Mortgage loan originators (MLOs) employed by a mortgage lender must be registered with the NMLS
  - MLOs employed by a mortgage lender must be state-licensed if the mortgage lender is not a federal agency–regulated institution
- **Mortgage broker**
  - A person or business entity who conducts loan originator activities through one or more licensed loan originators
  - Does not make loans
  - Does not service loans
- **Mortgage loan originator (MLO)**
  - A person who solicits mortgage loans or accepts applications for mortgage loans
  - Negotiates the terms of new or existing mortgage loans on behalf of a borrower or lender
  - Loan originator license is required
  - If a loan application is approved, MLO earns a loan origination fee
- **SAFE Mortgage Licensing Act**
  - Sets a minimum standard for licensing and registering mortgage loan originators
  - Requires employees of financial institutions regulated by a federal banking agency who engage in residential mortgage loan origination to register with the Nationwide Mortgage Licensing System (NMLS)
  - MLOs who are not employed by agency-regulated institutions are licensed by the state
- **Secondary market is where existing mortgages are purchased and sold**
  - Portfolio lenders hold mortgage loans in its portfolio and service the loans
  - Most lenders sell the loans in the secondary mortgage market
- **Two objectives of secondary mortgage market**
  - Circulates the mortgage money supply
  - Standardized loan requirements

- **Government-sponsored enterprises**
  - Fannie Mae buys conventional, FHA, and VA loans
  - Freddie Mac buys conventional mortgage loans
  - Ginnie Mae is a government corporation under HUD and a guarantor on pools of FHA and VA mortgage loans
- **Mortgage fraud**
  - Straw buyer
  - No documentation loans
  - Red flags
- **Equal Credit Opportunity Act (ECOA)**
  - Enforced by the Consumer Financial Protection Bureau
  - Requires financial institutions engaged in extending credit to make credit available without discrimination on the basis of race, color, religion, national origin, sex, marital status, age, or receipt of public assistance
- **Truth in Lending Act**
  - Implemented by Federal Reserve Regulation Z
  - Lenders must provide a Truth in Lending disclosure statement
  - Disclosure of full credit costs includes the amount of the loan, the APR, finance charges, a payment schedule, and total repayment amount over the lifetime of the loan
- **Advertisements containing triggering terms must disclose**
  - Amount or percentage of down payment
  - Terms of repayment
  - Annual percentage rate
- **Three-business-day right of rescission**
  - Does *not* apply to first mortgages
  - Applies to most consumer loans, including home equity lines of credit, second mortgages, and refinance loans
- **Real Estate Settlement Procedures Act (RESPA)** was enacted to ensure buyers are informed regarding the amount and type of charges they will pay at closing
  - Closing disclosure at least three business days prior to loan closing
  - Information booklet concerning settlement costs no later than third business day after application
  - Loan estimate no later than third business day after loan application
  - Affiliated business relationship disclosure required before closing
  - Prohibits seller from requiring the buyer to use a particular title insurance company as a condition of sale
  - Limits amount lenders can require borrowers to place in escrow for property taxes and hazard insurance
  - Kickbacks, fee-splitting, and unearned fees are illegal under RESPA
- **TILA-RESPA integrated disclosure rule**
  - *Loan Estimate* form third business day after receiving loan application
  - *Closing Disclosure* form at least three business days prior to closing

(Study material for broker candidates only)

- Initial escrow statement required at closing
- Annual escrow statement required from the loan servicer once a year

- The **Federal Reserve System** is the central bank of the United States charged with maintaining the stability of the financial system using three economic tools
- **Open-market operations involve the purchase and sale of U.S. Treasury securities**
  - Fed purchases securities—money supply increases and interest rates decrease
  - Fed sells securities—money supply decreases and interest rates increase
- **Discount rate is the interest rate charged to banks to borrow money from the Fed**
  - Discount rate increased—money supply decreases
  - Discount rate decreased—money supply increases
- **Reserve requirement is the amount of funds that an institution must hold in reserve against deposit liabilities as determined by the Fed**
  - Reserve requirement increased—money supply decreases and interest rates increase
  - Reserve requirement decreased—money supply increases and interest rates decrease

IMPORTANT DATES AND TIME PERIODS TO REMEMBER

- **Three business days.** Number of days for lender to provide APR disclosure (or at time of loan application)
- **Three business days.** Number of days to give loan applicant an estimate of settlement costs (or at time of loan application)
- **Three business days.** Number of days borrower has the right to cancel the loan contract following signing loan documents for home equity lines of credit, second mortgages, and refinance loans

IMPORTANT FORMULAS TO REMEMBER

- **Calculate the housing expense ratio (HER) and the total obligations ratio (TOR)**

  Monthly housing expense (PITI) ÷ monthly gross income = HER

  Monthly total obligations ÷ monthly gross income = TOR

  EXAMPLE A borrower has a monthly gross income of $5,000, monthly housing expenses of $1,250, and total monthly obligations of $2,000. Calculate the HER and TOR for this borrower.

  $1,250 ÷ $5,000 = .25 or 25% HER
  $2,000 ÷ $5,000 = .40 or 40% TOR

- **Calculate a mortgage amortization**

  1. Principal balance × annual interest ÷ 12 = first month's interest
  2. Monthly mortgage payment – 1st month's interest = principal payment
  3. Beginning loan balance – principal paid = new principal balance

EXAMPLE What is the principal balance on a $100,000 mortgage at 4% interest after two monthly payments of $477.40? (Note: Round to dollars and cents.)

Month 1:

$100,000 × .04 ÷ 12	= $333.33 first month's interest
$477.40 – $333.33	= $144.07 principal paid month 1
$100,000 – $144.07	= $99,855.93 new principal balance after one payment

Month 2:

$99,855.93 × .04 ÷ 12	= $332.85 second month's interest
$477.40 – $332.85	= $144.55 principal paid month 2
$99,855.93 – $144.55	= $99,711.38 principal balance after two payments

- **Calculate total interest paid on a mortgage loan over an extended period of time**

1. Calculate number of payments paid to date
2. Calculate the total amount paid to date
3. Amount borrowed × percent paid off = principal paid to date
4. Total paid to date – principal repaid = total interest paid to date

EXAMPLE Monthly mortgage payments of $365.49 have been paid for 10 years. The original amount borrowed was $40,000. After 10 years 35% of the loan has been paid.

10 years × 12 payment a year	= 120 payments to date
$365.49 × 120	= $43,858.80 total paid to date
$40,000 × .35	= $14,000 principal paid to date
$43,858.80 – $14,000	= $29,858.80 interest paid to date

SECTION 15 REAL ESTATE APPRAISAL

(See Unit 16 in *Florida Real Estate Principles, Practices & Law* and Units 6–8 in *Florida Real Estate Broker's Guide*)

KEY TERM REVIEW

Appraisals are opinions of value based on supportable evidence and approved methods.

Assemblage is the combining of two or more adjoining properties into one tract; the *process* of consolidating properties.

Automated valuation models (AVMs) are data analyses compiled using a computer database of closed sales.

Cost is the amount to produce or acquire something.

Cost approach estimates value by taking cost minus depreciation plus site value, based on the theory that a knowledgeable purchaser will pay no more for a property than the cost of acquiring a similar site and constructing an acceptable substitute structure.

Curable depreciation occurs when a building component has been added or repaired and the owners are able to get their money back in added value.

Depreciation is loss in value caused by things such as wear and tear, poor design, or the structure's surroundings (proximity).

Economic life or *useful life* is the total estimated time in years that an improvement will add value.

Effective age is the age indicated by a structure's condition and utility.

Effective gross income (EGI) is the result of deducting vacancy and collection losses from annual potential gross income plus adding any income from miscellaneous sources.

Federally related transaction is any real estate–related financial transaction that a federal financial institution's regulatory agency has either contracted for, or regulates, and requires the services of an appraiser.

Gross income multiplier (GIM) can include income from sources other than rental income (based on annual income); it is the ratio between a property's gross annual income and its selling price.

Gross living area (GLA) *(Study material for broker candidates only)* is the square footage calculated by taking the exterior dimensions of a house and then subtracting the garage square footage and any other square footage that is not heated.

Gross rent multiplier (GRM) is the ratio between a property's gross monthly rental income and its selling price.

Highest and best use is the most profitable legal way that a property can be used.

Income approach develops an estimated market value based on the present worth of future income from the subject property.

Incurable depreciation occurs when a building component has been added or repaired but the owners are unable to get their money back in added value.

Investment value is the value of a property to a particular investor based on the investor's desired rate of return and risk tolerance.

Market value is the most probable price a property should bring in a competitive and open market with the buyer and seller each acting prudently and knowledgeably, assuming the price is not affected by undue stimulus.

Net operating income (NOI) is the income remaining after subtracting all relevant operating expenses from EGI.

Overimprovement occurs when an owner invests more money in a structure than the owner may reasonably expect to recapture.

Plottage is the *added value* as a result of assembling (combining) two or more properties into one large parcel.

Potential gross income (PGI) is total annual income a property would produce if it were fully rented and no collections losses were incurred.

Price is the amount paid for something.

Principle of substitution means that a prudent buyer or investor will pay no more for a property than the cost of acquiring an equally desirable substitute property.

Progression is the principle that states the value of an inferior property is enhanced by its association with superior properties of the same type.

Purpose of appraisals *(Study material for broker candidates only)* is to determine the problem to be solved and the type of value to be estimated.

Reconciliation is a process of weighted averaging used in the sales comparison approach to bring the adjusted values of several comparable properties into a single estimate of value.

Regression is the principle that states the value of a superior property is negatively affected by its association with an inferior property of the same type.

Replacement cost is the amount of money required to replace a structure having the same use and functional utility as the subject property, using modern, available, or updated materials.

Reproduction cost is the amount of money required to build an exact duplicate of the structure.

Sales comparison approach is a method for estimating value by comparing similar properties with the subject property based on the theory that a knowledgeable purchaser will pay no more for a property than the cost of acquiring an equally acceptable substitute property.

Subject property is the property being appraised.

Uniform Standards of Professional Appraisal Practice (USPAP) is a set of guidelines (standards of practice) to follow when conducting appraisal services.

Vacancy and collection losses consist of the expected income loss that will result from occasional turnover of tenants and periodic vacancies, as well as the likelihood that not all of the rental income will be collected.

Value is the worth of something.

KEY CONCEPTS

- **Appraisal Foundation**
  - Appraiser Qualifications Board (AQB) endorses uniform examination
  - Appraisal Standards Board (ASB) develops USPAP
  - Appraisal Subcommittee (ASC) maintains a National Registry of State Certified and Licensed Appraisers
- **State certified appraisers**
  - Certified residential appraiser
  - Certified general appraiser
- **Federally related transaction**
  - Any real estate–related financial transaction that a federal financial institutions regulatory agency has either contracted for or regulates and that requires the services of an appraiser
  - Appraisals for real estate–related financial transactions require a state-certified or licensed appraiser unless the transaction is exempted from requirement
  - Fannie Mae, Freddie Mac, HUD, and the VA require the use of state-certified or licensed appraisers for all loans regardless of the amount of the loan
  - All appraisals for federally related transactions must be in writing and conform to the USPAP
- **Real estate licensees may prepare appraisal reports**
  - Provided *not* a federally related transaction
  - Must abide by the *Uniform Standards of Professional Appraisal Practice (USPAP)*
  - May *not* refer to a CMA or a BPO as an appraisal
  - May *not* hold themselves out to be an appraiser
- **Cost, price, value**
  - *Cost* is the total expenditure to create an improvement including materials, labor, and land
  - *Price* is the amount paid in a particular transaction (the contract price)
  - *Value* is the worth of something between many market participants
- **Types of value**
  - *Assessed value* is the value used as a basis for property taxation
  - *Insurance value* is an estimate of the amount of money required to replace a structure
  - *Investment value* is the price investors would pay, given their own financing requirements and income tax situation
  - *Liquidation value* is the value associated with a rapid sale
  - *Going-concern value* is the value of an income-producing property or business characterized by a significant operating history

- Salvage value is value at end of structure's useful life
- *Market value* is the most probable price that a property should bring in a competitive and open market under all conditions requisite to a fair sale, the buyer and seller each acting prudently and knowledgeably, and assuming the price is not affected by undue stimulus

- **Characteristics of value (DUST)**
  - **D** Demand
  - **U** Utility
  - **S** Scarcity
  - **T** Transferability
- **Principle of substitution**
  - The maximum value of a property tends to be set by cost of acquiring an equally desirable substitute property
  - Sets an upper limit of value
- **Highest and best use**
  - Most profitable single use of a property
  - Use must be legally permissible, physically possible, and financially feasible
  - Highest and best use of land as though vacant
  - Highest and best use of a property as improved
- **Increasing and decreasing returns**
  - Relationship between cost of an improvement and its contribution to value
  - Overimprovement
- **Conformity** based on concept that a property in harmony with surroundings has greater contributory value
- **Assemblage** and **plottage**
- **Progression** and **regression**
- **The appraisal process** *(Study material for broker candidates only)*
  - Define the problem
  - Preliminary analysis; select and collect data
  - Analyze highest and best use
  - Apply the three approaches to value
  - Reconcile the three values into a final estimate of value
  - Report the estimated value
- **Three approaches to value**
  - Sales comparison
  - Cost approach
  - Income approach
- **Relevance of approaches**
  - Sales comparison most relevant for valuing vacant lots
  - Cost approach most relevant for special-purpose property
  - Income approach most relevant for apartment complex

- **Sales comparison approach**
  - Used primarily for single-family residential and vacant land
  - Value is estimated by studying the sale prices of similar (*comparable*) properties
  - Sale prices of the comps are adjusted to infer value of the subject property
  - If a comparable is superior to the subject, adjust comp *down* (subtract)
  - If a comparable is inferior to the subject, adjust comp *up* (add)
  - Adjusted sale prices of comparables are reconciled into an estimated value of the subject property using a weighted average
- **Steps in cost approach**
  - Estimate the reproduction cost of the improvements (can use replacement cost)
  - Estimate amount of accrued depreciation (age-life method)
  - Estimate the value of the site
  - Add land value to the depreciated cost of the structure
- **Three types of depreciation in cost approach**
  - *Physical deterioration* is ordinary wear and tear caused by use
  - *Functional obsolescence* is poor design, obsolete equipment, and so forth
  - *External obsolescence* is caused by neighborhood influences *external* to the property
- **Income approach**
  - Measures a flow of income projected into the future
  - Principal of anticipation (value is created by the expectation of an income stream into the future)
- **Steps in the income approach**
  - Estimate annual potential gross income (PGI)
  - Deduct vacancy and collection loss and add other income to derive effective gross income (EGI)
  - Deduct operating expenses (fixed, variable, and reserves) to derive net operating income (NOI)
  - Compare net operating incomes of properties similar to the subject property and divide each NOI by the property's sale price to derive a capitalization rate
  - Apply the cap rate to the subject property's projected annual net income to estimate value
- **Reconciling the value indications** into a final value estimate
  - Weighted average
- **Gross rent multiplier (GRM)**
  - Relates sale price to monthly rental income
  - Applies to rental income only (usually monthly)
  - Sale price divided by gross monthly rent equals GRM

- **Gross income multiplier (GIM)**
  - Appropriate for small income-producing property
  - Refers to all income a property produces
  - Typically uses annual income
- **Comparative market analysis (CMA) categories of comparables**
  - Recently sold
  - Currently on the market
  - Recently expired listings
  - Common elements of comparison
  - Computer-generated CMAs
- **Automated valuation model (AVM)**
  - Used by lenders in situations where the expense of an appraisal may not be warranted
  - Do not meet USPAP standards
  - Do not involve property inspection

IMPORTANT FORMULAS TO REMEMBER

- **Calculate average price per square foot and apply to estimate land value**

1. Estimate the square footage of each comparable lot
2. Sale price ÷ total square feet = price per square foot
3. Average the price per square foot of the comparables
4. Subject property square feet × average price per square foot = estimated value of subject lot

EXAMPLE

Sale	Sale Price		Dimensions
1	$25,000		100' × 120'
2	$28,500		110' × 120'
3	$29,000		100' × 140'
1	100' × 120' = 12,000 square feet		
2	110' × 120' = 13,200 square feet		
3	100' × 140' = 14,000 square feet		
1	$25,000 ÷ 12,000 per square foot	= $2.08 (rounded to dollars and cents)	
2	$28,500 ÷ 13,200	= $2.16	
3	$29,000 ÷ 14,000	= $2.07	

$2.08 + $2.16 + $2.07 = $6.31 ÷ 3 sales = $2.10 average price per square foot
Assume subject lot is 115' × 130' and there are no other adjustments required:
115' × 130' = 14,950 square feet × $2.10 = $31,395 estimated market value or $31,400 (rounded)

- **Calculate the estimated market value of the subject property using the sales comparison approach**

1. Comp is *inferior add* value (CIA)
2. Comp is *better subtract* value (CBS)

EXAMPLE Subject property is a three-bedroom, two-bath, two-car garage home with a pool.

A comparable property is a four-bedroom, two-bath, two-car garage home with no pool but it has a screened-in porch.

The appraiser estimates that the fourth bedroom adds $15,000 value, a pool adds $12,000 value, and a screened-in porch adds $2,000 value. The comparable sold for $165,000. Calculate the estimated market value of the subject property based on this information only.

Feature	Subject	Comparable	Value Adjustment
Bedrooms	3	4	($15,000)
Pool	Yes	No	+ $12,000
Porch	No	Yes	($2,000)
Net adjustment			($5,000)

$165,000 – $5,000 net adjustment = $160,000 estimated market value of subject property

- **Calculate accrued depreciation using effective age and total economic life**

(Effective age ÷ total economic life) × reproduction cost new = accrued depreciation

EXAMPLE The effective age of a structure is five years old. Total economic life is estimated at 60 years. Reproduction cost new is $250,000.

(5 ÷ 60) = .0833 (rounded to four decimal places)
.0833 × $250,000 = $20,825 accrued depreciation

- **Calculate estimated property value using the cost approach**

Reproduction new cost of the building – accrued depreciation = building value

Building value + site value = depreciated value of the property

EXAMPLE A house has a living area of 2,200 square feet and a garage area of 420 square feet. The cost to construct living area today is $90 per square foot and $55 per square foot for the garage area. The home has an effective age of five years and has a useful life of 50 years. The lot is appraised at $32,000.

2,200 × $90 = $198,000 reproduction cost new of the living area
420 × $55 = $23,100 reproduction cost new garage area
$198,000 + $23,100 = $221,100 reproduction cost new of structure
(5 ÷ 50) × $221,100 = .10 × $221,100 = $22,110 accrued depreciation
$221,100 – $22,110 depreciation + $32,000 land = $230,990 depreciated value of the property using the cost approach

- **Calculate estimated property value using the income approach**

NOI ÷ cap rate = value

EXAMPLE The net operating income of a rental property is $80,000, and the capitalization rate is 8%.
$80,000 ÷ .08 = $1,000,000 value using income approach

- **Calculate the capitalization rate using the income approach**

NOI ÷ value = cap rate

EXAMPLE The net operating income of a retail store is $66,000, and the store recently sold for $550,000.
$66,000 ÷ $550,000 = .12 or 12% cap rate

- **Calculate the NOI using the income approach**

Value × cap rate = NOI

EXAMPLE You invest $335,000 in a property that should produce a 9% rate of return.
$335,000 × .09 = $30,150 NOI

- **Calculate estimated property value using the gross rent multiplier**

Sale price ÷ monthly rent = GRM

GRM × monthly rent = property value

EXAMPLE

Sale	Sale Price	Monthly Rent
1	$93,600	$650
2	$95,500	$675
3	$82,000	$565

(Round to nearest whole number):
$93,600 ÷ $650 = 144 GRM
$95,500 ÷ $675 = 141 GRM
$82,000 ÷ $565 = 145 GRM
144 + 141 + 145 = 430 ÷ 3 = 143 market GRM
Subject property has a market rent of $625:
$625 × 143 = $89,375 value

- **Calculate GIM using the gross income multiplier**

Sale price ÷ annual income = GIM

EXAMPLE If the annual income of a commercial property is $120,000 and the sale price is $900,000, what is the GIM?
$900,000 ÷ $120,000 = 7.5 GIM

SECTION 16 REAL ESTATE INVESTMENTS AND BUSINESS OPPORTUNITY BROKERAGE

(See Unit 17 in *Florida Real Estate Principles, Practices & Law* and Units 9 and 15 in *Florida Real Estate Broker's Guide*)

KEY TERM REVIEW

Appreciation is an increase in the worth or value of property.

Asset is anything of value.

Balance sheet *(Study material for broker candidates only)* shows the company's financial position at a stated moment in time.

Basis is an investor's initial cost of a property.

Capital gain (loss) is the difference between the adjusted basis of property and its net selling price.

Cash flow is the total amount of money generated from an investment after expenses have been paid.

Current ratio *(Study material for broker candidates only)* is the measure of the business's ability to meet short-term obligations and is calculated by dividing the business's current assets by its current liabilities.

Discounted cash flow analysis *(Study material for broker candidates only)* is an investment valuation technique that considers anticipated changes in cash flows over years, projects the current value of net proceeds from the sale of the property in the future, and accounts for the time value of money.

Equity is the property's value minus debt.

Going concern value is the value of an established business property compared with the value of just the physical assets of a business not yet established.

Goodwill is the intangible asset attributed to a business's reputation and the expectation of continued customer loyalty.

Internal rate of return (IRR) *(Study material for broker candidates only)* is the discount rate at which present values of future cash flows equal the down payment.

Inventory turnover ratio *(Study material for broker candidates only)* is an analysis of a business's management of inventory and is calculated by dividing the cost of goods sold by the ending inventory.

Leverage is the use of borrowed funds to finance the purchase of an asset.

Liquidation analysis is the valuation method used for a business that is going out-of-business

Liquidity refers to the ability to sell an investment quickly without loss of one's investment.

Net present value (NPV) *(Study material for broker candidates only)* is the present value of future cash flows (at a discount rate) minus the investor's down payment.

Quick ratio *(Study material for broker candidates only)* is a more conservative measure compared with the current ratio, of the business's ability to meet short-term obligations because it does not include inventory in current assets. Divide current assets (minus inventory) by current liabilities.

Real Estate Investment Trust (REIT) offers investors the opportunity to invest in a pool of income-producing properties under professional management.

Risk is the chance of losing all or part of an investment.

Tax shelter is an investment that shields income from payment of income taxes.

KEY CONCEPTS

- **Investment terminology**
  - Appreciation
  - Assets
  - Cash flow
  - Equity
  - Leverage (positive or negative)
  - Liquidity
  - Basis
  - Capital gain (or loss)
  - Tax shelter
  - Real estate investment trust (REIT)
  - Risk
- **Types of real estate investments**
  - Residential
  - Commercial
  - Industrial
  - Agricultural
  - Business opportunities
- **Advantages of real estate as an investment**
  - Usually above-average rate of return
  - Tax advantages
  - Hedge against inflation
  - Leverage of borrowed money
  - Equity buildup
- **Disadvantages of investing in real estate**
  - Lack of liquidity (illiquid)
  - More localized market
  - Expenses associated with expertise
  - Need for active management
  - Relatively high degree of risk

- **Risks associated with general business conditions**
  - *Business risk* (or *operating business risk*) is the degree of variance between budgeted (projected) income and expenses and actual income and expenses
  - *Financial risk* (or *operating financial risk*) is associated with the ability of a property to pay operating expenses from operations, borrowing, and equity
  - *Purchasing-power risk* is related to inflation
  - *Interest-rate risk* is the risk of rising interest rates
- **Risks that affect return**
  - *Liquidity risk* is the possible loss that may be incurred if the investment has to be converted quickly into cash
  - *Safety risk* is composed of market risk and risk of default
- **Leverage** is the use of borrowed funds to finance the purchase of an asset
  - *Positive leverage* occurs when the benefits exceed the cost of borrowing
  - *Negative leverage* occurs if the borrowed funds cost more than they are producing
- **Similarities between business brokerage and real estate brokerage**
  - Sale of real property or the assignment of a lease (transfer of interest in real property) is an integral part of a business brokerage transaction
  - A real estate license is required to deal in business brokerage
- **Differences between business brokerage and real estate brokerage**
  - Assets include personal property and goodwill
  - Value of real estate and value of going concern may be different
  - Wider geographic market for business brokerage
- **Expertise required in business brokerage**
  - Corporate finance
  - Business accounting
  - Valuation of businesses
- **Corporate finance** includes knowledge of
  - Classes and characteristics of corporate stock
  - Securities analyses and valuation
  - Management of working capital
  - Budgeting
- **Business accounting**
  - Income statement analysis
  - Balance sheet analysis
  - Asset depreciation
  - Taxation
- **Valuation of businesses**
  - Comparable sales analysis
  - Cost approach
  - Income analysis (best approach for valuing a business)
  - Liquidation analysis

- **Steps in the sale of a business**
  - Listing
  - Identify all assets of the business
  - Valuation of the business
  - Deduct liabilities
  - Valuation of stock
  - Legal compliance with all pertinent laws
  - Market (advertise) the business
  - Secure a buyer
  - Enter into a contract with both parties
  - Due diligence period
  - Closing preparation
  - Date of closing the transaction
- **Basic business appraisal** *(Study material for broker candidates only)*
  - Cash basis accounting recognizes income when it is received and expenses when they are paid
  - Accrual basis accounting recognizes income when it is earned and expenses when they are incurred
  - FIFO (first-in, first-out) is the inventory accounting method that shows the highest profit when costs are rising
  - LIFO (last-in, first-out) is the inventory accounting method that shows the least profit when costs are rising

IMPORTANT FORMULAS TO REMEMBER

- **Calculate an investor's equity**

  Current market value – mortgage debt = equity

  EXAMPLE An investor owns a business property with a value of $1,200,000 and a mortgage of $800,000.
  $1,200,000 – $800,000 = $400,000 equity

The following formulas are for broker candidates only

- **Calculate before-tax cash flow (BTCF)**

  Net operating income (NOI) – annual debt service (ADS) = before-tax cash flow (BTCF)

  EXAMPLE An office building has an NOI of $126,000 and annual debt service of $90,000. Calculate the before-tax cash flow (BTCF).
  $126,000 – $90,000 = $36,000 BTCF

- **Calculate after-tax cash flow (ATCF)**

  Before-tax cash flow (BTCF) – income taxes = after-tax cash flow (ATCF)

  EXAMPLE A property with a before-tax cash flow (BTCF) of $36,000 incurs an annual income tax liability of $14,518. Calculate the after-tax cash flow (ATCF).
  $36,000 – $14,518 = $21,482 ATCF

- **Calculate cash breakeven ratio**

Operating expenses – reserves + annual debt service (ADS) ÷ potential gross income (PGI) = cash breakeven ratio

EXAMPLE An office property has a PGI of $350,000. Operating expenses are estimated to be $189,000 (including $32,000 in reserves). The annual debt service (ADS) is $90,000. Calculate the cash breakeven ratio.
$189,000 – $32,000 + $90,000 ÷ $350,000 = .71 or 71% cash breakeven ratio

- **Calculate debt service coverage ratio**

Net operating income (NOI) ÷ annual debt service (ADS) = debt service coverage ratio

EXAMPLE A property has an NOI of $126,000 with annual debt service (ADS) of $90,000. Calculate the debt service coverage ratio.
$126,000 ÷ $90,000 = 1.4 or 140% debt service coverage ratio

- **Calculate equity dividend rate (EDR)**

Before-tax cash flow (BTCF) ÷ equity (down payment) = EDR

EXAMPLE An investor purchased a property with a before-tax cash flow (BTCF) of $36,000 with a down payment of $240,000. Calculate the equity dividend rate.
$36,000 ÷ $240,000 = .15 or 15% EDR

- **Calculate operating expense ratio**

Operating expenses ÷ effective gross income (EGI) = operating expense ratio

EXAMPLE An office building with an effective gross income (EGI) of $315,000 has annual operating expenses of $189,000. Calculate the operating expense ratio.
$189,000 ÷ $315,000 = .6 or 60% operating expense ratio

SECTION 17 TAXES AFFECTING REAL ESTATE

(See Unit 18 in *Florida Real Estate Principles, Practices & Law* and Unit 14 in *Florida Real Estate Broker's Guide*)

KEY TERM REVIEW

Adjusted basis is the owner's original cost plus buying expenses and capital improvements.
Ad valorem means taxed according to value.
Assessed value is the value of a property for property tax purposes.
Assessment limitation (SOH benefit) is the accumulated difference between the assessed value and the market value of a homesteaded property due to the annual limit on increases in assessed value.
Boot is additional capital or personal property included in a like-kind exchange.
Capital gain is profit from the sale of property.
Debt service is the amount of money needed to meet the periodic payments of principal and interest on a loan that is being amortized.
Depreciation is a key deduction when calculating taxable income from investment property because it reduces taxable income without requiring a cash outlay.
Exempt property includes property belonging to churches and nonprofit organizations.
Green Belt Law was designed to protect farmers from having taxes increased just because the land might be in the path of urban growth.
Home acquisition loan *(Study material for broker candidates only)* is a loan used to buy, construct, or improve a residence.
Home equity loan *(Study material for broker candidates only)* usually a second mortgage, allows the borrower to take out a lump sum or to access a line of credit.
Immune property is city, county, state, and federal government property.
Installment sale method is a way to report gain for income tax purposes as the gain is from the sale of investment property.
Just value is the fair and reasonable value based on objective valuation methods for property tax purposes.
Like-kind exchanges allow investors to defer paying taxes by exchanging real property.
Long-term capital gain *(Study material for broker candidates only)* is a gain on a capital asset that has been held for more than one year, resulting in a more favorable capital gains tax rate.
Mill is one one-thousandth of a dollar or one-tenth of a cent.
Passive income *(Study material for broker candidates only)* is income derived from rental properties or other trades or businesses in which a taxpayer does not materially participate.

Short-term capital gain *(Study material for broker candidates only)* is profit from the sale of a property that is owned for 12 months or less taxed at the owner's marginal tax rate.

Special assessments are one-time taxes levied on properties to help pay for some public improvement that benefits the property.

Taxable income is the amount of income that remains after all applicable deductions and adjustments are applied.

Taxable value is the nonexempt assessed value that is determined by subtracting the applicable exemptions from the assessed value.

Tax rate is the millage rate multiplied by taxable value to determine the annual property taxes due.

KEY CONCEPTS

- **Real property taxation process**
  - Property taxes are ad valorem taxes (according to value)
  - Assessed value of all properties within the county
  - Levied on a calendar-year basis
  - Paid in arrears (at end of tax year)
  - Becomes a lien on January 1st each year
  - Property tax liens are superior to any other lien regardless of date
- **Steps in protest procedure**
  - Contact the county property appraiser's office within 25 days to seek an adjustment
  - Appeal to the Value Adjustment Board
  - Litigation
- **Property tax exemptions**
  - *Immune* (government)
  - *Exempt* (churches and nonprofits)
  - *Partially exempt* (homesteaded property)
- **Homestead tax exemption**
  - Florida residents who hold title to a home in Florida and use the home as their permanent residence may homestead the property
- **Calculating homestead exemption**
  - First $25,000 of assessed value: $25,000 exemption from city, county, and school board taxes
  - Assessed value of $25,001 up to $50,000: no additional exemption
  - Assessed value between $50,001 up to $75,000: $25,000 additional exemption from city and county taxes only, applied to the amount of assessed value that exceeds $50,000
  - Assessed value greater than $75,000: $25,000 exemption from city, county, and school board taxes; and $25,000 additional exemption from city and county taxes
  - First-time applicants must file for homestead by March 1
- **Additional $500 exemptions on homesteaded property**
  - Widows and widowers

- Legally blind persons
- Nonveterans who are totally and permanently disabled

- **$5,000 disabled veteran exemption** for veterans who are at least 10% disabled by military service-connected injury
- **Green Belt Law**
  - Shields agricultural property from higher tax assessments
  - Designed to protect farmers from having taxes increase just because their land might be suited for development
- **Save Our Home amendment** caps how much the assessed value of homesteaded property may increase each year by the lesser of 3% annually or the CPI for the preceding year
- **Tax rates**
  - Cities, counties, and school boards are capped at 10 mills each
  - One mill is written in decimals as .001
  - Taxable value multiplied by the tax rate equals annual property taxes due
- **Special assessments**
  - A one-time tax on improvements such as sidewalks, street paving, and so forth
  - Law requires that improvements benefit the property by resulting in increased value
  - Street paving assessment is calculated on per foot cost of the improvement
- **Nonpayment of property taxes**
  - Property taxes constitute a lien superior to all other liens on real property
  - Property taxes become a lien on January 1 of each year
  - Property taxes for the previous year become delinquent on April 1
  - Tax certificates are issued for each delinquent property
  - Tax certificate auction
  - Redemption of tax certificates
  - Tax deed process
- **Tax advantages of owning a principal residence**
  - Mortgage interest
  - Property taxes
  - IRA withdraws for first-time homebuyers
  - Exclusion of gain from the sale of a principal residence
- **Additional tax benefits to homeowners**
  - Interest on home equity loans is deductible
  - Mortgage origination fees are deductible
- **Sale of real property**
  - Adjusted basis
  - Amount realized
  - Exclusion of gain from the principal residence

- **Purchase of real property from foreign sellers**
- **Investment property**
  - Types of income
  - Determining taxable income
  - Debt service
  - Depreciation components
- **Three deductions from taxable income on investment property**
  - Operating expenses (*not* reserve for replacements)
  - Financing expense
  - Depreciation (key to sheltering income from taxation)
- **Straight-line method of depreciation for investment real estate**
  - 27½ years for residential rental property
  - 39 years for nonresidential income-producing property
  - Depreciate structure *only* (never land)
  - Depreciable basis of property is the initial cost of the asset plus acquisition costs minus the land value
- **Capital gains and losses**
  - Tax on gain at time of sale
  - Installment sale method
  - Like-kind exchange

IMPORTANT DATES AND TIME PERIODS TO REMEMBER

- **January 1.** Date each year that property taxes become a lien on real property
- **March 1.** Last day for first-time applicants to file for homestead exemption
- **April 1.** Property taxes from the previous year become delinquent
- **27½ years.** Useful asset life for residential rental property
- **39 years.** Useful asset life for nonresidential income property

IMPORTANT FORMULAS TO REMEMBER

- **Calculate the tax rate**

(Budget – nonproperty revenue) ÷ (assessed value – exemptions) = tax rate

EXAMPLE County budget is $9,500,000. Nonproperty revenue totals 2,500,000. Total assessed valuation is $850,000,000. Exemptions total $125,000,000.

1. Calculate the budget less the nonproperty revenue
   $9,500,000 budget – $2,500,000 revenue = $7,000,000
2. Calculate the assessed value less exemptions
   $850,000,000 – $125,000,000 = $725,000,000
   Remaining budget ÷ property revenue
   $7,000,000 ÷ $725,000,000 =
   (Note: Drop last set of zeros in each number before dividing.)
   $7,000 ÷ $725,000 = .0096 or 9.6 mills

- **Calculate property taxes due**

3. Calculate total city, county, and school mills
4. $25,000 base exemption + $500 blind exemption (if applicable) applies to the assessed value up to $50,000
5. An additional $25,000 exemption applies to the assessed value greater than $50,000 on city and county taxes
6. Assessed value – applicable exemptions equals taxable value
7. Taxable value × tax rate = taxes due
8. Additional $25,000 exemption × school board mills = additional taxes due
9. Add values from steps 5 and 6 to find total property taxes due

EXAMPLE The city rate is 8 mills, the county rate is 7.5 mills, and the school board rate is 5 mills. The property is homesteaded and the owner is legally blind. The assessed value is $320,000.

$320,000 assessed value – $25,500 base exemption and blind exemption = $294,500 taxable value for school taxes only
$294,500 × .005 mills = $1,472.50 school taxes
$320,000 assessed value – $50,500 total homestead exemption = $269,500 taxable value for city and county taxes
8 mills city + 7.5 mills county = 15.5 mills = .0155
$269,500 × .0155 = $4,177.25 city and county taxes
$4,177.25 + $1,472.50 = $5,649.75 total taxes due

- **Calculate tax savings realized from allowable exemptions**

Homestead exemptions × millage rate = property taxes due

10. Multiply base exemption + blind exemption by total mills
11. Multiply the additional $25,000 exemption by city and county mills
12. Add values from steps 1 and 2 to find total tax savings

EXAMPLE $25,500 × .0205 = $522.75 savings
8 + 7.5 = 15.5 mills or .0155
$25,000 × .0155 = $387.50 savings
$522.75 + $387.50 = $910.25 total savings

- **Calculate the cost of a special assessment**

13. Calculate total cost of paving
14. Calculate cost of homeowners' share
15. Divide cost by 2 (*Assume* cost is split with owner across the street)

EXAMPLE The lot measures 125' by 150'. The cost to pave the street is $60 per foot. The city will pay 45% of the cost.

125 front feet × $60 = $7,500 total cost of paving
$7,500 × .55 = $4,125 homeowners' share
$4,125 ÷ 2 = $2,062.50

- **Calculate annual depreciation allowance on residential rental property**

16. Calculate the value of the building without the land
17. Building ÷ 27.5 years = annual depreciation

EXAMPLE Property was purchased for $450,000 and the site is valued at 20%. Sale occurred in January. (Round depreciation to nearest dollar.)

$450,000 × .80 = $360,000 building
$360,000 ÷ 27.5 = $13,090.91 (round to) $13,091 annual depreciation

- **Calculate annual depreciation allowance on nonresidential income property**

18. Calculate the value of the building without the land
19. Building ÷ 39 years = annual depreciation

EXAMPLE Income property was purchased for $450,000 and the site is valued at 20%. Sale occurred in January. (Round depreciation to nearest dollar.)

$450,000 × .80 = $360,000 building
$360,000 ÷ 39 = $9,230.77 (round to) $9,231 annual depreciation

- **Calculate taxable income for an investment property**

Net operating income (NOI) + reserve for replacements – mortgage interest – annual depreciation = taxable income

EXAMPLE An apartment building produced a net operating income of $245,000 for the previous year. Operating expenses for that year were $133,500 including $26,000 for reserve for replacements. The owner paid $71,250 in mortgage interest, and the annual depreciation was $59,395. Calculate the taxable income for the property.

$245,000 NOI + $26,000 reserves – $71,250 interest – $59,395 depreciation = $140,355 taxable income

SECTION 18 REAL ESTATE MARKETS AND ANALYSIS

(See Unit 15 in *Florida Real Estate Principles, Practices & Law*)

KEY TERM REVIEW

Buyer's market occurs when the supply and demand equilibrium is upset by excess supply; more supply available than buyers (supply exceeds demand).
Demand has to do with the desire and ability to purchase or rent goods and services.
Household is any person or group of persons occupying a separate housing space.
Seller's market occurs when the supply and demand equilibrium is upset with excess demand; more buyers competing for a limited supply (demand exceeds supply).
Situs is the relationship and influence created by location of a property that affect value.
Supply is the amount and type of real estate available for sale or rent at differing price levels in a given real estate market.
Vacancy rate is the percentage of rental units that are not occupied.

KEY CONCEPTS

- **Physical characteristics of real estate**
  - *Immobility* (the geographic location is fixed and therefore its value is largely influenced by the surrounding area)
  - Land is *indestructible* (durable)
  - Real estate is *unique* ; there is no standard product; no two parcels are identical for they are at least in different locations (nonhomogeneous)
- **Economic characteristics of real estate**
  - Government controls influence the market through zoning, building codes, and taxes
  - Relationship between supply, demand, and price
  - The market is slow to respond to change in supply and demand
  - Area preference (situs)
- **Variables that influence supply**
  - Availability of skilled labor
  - Availability of construction loans and financing

  - Availability of land
  - Availability of materials
- **Variables that influence demand**
  - Price of real estate
  - Population numbers and household composition
  - Income of consumers
  - Availability of mortgage credit
  - Consumer taste or preferences
- **Interpreting market conditions**
  - Price and supply are inversely (oppositely) related
  - When supply goes down, prices go up (seller's market)
  - When supply goes up, prices go down (buyer's market)
  - When prices *rise*, demand goes *down*
  - When prices *decrease*, demand goes *up*
- **Market indicators**
  - Price levels and building permits
  - Vacancy rates
  - Sales volume
- **Calculate occupancy and vacancy rates**

IMPORTANT FORMULAS TO REMEMBER

- **Calculate vacancy rate**

  Units not occupied ÷ total available units = vacancy rate

  EXAMPLE An apartment complex has 550 units of which 517 are occupied. Calculate the vacancy rate.

  550 – 517= 33 unoccupied units
  33 ÷ 550 = .06 or 6% vacancy rate

SECTION 19 REAL ESTATE–RELATED COMPUTATIONS AND CLOSING OF TRANSACTIONS

(See Unit 14 in *Florida Real Estate Principles, Practices & Law* and Unit 13 in *Florida Real Estate Broker's Guide*)

KEY TERM REVIEW

Arrears means paid at the end of the period for which payment is due.
Credit means to be reimbursed for an expense.
Debit means to be charged for an expense.
Preclosing inspection is a final walk-through with the sales associate to verify that repairs have been completed and that the property is left in good condition.
Profit is how much one makes over and above cost.
Proration means to divide various debits (charges) and credits between buyer and seller; a proration is a *shared expense* between the buyer and seller.
Title closing is the consummation of a real estate transaction, when the seller delivers title to the buyer in exchange for payment from the buyer of the purchase price.

KEY CONCEPTS

- **Sale commissions**
  - Simple commission based on sale price
  - Commission based on co-broke sale
  - Graduated commission
  - Net
- **Percentage applied to selling price, cost, and profit**
  - Calculate percentage profit (loss)
- **Preliminary steps to closing**
  - Earnest money is deposited
  - Additional deposit if required
  - Loan application
  - Contingencies
  - Appraisal
  - Loan approval
  - Title insurance

- Termite inspection
- Home inspection
- Required repairs are ordered
- Survey is ordered
- Buyer hazard insurance
- Preclosing inspection
- Review closing documents
- Amount of funds needed from buyer to close
- Earnest money to closing agent

■ **Prorated expenses**
- Debit to one party and a credit to the other party
- Dollar amount of the debit and credit are the same
- 360-day method (each month is counted as 30 days—even February and 31-day months)
- 365-day method (based on actual number of days in each month)

■ **County and city property taxes**
- Buyer is credited at closing for time seller owned property
- Debit seller, credit buyer
- Items paid in arrears use seller days to calculate proration

■ **Prepaid rent**
- Items paid in advance use buyer days to calculate proration
- Debit seller, credit buyer

■ **Mortgage interest on assumed mortgage**
- Interest is paid in arrears
- Use seller days to calculate proration
- Debit seller, credit buyer

■ **State transfer taxes**
- Documentary stamp tax on deeds is paid on full purchase price: $.70 ($.60 in Dade County) per $100 or fraction thereof
- Documentary stamp tax on notes is paid on amount of debt: $.35 per $100 or fraction thereof
- Intangible tax is paid on new debt: $.002 per $1 of new debt
- State transfer tax is an expense
- Enter as a debit to person paying expense

■ **Other charges**
- Preparation of documents
- Recording fees
- Broker's commission
- Title insurance

IMPORTANT FORMULAS TO REMEMBER

- **Calculate simple sale commission**

  Purchase price × percent of commission = commission

  EXAMPLE Purchase price is $80,000. Commission rate is 6%
  $80,000 × .06 = $4,800 total commission due

- **Calculate the net to the seller**

  Sale price × (100% – commission rate)

  EXAMPLE Sale price is $85,000 and commission rate is 8%
  $85,000 (100% – 8%)
  $85,000 × .92 = $78,200 net to seller

- **Calculate sale price given the amount seller wants to net and the mortgage amount**

  (Seller's net + mortgage amount) ÷ (100% – commission rate)

  EXAMPLE The seller wants to net $100,000. There is an existing mortgage of $45,000 and the broker wants to earn 7% commission
  ($100,000 + $45,000) ÷ (100% – 7%)
  $145,000 ÷ .93 = $155,913.98 (round to $155,914) sale price

- **Calculate a graduated commission**

  1. Sale price portion × first rate = commission due
  2. Sale price portion × second rate = commission due
  3. Sum the two commissions

  EXAMPLE The broker agrees to 8% on the first $500,000 of sale price and 10% on the balance. The property sells for $820,000.
  $500,000 × .08 = $40,000
  $320,000 × .10 = $32,000
  $40,000 + $32,000 = $72,000

- **Calculate broker's share of commission**

  Full commission × broker's split = commission due broker

  EXAMPLE The broker agreed to pay the sales associate 55% of the total commission. The property sold for $200,000. Commission rate was 8%.
  $200,000 × .08 = $16,000
  100% – .55 = .45
  $16,000 × .45 = $7,200 broker's split

- **Calculate percentage of profit**

  1. Calculate total cost
  2. Calculate amount made on sale
  3. Amount made on sale ÷ total cost = percentage of profit

EXAMPLE Investor purchased two lots for $25,000 each. He subdivided them into five lots and sold them for $12,000 each.
2 × $25,000 = $50,000 total cost
5 × $12,000 = $60,000 – $50,000 = $10,000 amount made on sale
$10,000 ÷ $50,000 = .20 or 20%

- **Calculate percentage of profit given lot dimensions and cost per front foot**

1. The first dimension is always front feet
2. Front feet × cost per front foot = total cost

EXAMPLE Developer purchased four lots each 100' × 150' at $250 per front foot. She subdivided the lots into six lots and sold them for $25,000 each.
100' × $250 × 4 lots = $100,000 total cost
6 × $25,000 = $150,000 – $100,000 = $50,000 amount made on sale
$50,000 ÷ $100,000 = .50 or 50%

- **Calculate a rent proration**

1. Rent is paid in *advance* (usually at the 1st of the month) therefore the unused portion of advance rent belongs to the buyer
2. Monthly rent ÷ days in month = rent per day
3. Rent per day × days owed buyer = amount of proration (credit buyer, debit seller)

Note: Prorations are calculated using either 30 days for each month (360-day method) or using the actual number of days in each month (365-day method).

EXAMPLE The scheduled date for closing a duplex is October 12. Total rent collected on the first of the month was $875. Day of closing belongs to buyer. Use actual number of days method.
$875 ÷ 31 = $28.2258 per day (rounded to four decimal places)
$28.2258 × 20 days = $564.516 or $564.52 (rounded)
Debit seller (seller already received entire month's rent) $564.52
Credit buyer (buyer is due rent for day of closing through remainder of month) $564.52

- **Calculate a property tax proration**

1. Property taxes are paid *in arrears* ; therefore the seller has usually not paid the property taxes at time of closing
2. Calculate number of days the seller *owes* for the calendar year

EXAMPLE Property taxes are $1,250. Closing date is March 10. Day of closing belongs to seller. Use 365-day method.
Total days charged seller:
31 January + 28 February + 10 March = 69 days
$1,250 ÷ 365 = $3.4246575
$3.4246575 × 69 days = $236.30137 or $236.30 rounded
Debit seller (seller has not paid the property taxes) $236.30
Credit buyer (buyer will pay entire tax bill in November) $236.30

- **Calculate a mortgage interest proration on an assumed mortgage**

1. Mortgage payments are normally paid monthly
2. Mortgage interest is usually paid *in arrears*

3. Proration is based on daily *interest* not monthly payment of principal and interest
4. Calculate daily interest charge

EXAMPLE Closing day is May 8. Buyer is assuming mortgage with an outstanding balance of $93,600 at 6% interest. Seller paid interest on the mortgage through April 30th. Day of closing is charged to the buyer. Use 365-day method.
Seller owes interest for seven days (May 1 through midnight May 7)
$93,600 × .06 = $5,616 annual interest ÷ 365 days = $15.386301 per day
$15.386301 × 7 days = $107.70 *debit seller* (because seller has not paid May interest) = $107.70 *credit buyer* (because buyer will pay entire month's interest when it becomes due on May 30th)

- **Calculate documentary tax on deeds**

1. Tax is paid on full purchase price
2. Rate is $.70 per hundred dollar increments ($.60 in Dade County)
3. If not an even $100 increment, round *up* to next even $100 increment
4. Typically seller pays the tax on the deed (entered as a *debit* to seller)

EXAMPLE Sale price is $175,000.
$175,000 ÷ $100 = 1,750 × $.70 = $1,225 doc stamps on deed

- **Calculate documentary tax on notes**

1. Tax is paid on note amount of *new* and *assumed* mortgage notes
2. Rate is $.35 per hundred dollar increments
3. Typically buyer pays doc stamps on notes (entered as a *debit* to buyer)

EXAMPLE Buyer assumes the existing first mortgage of $85,530 and the seller takes back a purchase money mortgage in the amount of $15,000.
Doc stamps on assumed mortgage:
$85,530 ÷ $100 = 855.3 round up to 856 × $.35 = $299.60 doc stamps on assumed note
Doc stamps on purchase money (2nd) mortgage:
$15,000 ÷ $100 = 150 × $.35 = $52.50 doc stamps on new note

- **Calculate intangible tax on new debt (note)**

1. Taxed on new debt only
2. Rate is 2 mills ($.002) per dollar of new debt
3. Typically buyer pays intangible tax (entered as a *debit* to buyer)

EXAMPLE Calculate intangible tax on purchase money mortgage of $15,000
$15,000 × $.002 = $30 intangible tax

Note to Readers

For a more complete description of math as it specifically applies to real estate, see the author's *Real Estate Math: What You Need to Know*, Dearborn™ Real Estate Education. This self-study book covers the basics of math and provides practice opportunities in all areas. Step-by-step solutions to the math problems are included in *Real Estate Math: What You Need to Know*.

REAL ESTATE LAW, FLORIDA REAL ESTATE LICENSE LAW SECTIONS

Real Estate License Law and Qualifications for Licensure: Florida Real Estate Principles, Practices & Law (Unit 2); Florida Real Estate Broker's Guide (Unit 1)

1. An individual does *not* intend to engage in real estate activity. However, he does plan to be an officer of a real estate brokerage corporation. Which status BEST describes this situation?
   a. Active sales associate license
   b. Active broker license
   c. Registered with the DBPR
   d. Inactive sales associate license

2. An individual who has fulfilled all of the academic and experience requirements for real estate brokers but who operates as a sales associate in the employ of a supervising broker is an
   a. active sales associate.
   b. active broker.
   c. inactive broker.
   d. active broker associate.

3. A member of the U.S. armed forces is transferred to active duty in Jacksonville, Florida. The service member's spouse holds a valid New York real estate license. The service member's spouse desires a Florida real estate license. Which statement is TRUE?
   a. The spouse must complete the prelicense education requirement.
   b. The spouse must pass the Florida-specific real estate law license exam.
   c. Upon application for a license, the DBPR must issue the spouse a Florida real estate license.
   d. The spouse is eligible for a Florida license provided Florida has a mutual recognition agreement with the state of New York.

4. A nonresident who holds a Florida real estate license MUST
   a. consent, once licensed, to having all documents notarized that become part of future real estate transactions in which the nonresident licensee is involved.
   b. complete all required post-licensing and continuing education requirements.
   c. become a Florida resident within the initial license period.
   d. accept permanent revocation of the license should any violation of the real estate license law be upheld.

5. An individual who has earned a four-year degree or higher in real estate is NOT exempt from which education requirement?
   a. Sales associate prelicense course
   b. Continuing education
   c. Broker prelicense course
   d. Sales associate post-license course

6. Which activity is NOT a real estate service?
   a. Mortgaging real property
   b. Advertising real property
   c. Renting real property
   d. Auctioning real property

7. Which statement is FALSE regarding mutual recognition agreements?
   a. The agreements are intended to recognize the education and experience that real estate licensees have acquired in other states or nations.
   b. Mutual recognition applicants are required to take an examination on Florida real estate laws.
   c. Mutual recognition applicants may be Florida residents or nonresidents.
   d. Mutual agreements allow Florida real estate licensees to have an equal opportunity for licensure in jurisdictions with which agreements are concluded.

8. A sales associate sells real estate on the weekend for brokerage company A. She also works as a sales associate for brokerage company B. She is paid on a commission basis at both brokerage company A and brokerage company B. Which statement applies to this situation?
   a. As long as the broker for brokerage company A is also an owner-developer, this is an acceptable arrangement.
   b. The sales associate is in violation of Chapter 475, F.S.
   c. The sales associate must register both employers with the DBPR.
   d. This is legal, provided the sales associate is issued a multiple license.

9. Which of the criteria listed below is NOT required to hold a Florida real estate license?
   a. Proof of U.S. citizenship
   b. 18 years of age or older
   c. High school diploma or GED
   d. U.S. Social Security number

10. A man owned two farms and a home when he died intestate. The court appointed a personal representative to dispose of any portions of the decedent's estate that might be subject to estate taxes and debts of the deceased. The personal representative
    a. must have the clerk of the circuit court auction any property sold.
    b. must register with the DBPR if he expects to be paid for his work.
    c. may advertise, negotiate, and sell the property and be compensated for his work without registering with the DBPR.
    d. must dispose of all real property through an active real estate broker.

11. A licensed real estate sales associate did NOT complete the post license education requirement eight months ago. Which statement applies to this situation?
    a. The licensee may be eligible for an extension due to physical hardship.
    b. The licensee must request an extension in writing to the Commission.
    c. The Commission has no legislative authority to extend the post-license requirement beyond six months.
    d. The Commission has the authority to allow the licensee to complete the post license education requirement if the licensee can document an economic hardship that prevented the licensee from completing the course.

12. A license applicant has completed the 63-hour sales associate prelicense course. Within what period of time after being issued a course completion slip for the prelicense course MUST the applicant pass the state license exam?
    a. Indefinitely
    b. Two years
    c. One year
    d. Six months

13. What type of evidence unless refuted by evidence to the contrary will prove a case?
    a. Prima facie
    b. Notarized
    c. Case law
    d. Enforceable

14. Which Florida statute governs the DBPR and the professions under the DBPR?
    a. Chapter 120, F.S.
    b. Chapter 455, F.S.
    c. Chapter 475, F.S.
    d. Chapter 492, F.S.

15. The three real estate license categories do NOT include
    a. sales associate.
    b. broker.
    c. broker associate.
    d. owner-developer.

Real Estate License Law and Commission Rules: Florida Real Estate Principles, Practices & Law (Unit 3); Florida Real Estate Broker's Guide (Unit 1)

16. Florida Statutes prohibit members from serving on the Commission for more than
    a. one two-year term.
    b. one four-year term.
    c. two consecutive four-year terms.
    d. three consecutive two-year terms.

17. The Commission's authority to promulgate administrative rules is part of its
    a. judicial powers.
    b. executive powers.
    c. quasi-judicial powers.
    d. quasi-legislative powers.

18. Which statement regarding the Division of Real Estate (DRE) is FALSE?
    a. The DRE offices are located in Orlando, Florida.
    b. The DRE's ministerial duties involve recordkeeping.
    c. The director of the DRE is appointed by the FREC chairperson.
    d. The Department of Business and Professional Regulation employs the DRE personnel to support FREC activities.

19. The Commission is obligated to report any criminal violation of Chapter 475, F.S., when knowledgeable of such violations, to the
    a. state's attorney having jurisdiction.
    b. secretary of the DBPR.
    c. local police.
    d. Division of Professions.

20. The Commission is NOT empowered to impose which disciplinary action against a licensee?
    a. Suspend a license
    b. Revoke a license
    c. Impose an administrative fine
    d. Sentence a licensee to six months' imprisonment

21. The licensee status that results when a license is not renewed at the end of the license period is referred to as
    a. canceled.
    b. delinquent.
    c. involuntary inactive.
    d. voluntary inactive.

22. An active broker accompanies her husband when he goes on active military duty in Ohio for five years. She is not active in real estate in Ohio. To obtain a current Florida broker's license within two years of her husband's discharge, she
    a. must first complete seven hours of continuing education for each inactive year.
    b. must first complete 14 hours of continuing education.
    c. must first complete 28 hours of reactivation education.
    d. need not complete any continuing education or reactivation education for those five years.

23. A sales associate's license expired 20 months ago. What MUST this sales associate do to again work as a real estate sales associate?
    a. Complete Course I and pass the end-of-course exam
    b. Complete 14 hours of continuing education
    c. Complete a 28-hour Commission-prescribed education course
    d. Pass the state license exam

24. The only active general partner in a real estate partnership did not account properly for his escrowed funds. His license was suspended. All of the licenses of the sales associates in that partnership are
    a. suspended.
    b. canceled.
    c. placed in involuntary inactive status.
    d. not affected.

25. A broker wishes to be issued several broker licenses for business reasons. She may
    a. only be issued one broker license.
    b. be issued one broker license only, but have several broker associate licenses.
    c. be issued a group license.
    d. request multiple licenses.

26. Which FREC power is part of the FREC's quasi-judicial responsibilities?
    a. Foster education of licensees
    b. Regulate professional practices
    c. Make determination of violations
    d. Establish fees

27. An owner-developer employs five licensed sales associates and pays each sales associate a commission for sales of the owner-developer's lots. Which is TRUE of the owner-developer?
    a. The owner-developer must hold an active broker license.
    b. The owner-developer must register with the DBPR but does not have to be licensed.
    c. The owner-developer may only pay the sales associates a salary, not a commission.
    d. The owner-developer must apply for multiple licenses.

28. A broker decides to relocate his real estate brokerage office. He notifies the Commission of the change in business address. He also informs the Commission of the names of three sales associates who are no longer associated with his brokerage. The sales associates' licenses will be
    a. suspended until they find new employment.
    b. placed in involuntary inactive status.
    c. null and void.
    d. canceled.

Authorized Relationships, Duties, and Disclosure: Florida Real Estate Principles, Practices & Law (Unit 4); Florida Real Estate Broker's Guide (Unit 10)

29. Which information would be considered a material fact in a real estate transaction that MUST be disclosed to prospective buyers?
    a. A murder-suicide occurred in the residence.
    b. Two home invasions have occurred in the neighborhood.
    c. The homeowners were caregivers for a family member diagnosed with acquired immune deficiency syndrome.
    d. There are ¼" wide cracks in the foundation of the residence that have been filled in with concrete.

30. A real estate broker, when working in a single agent relationship, is typically authorized by a principal to act as a
    a. designated agent.
    b. special agent.
    c. general agent.
    d. nonagent.

31. A broker is a single agent for a buyer who has entered into a written contract to purchase a new house from a builder. The builder is unable to complete construction by the required date. The builder and the buyer agree to rescind the contract. What must the broker do with the cancelled contract?
    a. The broker must retain the contract and brokerage disclosures for five years.
    b. The broker is not required to keep builder contracts.
    c. The broker is not required to keep the contract because it was rescinded.
    d. The broker must retain the contract and brokerage disclosures for two years.

32. The property owner of a listed property has instructed the broker not to show the property when the owner is out of town. A potential buyer asks the sales associate to show the listed property; however, the owner is out of town. How should the sales associate handle the situation?
    a. Show the buyer the property because the owner will not find out.
    b. Explain to the buyer that the sales associate cannot show the property until the owner returns.
    c. The sales associate can show the property anytime unless the owner put his instructions in writing.
    d. Show the buyer the property provided the buyer has been prequalified and is a serious buyer.

33. A sales associate has been told by her real estate broker to commit an unlawful act. The sales associate should
    a. indicate her concern but comply with her employing broker.
    b. notify the FREC.
    c. refuse and withdraw from the relationship.
    d. comply because of the fiduciary obligation involved.

34. The broker and the seller agree to single agency representation. The broker MUST
   a. give the seller the no brokerage relationship notice.
   b. have the seller indicate in writing that the seller was informed of all the agency relationship options.
   c. have the seller sign the transition to single agent notice.
   d. give the seller the single agent notice.

35. A sales associate or broker associate owes fiduciary duties
   a. only to the broker if working as an employee of the broker.
   b. to the principal as does the broker, including those situations where the sales associate, for tax purposes, is an independent contractor.
   c. to the buyer when working for a transaction broker.
   d. to all of the individuals in the above situations.

36. The buyer's or seller's signature is required on which brokerage relationship disclosure before the licensee may continue?
   a. No brokerage relationship notice
   b. Single agent notice
   c. Consent to transition to transaction broker notice
   d. Transaction broker notice

37. The brokerage relationship disclosure requirements in Chapter 475, F.S., do NOT apply to
   a. agricultural property of 10 acres or less.
   b. an agreement to lease a residential condominium.
   c. improved residential property of no more than four units.
   d. an unimproved site intended for development as a residential duplex.

38. In Florida, which brokerage relationship is NOT legal?
   a. Nonrepresentation—facilitator
   b. Single agent—principal
   c. Transaction broker—customer
   d. Dual agent in a residential transaction

39. A transaction broker may disclose, without exception
   a. to the buyer, that the seller will accept a price less than the listed price.
   b. the motivation of the other party for buying or selling the property.
   c. to the buyer, the listed price and physical characteristics of the home.
   d. to the seller, the race of the prospective buyer.

40. A transaction broker of residential property has which duty(ies) and responsibility(ies)?
   a. Undivided loyalty to both the buyer and seller
   b. Full disclosure between buyer and seller
   c. To disclose any latent defects to the buyer
   d. Obedience to the buyer and seller

41. Which statement applies to designated sales associates?
   a. Designated sales associates have the duties of a single agent.
   b. Designated sales associates work as nonrepresentatives in transactions involving commercial property.
   c. Designated sales associates are sales associates working under a broker who has been issued multiple licenses.
   d. Designated sales associates have earned a designation awarded by a professional organization.

42. Duties owed in a no brokerage relationship include
   a. loyalty.
   b. accounting for all funds.
   c. confidentiality.
   d. obedience.

43. Unwritten law is also called
   a. statutory law.
   b. administrative law.
   c. common law.
   d. promulgated law.

44. When purchasing a commercial property from a seller without the services of a real estate professional, a buyer would be well advised to carefully verify information conveyed regarding the property. This is sometimes referred to as
    a. constructive notice.
    b. eminent domain.
    c. caveat emptor.
    d. lis pendens.

Real Estate Brokerage Activities and Procedures: Florida Real Estate Principles, Practices & Law (Unit 5); Florida Real Estate Broker's Guide (Units 2 and 4)

45. Real property ads and yard signs of a licensed broker MUST include the name of the
    a. broker associate who obtained the listing.
    b. broker only.
    c. seller or broker's principal.
    d. brokerage firm.

46. During a lunch meeting, three brokers discuss how to increase their businesses. They decide that broker A will work exclusively northeast of downtown, broker B will work exclusively northwest of downtown, and broker C will work exclusively south of downtown. This is a
    a. violation of antitrust laws called market allocation.
    b. violation of antitrust laws called price-fixing.
    c. common, acceptable practice among brokers.
    d. violation of the statute of frauds.

47. A broker associate is ordering business cards. May she put "broker" on the card instead of "broker associate"?
    a. Yes, because she is broker-qualified.
    b. Yes, with the consent of her broker.
    c. No, she must use the title "broker associate."
    d. This is a matter of personal taste.

48. A sales associate is selling her own property "by owner." Which statement is TRUE regarding real estate licensees selling property "by owner?"
    a. The licensee must disclose in the ad that she is a real estate licensee.
    b. The licensee must include the name of her broker in the ad.
    c. The property must be listed with the sales associate's broker.
    d. The licensee should disclose to a buyer prospect the fact that she holds a real estate license at the first point of meaningful negotiation.

49. Commingling occurs when a broker
    a. deposits earnest money in a personal account.
    b. employs unlicensed persons to obtain listings and sales.
    c. attempts to channel persons of a particular race to a certain neighborhood.
    d. deposits up to $1,000 of personal funds in a sales escrow account.

50. Rebecca K. Sammis, broker of Executive Homes Inc., is ordering the sign for her new office. She is NOT required to have what information on her sign?
    a. Licensed Real Estate Broker
    b. Executive Homes Inc.
    c. 1000 N. Gulf to Bay Blvd.
    d. Rebecca K. Sammis

51. A sales associate receives a good-faith deposit on Monday morning. The broker is in the office that day, so he gives the deposit to his broker that same day. By the end of business on what day must the broker deposit the funds into the escrow account?
    a. Tuesday
    b. Wednesday
    c. Thursday
    d. Friday

52. If both buyer and seller claim the earnest money deposit in a broker's escrow account, how much time does the broker have to notify the FREC in writing?
    a. 5 calendar days
    b. 15 business days
    c. 7 calendar days
    d. 30 business days

53. An escrow account may NOT be in
   a. a Florida-based title company having trust powers.
   b. a credit union located in Florida.
   c. a qualified Florida attorney's trust account if designated in the contract.
   d. an insurance company located in Florida.

54. Which statement is FALSE regarding unearned fees?
   a. Payment of an unearned fee is also called a kickback.
   b. Real estate licensees are prohibited from sharing part of their commission with the buyer or seller in a real estate contract unless the buyer or seller is a real estate licensee.
   c. Payment of an unearned fee must not violate RESPA.
   d. An owner of an apartment complex may pay a finder's fee of up to $50 to an unlicensed person who is tenant of the apartment complex for the referral of a prospect who decides to rent an apartment in the complex.

55. State and federal telemarketing laws restrict telephone solicitation calls to what hours?
   a. 8:00 am to 5:00 pm
   b. 8:00 am to 6:00 pm
   c. 8:00 am to 9:00 pm
   d. 9:00 am to 8:00 pm

56. A dispute over escrowed funds arises between the buyer and seller. The broker notifies the FREC of the conflicting demands and requests that the Commission issue an escrow disbursement order; however, the FREC declines. Which alternative method CANNOT be used to resolve the matter?
   a. Petition for review or appeal
   b. Mediation
   c. Arbitration
   d. Litigation

57. A broker of a large office hired a certified public accountant (CPA) and a full-time bookkeeper to manage the escrow account. Which statement is TRUE regarding this situation?
   a. The broker is relieved of liability in the event there is an escrow violation because a certified CPA has been hired to manage the escrow account.
   b. Both the CPA and the bookkeeper must also hold a real estate license if they are going to write checks on the escrow account.
   c. The broker is required to personally prepare the monthly escrow account reconciliation statement.
   d. The broker must be a signatory on the escrow account.

58. A broker has an agreement with a local rental car agency. The agreement stipulates that the broker will pay a $25 referral fee to the rental car agency for each prospective buyer referred to the broker. Which applies?
   a. This is a legal kickback or rebate.
   b. This is legal, provided the broker informs each prospect of the agreement.
   c. Florida Real Estate Law prohibits all kickbacks and rebates.
   d. The broker is in violation of Chapter 475, F.S., because he has promised to compensate an unlicensed person for the referral of real estate business.

59. In which situation is the broker NOT exempt from the notice requirements regarding conflicting demands?
   a. A sale of HUD-owned property that uses a HUD sale contract
   b. A dispute over escrow funds related to a property inspection
   c. A buyer's cancellation of a residential condominium purchase agreement within the allowable time period for review
   d. A buyer's inability to secure financing for the purchase according to the terms of the contract

60. A prospective tenant was recently transferred to Jacksonville. He was not familiar with the city so he purchased a rental list for $100 from a local real estate company. The prospective tenant referred to the list while looking for an apartment but was unable to locate a suitable unit. He has requested a refund of his $100. Which applies?
    a. He is entitled to a refund of his $100 if requested in writing within 30 days.
    b. He is entitled to a refund of $75 if requested either verbally or in writing within 30 days.
    c. He is not entitled to a refund because there was nothing wrong with the list.
    d. The broker is guilty of a first degree misdemeanor.

61. The owner of an office building has signed an exclusive listing agreement with a broker. The listing agreement contains information about the broker's lien rights in accordance with Part III of 475, F.S. If the owner sells the property without paying the broker a commission, the broker
    a. may record a lien on the office building within 30 days of closing.
    b. cannot record any lien without first obtaining a court judgment.
    c. may place a lien against the seller's net proceeds from the sale.
    d. may record a lien with an effective date of the listing agreement.

62. A sales associate has hired a licensed personal assistant to help increase the sales associate's business. The licensed assistant will receive $12 an hour for administrative work and 35% of any commissions earned. The licensed assistant
    a. cannot perform any services of real estate.
    b. must be paid by the sales associate's broker for all administrative work and commissions.
    c. may be paid by the sales associate for administrative work but must be paid by the broker for commissions earned.
    d. may be paid by the sales associate for the administrative work and for the 35% commission.

63. May escrow funds be moved from a non-interest-bearing account to an interest-bearing account?
    a. No, to do so would be a violation of Chapter 475, F.S.
    b. No, funds may not be removed from the noninterest-bearing account until title closing.
    c. Yes, the broker is free to move the funds from one escrow account to another escrow account.
    d. Yes, provided the broker secures the written permission of all interested parties to the contract before moving the funds.

64. A real estate sales associate might lawfully accept an extra commission for a difficult sale from
    a. an appreciative seller.
    b. a thankful buyer.
    c. the broker-employer.
    d. the mortgage lender.

65. If a licensee accepts a postdated check as an earnest money deposit on real property, which applies?
    a. The FREC must be notified within 24 hours.
    b. The seller's approval must first be obtained.
    c. The sales associate must get approval from the listing broker.
    d. The postdated check may not be drawn on an out-of-state bank account.

66. Which statement is TRUE regarding a sales associate forming a professional association?
    a. Only brokers may form a professional association.
    b. Sales associates may form a professional association in their legal name only.
    c. Forming a professional association allows the sales associate to work independently of the broker.
    d. It is a violation of license law for a sales associate to form a professional association.

67. A sales associate has helped a buyer locate a home for which the buyer has made an offer to purchase. The buyer gives the sales associate an earnest money check of $2,500 payable to a title company. Which applies?
   a. The sales associate must indicate the name, address, and telephone number of the title company on the purchase and sale agreement.
   b. The sales associate's employing broker must deposit the $2,500 in the broker's escrow account within three business days.
   c. The earnest money check must be made payable to the broker's trust account.
   d. Within five business days after the deposit has been made, the sales associate's broker must make a written request to the title company for written verification of receipt of the deposit.

68. A real estate broker maintains an escrow account for sales transactions and a separate property management escrow account. The broker is allowed to deposit his own funds in the two accounts up to a maximum of
   a. $6,000.
   b. $5,000.
   c. $2,000.
   d. $1,000.

69. Which business entity would obligate all principals as personally liable for organization-incurred debts?
   a. General partnerships
   b. Limited partnerships
   c. Limited liability companies
   d. Corporations for profit

70. The legal term that applies when two real estate brokers share office space in such a manner that the public is deceived into believing that a partnership exists is referred to as a
   a. quasi-partnership.
   b. limited partnership.
   c. quasi-corporation.
   d. quasi-joint venture.

71. A licensed real estate sales associate and broker desire to open a new real estate brokerage firm as general partners. Which statement applies to this situation?
   a. The partnership must be registered as a joint venture.
   b. They may register the partnership with the broker as the required active broker partner and the sales associate as a junior partner.
   c. They may not register as a partnership; however, they can incorporate and register as a corporation with the sales associate as vice president and the broker as president.
   d. A sales associate may not be a general partner in a real estate brokerage partnership.

72. Which entity or individual may NOT be licensed under a trade name?
   a. Brokerage corporation
   b. Brokerage partnership
   c. Real estate broker associate
   d. Limited liability brokerage corporation

73. A joint venture usually is created to
   a. simplify appraisals.
   b. carry out a single project.
   c. quiet title.
   d. take advantage of business opportunities.

74. On July 1, a broker received conflicting demands from a buyer and seller regarding a good faith deposit. Twelve business days later, the broker is unable to resolve the conflict between the parties and notifies the FREC. How many days does this broker have remaining to implement a settlement procedure?
   a. 10 business days
   b. 15 business days
   c. 18 business days
   d. 30 business days

75. Which statement is FALSE regarding the Junk Fax Prevention Act concerning unsolicited advertisements to fax machines?
   a. All faxes must include the date and time the fax is sent.
   b. The Junk Fax Act regulates unsolicited advertisements to residential fax machines only.
   c. Faxes that contain an unsolicited advertisement must include an opt-out notice.
   d. The registered name of the company sending the fax must be included on all faxes.

76. A personal assistant MUST hold a real estate license to
   a. fill out and submit listings and changes to an MLS.
   b. write ads for approval of the licensee and the supervising broker.
   c. conduct listing presentations on behalf of the sales associate.
   d. place signs on property.

Violations of License Law, Penalties, and Procedures: Florida Real Estate Principles, Practices & Law (Unit 6); Florida Real Estate Broker's Guide (Unit 5)

77. An applicant was issued a sales associate's license by mistake. She has been informed that the license has been revoked. Which applies?
   a. This action is referred to as "revoke without prejudice."
   b. The applicant is not allowed to reapply for a sales associate's license for one year.
   c. The applicant has been disciplined for a violation of Chapter 475, F.S.
   d. Revocation means that the applicant may not be licensed in Florida for five years.

78. Which statement concerning a consumer complaint is FALSE?
   a. A complaint is considered to be legally sufficient if it contains facts that indicate a violation of license law has occurred.
   b. The DBPR will investigate an anonymous complaint that is in writing and legally sufficient.
   c. A person may file a complaint online.
   d. The person named in a complaint must be a real estate licensee.

79. If a legally sufficient complaint has been filed, investigated, and found valid, the next step in the complaint process is
   a. an informal proceeding.
   b. a formal hearing.
   c. probable cause determination.
   d. final order issuance.

80. False advertising concerning real estate information is what type of penalty?
   a. First-degree misdemeanor
   b. Second-degree misdemeanor
   c. Third-degree misdemeanor
   d. Third-degree felony

81. A sales associate put a "for sale by owner" sign on his property with no intention of selling his home. The licensee used the sign as a way to reach prospective buyers for his listed properties. The FREC may find the sales associate guilty of which violation?
   a. Failure to account for and deliver
   b. Commingling
   c. Misrepresentation
   d. Conversion

82. A sales associate was issued a citation. How many days does the licensee have to either pay the citation or file an objection to the alleged violation?
   a. 30
   b. 45
   c. 60
   d. 90

83. Which statement is TRUE regarding a real estate sales associate who is convicted of driving under the influence (DUI)?
   a. The sales associate does not need to report the DUI conviction because only felony convictions need to be reported to the Commission.
   b. The sales associate must report the DUI conviction within 30 days to the Commission.
   c. The sales associate's employer is required to notify the DBPR of the DUI conviction.
   d. Only real estate applicants are required to disclose criminal offenses to the DBPR.

84. A sales associate disputes the facts and allegations in a formal complaint. Which statement is TRUE regarding this situation?
   a. The sales associate should request the matter be heard in an informal hearing.
   b. The sales associate should refuse to sign the election of rights in protest.
   c. The matter must be heard in a formal hearing before an administrative law judge.
   d. The sales associate should file an objection to the formal complaint and mail it to the DBPR Secretary.

85. A DBPR investigator is authorized, in cases that involve a first-time offense of a minor violation, to issue
   a. a cease and desist order.
   b. a notice of noncompliance.
   c. a letter of guidance.
   d. an administrative fine.

86. Which action would likely result in a charge of conversion?
   a. The sales associate did not indicate on the contract for sale and purchase that the earnest money check was postdated.
   b. The broker deposited the rental security deposit checks into the operating account.
   c. The broker did not review the monthly reconciliation statements prepared by the accountant when a shortage occurred.
   d. A broker placed escrow funds in the operating account and used the funds to cover office expenses.

87. A broker followed the instructions in an escrow disbursement order (EDO). The broker was later sued by a party to the real estate transaction. The lawsuit resulted in a civil judgment and a payment of $10,000 from the recovery fund. As a consequence, the FREC
   a. will take no action against the broker.
   b. will probably suspend the broker's license.
   c. will seek reimbursement of $10,000.
   d. is required to suspend the broker's license.

88. Which statement regarding the recovery fund is FALSE?
   a. Licensees must hold an active license at the time of the alleged act.
   b. An unlicensed spouse of the offending licensee is eligible for reimbursement.
   c. A final judgment must be issued against the licensee and the consumer must make an attempt to collect on the judgment.
   d. Punitive damages and interest cannot be reimbursed from the recovery fund.

89. A claimant has obtained a judgment against a licensee. The judgment includes liquidated damages of $15,000, punitive damages of $12,500, and attorney fees of $2,500. The claimant may be awarded what amount from the recovery fund?
   a. $15,000
   b. $17,500
   c. $30,000
   d. $50,000

90. Which statement is FALSE regarding the probable-cause panel?
   a. At least one member must be a professional member.
   b. A former Commissioner with an inactive real estate license may serve on the panel.
   c. A consumer member may serve on probable-cause.
   d. The FREC chairperson appoints the probable-cause panel.

91. A licensee has been issued an administrative complaint. The licensee has signed the election of rights indicating that he does not dispute the allegations of fact and he requests an informal hearing. How much prior notice of a hearing MUST be given to the licensee-respondent?
   a. 14 days
   b. 15 days
   c. 30 days
   d. 45 days

92. An agreement as to the facts of the case and the penalty reached between the DRE attorneys and the licensee is called
    a. a summary order.
    b. an informal hearing agreement.
    c. a settlement stipulation.
    d. a mediation order.

93. Which violation is a third-degree felony?
    a. Provide inaccurate and out-of-date rental information for compensation
    b. False and misleading advertising
    c. Reproduction or theft of a real estate license exam
    d. Failure to account for and deliver escrow funds

94. The maximum payment from the Real Estate Recovery Fund for a judgment issued in connection with a single real estate transaction is
    a. $50,000.
    b. $75,000.
    c. $100,000.
    d. $150,000.

95. A broker followed the instructions of an escrow disbursement order. The seller sued the broker. Which expense associated with the EDO CANNOT be reimbursed from the recovery fund?
    a. Seller's attorney fees
    b. Broker's attorney fees
    c. Compensatory damages
    d. Punitive damages

GENERAL REAL ESTATE LAW SECTIONS

Federal and State Laws Pertaining to Real Estate: Florida Real Estate Principles, Practices & Law (Unit 7); Florida Real Estate Broker's Guide (Units 2, 12, 17, and 18)

96. The United States Supreme Court ruling in *Jones v. Mayer,* as it pertains to real property, focuses on
    a. discrimination.
    b. truth-in-lending.
    c. informing buyers of latent defects.
    d. misrepresentation by land developers.

97. The Civil Rights Act of 1968 made discrimination illegal if based on any of these criteria EXCEPT
    a. age.
    b. race.
    c. sex.
    d. religion.

98. The Fair Housing Act of 1968 was part of the
    a. National Housing Act.
    b. Interstate Land Sales Full Disclosure Act.
    c. Truth in Lending Act.
    d. Civil Rights Act.

99. What landmark legislation ended racial segregation in public schools, in the workplace, and in public accommodations?
    a. Civil Rights Act of 1866
    b. Civil Rights Act of 1964
    c. Fair Housing Act
    d. Equal Opportunity Act

100. A protected class under the Fair Housing Act is
    a. age.
    b. occupation.
    c. national origin.
    d. marital status.

101. The act of inducing homeowners to sell by stating that minority persons might move into a neighborhood is called
    a. blockbusting.
    b. redlining.
    c. steering.
    d. ethnic zoning.

102. The act of refusing to make mortgage loans or stating different mortgage terms or conditions based on racial groups is called
    a. blockbusting.
    b. redlining.
    c. steering.
    d. overwriting.

103. The act of channeling buyers to a particular area either to maintain or to change the character of a neighborhood is called
    a. blockbusting.
    b. redlining.
    c. steering.
    d. riparian right.

104. Developers selling lots in a subdivision of 25 or more lots that is nationally promoted through advertising must provide potential buyers, prior to their signing a purchase contract, with a
    a. Statement of Record.
    b. Settlement Statement.
    c. copy of Regulation Z.
    d. Property Report.

105. Under which circumstance may a real estate licensee lawfully refuse to show a listed property to a member of a protected class who has specifically requested to see the property?
   a. Never
   b. When the owner is out-of-town and has instructed the broker not to show the listed property when the owner is away on business
   c. When the owner has expressed his intent in writing to exercise his exemption under the Fair Housing Act
   d. When the licensee believes that showing the property to the prospective buyer will be considered steering

106. When a security deposit or advance rent is required by a landlord, the landlord may
   a. commingle such funds with personal funds and pay the tenant 75% of any interest earned.
   b. post a surety bond in the total amount of security deposits/advance rents or $50,000, whichever is less, and pay the tenant 5% per year simple interest.
   c. deposit such funds in a separate interest-bearing account, and pay the tenant at least 50% of the annualized average interest.
   d. place the funds in a broker's operating account.

107. A tenant in a 50-unit apartment complex paid a $1,200 security deposit. The tenant received a receipt for the $1,200. Three weeks later, the landlord informed the tenant by phone the name of the bank where the tenant's security deposit was being held. Why has the landlord violated F.S. 83?
   a. The landlord failed to notify the tenant in writing of the bank name, address, and other information concerning the $1,200 security deposit.
   b. The landlord collected a security deposit exceeding legal limits.
   c. The landlord failed to notify the tenant within 15 days of the manner in which his funds were held.
   d. A security deposit of $1,200 is an "unconscionable agreement or provision."

108. If a tenant vacates rented premises at the end of a lease, how many days does the landlord have by law to notify the tenant if the landlord intends to claim a part of the tenant's security deposit?
   a. 3
   b. 7
   c. 15
   d. 30

109. With which government agency do developers of subdivisions with 100 or more lots have to register?
   a. Consumer Financial Protection Bureau
   b. Department of Housing and Urban Development
   c. Department of Business and Professional Regulation
   d. Environmental Protection Agency

110. Any legal remedy sought by a tenant or a landlord under the Florida Residential Landlord and Tenant Act must be through the
   a. civil courts.
   b. criminal courts.
   c. Division of Florida Land Sales, Condominiums and Mobile Homes.
   d. Division of Real Estate.

111. If a brokerage office provides property management services to property owners, and collects and holds rental funds on behalf of the owner, how must the broker account for the advance rent and security deposits?
   a. If the broker posts a $50,000 surety bond, the broker may place the advance rent and security deposits in the broker's operating account.
   b. The broker may place the advance rent and security deposits in the broker's operating account and keep a record of the amount of funds held on each tenant's behalf.
   c. The broker must pay the tenants 5% interest on the funds held for the benefit of each tenant.
   d. The broker must deposit the advance rent and security deposits into an escrow account and prepare reconciliation statements for the account each month.

Property Rights: Estates and Tenancies, Condominiums, Cooperatives, and Time Sharing: Florida Real Estate Principles, Practices & Law (Unit 8); Florida Real Estate Broker's Guide (Units 11, 12, and 18)

112. The rights of an owner of land that abuts water are referred to as
   a. subsurface rights.
   b. navigational rights.
   c. riparian rights.
   d. reliction rights.

113. A tree growing near the corner of a lot is ordinarily considered to be
   a. real property.
   b. personal property.
   c. a fixture.
   d. chattel.

114. Real property can be converted into personal property by
   a. severance.
   b. substitution.
   c. accretion.
   d. attachment.

115. The owner of an automobile parts business rents space in a commercial shopping center. The business owner has installed shelving and display racks. The shelving is bolted to the floors and the racks are attached to the walls. The racks and shelving are
   a. real property.
   b. trade fixtures.
   c. property of the landlord.
   d. real estate.

116. How many days' notice is required to terminate a month-to-month tenancy at will?
   a. 3
   b. 7
   c. 15
   d. 30

117. An estate or interest in real property that can be measured by the lifetime of an individual is a type of
   a. fee simple estate.
   b. estate by the entireties.
   c. freehold estate.
   d. estate for years.

118. A father and his daughter bought a commercially zoned tract for cash. The property was deeded to them "with full and legal rights of survivorship." The father and daughter are
   a. tenants by the entireties.
   b. tenants in common.
   c. joint tenants.
   d. tenants in severalty.

119. A widower who owns a condominium unit holds a
   a. proprietary lease.
   b. proprietary estate.
   c. freehold estate.
   d. tenancy by the entireties.

120. A type of concurrent ownership that provides an undivided interest in the property with no right of survivorship is
   a. a tenancy in common.
   b. an estate in severalty.
   c. a joint tenancy.
   d. a conventional life estate.

121. Three persons were co-owners of a parcel of real property. One owner died, and his ownership passed to the two remaining co-owners. He was a
   a. tenant by the entirety.
   b. joint tenant.
   c. tenant in common.
   d. tenant at will.

122. A woman and her sister, who are both married, want to go into business together and are purchasing a parcel on which to build a restaurant. To protect each of their families, how should they take title?
   a. Joint tenancy
   b. Tenancy in common
   c. Estate for years
   d. Life estate

123. The ownership right that permits an owner of real property to sell, mortgage, dedicate, or otherwise dispose of all or any portion of the property is referred to as the right of
   a. control.
   b. disposition.
   c. exclusion.
   d. possession.

124. Besides husband-and-wife ownership, the MOST frequently used form of co-ownership of property is
 a. tenancy by the entirety.
 b. tenancy in common.
 c. joint tenancy.
 d. tenancy at will.

125. One criterion used to determine if an item in real property is a fixture is whether the real property would be damaged by removing the item in question. What "test" for fixtures does this describe?
 a. Intent of the parties
 b. Relationship of the parties
 c. Method or degree of attachment
 d. Adaptation of the item

126. Developers of new cooperative units must give buyers a disclosure which informs buyers that they may cancel within how many days of signing the contract?
 a. 3 business days
 b. 10 business days
 c. 10 calendar days
 d. 15 calendar days

127. Two buyers purchased a three-story building and took title as legal joint tenants. One died testate. The surviving owner now owns the building
 a. as a tenant by the entirety.
 b. in severalty.
 c. in absolute ownership under the law of descent.
 d. subject to the terms of the deceased owner's will.

128. Which disclosure document is required for the sale of condominiums from a developer of more than 20 residential units?
 a. Rules of the association
 b. Governance form
 c. Most recent year-end financial report
 d. Estimated operating budget

129. An interest in real property that exists for a designated period, created by a properly executed lease agreement, is
 a. a freehold estate.
 b. an estate for years.
 c. a tenancy at will.
 d. a fee simple estate.

130. The type of time-share ownership that the usage rights revert back to the developer-seller is
 a. interval ownership.
 b. right to use.
 c. ownership in severalty.
 d. life estate.

131. A mother deeded a beachfront villa to her son who suffered from a terminal illness. The deed specified that the property was to return to the mother or her heirs when the son died. The estate owned by the mother, or her heirs, is
 a. a conventional life estate.
 b. a fee simple estate.
 c. an estate for years.
 d. an estate in reversion.

132. Salaried employees sell time-share units for a large owner-developer in Ft. Myers, Florida. Each Christmas, the employees receive a year-end bonus based on sales production for the year. Must the employees be licensed as real estate sales associates?
 a. No, the employees are exempt from a real estate license because they work for an owner-developer.
 b. Yes, they must be licensed as real estate sales associates because part of the compensation is based on real estate sales production.
 c. No, they are exempt from a real estate license because the employees must hold a time-share license.
 d. Yes, they must be licensed as real estate sales associates because they perform services of real estate for an owner-developer.

133. In which document will a condominium owner find the rules and regulations?
 a. Bylaws of the association
 b. Declaration of condominium
 c. Frequently Asked Questions (FAQ) and Answers
 d. Master deed

134. What is the cancellation period for the purchase of a three-year-old residential condominium unit from a private party?
 a. 3 calendar days
 b. 3 business days
 c. 15 calendar days
 d. 15 business days

135. The estate in real property with the least bundle of rights is the
   a. tenancy at will.
   b. tenancy at sufferance.
   c. fee simple estate.
   d. estate for years.

136. Homeowners are protected from forced sale of their homesteaded property for nonpayment of which type of debt?
   a. Special assessment liens
   b. Vendors' lien
   c. Home equity line of credit
   d. Credit card bills

137. Which right is NOT included in the bundle of rights?
   a. Possession
   b. Control
   c. Inheritance
   d. Enjoyment

138. Lucy lives in Tall Towers Condominiums. She enjoys swimming in the condominium's pool each morning before going to work. The pool is referred to as
   a. chattel.
   b. proprietary rights.
   c. common elements.
   d. community property.

139. If I lease my lake front property to you for an indefinite period of time, your interest in real property would be
   a. an estate for years.
   b. a tenancy by the entireties.
   c. a tenancy at will.
   d. a tenancy at sufferance.

140. A condominium is created by
   a. recording a declaration in the public records.
   b. forming a corporation and filing the articles of incorporation with the Florida Department of State.
   c. filing a copy of the bylaws with the county property assessor's office.
   d. filing the building plans with the county.

141. The legal document that allows a purchaser of a cooperative to occupy a particular unit is referred to as
   a. an estate for years.
   b. a proprietary lease.
   c. a declaration of intent to occupy.
   d. a declaration of possession.

142. The statutory creation of a condominium building requires certain basic items of legal documentation, one of which is NOT the
   a. declaration of condominium.
   b. articles of incorporation of the association.
   c. common elements agreement.
   d. bylaws of the association.

143. The process of land buildup from water-borne rock, sand, and soil is
   a. accretion.
   b. alluvion.
   c. erosion.
   d. reliction.

144. Which condominium document is required to be given to prospective buyers only for new residential construction of more than 20 units?
   a. Frequently Asked Questions and Answers
   b. Bylaws
   c. Articles of Incorporation
   d. Prospectus

Title, Deeds, and Ownership Restrictions: Florida Real Estate Principles, Practices & Law (Unit 9); Florida Real Estate Broker's Guide (Units 15 and 18)

145. Which type of alienation is voluntary?
   a. Descent
   b. Will
   c. Escheat
   d. Eminent domain

146. Title by adverse possession must continue for at LEAST how many consecutive years without the owner's consent?
   a. 5
   b. 7
   c. 12
   d. 15

147. A nephew inherits his uncle's 1,150-acre cattle ranch. The legal term for the nephew in this situation is
    a. bequest.
    b. devisee.
    c. beneficiary.
    d. testator.

148. When a real property owner fails to occupy a property and the land is occupied by someone else for seven years, the basis for a title claim may be created by use of the legal principle of
    a. escheat.
    b. estoppel.
    c. adverse interest.
    d. adverse possession.

149. The purpose of recording a deed is to
    a. give the world actual notice of ownership.
    b. give the world constructive notice of ownership.
    c. establish a future right of redemption.
    d. bring the county records up to date as to ownership.

150. Legal title always passes from the seller to the buyer
    a. on the date of the execution of the deed.
    b. when the closing statement has been signed.
    c. when the deed is placed in escrow.
    d. when the deed is voluntarily delivered and voluntarily accepted.

151. The term *acknowledgment* refers to
    a. the stamp indicating delivery to the clerk of the court.
    b. public acknowledgment of true ownership by giving actual notice.
    c. a signer's formal declaration before an authorized official that the signer is executing the instrument as a free act and deed.
    d. the act of recording a legal document.

152. Each of these is a method of acquiring legal title to real property EXCEPT
    a. descent.
    b. quitclaim deed.
    c. eminent domain.
    d. novation.

153. The terms in each pair are synonymous EXCEPT
    a. vendee—purchaser.
    b. mortgagee—lender.
    c. lessor—landlord.
    d. grantee—seller.

154. Which statement does NOT describe an owner's title insurance policy?
    a. The premium is paid once only—at time of issue.
    b. The policy may not be transferred from one owner to another owner.
    c. Damages are paid for any defect in the title not listed as an exception.
    d. The policy is issued for an amount equal to the unpaid balance of the mortgage loan.

155. An owner sold her home to a married couple and gave them a warranty deed. The couple moved into the home but did not record the deed. Two days later, the seller died, and her heirs in another state sold the property without any knowledge of the previous sale. The heirs conveyed title to a single man, who did record the deed. Who owns the property?
    a. The couple
    b. The single man
    c. The deceased owner's heirs
    d. The couple and the single man as joint tenants

156. The essential elements of a deed do NOT include
    a. consideration.
    b. under seal.
    c. witnessing.
    d. delivery.

157. The clause in a deed that contains the words "bargains and sells" or similar words is the
    a. granting clause.
    b. habendum clause.
    c. encumbrances clause.
    d. seisin clause.

158. The clause in a deed that specifies the type of estate being transferred is the
    a. premises clause.
    b. seisin clause.
    c. habendum clause.
    d. granting clause.

159. Can a property owner give a sales associate power of attorney to draft a lease?
   a. Only brokers may act as a power of attorney.
   b. Yes, provided the power of attorney authorizes a licensee to perform such an act.
   c. No, only attorneys may draft leases for others.
   d. Yes, with the broker's consent.

160. Buyer and seller are discussing the type of deed that is to be conveyed. The buyers are requiring a guarantee that the seller owns the property and has a legal right to sell. This guarantee is part of which clause in the deed?
   a. Seisin
   b. Habendum
   c. Premises
   d. Encumbrance

161. A type of deed that contains the words "remise and release" or similar words is the
   a. special warranty deed.
   b. quitclaim deed.
   c. bargain and sale deed.
   d. personal representative's deed.

162. Private restrictions on ownership of real property include which restriction?
   a. Police power
   b. Deed restrictions
   c. Eminent domain
   d. Escheat

163. The covenant in a general warranty deed that promises that the grantor will obtain and deliver any legal instrument that might be required to make the title good in the future is the covenant of
   a. further assurance.
   b. quiet enjoyment.
   c. warranty forever.
   d. habendum et tinendum.

164. A buyer is purchasing a property that is part of a decedent's estate. Which type of deed will the buyer receive?
   a. Quitclaim deed
   b. Bargain and sale deed
   c. Personal representative's deed
   d. Committee's deed

165. Which pair does NOT belong together?
   a. Fee simple—Absolute
   b. Escheat—Testate
   c. Tenancy in common—No right of survivorship
   d. Joint tenancy—Undivided interest

166. The key difference between police power and eminent domain is whether
   a. the action was by a governmental agency.
   b. any compensation was paid to an affected owner.
   c. the owner's use was affected.
   d. the improvements are to be destroyed.

167. Against her will, an owner's farm was taken in order that a municipal water supply could be built. The legal principle justifying this action is called
   a. police power.
   b. eminent domain.
   c. escheat to the state.
   d. estoppel.

168. A specific garage parking space conveys with the title transfer of a condominium. The parking space is what type of property?
   a. Common element
   b. Appurtenance
   c. Deed restriction
   d. Devise

169. A person dies intestate without heirs. The principle of law applying to disposition of the person's real property is
   a. escheat.
   b. estoppel.
   c. easement.
   d. eminent domain.

170. An easement created by court order to allow the right of ingress and egress over another person's property to landlocked property is which type of easement?
   a. Easement by prescription
   b. Easement by condemnation
   c. Easement by necessity
   d. Easement by adverse possession

171. Necessary parts of a lease do NOT include
   a. the names of the parties to the lease.
   b. the term of the lease.
   c. an option to purchase.
   d. valuable consideration.

172. The Florida Residential Landlord and Tenant Act requires landlords to approve or deny the rental application of an active service member within how many days?
   a. 5 days
   b. 7 days
   c. 14 days
   d. 15 days

173. If a tenant legally subrogates or subordinates the rental space, it means that the tenant has
   a. assigned the lease.
   b. given up the lease.
   c. terminated the lease.
   d. subleased the lease.

174. Which type of statutory deed is typically used to clear clouds on the title?
   a. Quitclaim
   b. Bargain and sale
   c. General warranty
   d. Special warranty

175. A property owner builds a bridge across a stream he owns, but the footing on the other side extends onto his neighbor's property. The legal term for this action is
   a. easement.
   b. implied easement.
   c. encroachment.
   d. subrogation of space.

176. A neighbor succeeds in gaining legal use of an owner's property by open and continuous use of the land for over 20 years. The legal term for this result is
   a. encroachment.
   b. easement by prescription.
   c. accretion.
   d. adverse possession.

177. An instrument that transfers possession of real property but does not transfer ownership is
   a. a deed.
   b. an easement.
   c. a mortgage.
   d. a lease.

178. What is the legal term used to describe the deceased female creator of a will?
   a. Testator
   b. Bequest
   c. Testatrix
   d. Beneficiary

179. A type of contractual agreement having all essential elements of a contract plus a property description and a definite term of tenancy specified creates which type of interest in real property?
   a. Tenancy at will
   b. Leasehold
   c. Fee simple estate
   d. Life estate

180. All these terms apply to leasing EXCEPT
   a. eviction.
   b. assignment.
   c. subrogation.
   d. title.

181. Which government restriction on ownership represents the broadest power of government to limit the rights of property owners?
   a. Eminent domain
   b. Police power
   c. Escheat
   d. Government liens

182. Which statement is TRUE?
   a. All liens are encumbrances.
   b. All encumbrances are liens.
   c. Specific liens affect all personal property of the debtor.
   d. A property tax lien is a type of general lien.

183. Lenders will often use what type of deed to convey property to a new buyer that has been taken back through a foreclosure proceeding?
   a. Quitclaim deed
   b. General warranty deed
   c. Special warranty deed
   d. Bargain and sale deed

184. Which tax does NOT create a superior lien?
   a. Federal estate tax
   b. Income tax
   c. Property tax
   d. Special assessment tax

185. Which statement is TRUE with respect to the assignment of a lease?
   a. The original lessee is not liable for the payment of the rent.
   b. It is the same as a sublease.
   c. The original lessee would still retain a right to use the property for a limited time.
   d. The entire leasehold is transferred.

186. A sublease will result in a lease of
   a. the entire premises by a new tenant.
   b. a portion of the leased rights and interests.
   c. the entire premises located below ground level.
   d. all of the leased premises for the full duration of the remainder of the original lease.

187. Which lien is NOT a specific lien?
   a. Mortgage lien
   b. Construction lien
   c. Property tax lien
   d. Income tax lien

188. A railroad company may use which method to acquire land?
   a. Escheat
   b. Police power
   c. Eminent domain
   d. Auction

189. Which encumbrance constitutes a lien on real property?
   a. Easement
   b. Encroachment
   c. Restriction
   d. Mortgage

190. Normally, the priority of a mortgage lien is determined by
   a. the order in which other liens are filed or recorded.
   b. the order in which the cause of action arose.
   c. the size of the claim.
   d. a court of law.

191. Unless a written agreement exists to change the usual order of priority, the mortgage with the highest priority is the
   a. construction loan mortgage.
   b. mortgage that was recorded first.
   c. mortgage for the greatest amount.
   d. mortgage containing the subordination agreement.

192. A real property tax is an example of a
   a. specific voluntary lien.
   b. specific involuntary lien.
   c. general voluntary lien.
   d. general involuntary lien.

193. A lawsuit against a farmer is pending. The court rules that her vegetable farm be seized and held as security in case of a judgment against the farmer. This legal action is called
   a. lis pendens.
   b. adverse possession.
   c. attachment.
   d. assignment.

194. A type of lien that results when a seller accepts a mortgage as part of the purchase price for a home is a
   a. general lien.
   b. vendor's lien.
   c. construction lien.
   d. home equity lien.

195. Which term describes the beneficial interest in real estate that implies that an individual will receive legal title at a future date?
   a. Legal title
   b. Equitable title
   c. Cloud on title
   d. Marketable title

Real Estate Contracts: Florida Real Estate Principles, Practices & Law (Unit 11); Florida Real Estate Broker's Guide (Unit 11)

196. A buyer and a seller make an oral agreement regarding the sale of the seller's property. This contract normally would be unenforceable in a court of law based on the
   a. laws of agency.
   b. statute of frauds.
   c. statute of limitations.
   d. real estate licensing laws.

197. Essential elements of a real estate contract include all EXCEPT
   a. consideration.
   b. offer and acceptance.
   c. in writing and signed.
   d. recordation.

198. To be valid, a real estate sale contract MUST contain
   a. an earnest money deposit.
   b. an offer and acceptance.
   c. evidence of two witnesses' signatures.
   d. a notary's seal.

199. A properly executed contract that has as its purpose an illegal objective is
   a. valid and enforceable.
   b. valid but not enforceable.
   c. legal but depends on voluntary performance.
   d. void.

200. Which contract is NOT covered under the statute of frauds?
   a. 6-month lease agreement
   b. Option contract
   c. Mortgage
   d. 18-month listing agreement

201. A real estate sale contract becomes valid or in effect when it has been signed by the
   a. broker and buyer.
   b. buyer and spouse.
   c. seller and two witnesses.
   d. buyer and seller.

202. A broker promises to give a $20,000 bonus to the first sales associate who sells 20 homes. Which type of contract is this?
   a. Unilateral contract
   b. Bilateral contract
   c. Executed contract
   d. Implied contract

203. A real estate licensee is interested in obtaining an option on property as the true optionee. Which statement is FALSE regarding a real estate licensee's obligations?
   a. The licensee must divest (relinquish) the role as licensee for this transaction.
   b. In the option contract, the licensee must pledge a nominal consideration.
   c. The licensee must inform the owner that the licensee is personally interested in acquiring an option on the property.
   d. The licensee must inform the owner that the licensee is not functioning as a real estate agent in this transaction.

204. Which statement is TRUE regarding an "as is" provision in a sale contract?
   a. An "as is" provision relieves the seller of liability for failure to disclose material defects.
   b. The "as is" provision can be used to eliminate the duty to disclose material defects.
   c. The "as is" provision does *not* eliminate the duty to disclose all known material defects.
   d. The "as is" provision may not be used for residential real estate transactions.

205. A parol contract is also called
   a. a written contract.
   b. a unilateral contract.
   c. an express contract.
   d. an informal contract.

206. When a real estate sale contract has been signed by the purchaser and given to the seller's broker along with an earnest money check,
   a. this transaction constitutes a valid contract in the eyes of the law.
   b. the purchaser can sue the seller for specific performance.
   c. the buyer has given a written offer.
   d. the earnest money will be returned if the buyer defaults.

207. A buyer signs a contract to purchase a seller's home for $370,000. The listing broker submits the contract to the seller, but the seller insists on the listed price of $380,000. The broker prepares a new contract for $380,000 that the buyer refuses to sign. The seller then instructs the broker to take the buyer's original offer of $370,000 back to the buyer because the seller has decided to accept the offer. The buyer has changed his mind and refuses to accept the contract. The result is
   a. no valid contract exists.
   b. an enforceable contract exists.
   c. the buyer, having refused the contract, must pay the broker's commission.
   d. the seller owes the broker a sales commission.

208. A buyer signs a contract to purchase a property that is subject to a mandatory homeowners association. The buyer did not receive a disclosure concerning the association before signing the sale and purchase contract. Which statement is TRUE?
   a. The buyer may cancel the sale contract within three days of signing the contract.
   b. The buyer may cancel the sale contract within three days unless the buyer waives this right in the contract.
   c. The buyer may cancel the sale contract within three days after receiving the disclosure.
   d. The buyer may cancel the sale contract within three days after closing.

209. When an offeror withdraws an offer before acceptance, the offeror has
   a. abandoned the offer.
   b. revoked the offer.
   c. counteroffered.
   d. breached the contract.

210. A property owner and a broker decide to sell $20 lottery tickets to prospective customers for a chance to win the owner's property. They announce that if 1,000 tickets are sold, the winning ticket will get the property free and clear. However, if less than 1,000 tickets are sold, the winning ticket will get the property for a price of $200,000 minus the value of the tickets sold. Which statement is TRUE?
   a. The owner and broker have devised an innovative marketing plan.
   b. The broker may be charged with fraudulent and dishonest dealing by trick, scheme, or device.
   c. The broker must file the lottery plan with the Florida state lottery.
   d. The broker may be charged with a violation of the statute of frauds.

211. The phrase "time is of the essence" means
   a. the buyer wants to take possession quickly.
   b. the seller wants to close quickly.
   c. actions are required by dates set forth in the agreement.
   d. a specified period of time must lapse before the contract can legally be concluded.

212. A seller and a buyer enter into a real estate contract. The seller defaults. The buyer sues the seller to go through with the contract. This action is known as a suit for
   a. specific performance.
   b. damages.
   c. unliquidated damages.
   d. declaratory judgment.

213. Which statement is TRUE regarding listing agreements?
   a. The sales associate earns the commission.
   b. An exclusive-agency listing provides for the broker to earn a commission no matter who is the procuring cause.
   c. Procuring cause disputes between licensees are typically settled in small claims court.
   d. If required to effect a sale, the commission is earned only if the buyer closes on the property.

214. The statute that requires an injured party to bring an action within a specific period of time after the injury is the statute of
   a. obligations.
   b. limitations.
   c. frauds.
   d. specific enforcement.

215. Which written instrument authorizes a person to act for and on behalf of another person?
   a. Attorney-in-fact
   b. Lis pendens
   c. Option
   d. Power of attorney

216. If a broker is given the right to sign a real estate sale contract that will be binding on the seller, the broker is
   a. an attorney-in-fact.
   b. given general power of attorney.
   c. a special agent trustee.
   d. the attorney of record.

217. A real estate licensee is NOT authorized to draw which contract?
   a. Option
   b. Buyer-brokerage
   c. Lease
   d. Sale and purchase

218. A listing to sell property and obtain a specified amount for the owner-principal is called
   a. an open listing.
   b. an exclusive right-to-sell listing.
   c. an implied listing.
   d. a net listing.

219. The term *procuring cause* is most significant in which type of listing?
   a. Open
   b. Exclusive-agency
   c. Exclusive right-to-sell
   d. Net

220. If a property has been cited as being in violation of building code, the seller must provide a disclosure to the buyer. Which statement is TRUE regarding the disclosure?
   a. The seller must correct the violation before closing or credit the buyer with the cost to correct.
   b. The seller must deposit with the closing agent an amount equal to the cost to clear the violation.
   c. If the seller does not clear the violation before closing, it becomes the buyer's responsibility to clear the violation.
   d. The seller must notify the code enforcement agency of the new owner's name and address within 30 days after closing.

221. In a valid option contract to purchase real estate, the optionee
   a. is the prospective seller of the property.
   b. must purchase the property within the option period.
   c. has no obligation to purchase the property.
   d. is limited to a refund of the option consideration if the option is exercised.

222. Any contract that obligates both parties to perform in accordance with the terms of the contract is
   a. an unenforceable contract.
   b. a unilateral contract.
   c. a bilateral contract.
   d. a voidable contract.

223. A broker mailed a signed purchase offer to a property owner. Instead of signing the purchase offer contract, the owner sent the broker a telegram accepting the offer. Which is correct?
   a. There has been a valid offer but not a legal acceptance.
   b. There is a valid contract between the buyer and seller.
   c. There has been a valid offer and a telegraphic acceptance but not an enforceable contract.
   d. To be enforceable, a contract must contain the offer and acceptance within the same instrument.

224. A 17-year-old high school student has entered into a contract to purchase an adult's car. This is
   a. a void contract.
   b. an illegal contract.
   c. an option contract.
   d. a voidable contract.

225. A seller and a buyer negotiated the sale and purchase of the seller's condominium over a two-week period. Finally, they reached a meeting of the minds regarding the purchase price and terms of the sale. What type of contract exists at this point?
   a. Implied contract
   b. Express contract
   c. Executed contract
   d. Option contract

226. A broker MUST give a copy of the written listing agreement to the seller
   a. at the time of acceptance.
   b. by the end of the next business day.
   c. within 24 hours of execution.
   d. by the end of the third business day.

227. In an assignment of a real estate contract, the person assigned the legal rights is the
   a. assignee.
   b. assignor.
   c. vendor.
   d. optionor.

228. In case of breach by the buyer, most real estate sale contracts include a provision that the earnest money be regarded as
   a. liquidated damages to the broker.
   b. liquidated damages to the seller.
   c. unliquidated damages to the seller.
   d. unliquidated damages in escrow.

229. A seller who wishes to recover monetary damages equal to the extent of loss suffered in excess of the earnest money deposit may
   a. sue for specific performance.
   b. sue for compensatory damages.
   c. seek compensation from the Real Estate Recovery Fund.
   d. sue the broker for breach of duty to perform.

230. Which reason would NOT make a valid contract to purchase and sell real estate unenforceable?
   a. It violates the statute of frauds.
   b. The time frame extends beyond the statute of limitations.
   c. The property is destroyed.
   d. No earnest money was pledged.

Planning, Zoning, and Environmental Hazards: Florida Real Estate Principles, Practices & Law (Unit 19); Florida Real Estate Broker's Guide (Unit 16)

231. The requirement that the infrastructure for sanitary sewers, potable water, and waste treatment facilities be in place before new development is allowed is the
   a. community impact provision.
   b. infrastructure provision.
   c. concurrency provision.
   d. Florida building code.

232. A strip of land that separates one type of land use from another is
   a. a nonconforming use.
   b. a buffer zone.
   c. a boundary.
   d. an easement.

233. City planning commissions are usually NOT delegated which authority?
   a. Subdivision plat approval
   b. Zoning change approval
   c. Sign control
   d. Site plan approval

234. Zone R-1A typically refers to
   a. rural areas.
   b. railroad yards.
   c. single-family dwellings.
   d. light industry.

235. Government regulations that establish construction requirements are termed
   a. health ordinances.
   b. building codes.
   c. master plans.
   d. zoning regulations.

236. An example of a granted variance could be a
   a. house whose owner established a business in the home that is zoned single-family residence.
   b. business in an area that has been rezoned residential.
   c. house next to a service station.
   d. shopping center that has fewer than the number of parking spaces required per square foot of rentable space.

237. The Zoning Board of Adjustment will only grant a variance if the property owner demonstrates that
   a. a hardship exists or would be created if required to comply with the zoning code.
   b. the owner has a physical hardship.
   c. the owner has a mental hardship.
   d. an economic hardship would be created by complying with the zoning code.

238. A grandfather clause in a zoning ordinance probably would allow an owner to
   a. reshingle the roof of a structure that is a nonconforming use.
   b. enlarge a building that is a nonconforming use.
   c. rebuild a structure 60% destroyed by fire that is a nonconforming use.
   d. convert a three-room structure into two large rooms.

239. Which procedure is NOT used by a local municipality to enforce building codes?
   a. Issue certificates of occupancy
   b. Issue building permits
   c. Conduct building inspections
   d. Conduct condemnation proceedings

240. When a new home is constructed, the structure is inspected to make sure it is built in compliance with building codes for wind-load strength, ventilation, and so forth. If the inspection is successful, the building inspector will issue a
    a. certificate of occupancy.
    b. building permit.
    c. lis pendens.
    d. notice of commencement.

241. Which statement describes a planned unit development?
    a. Clustering homes together on smaller lots to allow for open green spaces
    b. Single-family dwelling units predominate
    c. Shopping areas included, but not professional offices
    d. Organized rejuvenation of depressed urban areas

242. Industrial zoning is used to control
    a. density per acre.
    b. intensity of use.
    c. emissions and effluents.
    d. minimum lot size.

243. The DBPR licenses
    a. asbestos specialists.
    b. radon testers.
    c. lead-based paint inspectors.
    d. mold assessors.

244. A special flood hazard area is
    a. a wetland area.
    b. a 100-year flood plain.
    c. an area designated in a named storm's path.
    d. an area that is prone to pour drainage after rainy weather.

REAL ESTATE PRINCIPLES AND PRACTICES SECTIONS

The Real Estate Business: Florida Real Estate Principles, Practices & Law (Unit 1)

245. Business brokers
   a. must be licensed as real estate licensees.
   b. are not required to qualify as real estate licensees.
   c. must hold a business brokerage license.
   d. are required to be licensed as a real estate broker only if the sale of a business involves the sale of real property.

246. The term *dedication* refers to
   a. the initial stage of subdivision development ("ceremonial start-up").
   b. the transfer of certain subdivision areas from private to public ownership.
   c. recordation of a subdivision plat at the county courthouse.
   d. a covenant placed in the deeds to all subdivision lots.

247. The practice of using five or six model homes to sell houses in a subdivision is associated with
   a. speculative (spec) building.
   b. tract building.
   c. custom building.
   d. mass market building.

248. A property manager
   a. exclusively finds tenants for property in exchange for a fee.
   b. is synonymous with rental agent.
   c. is responsible for leasing, managing, marketing, and overall maintenance of property.
   d. who manages apartment units and commercial property must hold a CAM license.

249. Follow-up refers to which activity?
   a. Making sure all of the inspections are completed prior to closing
   b. Returning all phone calls to the buyer and seller in a timely manner
   c. Keeping in touch with the new homeowner who purchased the home through the sales associate
   d. Attending the title closing and collecting the commission check

250. A licensed real estate broker may
   a. not appraise real property unless the broker is a licensed appraiser.
   b. prepare CMAs only in the scope of listing property.
   c. not charge for a comparative market analysis (CMA).
   d. not appraise property that involves a federally related transaction unless the broker is also a licensed or state-certified appraiser.

251. A subdivision plat map
   a. is a map provided to prospective buyers by local real estate offices.
   b. indicates the size and location of individual lots, streets, and utilities.
   c. is developed by the tax assessor's office for tax assessment purposes.
   d. depicts the side and front elevations of structures.

252. A property owner who does NOT reside on the property and who often relies on a professional property management company to manage the investment is
   a. a property manager.
   b. an absentee owner.
   c. a real estate licensee.
   d. a nonresident owner.

253. The creation of a database of prospective customers for the purpose of directed advertising is called
   a. target marketing.
   b. software development.
   c. follow-up.
   d. business opportunity marketing.

254. A valuation product used by lenders involved in short sales of distressed property is called a
   a. comparative market analysis.
   b. certified appraisal.
   c. nonconforming valuation estimate.
   d. broker's price opinion.

Legal Descriptions:
Florida Real Estate Principles, Practices & Law (Unit 10)

255. The legal description method that uses direction, distance, and a POB is the
   a. metes-and-bounds method.
   b. government survey method.
   c. rectangular method.
   d. lot-and-block numbers method.

256. The section number located due west of Section 6 is
   a. 7.
   b. 5.
   c. 3.
   d. 1.

257. Which description is MOST nearly due north?
   a. N 89° 30' E
   b. N 0° 45' E
   c. N 0° 30' W
   d. N 1° 15' W

258. The compass direction that is the straight-line opposite of S 45° E is
   a. N 45° E.
   b. N 45° W.
   c. S 45° W.
   d. S 45° E.

259. In Florida, the principal meridian and base line intersect in Tallahassee because
   a. the state government is located there.
   b. the governor in office in 1831 decreed that it be there.
   c. Florida State University is located there.
   d. it is the basic reference point selected by the federal government.

260. Which statement is FALSE concerning townships?
   a. Each township is composed of 36 sections.
   b. A township is six miles square.
   c. There are 640 acres in a township.
   d. Townships are located by referring to principal meridians and base lines.

261. The SW¼ of the SE¼ of the NW¼, of Section 10, Township 3 South, Range 5 East, describes a tract of
   a. .125 acre.
   b. .5 acre.
   c. 10 acres.
   d. 64 acres.

262. In Florida, Range 2 East is closest to
   a. Tallahassee.
   b. Jacksonville.
   c. Miami.
   d. Pensacola.

263. Which description describes a check?
   a. A fractional piece of land less than a quarter section located along the banks of lakes and streams
   b. A square 24 miles on each side created by intersecting guide meridians and correction lines, containing 16 townships
   c. A square 6 miles on each side containing 36 square miles
   d. A square containing 160 acres, measuring 2,640 feet by 2,640 feet

264. A range is numbered to the
   a. north or south of a principal meridian.
   b. east or west of a principal meridian.
   c. north or south of a base line.
   d. east or west of a township or tier.

265. Which statement is TRUE about the sections in a township?
   a. Section 13 lies to the north of Section 24.
   b. Section 1 is, by law, set aside for school purposes.
   c. Section 31 lies in the southeast corner of the township.
   d. Section 7 lies to the east of Section 8.

266. Which type of legal description is used only in developed subdivisions?
   a. Government survey
   b. Metes-and-bounds
   c. Lot and block
   d. Tax assessor's map

267. How many acres are contained in a parcel described as the SE¼ of the NW¼ and the S½ of the NE¼ of a certain section?
   a. 5
   b. 40
   c. 80
   d. 120

Residential Mortgages:
Florida Real Estate Principles, Practices & Law (Unit 12);
Florida Real Estate Broker's Guide (Unit 12)

268. Which method of settling a default involves a conveyance of the title to the lender?
   a. Judicial foreclosure
   b. Deed in lieu of foreclosure
   c. Satisfaction of mortgage
   d. Quasi judicial procedure

269. When a promissory note is executed, it becomes
   a. security for the debt.
   b. evidence of the debt.
   c. a legal obligation of the creditor.
   d. a conveyance of interest in real property.

270. A mortgage clause (in title theory states) that provides for the transfer of title to real property to the borrower once the mortgage debt has been repaid is the
   a. defeasance clause.
   b. novation.
   c. right to reinstate.
   d. hold harmless clause.

271. Which legal instrument would contain the interest rate, loan amount, maturity date, and payment schedule?
   a. Deed
   b. Closing statement
   c. Lease
   d. Note

272. The mortgagor is the person who
   a. holds the property as security for the loan.
   b. lends the money.
   c. signs the note.
   d. receives the monthly payments.

273. A first mortgage holder can agree to take a lower lien priority using which instrument?
   a. Junior mortgage
   b. First right of refusal
   c. Satisfaction of mortgage
   d. Subordination agreement

274. A buyer purchases a home worth $450,000. She finances the purchase with a mortgage loan of $360,000. What is the loan-to-value ratio?
   a. 20%
   b. 30%
   c. 75%
   d. 80%

275. Which mortgage clause legally allows the lender to declare the entire unpaid sum due when the debtor defaults?
   a. Acceleration clause
   b. Due-on-sale clause
   c. Defeasance clause
   d. Prepayment penalty clause

276. A property owner defaulted on the mortgage. Prior to foreclosure, the owner paid the lender the missed mortgage payments, plus the expenses incurred by the lender as a result of the default. Which mortgage provision allows the borrower to make mortgage payments as specified in the promissory note?
   a. Right to reinstate
   b. Defeasance clause
   c. Acceleration clause
   d. Promise to repay

277. Which clause is typically found in a mortgage loan to finance income-producing property?
   a. Partial release clause
   b. Receivership clause
   c. Subordination clause
   d. Prepayment penalty clause

278. A lender promises to make a loan to an owner of a new apartment building once construction of the building is complete. This is called
   a. an estoppel certificate.
   b. a defeasance clause.
   c. a subordination agreement.
   d. a takeout commitment.

279. Which statement regarding a due-on-sale clause is NOT true?
    a. The clause allows the mortgagee to call the outstanding loan balance plus accrued interest due.
    b. The lender initiates the clause if all or part of the property is sold or transferred without the lender's prior consent.
    c. The clause prevents another party from assuming the mortgage and requires the mortgage debt to be paid in full when the property is sold.
    d. The clause releases the mortgagor from personal liability on the sale of the property.

280. When a loan is paid off in a lien theory state such as Florida, the lender is required to give the borrower
    a. a deed of reconveyance.
    b. a certificate of title.
    c. a satisfaction of mortgage.
    d. an opinion of title.

281. A closing agent, who is preparing for a closing, wants to verify the balance of an existing mortgage before cutting a check to pay the lender in full at closing. Which document verifies this information?
    a. Broker's reconciliation statement
    b. Due on sale clause
    c. Estoppel certificate
    d. Novation

282. The amount of a loan expressed as a percentage of the value of real property offered as security is the
    a. loan-to-value ratio.
    b. amortization schedule.
    c. leverage ratio.
    d. debt-service coverage ratio.

283. The borrower's monthly mortgage payment consists of
    a. principal, interest, taxes, and insurance (PITI).
    b. principal amount, interest rate, property taxes, and loan term.
    c. principal amount, interest rate, loan term, and monthly payment.
    d. principal, interest, insurance, and down payment.

284. The seller has an existing first mortgage. In order to limit exposure to further liability, the seller should find a buyer ready to
    a. take title subject to the mortgage.
    b. subordinate the buyer's position to the mortgage.
    c. assume the mortgage and note.
    d. obtain new financing.

285. A buyer assumed an existing recorded $82,000 mortgage as part of a real estate purchase. This action will necessitate
    a. a new mortgage instrument.
    b. a new promissory note.
    c. payment of an intangible tax to the state.
    d. the seller remaining primarily liable for the debt.

286. A financing device that grants a buyer "equitable title" without a deed from grantor to grantee is called
    a. a wraparound mortgage.
    b. a purchase money mortgage.
    c. an option contract.
    d. a land contract.

287. A borrower does not give up possession of a property but does use the property as collateral for a loan. This process is called
    a. estoppel.
    b. hypothecation.
    c. redemption.
    d. subordination.

288. A buyer is assuming the seller's existing mortgage. Which agreement relieves the seller of liability for the assumed mortgage?
    a. Assignment
    b. Estoppel certificate
    c. Novation
    d. Hypothecation

289. A buyer decides to purchase a property for $255,000. Which down payment will create the lowest risk for the mortgagee?
    a. $12,750
    b. $25,500
    c. $38,250
    d. $51,000

290. Mortgage ownership is transferred from one individual to another by executing
    a. an assignment of mortgage.
    b. an estoppel certificate.
    c. a lis pendens.
    d. an option contract.

291. A recorded legal document that gives constructive notice that an action affects title to a parcel of real property is called
    a. a lis pendens.
    b. a writ of mandamus.
    c. an injunction.
    d. an attachment.

292. To compute the dollar value of a loan discount, each discount point is equal to
    a. 1% of the amount loaned.
    b. one-eighth of 1% of the amount to be loaned.
    c. 1% of the appraised value plus closing costs.
    d. 1% of the purchase price.

293. A buyer obtains a mortgage of $200,000. The lender makes the loan at 4% interest plus 2 discount points. What is the approximate yield on the mortgage loan?
    a. 4%
    b. 4.25%
    c. 4.5%
    d. 6%

294. Which fee does a lender charge for processing a mortgage application?
    a. Commitment fee
    b. Loan origination fee
    c. Funding fee
    d. Transfer fee

Types of Mortgages and Sources of Financing: Florida Real Estate Principles, Practices & Law (Unit 13)

295. Which parties are most involved in the secondary market?
    a. Mortgage broker and mortgage lender
    b. Mortgagor and mortgagee
    c. Mortgage broker and mortgagee
    d. Fannie Mae and Ginnie Mae

296. Which statement BEST describes Fannie Mae's function?
    a. It regulates lending terms and policies of member banks.
    b. It absorbs any losses incurred by Ginnie Mae.
    c. It acts as a secondary market in purchases of FHA, VA, and conventional loans.
    d. It insures FHA loans.

297. If the Fed decides to sell securities through open-market bulk trading, the result will be
    a. an increase of money in circulation.
    b. a decrease of money in circulation.
    c. a relaxing of interest rates.
    d. an increase in the discount rate.

298. Fannie Mae does NOT
    a. purchase conventional loans.
    b. sell mortgages to institutions.
    c. buy FHA and VA loans.
    d. originate federal loans.

299. A shorter loan term results in
    a. smaller monthly payments.
    b. more interest paid over the life of the loan.
    c. less principal paid over the life of the loan.
    d. less total interest paid during the loan term.

300. An economic indicator that is used to adjust the interest rate on an adjustable rate mortgage is
    a. the discount rate.
    b. Fannie Mae.
    c. the index.
    d. the margin.

301. Freddie Mac is a
    a. part of Ginnie Mae.
    b. subsidiary of Fannie Mae.
    c. secondary market for SAs.
    d. government insurance program.

302. The discount rate is BEST defined as the
    a. interest rate charged borrowers when the mortgage is discounted.
    b. interest rate charged banks for borrowing money from the Federal Reserve.
    c. up-front cost charged borrowers to increase the yield on mortgage loans.
    d. interest rate charged on VA loans.

303. The total amount the interest rate may increase over the life of an adjustable-rate mortgage loan is the
    a. ceiling.
    b. lifetime cap.
    c. margin.
    d. calculated interest rate.

304. All nationally chartered commercial banks must be members of the
    a. Federal National Mortgage Association.
    b. Government National Mortgage Association.
    c. Federal Reserve System.
    d. Federal Home Loan Mortgage Corporation.

305. Who is required to obtain a Florida mortgage loan originator's (MLO) license?
    a. An employee of a national bank who arranges mortgage loans for bank customers
    b. An employee of a federal credit union who coordinates loans for credit union members
    c. An agent of a state-regulated mortgage lender who takes loan applications from consumers
    d. An agent of a federal savings association who makes loans to customers of the association

306. Which type of mortgage loan is a nonconventional mortgage loan?
    a. Adjustable rate
    b. Home equity
    c. FHA-insured
    d. 30-year fixed rate

307. The law that makes it illegal to deny credit on the basis of age is the
    a. Equal Credit Opportunity Act.
    b. Consumer Credit Protection Act.
    c. Fair Housing Act.
    d. Civil Rights Act of 1968.

308. The Truth in Lending Act is implemented by
    a. Regulation Z.
    b. RESPA.
    c. Regulation D.
    d. a Property Report.

309. The MOST important objectives of the federal Truth in Lending Act are to ensure disclosure of finance charges and
    a. to inform buyers of probable closing expenses where known.
    b. the use of a closing disclosure.
    c. the annual percentage rate (APR).
    d. to provide borrowers with a RESPA settlement cost booklet.

310. The TILA-RESPA rule does NOT require that
    a. buyers receive the loan estimate within three business days of loan application.
    b. a closing disclosure be used for a loan to purchase a mobile home.
    c. lenders provide prospective borrowers with a closing disclosure at least three business days before loan closing on a loan secured by a four-family dwelling.
    d. buyers receive a closing disclosure at least three business days prior to loan closing on loans secured by 25 or more acres.

311. Which real estate loan transaction is exempt from the provisions of TILA-RESPA?
    a. Purchase of a home for personal use with FHA financing
    b. Reverse mortgage loan
    c. Purchase of a four-unit apartment building
    d. Purchase of a condominium with VA financing

312. One mortgage clause NOT normally found in a VA or FHA mortgage is the
    a. subordination agreement.
    b. redemption clause.
    c. acceleration clause.
    d. prepayment penalty clause.

313. Which information is the BEST indicator of a loan applicant's willingness to repay debt?
    a. Housing expense ratio
    b. Credit score
    c. W-2 income data
    d. Total obligations ratio

314. Which statement is TRUE concerning VA loans?
   a. A down payment is required on all VA loans.
   b. Veteran borrowers are charged mortgage insurance premiums (MIP).
   c. The VA has the authority to partially guarantee mortgage loans made to veterans by private lenders.
   d. The veteran must secure an estoppel certificate from the VA to begin the loan process.

315. The VA loan guarantee is referred to as the
   a. maximum entitlement.
   b. certificate of guarantee.
   c. certificate of reasonable value.
   d. minimum cash investment.

316. The minimum cash investment on an FHA mortgage loan is
   a. set by lenders.
   b. 3.5% of the purchase price or the appraised value.
   c. dependent on the borrower's qualifying ratios.
   d. 0% on a loan not exceeding $424,100.

317. Which statement is TRUE regarding FHA loans?
   a. New FHA home mortgages are available to qualified investors.
   b. FHA makes loans to qualified borrowers.
   c. FHA insures mortgage loans.
   d. Down payments are not required on FHA loans.

318. FHA requires borrowers to pay
   a. a funding fee.
   b. one-twelfth of the estimated property taxes with each monthly payment.
   c. discount points.
   d. a user's fee.

319. A loan amortization schedule shows monthly payments of
   a. principal.
   b. interest.
   c. principal and interest.
   d. principal, interest, taxes, and insurance.

320. Which pair of terms does NOT belong together?
   a. FHA—mortgage insurance premium
   b. VA—minimum cash investment
   c. Conventional—PMI more than 80%
   d. VA—funding fee

321. An increase in the mortgage money supply is called
   a. the secondary mortgage market.
   b. disintermediation.
   c. intermediation.
   d. a buyer's market.

322. Assume that a buyer is making fully amortized payments of $700 per month on a purchase money mortgage. Which applies?
   a. The amount applying to principal decreases each month.
   b. The interest payment remains constant.
   c. Interest and principal remain constant.
   d. The amount applying to interest decreases each month.

323. Mortgage loan payments made in regular installments of interest only with the full principal amount plus accrued interest paid at one time at the end of the loan period describes
   a. a blanket mortgage.
   b. a package mortgage.
   c. a term mortgage.
   d. an adjustable-rate mortgage.

324. A partial release clause is unique to which type of mortgage?
   a. Balloon mortgage
   b. Blanket mortgage
   c. Reverse mortgage
   d. Partially amortized mortgage

325. A home equity conversion mortgage is also called a
   a. home equity loan.
   b. reverse mortgage.
   c. partially amortized mortgage.
   d. blanket mortgage.

326. Which type of mortgage requires a total obligations ratio and a housing expense ratio?
   a. VA-guaranteed
   b. Conventional
   c. FHA-insured
   d. Jumbo

327. Which type of mortgage loan requires a balloon payment at the end of the loan term?
   a. Amortized
   b. Adjustable-rate
   c. Package
   d. Partially amortized

Real Estate Appraisal: Florida Real Estate Principles, Practices & Law (Unit 16); Florida Real Estate Broker's Guide (Units 6–8)

328. Plottage can BEST be described as the
   a. recorded instrument that identifies the individual lots in a developed subdivision.
   b. development of raw land.
   c. process of combining two or more small lots into one large tract to enhance potential development.
   d. increase in value that results from combining contiguous lots so that the value of the combined properties is greater than the sum of the individual lot values.

329. Market value is the
   a. highest price in terms of money a property will bring.
   b. most probable price that a property should bring.
   c. best estimate of local market value available from recent sales.
   d. highest number of dollars a property will bring from informed buyers.

330. Which statement is TRUE regarding the provisions of the USPAP?
   a. Comparative market analyses are exempt from compliance with the USPAP.
   b. Appraisals prepared by real estate sales associates are exempt from compliance with the USPAP.
   c. Only state-certified or licensed appraisers are required to use the USPAP.
   d. The USPAP establishes disciplinary guidelines for USPAP violations.

331. If the capitalization rate remains constant, but net operating income is increased, how will the property value be affected?
   a. Not enough data is provided to answer this question.
   b. Property value remains constant.
   c. Property value decreases.
   d. Property value increases.

332. The amount of dollars spent to create an improvement is called
   a. price.
   b. cost.
   c. retail value.
   d. probable value.

333. Characteristics of real estate value do NOT include
   a. utility.
   b. cost.
   c. transferability.
   d. scarcity.

334. The MOST suitable appraisal method for a vacant lot in a choice subdivision is the
   a. sales comparison approach.
   b. comparative market analysis.
   c. cost-depreciation approach.
   d. income capitalization approach.

335. Which pair is MOST appropriate in estimating value?
   a. Apartment building—Cost approach
   b. Hospital—Income approach
   c. Single-family dwelling—Cost approach
   d. Raw land—Sales comparison approach

336. A post office of historic value and unique construction is BEST appraised by which approach to estimating value?
   a. Income approach
   b. Market approach
   c. Cost approach
   d. Comparability approach

337. The MOST relevant approach to appraising an apartment complex would focus on
   a. comparative market analysis.
   b. present value of future income.
   c. cost to reproduce.
   d. comparable sales.

338. If a comparable property is superior in lot size compared with the subject property, the price of the
   a. comparable is adjusted upward.
   b. comparable is adjusted downward.
   c. subject is adjusted downward.
   d. subject is adjusted upward.

339. Land value is obtained separately when using which approach to estimating value?
  a. Income approach
  b. Cost approach
  c. Market approach
  d. Multiplier approach

340. The factor by which annual rent from a commercial property is multiplied to obtain an estimate of the property's value is called the
  a. rental index.
  b. net rent multiplier.
  c. net operating income.
  d. gross income multiplier.

341. Which factor is used in determining gross rent multipliers?
  a. Capitalization rate
  b. Net income
  c. Gross monthly income
  d. Net operating income

342. Which type of value BEST describes the amount of dollars a property will bring in a foreclosure sale?
  a. Market
  b. Liquidation
  c. Salvage
  d. Investment

343. When measuring the square footage of a house, an appraiser uses
  a. net rentable area.
  b. exterior dimensions.
  c. room sizes.
  d. interior dimensions, excluding partitions.

344. For real property to be depreciated, it MUST
  a. be free and clear.
  b. be owned in fee simple.
  c. be in good condition.
  d. have improvements.

345. Over which factor of depreciation does a property owner have the LEAST control?
  a. Ordinary wear and tear
  b. Exterior facade
  c. A poorly designed traffic pattern
  d. Forces outside the property boundaries

346. When the estimate of value is adjusted because of an outdated kitchen, it is called
  a. external obsolescence.
  b. functional obsolescence.
  c. curable physical deterioration.
  d. incurable physical deterioration.

347. Which factor is NOT a cause of physical deterioration depreciation?
  a. Lack of maintenance
  b. Wear and tear due to use
  c. Layout of the traffic pattern
  d. Exposure to the elements

348. Which statement is TRUE concerning loss in value due to depreciation?
  a. Extra-large, load-bearing columns in a large but old, one-floor store represent incurable functional obsolescence.
  b. An unattractive storefront window represents incurable physical deterioration.
  c. An unattractive storefront window represents curable external obsolescence.
  d. Extra-large, load-bearing columns in a large but old, one-floor store represent curable functional obsolescence.

349. You have just learned that the nearby airport has obtained government approvals to redirect the flight path of planes over your subdivision. The effect on your subdivision is called
  a. functional obsolescence.
  b. external obsolescence.
  c. physical deterioration.
  d. environmental obsolescence.

350. Which characteristic might be classified as functional obsolescence?
  a. Exterior needs repainting.
  b. Property fronts on a busy expressway.
  c. Property has a one-car garage.
  d. Neighborhood is 60 years old.

351. Correction of an incurable element of physical deterioration or functional obsolescence results in a value increase that is
  a. less than the cost to cure the defect.
  b. equal to the cost to cure the defect.
  c. greater than the cost to cure the defect.
  d. unrelated to the cost to cure the defect.

352. The period of time through which a property gives benefits to its owner is BEST described as its
   a. investment duration.
   b. physical life.
   c. value duration.
   d. economic life.

353. A smaller well maintained home in a subdivision of larger homes will tend to benefit from its proximity to the larger homes. Which principle of value applies?
   a. Progression
   b. Increasing and decreasing returns
   c. Principle of substitution
   d. Conformity

354. What is the correct sequence to arrive at an estimate of value using the income capitalization approach?
   a. Determine effective gross income; find net operating income; find operating expenses; determine potential gross income
   b. Determine effective gross income; find operating expenses; determine potential gross income; find net operating income
   c. Determine potential gross income; determine effective gross income; find operating expenses; find net operating income
   d. Determine potential gross income; find net operating income; determine effective gross income; find operating expenses

355. Which valuation must conform to the *USPAP*?
   a. Broker's price opinion
   b. Comparative market analysis
   c. Appraisal for an FHA loan
   d. All valuation reports listed above must conform to the *USPAP*.

Real Estate Investments and Business Opportunity Brokerage:
Florida Real Estate Principles, Practices & Law (Unit 17); Florida Real Estate Broker's Guide (Units 9 and 15)

356. If an investment property is considered to lack liquidity, this means that the property
   a. is debt-ridden.
   b. has no access to a public water supply.
   c. cannot be sold quickly at full value.
   d. represents a substantial risk to the investor.

357. When associated with real estate finance, the term *leverage* means
   a. the use of a purchaser's funds to gain concessions from a seller.
   b. the use of borrowed funds to minimize the necessity for a borrower to use his own money.
   c. a lender's use of current conditions in the mortgage market to obtain the highest interest rate and best terms for each new mortgage.
   d. a prospective borrower's use of various mortgage rates and terms obtained by shopping for a mortgage loan.

358. Which characteristic is an advantage of real estate investments?
   a. Market is local in nature
   b. Need for property manager
   c. Requires active management
   d. IRS tax treatment

359. The financial report that indicates a firm's financial position at a stated moment in time is the
   a. profit and loss report.
   b. income statement.
   c. balance sheet.
   d. cash flow statement.

360. The intangible advantage a business enjoys over its competitors is known as
   a. liquidity.
   b. leverage.
   c. cash flow.
   d. goodwill.

361. The going concern value of a business
   a. is equal to the value of its real estate holdings.
   b. excludes goodwill.
   c. is the worth of an established business property.
   d. is equal to working capital plus cash flow.

362. The effect of positive leverage is to increase the
   a. borrower's return on equity.
   b. lender's yield.
   c. the loan-to-value ratio.
   d. amount borrowed.

363. Widely accepted appraisal techniques for appraising businesses does NOT include
   a. comparable sales analysis.
   b. cost approach.
   c. leverage analysis.
   d. liquidation analysis.

364. Which characteristic is a disadvantage of real estate investments?
   a. Leverage of borrowed funds
   b. Return on investment
   c. Degree of risk
   d. Tax treatment

365. The total amount of spendable income generated from an investment is
   a. cash flow.
   b. equity.
   c. leverage.
   d. appreciation.

366. The difference between the adjusted basis of a property and its net selling price is called
   a. a tax shelter.
   b. capital gain.
   c. cash flow.
   d. equity.

367. Which type of risk is the probability that projected income will NOT be adequate to meet operating expenses?
   a. Market risk
   b. Business risk
   c. Purchasing-power risk
   d. Interest-rate risk

368. The type of real estate investment that involves the sale or lease of a business is called
   a. commercial real estate.
   b. syndication.
   c. real estate investment trusts.
   d. business opportunities.

369. Which characteristic applies to both real estate brokerage and business brokerage?
   a. Assets include good will
   b. Wider geographic market
   c. Going-concern value may differ from real estate value
   d. Sale of real property or an assignment of a long-term lease

Taxes Affecting Real Estate:
Florida Real Estate Principles, Practices & Law (Unit 18);
Florida Real Estate Broker's Guide (Unit 14)

370. Which deduction from gross income is NOT allowed when calculating the taxable income on investment property?
   a. Operating expenses
   b. Mortgage interest
   c. Depreciation
   d. Reserve for replacements

371. For tax purposes, the installment sale method
   a. relieves the seller of paying tax on a capital gain before it is received.
   b. requires that a capital loss be deferred.
   c. requires that any capital gain or loss be deferred.
   d. requires that a qualified loss be recognized in the year of the final installment payment.

372. Property taxes become a lien on real property on the first of which month?
   a. January
   b. March
   c. April
   d. November

373. The Value Adjustment Board is composed of
   a. two county commissioners, one school board member, and two citizen members.
   b. two county commissioners and three school board members.
   c. three county commissioners and two certified property appraisers.
   d. two county commissioners and three certified property appraisers.

374. A homeowner was upset by the assessed value assigned to his home by the county property appraiser. He decided to protest the assessment and within prescribed time limits appealed to the Value Adjustment Board. Why did the Board refuse to hear the homeowner's appeal?
   a. Such a protest requires that the homeowner seek litigation in the courts.
   b. The homeowner should have first registered his protest with the county property appraiser.
   c. The Board is not authorized to review assessments made by the county property appraiser.
   d. The property must first be reappraised before the Board can determine the validity of the assessment.

375. A 66-year-old widow is totally disabled due to a serious heart condition. The assessed value of her homesteaded property is $189,500. How much is her homestead exemption for city and county taxes (non-school taxes)?
   a. $25,500
   b. $26,000
   c. $50,000
   d. $51,000

376. A fast-growing church has just purchased an adjacent apartment building and plans to convert it to a retirement home. Disregarding other factors, property owners in that area probably would be affected by
   a. lower taxes.
   b. higher taxes.
   c. subrogation of space.
   d. increased property values.

377. Which property is neither exempt nor immune from ad valorem property taxes?
   a. County hospital
   b. New church
   c. High school
   d. Undeveloped farmland

378. A lower assessment for land classified as being for agricultural purposes is protected by laws known as
   a. green belt laws.
   b. homestead laws.
   c. constitutional homestead laws.
   d. blue belt laws.

379. Property taxes for the current year become payable on
   a. January 1.
   b. March 1.
   c. April 1.
   d. November 1.

380. The term *mill* is MOST frequently associated with
   a. mortgages.
   b. interest rates.
   c. tax rates.
   d. listings.

381. In the formula for determining the tax rate for a government taxing unit, the approved budget minus nonproperty tax revenue is divided by
   a. total assessed property valuation.
   b. total assessed property valuation minus exemptions.
   c. property tax revenues from the district.
   d. net proceeds from all taxes levied in the district.

382. When a city or county government in Florida must collect delinquent taxes on a property, it issues a
   a. property tax certificate.
   b. tax lien.
   c. tax deed.
   d. special assessment.

383. The purpose of Florida's Save Our Home amendment is to
   a. limit the amount of increase in assessed value of homesteaded property.
   b. reduce the amount of government sponsored mortgage foreclosures.
   c. provide incentives for revitalization of inner city neighborhoods.
   d. limit the millage rate that may be applied to residential property.

384. Income tax benefits to homeowners are available only if
   a. applied for in the year of purchase.
   b. deductions are itemized annually.
   c. at least one spouse is 55 years of age or older.
   d. applied for within two years before or after selling the former principal residence.

385. Special assessments are
  a. used to help pay for some public improvement that benefits the property.
  b. levied on a calendar year basis.
  c. based on assessed value.
  d. charged to everyone in a specific tax district.

386. A single person bought his home 18 months ago and is now relocating to another city because of a change in employment. Is he entitled to an exclusion of gain from the sale of his home?
  a. Yes, he is entitled to a $500,000 exclusion.
  b. He is entitled to a reduced exclusion because he did not occupy the residence for at least two years.
  c. Yes, he is entitled to a $250,000 exclusion.
  d. He is entitled to an exclusion, provided he purchases another home within 24 months.

387. One result of the current tax law is that homeowners
  a. pay capital gains tax at an 8% lower rate on their home sales.
  b. may use a one-time $500,000 exclusion if they file their taxes jointly.
  c. are not required to reinvest the sale proceeds in a new residence to claim the exclusion.
  d. are permitted to use the $125,000 over-55 exclusion more than once.

388. Tax advantages of home ownership include all EXCEPT
  a. deduction of mortgage interest paid on a second home.
  b. depreciation allowance.
  c. deduction of property taxes on principal residence.
  d. exclusion of up to $250,000 of gain ($500,000 for married couples filing jointly).

389. What number of years has the IRS established as the useful asset life for nonresidential income-producing property for calculating depreciation?
  a. 15
  b. 27.5
  c. 39
  d. 47

390. The purpose of a TRIM notice is to
  a. reduce property taxes.
  b. cut government waste.
  c. inform property owners of the tax bill they can expect in November.
  d. give owners an opportunity to pay taxes early.

391. The maximum Save Our Home benefit that may be transferred to a new homestead is
  a. $25,000.
  b. $50,000.
  c. $51,000.
  d. $500,000.

392. A member of the Armed Services died while on active duty. The surviving spouse is entitled to a homestead deduction of
  a. an additional $500 from the assessed value.
  b. an additional $5,000 from the assessed value.
  c. a 100% tax exemption from property taxes EXCEPT for school board taxes.
  d. a 100% tax exemption.

393. If a property owner's request to the county property appraiser for a tax adjustment is rejected, the property owner may appeal to the Value Adjust Board within what period of time after the TRIM notice is mailed?
  a. 15 days
  b. 25 days
  c. 30 days
  d. By November 1

Real Estate Markets and Analysis: Florida Real Estate Principles, Practices & Law (Unit 15)

394. A physical characteristic of real estate is
  a. the market is slow to respond to change in supply and demand.
  b. land is immobile.
  c. area preference.
  d. government control such as zoning regulations.

395. The statement that land is nonhomogeneous refers to which characteristic of the real estate market?
  a. Real estate is immobile.
  b. Land is indestructible.
  c. Real estate is unique.
  d. The market is slow to respond to changes in supply and demand.

396. To better estimate the demand for dwelling space, most experts charged with analysis of populations will use as a basis for their analysis
   a. total population size.
   b. the household.
   c. average family income.
   d. average family size.

397. Which variable influences supply?
   a. Price of real estate
   b. Income of consumers
   c. Availability of labor
   d. Mortgage credit availability

398. When the supply and demand equilibrium is upset by excess demand, which market activity results?
   a. Pressure to relax interest rates
   b. Buyer's market develops
   c. Seller's market develops
   d. Drop in housing starts

399. Economic characteristics of real estate include
   a. durability of land.
   b. immobility of real estate.
   c. uniqueness of real estate.
   d. situs.

400. When the supply of apartment units increases relative to demand, rents
   a. increase.
   b. decrease.
   c. remain stable.
   d. become noncompetitive.

Real Estate–Related Computations and Closing of Transactions:
Florida Real Estate Principles, Practices & Law (Unit 14 Narrative); Florida Real Estate Broker's Guide (Unit 13)

401. An item that is credited to the seller is the
   a. purchase money mortgage.
   b. assumed mortgage.
   c. seller prepaid items.
   d. unpaid property tax.

402. Which statement is FALSE regarding buyer hazard insurance?
   a. Buyers who finance the purchase with a mortgage must provide proof of homeowners insurance coverage at closing.
   b. Most insurance companies allow the buyer to purchase insurance up to 30 days in advance.
   c. If a tropical storm is named, the insurance company will suspend issuing insurance policies until the storm passes.
   d. The buyer can save money by waiting until the closing to purchase hazard insurance.

403. The day of closing
   a. is always charged to the seller.
   b. if belonging to the seller, means that the seller is charged one extra day.
   c. is always charged to the buyer.
   d. if belonging to the seller, means that the seller is charged one less day.

404. When mortgage interest paid in arrears on a loan assumption is prorated, the amount up to the day of closing is
   a. debited to the seller, credited to the buyer.
   b. debited to the seller.
   c. debited to the buyer, credited to the seller.
   d. not shown on the closing statement.

405. Which statement is TRUE with respect to closing statement entries?
   a. Brokerage commission is usually entered as a debit to seller and a credit to buyer.
   b. The earnest money deposit is entered as a credit to the buyer.
   c. Title insurance expense, when applicable, is usually entered as a debit to seller and a credit to buyer.
   d. Abstract continuation expense, when applicable, is usually entered as a debit to buyer.

406. After contracting to sell and unless otherwise agreed, the seller is responsible for
   a. existing liens and title insurance.
   b. lis pendens.
   c. existing liens and documentary stamps on the note.
   d. existing liens.

407. When monthly rent paid in advance is prorated, how is the calculated figure entered on the closing statement?
   a. Debit to the seller, credit to the buyer
   b. Debit to the seller
   c. Debit to the buyer, credit to the seller
   d. Credit to the buyer

MATH PROBLEMS

408. What did a new home cost if the state documentary stamp tax on the deed was $546?
   a. $74,500
   b. $78,000
   c. $156,000
   d. $273,000

409. The county property appraiser has assigned an assessed value of $117,500. The property is homesteaded. The county charges the following millage rates: city 10 mills, county 10 mills, and school district 6 mills. Calculate the property taxes.
   a. $1,755
   b. $1,905
   c. $2,405
   d. $2,845

410. A home has been assessed by the county property appraiser at $116,000. The property is homesteaded. The city, county, and school board district each charge 10 mills for a total millage rate of 30 mills. How much is saved by the homestead exemption?
   a. $750
   b. $1,250
   c. $1,500
   d. $3,480

411. An investor originally purchased a new home for $249,000. During the period of ownership, the investor spent $21,000 in capital improvements. The investor sold the home 15 years later for $325,000. The investor paid a brokerage fee of 6% of the sale price and paid out-of-pocket closing costs totaling $3,500. What is the investor's capital gain from the sale?
   a. $32,000
   b. $51,500
   c. $53,000
   d. $78,000

412. A lot is 180' × 225'. The city is assessing all lot owners on the street based on $24 per foot for paving. The city has agreed to pay 30% of the paving cost. What is the paving assessment for this lot?
   a. $648
   b. $1,296
   c. $1,512
   d. $3,024

413. A home sold for $108,400. The buyers paid $18,400 down, assumed a recorded mortgage of $72,000, and gave the sellers a new second mortgage in the amount of $18,000. How much will the buyers pay for state taxes resulting from these financial arrangements?
   a. Intangible tax $36; documentary stamp tax $252
   b. Intangible tax $36; documentary stamp tax $315
   c. Intangible tax $144; documentary stamp tax $230.40
   d. Intangible tax $180; documentary stamp tax $63

414. A married couple purchased a home for $287,500, made a down payment of 25%, and secured a new conventional mortgage loan for the balance. Calculate the intangible taxes due.
   a. $575.00
   b. $431.25
   c. $251.65
   d. $143.75

415. The documentary stamp tax charged for a property is $825.30. Calculate the purchase price.
   a. $57,750
   b. $82,500
   c. $117,900
   d. $195,835

416. A corporation purchased 1,600 acres of Florida ranch land from a foreign seller for $5,600,000. Current law requires the buyer to withhold from the seller and pay to the IRS approximately
   a. $560,000.
   b. $840,000.
   c. $1,120,000.
   d. $1,400,000.

417. The N½ of a standard section contains
   a. 80 acres.
   b. 160 acres.
   c. 320 acres.
   d. 640 acres.

418. A multifamily residential investment property is appraised at $235,000. Land value is 20% of the total appraised value. Calculate the annual depreciation deduction. (Round to the nearest dollar.)
   a. $6,065
   b. $6,836
   c. $7,581
   d. $8,545

419. A broker listed a parcel that measures 891 feet by 440 feet. How many acres are contained in the parcel?
   a. 4½
   b. 7¼
   c. 9
   d. 12

420. If a parcel described as the S½ of the SW¼ of Section 21 sold for $4,000 per acre, its sale price was
   a. $160,000.
   b. $280,000.
   c. $320,000.
   d. $640,000.

421. What is the cost per acre of a tract of land that sold for $1,306,800 and measures 4,000 feet by 2,000 feet?
   a. $8,712 per acre
   b. $7,116 per acre
   c. $6,246 per acre
   d. $4,356 per acre

422. A lot is 73 feet wide and 120 feet deep. What fraction of an acre is this lot?
   a. ½
   b. ⅓
   c. ¼
   d. ⅕

423. A buyer paid a state intangible tax of $248 on a $155,000 home. What was the mortgage loan amount, and how much was the state documentary stamp tax on the note?
   a. $124,000 loan amount; $434.00 documentary stamp taxes on the note
   b. $124,000 loan amount; $542.50 documentary stamp taxes on the note
   c. $70,857.14 loan amount; $141.71 documentary stamp taxes on the note
   d. $70,857.14 loan amount; $255.35 documentary stamp taxes on the note

424. The sale price on a home is $180,000. The buyer secured a $140,000 loan and paid $3,200 in closing costs and prepaid expenses. What is the loan-to-value ratio? (Round to the nearest whole percentage point.)
   a. 76%
   b. 78%
   c. 79%
   d. 80%

425. The loan-to-value ratio offered by a local financial institution is 75%. If a buyer wishes to acquire a lot selling for $129,500, the buyer will need to make a down payment of
   a. $1,727.
   b. $5,180.
   c. $25,780.
   d. $32,375.

426. A lender quotes a mortgage loan of $325,000 at 5% interest. The monthly payment is $1,744.67. How much of the second monthly payment will apply to the principal reduction?
   a. $390.50
   b. $392.13
   c. $393.56
   d. $395.01

427. A lender quotes a mortgage loan of $260,000 at 4% interest. The monthly payment is $1,241.27. How much of the second monthly payment will apply to the principal reduction?
   a. $374.60
   b. $375.85
   c. $865.42
   d. $866.67

428. What is the FHA housing expense ratio for a borrower with monthly housing expenses of $696, total monthly gross income of $2,400, and total monthly obligations of $960?
   a. 29%
   b. 33%
   c. 38%
   d. 40%

429. A buyer purchased a mobile home appraised at $60,000 with closing costs of $2,500. The loan is for $50,000. If the seller paid a $2,500 discount, how many points were charged by the lender?
   a. 3 points
   b. 4 points
   c. 5 points
   d. 6 points

430. A buyer applied for a 30-year, fixed-rate $105,000 mortgage. The lender will grant the loan if the buyer will pay interest at the rate of 4.5% plus three points and a 1% loan origination fee. What are the total loan charges if the buyer decides to take the loan offer?
   a. $525
   b. $1,444
   c. $3,150
   d. $4,200

431. A building was sold for $90,000. The buyer paid 10% cash and obtained a loan for the balance. The lending institution charged a 1% loan origination fee. The total cash used by the buyer for this purchase was
   a. $9,900.
   b. $9,810.
   c. $9,000.
   d. $810.

432. A 43,560 square-foot lot is to be subdivided. One-fourth of the lot is made up of a retaining pond, and one-eighth of the lot will be used for a road. How many square feet of usable area are left?
   a. 5,445 sq. ft.
   b. 10,890 sq. ft.
   c. 16,335 sq. ft.
   d. 27,225 sq. ft.

433. The seller wants to net $100,000. If the broker wants to earn 6% commission and the seller's closing costs are estimated at $5,000 (not including commission), for what price MUST the property sell?
   a. $105,000
   b. $111,000
   c. $111,383
   d. $111,702

434. The broker agreed to pay his sales associate 45% of the total commission. The property sold for $320,000 and the commission rate was 7%. The property was sold "in house." What was the broker's share of the commission?
   a. $22,400
   b. $12,320
   c. $11,200
   d. $10,080

435. A developer purchased five lots each measuring 110' × 150'. The lots cost $325 per front foot. The developer subdivided the lots into eight lots and then sold them for $28,000 each. How much profit did the developer earn (rounded)?
   a. 10%
   b. 15%
   c. 20%
   d. 25%

436. If two brokers split the 7% commission 50/50 on a property that sold for $98,400, what did each receive?
   a. $3,444
   b. $4,200
   c. $6,888
   d. $8,400

437. Three tracts are 2¾ acres, 3⅚ acres, and 4⅚ acres in size. Together, they represent
  a. 10 acres.
  b. 10$\frac{1}{12}$ acres.
  c. 11 acres.
  d. 11½ acres.

438. Monthly mortgage payments of $450 have been paid for 15 years. The original mortgage amount was $45,000. After 15 years, 50% of the loan has been paid. What is the total amount of interest paid to date?
  a. $6,750
  b. $22,500
  c. $58,500
  d. $60,450

439. A commercial property leases for $200,000 per year. Miscellaneous income derived from the property totals $12,000 per year. The property recently sold for $1,395,000. What is the GIM?
  a. 6.6
  b. 6.8
  c. 7.0
  d. 7.5

440. Some years ago, a couple built their home for $70,000 on a lot that cost them $30,000. If building costs have doubled and lot prices have increased 300%, how much has their original investment of $100,000 appreciated?
  a. 130%
  b. 160%
  c. 260%
  d. 500%

441. An investor owns a five-unit apartment building. Over a period of time, the investor has found that the expenses to operate the apartment building have averaged 55% of the gross income. If one apartment rents for $920 per month, another for $940 per month, and the remaining three apartments rent for $900 per month each, what are the annual gross and net incomes for the investor's apartment building?
  a. $4,560 gross income; $2,508 net income
  b. $4,560 gross income; $2,052 net income
  c. $54,720 gross income; $30,096 net income
  d. $54,720 gross income; $24,624 net income

442. If a capitalization rate of 10.5% is used, what is the market value of an investment property assuming a net income of $8,424?
  a. $49,371.43
  b. $80,228.57
  c. $98,057.14
  d. $178,285.71

443. A residential zoning category requires at least 15,000 square feet per lot. The developer is reserving 25% of the land to streets, sidewalks, and a community center. The tract of land for development consists of 200 acres. How many residential lots are available for development?
  a. 145
  b. 150
  c. 435
  d. 580

444. A married couple sign a contract to purchase a $280,000 home and make an earnest money deposit of $5,000. The seller has agreed to pay a 7% commission to the listing broker. The buyers will receive a credit of $2,734 for the seller's portion of the ad valorem taxes. If the buyers obtain an 80% conventional loan at 5% interest with 3 points to be paid by them, how much will be due from the buyers at closing?
  a. $54,986
  b. $56,666
  c. $74,586
  d. $222,986

445. While working for a broker, a sales associate acquired a listing for $294,900 at a 6% commission rate. A second sales associate, who works for another brokerage office, found the buyer for the property. The listing and selling brokers agree to a 50-50 split between the two offices. The property sold for $289,000. The selling broker kept 45% of the commission received by the selling office. How much did the selling office's sales associate receive?
  a. $3,901.50
  b. $4,335.00
  c. $4,358.00
  d. $4,768.50

446. A developer sold a lot for $36,000. This represented a loss of 10%. What was the cost of the lot?
   a. $32,400
   b. $39,600
   c. $40,000
   d. $42,800

447. A real estate office sold 180 homes this year. This was 20% more sales than last year. How many homes did the office sell last year?
   a. 140
   b. 144
   c. 150
   d. 154

448. If a $5,600 sale commission is split 60/40 between the listing broker and the selling broker, and each broker splits his share of the commission 50/50 with respective listing and selling sales associates, how much more will the listing broker earn from the sale than the selling broker?
   a. $3,360
   b. $2,240
   c. $1,120
   d. $560

449. A buyer has made an earnest money deposit of $10,150 on a house selling for $94,500. A local lender has agreed to lend 85% of the selling price at 4½% interest for 30 years. If the buyer's closing costs amount to $1,575, how much more cash must the buyer produce at closing?
   a. $5,600
   b. $7,175
   c. $12,889
   d. $14,175

450. A homesteaded property is assessed at $274,500. The millage is 7 mills for county schools and 18 mills for all non-school taxing authorities. What are the property taxes owed on this property?
   a. $4,041.00
   b. $5,612.50
   c. $5,787.50
   d. $6,862.50

451. An investor bought half of a quarter-section of land for $160,000. She plans to develop the property into a residential subdivision. Local zoning will require all lots in the community to be not less than 100' × 120' in size, and the engineering firm employed by the investor has informed her that approximately 484,800 square feet of the tract will be required for parks, streets, storm sewers, and other development purposes. The engineering firm has also estimated that total development costs and associated expenses will amount to five times the raw land costs. The investor wants to make a profit of 10% based on total costs. How much must the investor average per lot to accomplish her profit objective?
   a. $3,200
   b. $3,641
   c. $3,840
   d. $4,224

452. Closing date is July 8. The buyer is assuming the seller's mortgage loan that has a principal balance of $217,500 at 3½% interest. The day of closing is charged to the buyer. What is the proration and how is it entered on the Closing Disclosure?
   a. $145.99 credit seller; $145.99 debit buyer
   b. $145.99 debit seller; $145.99 credit buyer
   c. $166.85 credit seller; $166.85 debit buyer
   d. $166.85 debit seller; $166.85 credit buyer

453. An appraiser has assigned the following weights to three adjusted sale prices:

   Comparable 1: $334,500—45% weight
   Comparable 2: $327,500—35% weight
   Comparable 3: $317,900—20% weight

   What is the reconciled estimated market value of the subject property?
   a. $326,633
   b. $328,730
   c. $332,537
   d. $334,500

454. A homesteaded property is located in Ocala, Florida, in Marion County. The city tax rate is 7.2 mills, the county tax rate is 8.1 mills, and the school district tax rate is 5 mills. The homeowner is a blind widow and has qualified for homestead exemption. The home has been assessed at $235,000. What does the property owner owe in property taxes?
   a. $2,815.20
   b. $2,894.65
   c. $3,860.20
   d. $3,870.35

455. A closing date of April 30 is set, with prorations (using the 365-day method) effective at midnight on the day of closing. The property taxes are estimated to be $1,095. What entry is this on the closing disclosure for the seller?
   a. Debit for $360
   b. Debit for $735
   c. Credit for $360
   d. Credit for $735

456. A homesteaded property is located in Jacksonville, Florida, in Duval County. The city tax rate is 8.1 mills, the county tax rate is 8.9 mills, and the school district tax rate is 5 mills. The homeowner is a blind widow and has qualified for homestead exemption. The home has been assessed at $199,000. What are the property taxes owed on this property?
   a. $2,516
   b. $3,256
   c. $3,278
   d. $3,381

457. A single-family residence is available for listing. A comparable home recently sold for $140,000. Compared with the subject property, the comparable has a superior location ($12,500), is smaller ($8,000), and is three years older ($5,000). What is the subject property's value based solely on the information given?
   a. $139,500
   b. $140,500
   c. $144,500
   d. $157,500

458. A house cost $89,500 to build. When new, the building was estimated to have a 50-year useful life. Using straight-line depreciation, what is the accumulated depreciation after four years?
   a. $1,790
   b. $7,160
   c. $8,200
   d. $8,741

459. The scheduled date for closing a duplex is June 15. Rent collected on the first of each month is $600 per unit. Day of closing belongs to the buyer. How will the proration be entered on the closing disclosure?
   a. $320 debit seller; $320 credit buyer
   b. $600 debit seller; $600 credit buyer
   c. $640 debit seller; $640 credit buyer
   d. $640 debit seller; $560 credit buyer

460. Based on the following, what is the estimated market value of a lot 100' × 110' in the Cove Hill Subdivision?

   Comparable Sales Data
   Sale 1: lot 100' × 120' adjacent to subject lot, sold one week ago for $36,720
   Sale 2: lot 100' × 100' located four blocks away, sold three months ago for $29,800
   Sale 3: lot 110' × 110' located on same street, four lots removed, sold two weeks ago for $36,800
   Sale 4: lot 90' × 110' across the street, sold one month ago for $29,700
   a. $30,130
   b. $32,880
   c. $33,220
   d. $35,400

461. An appraiser has been asked to appraise a building lot in a quality subdivision. His research efforts reveal that five lots have been sold in the past four months in the same neighborhood as the subject lot.

Sale No.	Lot Size	Price	Price per sq.ft.
1.	100' × 130'	$5,600	________
2.	104' × 132'	$5,800	________
3.	102' × 130'	$5,600	________
4.	102' × 130'	$5,600	________
5.	100' × 132'	$5,400	________

If the lot being appraised is 110' × 130', what would the total market value be if based on the average price per square foot of the five previous sales, with no adjustments for time or location?
a. $5,600
b. $6,023
c. $24,000
d. $32,200

462. The sellers are asking $144,000 for their 1,800-square-foot home. The asking price per square foot is
a. $65.
b. $76.
c. $80.
d. $86.

463. A rental house produces $875 per month in gross income. The house costs $113,750. What is the monthly gross rent multiplier?
a. .00769
b. 10.83
c. 130
d. 375

464. A landlord owns an 1,800-square-foot rental house that rents for $.70 per square foot per month. If the GRM (monthly) for that property is 120, what is the market value of the property?
a. $105,000
b. $126,450
c. $140,720
d. $151,200

465. A licensee has been asked to determine the current market value of a six-year-old building with a reproduction cost of $480,000. When new, the economic life of the structure was estimated to be 40 years. If the site value is known to be $100,000, what is the current market value of the entire property?
a. $493,000
b. $508,000
c. $568,000
d. $580,000

466. A sales associate measured the exterior of a home and found it to be 40' × 60'. Disregarding other factors, what is the cost per square foot if the house sold for $202,080?
a. $82.35
b. $83.60
c. $84.20
d. $85.50

467. If a building has an estimated economic life of 20 years, the percentage loss of economic life per year is
a. 2%.
b. 4%.
c. 5%.
d. 20%.

468. An office that measures 20' × 40' rents for $840 per month. The annual rent per square foot is
a. $9.52.
b. $10.50.
c. $11.43.
d. $12.60.

469. A landlord leases 12 apartments in Crow Hollow for a total net monthly rental of $4,800. If this figure represents a 12% annual return on investment, what was the original cost of this property?
a. $240,000
b. $480,000
c. $576,000
d. $720,000

470. An apartment building has eight units, each of which rents for $475 per month. A vacancy rate of 10% persists year after year. Total operating expenses average $1,875 per month. If a capitalization rate of 12% is appropriate, what is the market value of the property?
   a. $154,500
   b. $192,500
   c. $342,000
   d. $380,000

471. An office building produces an effective gross income of $96,400. Building operating expenses total $36,600, and the monthly mortgage payment is $2,240. What is the building's net operating income?
   a. $32,920
   b. $57,560
   c. $59,800
   d. $69,520

472. A contractor builds a two-story warehouse measuring 120 feet × 150 feet. Ten percent of the space is allocated to elevators and landings. The contractor plans to store bins of construction material that each measure 10 feet × 12 feet. How many bins will the building accommodate?
   a. 120
   b. 220
   c. 250
   d. 270

473. A building is valued at $185,000 when NOI is capitalized at a rate of 8%. NOI is 40% of effective gross income. Calculate the effective gross income.
   a. $14,800
   b. $24,667
   c. $32,000
   d. $37,000

474. Examination of documentary stamps on recently recorded deeds provided the following sale prices. Data obtained from property managers produced the income figures. Use the information given to determine the correct overall capitalization rate for the comparable apartment properties. (Round all decimals to three numbers before final rounding to two places.)

Comparable Properties	NOI	Sale Prices
Apt. Project 1	$39,400	$345,000
Apt. Project 2	$45,680	$464,000
Apt. Project 3	$36,800	$386,000
Apt. Project 4	$43,790	$424,000

   a. 9.77%
   b. 10.25%
   c. 10.50%
   d. 11.00%

475. A buyer obtains a mortgage loan of $340,000, and the lender agrees to make the loan at 4% interest with the buyer to pay 3 points at closing. What is the lender's effective yield on the loan?
   a. 4.0%
   b. 4.25%
   c. 4.375%
   d. 4.75%

476. The buyers paid a cash down payment of $55,000 and applied for a $145,000 loan. What is the LTV ratio?
   a. 27.5%
   b. 37.9%
   c. 72.5%
   d. 80.0%

477. What is the net operating income of a building if the operating expenses are $8,350, the effective gross income is $26,750, and the mortgage payment is $11,100?
   a. $18,400
   b. $11,100
   c. $7,300
   d. $6,900

478. What is the net operating income for a property that produces a potential gross income of $26,750, has fixed operating expenses of $8,350, has a mortgage payment of $11,100, and has a reserve for replacements of $450?
   a. $6,850
   b. $17,950
   c. $18,400
   d. $19,900

479. Which property has the highest assessed value?
   a. Market value $49,500; assessed at 100% of value
   b. Market value $66,900; assessed at 75% of value
   c. Market value $81,400; assessed at 60% of value
   d. Market value $119,600; assessed at 40% of value

480. A seller sold his home and agreed to a June 16, 20XX, closing date. The last day for which interest was paid on the $105,500 remaining balance of the 8%, 30-year conventional mortgage was April 30, 20XX. If the total monthly mortgage payment was $774.14, what amount of prorated mortgage interest would appear on the closing statement as a debit to the seller? (Use the 365-day method of proration and charge the day of closing to the buyer.)
   a. $1,054.76
   b. $1,063.52
   c. $1,086.64
   d. $1,406.66

481. The borrowers have a combined gross monthly income of $2,350. They have applied for an FHA loan that will require monthly housing expenses of $658. They have other credit obligations of $282 per month. Will they meet the established FHA standards/ratios for housing expenses and total obligations?
   a. No, their housing expense ratio exceeds FHA maximums.
   b. They meet the housing expense ratio standard but not the total obligations ratio standard.
   c. No, they do not meet either standard/ratio.
   d. Yes, they meet the FHA standards for both ratios.

482. A 10-year-old structure has an effective age of eight years. Total economic life is estimated to be 55 years. Reproduction cost new of the structure is $300,000. What is the accrued depreciation for this structure?
   a. $22,450
   b. $35,890
   c. $43,500
   d. $45,500

483. An investor owns a business property with a value of $1,500,000. The market capitalization rate is 8%. Operating expenses total 30% of potential gross income. The investment is leveraged with a $1,250,000 mortgage. What is the investor's equity?
   a. $100,000
   b. $120,000
   c. $250,000
   d. $450,000

484. A buyer is purchasing a home from the seller for $190,000. The buyer gets a first mortgage loan with a loan-to-value ratio of 60%. The seller takes back a purchase money mortgage for 43% of the balance. How much money does the buyer need for a down payment?
   a. $36,000
   b. $49,020
   c. $32,680
   d. $43,320

485. An appraiser has assigned the following weights to three adjusted sale prices:
   - Comparable 1: $319,900 45% weight
   - Comparable 2: $312,500 35% weight
   - Comparable 3: $308,500 20% weight

   What is the reconciled estimated market value of the subject property?
   a. $313,633
   b. $314,050
   c. $315,030
   d. $319,900

486. An investor is considering the purchase of an office building. The building has four rentable offices. The operating expenses are $30,000 per year. The investor has $150,000 to invest that she wants to receive a 20% return. What monthly rent must she charge per office to get the desired return?
   a. $1,500
   b. $1,250
   c. $800
   d. $625

487. An apartment building has 10 apartments that rent for $220 per month and six apartments that rent for $185 per month. The building also has four apartments that rent for $35 per week. What is the annual gross rental income?
   a. $4,700
   b. $26,400
   c. $39,720
   d. $47,000

488. A lot that measures 140' by 160' contains what percentage of an acre?
   a. 1.94%
   b. 194%
   c. .514%
   d. 51.4%

BROKER INVESTMENT PROBLEMS

Questions 489–503 test mastery of broker math in the *Florida Real Estate Broker's Guide.*

Use the following information to answer problems 489–499:

An investor purchased an apartment building in January for $350,000. The contract specified that $300,000 of the purchase price was allocated to the building and $50,000 of the purchase price was for the land. The investor made a down payment of $50,000 and financed the remainder of the purchase with a loan. The mortgage is for 30 years at 7% interest with a monthly payment of $1,995.91. The apartment building consists of 12 apartments that each rent for $650 per month. Vacancy and collection losses are estimated at 5%. Operating expenses are 30% of the effective gross income and include reserves of $10,000.

489. What is the potential gross income for this investment property?
   a. $82,950
   b. $85,700
   c. $93,600
   d. $95,800

490. What is the effective gross income for this investment property?
   a. $78,920
   b. $88,920
   c. $90,750
   d. $93,600

491. What is the dollar amount of the total operating expenses?
   a. $15,875
   b. $16,676
   c. $26,676
   d. $28,080

492. What is the net operating income for this property?
   a. $50,925
   b. $52,244
   c. $60,840
   d. $62,244

493. What is the annual debt service for this property? (Round to nearest dollar.)
   a. $23,951
   b. $23,979
   c. $24,276
   d. $24,500

494. What is the debt service coverage ratio for this property? (Round to two decimal places.)
   a. 2.00
   b. 2.20
   c. 2.50
   d. 2.60

495. What is the before-tax cash flow for this property?
   a. $23,851
   b. $28,935
   c. $36,340
   d. $38,293

496. What is the operating expense ratio for this property?
   a. .28
   b. .29
   c. .30
   d. .32

497. What is the equity dividend rate for this property expressed as a percent?
   a. 24.9%
   b. 35.5%
   c. 48.7%
   d. 76.6%

498. What is the annual IRS depreciation allowance for this property? (Round to nearest dollar.)
   a. $9,677
   b. $10,909
   c. $11,290
   d. $12,727

499. What is the cash breakeven ratio expressed as a percent for this property?
   a. 43.4%
   b. 44.9%
   c. 45.7%
   d. 54.1%

500. A home is appraised for $345,000. The owner's existing first mortgage has a balance of $181,435. The owner applies for a home equity mortgage loan and the lender agrees to make a loan with a maximum loan-to-value rate overall of 80%, including both mortgages. How much more can the owner borrow?
   a. $94,565
   b. $98,794
   c. $115,435
   d. $118,565

501. An investor buys an office building on a two-acre site for $995,000. Acquisition costs are: appraisal $4,500, survey $900, title insurance $3,400. The land value represents 20%. What is the depreciable basis of the investor's building?
   a. $786,540
   b. $796,000
   c. $800,945
   d. $803,040

502. An office property is purchased for $1,675,000. The building represents 80% of the value. What is the typical annual depreciation deduction for this building? (Round to nearest dollar.)
   a. $22,307
   b. $27,454
   c. $34,359
   d. $48,727

503. A retail business rents space in the regional mall under a percentage lease. The store pays a base rent of $3,250 and 5% of their monthly sales based on an overage clause. Above what annual sales level does the store pay rent in excess of the base rent?
   a. $65,000
   b. $197,500
   c. $741,000
   d. $780,000

CLOSING DISCLOSURE QUESTIONS FOR BROKER CANDIDATES

Using the following information, answer questions 504–511.

The buyer contracts to purchase a duplex from the seller for $115,650. The buyer gave a $10,500 binder deposit to the broker. A closing date of August 10 was set with the day of closing belonging to the buyer (not a leap year).

The buyer will assume the existing first mortgage of $47,950 at 9% interest payable in arrears as of August 1 this year. The current month's interest is to be prorated. The buyer is being charged an assumption fee of 1% to assume the first mortgage. The lender is requiring that the buyer obtain a one-year hazard insurance policy from a local insurance agent for $980 payable at closing.

The seller has an existing second mortgage with a balance of $23,000 as of August 1 this year. The interest rate is 10% with payments payable monthly in arrears. This mortgage will be paid off at closing, plus any accrued interest due the lender.

The buyer is receiving a new $20,000 second mortgage from a local credit union at 9% interest payable monthly in arrears. The lender is charging the buyer 1½ discount points and requires the August interest to be payable in advance at closing.

One apartment in the duplex was leased for one year on March 1 this year (monthly rent is due on the first of each month). The second apartment was leased for one year on May 15 this year (monthly rent is due on the 15th of each month). The rent for each apartment is $475 per month. The seller collected the first and last months' rent upon occupancy, along with a $450 security deposit for each apartment.

The parties have agreed to prorate the taxes. The assessed value of the property for both city and county taxes is $96,000. City taxes are 3 mills, county taxes are 4.5 mills, and school board taxes are 8.5 mills.

The seller agrees to pay attorney fees of $175, state documentary stamps on the deed, a 7½% commission to the broker, and $60 for a termite inspection.

The buyer agrees to pay his attorney $140, the applicable state documentary stamps on the mortgage note(s), the intangible tax on the new second mortgage, $15 for recording the mortgage, $20 for recording the deed, and $1,260 for a title insurance policy.

Used with permission of Andy Gray Schools of Real Estate, Inc.

504. How much is the buyer charged for state documentary stamps and intangible taxes for financing, and where will the information appear on the closing disclosure?
   a. $110.00; page two
   b. $208.00; page three
   c. $278.00; page two
   d. $682.95; page three

505. What is the proration for property taxes, and where will the information appear on the closing disclosure?
   a. Credit seller $605.98; debit buyer $605.98; page three
   b. Credit buyer $930.02; debit seller $930.02; page three
   c. Credit seller $934.22; debit buyer $934.22; page two
   d. Credit buyer $984.26; debit seller $984.26; page two

506. How much will the buyer pay in prepaid interest for the month of August, and on which page of the closing disclosure will that appear?
   a. $108.49; page three
   b. $108.49; page two
   c. $260.11; page three
   d. $260.11; page two

507. What is the rental proration, and where will it appear on the closing disclosure?
   a. Credit buyer $413.71; debit seller $413.71; page three
   b. Credit buyer $427.50; debit seller $427.50; page two
   c. Credit seller $522.50; debit buyer $522.50; page three
   d. Credit seller $536.29; debit buyer $536.29; page two

508. How will the binder deposit appear on the closing disclosure?
   a. Entered on page three as a $10,500 credit for the buyer
   b. Entered on page three as a $10,500 credit for the buyer and a $10,500 debit for the seller
   c. Entered on page two as a $10,500 credit for the buyer
   d. Entered on page two as a $10,500 credit for the seller and a $10,500 debit for the buyer

509. How much will the seller pay for documentary stamps for the sale and for brokerage commission? On which page of the closing disclosure will the entries appear?
   a. Documentary stamps are $809.55; commission is $8,673.75; page two
   b. Documentary stamps are $809.55; commission is $8,670.00; page three
   c. Documentary stamps are $809.90; commission is $8,673.75; page two
   d. Documentary stamps are $809.90; commission is $8,670.00; page three

510. How much will the buyer pay in an assumption fee and for discount points? Where will those entries be entered on the closing disclosure?
   a. Assumption fee: $200.00; discount points: $719.25; page three
   b. Assumption fee: $479.50; discount points: $1,734.75; page three
   c. Assumption fee: $300.00; discount points: $479.50; page two
   d. Assumption fee: $479.50; discount points: $300.00; page two

511. How much is the seller's payoff for the existing second mortgage? Where will the payoff appear on the closing disclosure?
   a. $23,000.00; page three
   b. $23,061.83; page three
   c. $23,000.00; page two
   d. $23,061.83; page two

100 MULTIPLE-CHOICE QUESTION EXAM 1

Instructions. Before taking the state license examination, prepare by taking the Practice Exams in this book. Doing so will allow you to test your knowledge, to practice your exam-taking strategies, and to reduce your anxiety. Take the practice exam under timed conditions, and then review both your right and your wrong answers. This exam is designed as a representative test: Questions are from all major subject areas; they are of the type and in the form used on state exams for sales associates and brokers; and the degree of difficulty is on a par with, or is slightly more difficult than, the typical licensing exam. Thus, successful completion (75 or higher) under simulated exam conditions (three uninterrupted hours using no reference material) should indicate your readiness for the state exam. Darken your answers in the spaces on the Answer Sheet provided on page 217. The correct answers (with textbook unit number references) for this exam are in the Practice Exam 1 Answer Key at the end of this book, complete with explanations of the correct answers.

1. An independent special district authorized by statute to issue bonds to raise funds to construct infrastructure for a residential development is referred to as a
   a. community association.
   b. special tax district.
   c. community development district.
   d. homeowner's association.

2. A real estate licensee who is representing a tenant in a commercial rental wants to share part of her commission with the tenant. Which statement is TRUE regarding this situation?
   a. A licensee may share a commission with a party to a real estate sale and purchase agreement, but not with parties to lease agreements.
   b. Real estate licensees may share commissions with parties to residential lease agreements, but not with parties to commercial lease agreements.
   c. Real estate licensees may share their commission with a party to a lease agreement, provided it is disclosed to all interested parties.
   d. It is illegal for a real estate licensee to share commissions with a party to any real estate transaction unless the party is a real estate licensee.

3. When the value of a business's tangible assets is subtracted from its purchase price, the amount remaining represents the
   a. price paid for goodwill.
   b. accounts payable to the business.
   c. long-term liabilities of the business.
   d. sales tax collected but not yet remitted to the state.

4. Which type of estate in real property is held for a definite number of years?
   a. Fee simple estate
   b. Life estate
   c. Estate for years
   d. Estate by the entireties

5. In the government survey system of legal descriptions, a township measures
   a. 6 square miles.
   b. 6 miles square.
   c. 640 acres.
   d. 640 square miles.

6. An apartment building consists of 430 units. The complex is 90% occupied. How many units are vacant?
   a. 10
   b. 35
   c. 43
   d. 387

7. In Dade County, Florida, a tenant leased a two-bedroom, single-family home from the landlord in June for a one-year period. In November, the tenant told the landlord that she had no source of heat and requested he install a heater. The landlord said he would install the heater, but it would result in a rental increase of $50 per month. Which statement is correct?
   a. The landlord is required to provide heat, and the rent was established by lease.
   b. The landlord is entitled to increase the rent because the single-family home is exempt from the Florida Landlord and Tenant Act.
   c. The tenant is not entitled to any free additions or improvements because she should have inspected the premises prior to signing the lease.
   d. Winters are not cold enough in Dade County, Florida, to require landlords to heat rental units.

8. Listing agreements do NOT have which requirement?
   a. Written form
   b. Definite expiration date
   c. Description of the property
   d. Fee or commission charged

9. The "highest and best use as though vacant" is considered to be the use that will result in the greatest amount and longest duration of net income that accrues to the
   a. improvements on a property.
   b. land itself.
   c. lessee of commercial property.
   d. lessor of commercial property.

10. A seller has listed his property with a real estate company. The seller has informed the sales associate that he will not sell his condominium to college students. Which statement is TRUE regarding this situation?
   a. The seller can refuse to sell to college students, but the real estate licensee cannot refuse college students.
   b. The seller and his sales associate can be fined for violating the Fair Housing Act.
   c. Although this may be a poor business decision, it is not a violation of the Fair Housing Act.
   d. The licensee should withdraw from the listing and report the seller to the FREC.

11. A real estate company employs a receptionist. A buyer comes into the office and hands the receptionist an earnest money deposit on Wednesday (no legal holidays involved). Which statement applies to this situation?
   a. The broker must deposit the check into the escrow account no later than the end of business on Monday of the following week.
   b. The receptionist could be charged with providing real estate services without a license.
   c. The broker must deposit the check into the escrow account by the end of business on Friday.
   d. Only a licensed real estate sales associate is allowed to accept an earnest money deposit on behalf of the broker.

12. A broker's principal is away on vacation. The broker receives an offer of $267,000 for the principal's property. Before the principal returns, the broker receives a second offer of $264,000. The broker should
   a. refuse the lower offer.
   b. submit only the best offer when the principal returns.
   c. hold the lower offer until the first offer is accepted or rejected.
   d. submit both offers to the principal.

13. Which statement is FALSE regarding the renewal exemption for members of the U.S. armed forces?
   a. To be eligible for the exemption, the licensee cannot engage in real estate brokerage activity in the private sector for profit during the period of service in the armed forces.
   b. The service member is exempt for renewal provisions for two years after discharge from active duty.
   c. The renewal exemption applies to a licensed spouse provided the service member was stationed on active duty in Florida.
   d. The exemption applies to a licensed surviving spouse provided the member of the armed forces was serving on active duty at the time of death.

14. A licensed real estate broker and his wife jointly owned a two-person corporation for profit registered with the DBPR as an active real estate brokerage firm. The wife was registered as an officer of the corporation but had never qualified to be licensed. The broker and his wife mutually agreed to a divorce, and the court awarded the wife the profitable real estate brokerage corporation as part of the property settlement. The wife retained her married name, and the husband organized a new brokerage firm. Which is correct?
    a. As a result of the court's action, the wife may continue operating the brokerage firm if she chooses.
    b. The wife is entitled to the same rights and privileges as full owner of the firm as existed before the divorce.
    c. The wife need only request that her status be changed to active real estate broker.
    d. It is illegal for the wife to continue operating the firm.

15. A buyer gives the broker a $53,500 good-faith deposit. The broker defrauds the buyer of the $53,500. The buyer sues the broker and is awarded a judgment in the amount of $78,500 for the original $53,500 deposit plus $25,000 in punitive damages. The buyer was unable to collect the judgment from the broker, so he requests relief from the Florida Real Estate Recovery Fund. How much can the buyer receive from the Recovery Fund?
    a. $78,500
    b. $53,500
    c. $50,000
    d. $25,000

16. A sales associate has earned a commission of $2,400. The broker for whom she works pays her $2,000 and uses the remainder of her commission to pay office expenses with a promise to pay the remaining $400 when he can afford to do so. The broker is guilty of
    a. concealment.
    b. grand larceny.
    c. culpable negligence.
    d. conversion.

17. A community association manager (CAM) license is required to manage which type of property?
    a. 150 unit apartment building
    b. Retail strip stores
    c. Single-family dwellings
    d. 20 unit condominium complex

18. The Federal law that prohibits a seller from requiring the homebuyer to use a particular title insurance company as a condition of sale is the
    a. Truth in Lending Act.
    b. Equal Credit Opportunity Act.
    c. Florida "Little FTC Act."
    d. Real Estate Settlement Procedures Act.

19. A tenant continued to occupy the premises following expiration of the lease. The tenant continued to pay monthly rent to the landlord. The tenant is a
    a. lessor.
    b. life tenant.
    c. tenant at will.
    d. tenant at sufferance.

20. A broker receives conflicting demands from the buyer and seller. The broker properly notifies the FREC and requests an escrow disbursement order (EDO). However, before the order is issued, the buyer and seller sue one another. What must the broker do in this situation?
    a. The broker must notify the FREC of the situation within 10 business days.
    b. The broker need not do anything because the lawsuits are a separate action.
    c. The broker must follow the instructions of the EDO when received because it was timely filed.
    d. The broker must notify the FREC of the lawsuit within 15 business days.

21. The purpose of the Save Our Home amendment is to
    a. provide a procedure for retaining ownership of one's home after foreclosure proceedings are initiated.
    b. limit the increase in the assessed value of homestead property.
    c. provide low-cost mortgage financing for first-time homebuyers.
    d. reduce the amount of income taxes owed by homeowners.

22. The neighbor of a real estate broker referred his sister to the broker. The sister purchased a home costing $250,000. To show his appreciation, the broker may
    a. take the neighbor and his wife out to dinner.
    b. give the neighbor a bottle of his favorite wine.
    c. send the neighbor a small gift.
    d. express his thanks to the neighbor.

23. The appropriate type of brokerage relationship is determined by the
    a. listing agent.
    b. seller.
    c. broker.
    d. buyer.

24. A broker listed a commercial lot for $98,000. Later, the broker learned that a firm that owned the building adjoining the seller's lot was going to need the lot for expansion and would be willing to pay up to $130,000 for the lot. The broker told the seller that she wanted to terminate her brokerage relationship and buy the lot herself for $96,000 cash. The seller agreed to the offer and sold the lot to the broker, who then sold the lot to the neighboring firm. This is an example of
    a. a legitimate business transaction.
    b. conversion.
    c. culpable negligence.
    d. concealment.

25. What is the maximum allowable homestead exemption for a widow who is a veteran with a 25% disability due to service-connected injuries?
    a. $25,500
    b. $30,500
    c. $50,500
    d. $55,500

26. A contract for the sale and purchase of a property fails to close. Both the buyer and the seller make demands that they are entitled to receive the earnest money deposit. The matter is to be resolved in a court of law. The broker is not making a claim to receive any of the funds. Which court procedure is appropriate in this situation?
    a. Interpleader
    b. Declaratory judgment
    c. Compensatory damages
    d. Lis pendens

27. Which statement is FALSE regarding brokerage relationship disclosure requirements?
    a. A licensee who does an open house at a listed property must give each prospective buyer who attends the open house a no brokerage relationship notice.
    b. The single agent disclosure, when that relationship is chosen, must be made before, or at the time of, entering into a listing agreement or an agreement for representation, or before the showing of property, whichever occurs first.
    c. Brokers must retain brokerage relationship disclosure documents for five years for all residential transactions that result in a written contract to purchase and sell real property.
    d. If a transaction fails to close, the licensee should retain the brokerage relationship disclosure documents with the purchase and sale contract and other documents associated with the property and place them in the failed to close file.

28. The clause in a mortgage that ensures that the mortgage cannot be foreclosed so long as all payments are current and other conditions are fulfilled is the
    a. redemption clause.
    b. defeasance clause.
    c. right to reinstate clause.
    d. release clause.

29. When the probable-cause panel decides that a real estate licensee's activities may have been grounds for suspension or revocation, the DBPR files a
    a. formal complaint.
    b. stipulation.
    c. notice of noncompliance.
    d. writ of injunction.

30. An unlicensed out-of-state resident referred a prospective buyer to a Tallahassee, Florida, broker. The Tallahassee broker reimbursed the out-of-state resident for the out-of-pocket expenses associated with making the referral. Which statement applies to this situation?
    a. This is legal because the expenses were actually incurred.
    b. The out-of-state resident can accept the expense money as long as the out-of-state resident does not come to Florida.
    c. The expense money can be considered a referral fee and therefore must be disclosed to the prospective buyer before the out-of-state resident can accept the money.
    d. Both the out-of-state resident and the Tallahassee broker have violated Chapter 475 because it is illegal to pay an unlicensed person for performing real estate services.

31. Which brokerage relationship duty applies only to single agents?
    a. Account for all funds
    b. Exercise limited confidentiality
    c. Full disclosure
    d. Deal honestly and fairly

32. A real estate company is the exclusive representative of the developer of a new subdivision. The real estate company's sales staff will temporarily work out of a mobile home that the developer has placed in the subdivision until the model home is completed. Transactions will be closed at the main office. Does the real estate company need to register the mobile home as a branch office?
    a. License law prohibits the use of mobile homes as temporary shelters.
    b. The broker must make the mobile home stationary before registering it as a branch office.
    c. The broker must register the branch office and pay a fee before assigning any sales staff there.
    d. The mobile home is a temporary shelter and is not considered to be a branch office.

33. Which term is associated with additional land resulting from the gradual receding of water that now belongs to the property owner?
    a. Accretion
    b. Alluvion
    c. Reliction
    d. Erosion

34. A sales associate is employed by a developer to sell homes in a new subdivision. The developer is also building in two other subdivisions, which are organized as affiliated companies. The developer wants to have the sales associate sell homes in the other subdivisions. Which statement applies?
    a. The sales associate must work out of one subdivision but not all because sales associates must be registered with a single office.
    b. The sales associate may request and be issued a group license so that the associate can work in any of the developer's subdivisions.
    c. The developer must contact the DBPR and request a multiple license.
    d. The sales offices of the subdivisions are considered temporary shelters. Therefore, the sales associate doesn't need to do anything in order to work for the various affiliated entities.

35. A broker received an offer and an earnest money deposit on Thursday, July 10, at 9:30 am. The owner of the property will not be in town until Wednesday, July 16, to consider the offer. The broker's next normal banking day will be Monday, July 14; however, he has a large safe built into the wall of his office. FREC rules require the broker to
    a. hold the earnest money deposit in his safe until his principal can accept or reject the offer.
    b. hold the earnest money deposit in his safe until his banking day on Monday, July 14.
    c. deposit the earnest money in his escrow account by the close of business on Tuesday, July 15.
    d. deposit the earnest money in his escrow account by the close of business on Friday, July 11.

36. A buyer entered into a purchase and sale agreement to buy a seller's condominium. Two days later, the buyer canceled the contract and requested that the broker return the earnest money deposit. Which statement applies to this situation?
    a. The broker may return the earnest money deposit because it is within the buyer's three-day rescission period.
    b. The broker must get a release of the earnest money deposit from both the buyer and the seller before releasing the funds. Otherwise, the broker must notify the FREC of conflicting demands.
    c. This is a breach of contract, and the seller may be entitled to the earnest money deposit as liquidated damages.
    d. The broker must request the FREC to issue an escrow disbursement order.

37. A Georgia broker has a prospective buyer who wants to buy some land in Florida for the purpose of building between 100 and 150 luxury condominiums. The Georgia broker contacts a Florida broker to help locate some suitable tracts for the prospect to consider. Together, they work with the buyer and show her five separate tracts. Their cooperation pays off when the buyer purchases a 60-acre tract for $558,000 and they evenly divide a 10% commission. Which is MOST correct?
    a. If the Georgia broker's license is current, this is a legal arrangement.
    b. Only the Florida broker is legally entitled to a commission.
    c. Both brokers are legally entitled to a commission.
    d. Both brokers have violated Chapter 475, F.S.

38. For a limited partnership to register as a real estate broker with the DBPR, the limited partnership must
    a. file a copy of the partnership agreement with the DBPR.
    b. have all general partners who will deal with the public licensed as active brokers.
    c. register all unlicensed limited partners.
    d. register all sales associates who are general partners.

39. A broker who receives conflicting demands regarding the disbursement of escrowed property must notify the FREC within what period of time?
    a. 10 calendar days
    b. 15 business days
    c. 30 calendar days
    d. 30 business days

40. Which type of deed will provide the grantor the BEST assurance of no future liability?
    a. Warranty deed
    b. Special warranty deed
    c. Quitclaim deed
    d. Fiduciary's deed

41. In an effort to obtain more listings and subsequent commissions, a licensee urges people in an older neighborhood to sell because "a group belonging to a religious cult has recently moved into the neighborhood and property values will fall." This is an example of the illegal and unethical practice called
    a. redlining.
    b. blockbusting.
    c. reverse discrimination.
    d. steering.

42. The mandatory distance between lot lines and building improvements is known as
    a. zoning.
    b. variance.
    c. frontage.
    d. setback.

43. If the interest paid for borrowed funds is greater than the overall rate of return to an investor, this is an example of
    a. positive leverage.
    b. negative leverage.
    c. increased yield.
    d. increased cash reversion.

44. Two owner-developers are both active real estate broker licensees. Together they hire a certified accountant (CPA) who is not a licensee to supervise the overall development of a large tract of land they are jointly developing into a high-quality, recreation-oriented subdivision. The accountant is not experienced in selling real estate; however, he is an astute businessman and manages to exceed the first 18 months' sales projections in just nine months. As a reward for his achievement, the owner-developers agree to pay the accountant a bonus of 15% of the amount in excess of the first 12 months' sales projections. Which is MOST correct?
    a. This is a perfectly legal arrangement.
    b. All three individuals have violated Chapter 475, F.S.
    c. The developers have violated Chapter 475, F.S.
    d. The accountant has violated Chapter 475, F.S.

45. The Florida Vacation Plan and Timesharing Act applies to time-share plans consisting of
    a. more than seven time-share periods over at least a three-year period.
    b. more than three time-share periods over at least a seven-year period.
    c. more than seven time-share periods with no minimum span of time.
    d. two or more time-share periods with no minimum span of time.

46. A property management company represents a residential landlord who has obtained a writ of possession to evict a tenant. The writ has been executed by the sheriff. The tenant's belongings are inside the apartment. Which statement is TRUE regarding this situation?
    a. The landlord, or the property management company as agent, may remove the personal belongings and place them on the property line.
    b. Only the sheriff may remove the tenant's personal belongings.
    c. The property manager must notify the tenant by certified mail of the intent to remove the personal property.
    d. The landlord or property manager must get an executed judgment lien on the personal property before taking possession of it.

47. A widower is always looking for good, safe investments for his money. He decides to bid on a bungalow home at a foreclosure sale. The widower feels that the fair market value of the home is approximately $84,000. There is a first mortgage lien of $68,000 held by the lender who has initiated the foreclosure action. The property is homesteaded by the current owner. Property taxes are two years in arrears. Which statement applies?
   a. The widower's opening bid should be high enough to cover the existing first mortgage so that the mortgage lien can be satisfied from the sale proceeds.
   b. The widower will be responsible for the prior property tax liens.
   c. The mortgage lien and back taxes will not survive a foreclosure sale.
   d. Because this is homesteaded property, the home is protected from foreclosure.

48. Which statement does NOT describe a purchase money mortgage?
   a. It is alternative financing between buyer and seller that usually excludes a third party.
   b. It enables a buyer to purchase with less equity funds than required by a financial institution.
   c. It is given by the buyer to the seller for all or part of the purchase price of the property.
   d. The seller retains legal title until the buyer has made all the mortgage payments.

49. A real estate licensee evaluates real property for the purpose of obtaining a listing. The licensee must refer to the value as
   a. an estimate of value.
   b. a listing analysis.
   c. an appraised value.
   d. a comparative market analysis (CMA).

50. A woman works in an onsite apartment rental office. Her employer pays her an annual salary of $80,000 and an end-of-year bonus, which is based on the number of new tenants the woman finds for the apartments. The woman
   a. does not need a real estate license because she is paid a salary.
   b. does not need a real estate license unless the tenant leases are for longer than one year.
   c. does not need a real estate license because she works on site at the apartments.
   d. must be a licensed broker or a licensed sales associate working under a broker to perform these duties.

51. To be enforceable in court, a contract for the sale of real property must
   a. be signed by two competent witnesses.
   b. be in writing and signed by both parties.
   c. be acknowledged by an official of the court or a notary public.
   d. specify the type of deed that will convey the title.

52. When a buyer stipulates that he will agree to make each monthly mortgage payment on the house he is buying but takes no responsibility for the note, he is
   a. buying with an assumption of the mortgage.
   b. releasing the seller from his obligation regarding the mortgage.
   c. purchasing the house subject to the mortgage.
   d. assigning the mortgage.

53. Which estate is an example of a nonfreehold estate?
    a. Estate for years
    b. Life estate
    c. Fee estate
    d. Estate by the entireties

54. A married man purchased an investment property in his name only. If he later divorces, how will the investment property be treated?
    a. As community property
    b. As a nonmarital asset
    c. As a marital asset
    d. As joint property

55. A son, who is not licensed, helped his father by finding buyers for his father's lots. The son did not receive any money, but his father agreed to give the son a choice lot, free and clear, after the son found buyers for five lots. The son was offered a well-paying job some distance from home after he had found buyers for only three lots. The son took the job and did not earn his lot. Which statement is correct?
    a. The son need not have been licensed because his father owned the lots.
    b. The son violated Chapter 475, F.S., and is subject to fine or imprisonment.
    c. The son did not violate Chapter 475, F.S., because he received no compensation.
    d. The son and his father both violated Chapter 475, F.S., due to intent.

56. An 83-year-old widow owned a popular restaurant business. Her business assets consisted of goodwill, regular customers, all the restaurant equipment, and the building housing the restaurant. The land was leased and had 54 years remaining on a 99-year lease. The widow told her headwaiter that she would like his help in selling the business for $200,000. The widow agreed to give the headwaiter $7,000 if he found a buyer for the business. The headwaiter approached one of the regular customers who agreed to buy the business if the headwaiter would contract to manage the business. An agreement was reached, and the widow sold the business. When the widow learned that the headwaiter was going to take over as manager, the widow refused to pay the promised $7,000. Which is MOST correct?
    a. The headwaiter can force the widow to pay on the strength of a verbal contract.
    b. The widow's age would cause doubt to be cast on the compensation agreement.
    c. The headwaiter violated Chapter 475, F.S., and can be fined or jailed.
    d. Because the headwaiter received no compensation, he did not violate Chapter 475, F.S.

57. Curable functional obsolescence results in a change in value that is
    a. less than the cost to cure the defect.
    b. equal to the cost to cure the defect.
    c. greater than the cost to cure the defect.
    d. unrelated to the actual cost to cure the defect.

58. When a broker is unable to convince a property owner that the current market value is the price at which the property should be listed, the broker should
    a. take the listing at the owner's price and hope to sell the property.
    b. take the listing at the owner's price and later return to negotiate a reduction.
    c. diplomatically decline to accept the listing.
    d. take the listing and forget about it.

59. Which action will terminate a brokerage relationship?
    a. The seller rejected a buyer's full price offer.
    b. The sales associate was killed in an auto accident.
    c. The spouses owning a listed property file for divorce.
    d. The listing agreement expires.

60. Which offense is a misdemeanor of the first degree?
    a. False advertising
    b. Unlicensed practice of real estate
    c. Culpable negligence
    d. Collecting a fee for inaccurate and out-of-date rental information

61. Streets, parks, and school sites are transferred from developers to counties or communities by an act or process called
    a. subdivision.
    b. subrogation.
    c. descent.
    d. dedication.

62. A mortgage note provides legal evidence of a personal debt and also
    a. permits legal action to collect the debt wherever the mortgagee may be located.
    b. pledges all the assets of the mortgagor.
    c. neutralizes the defeasance clause in the mortgage.
    d. creates a lien on the property.

63. A broker has a farm listed for $164,000 with a negotiated sale commission of 6%. A retiree sees the For Sale sign and voluntarily offers $185,000 for the farm. The broker buys the farm from her seller for $160,000, and then she sells it to the retiree for $185,000. Later, the seller learns of the sequence of transactions. Which statement is MOST correct?
    a. The broker must reimburse the seller $25,000 plus any commission received.
    b. No legal or ethical violation has occurred.
    c. The broker's purchase price may be regarded as a legal option.
    d. The law does not apply to this transaction.

64. In determining market value, the principle of substitution is the basis for which approach to value?
    a. Comparable sales approach
    b. Cost-depreciation approach
    c. Income approach
    d. The principle of substitution is the basis for all three approaches

65. Which statement is FALSE regarding a new condominium complex?
    a. A declaration must be filed before any units may be sold.
    b. Each unit owner has a fractional, undivided interest in the common areas and facilities.
    c. Unit owners are responsible for their own mortgage payments.
    d. Unit ownership requires the purchase of shares of stock in the association.

66. When a new lending agreement releases the seller and substitutes the buyer as the party liable for the mortgage debt, this act is called
   a. subrogation.
   b. subject to the mortgage.
   c. novation.
   d. negative amortization.

67. How is mortgage interest on an assumed mortgage entered on the closing document?
   a. Debit buyer only
   b. Credit buyer only
   c. Debit buyer and credit seller
   d. Debit seller and credit buyer

68. The risk associated with an investment's ability to provide sufficient funds to pay operating costs is referred to as
   a. purchasing power risk.
   b. interest rate risk.
   c. business risk.
   d. financial risk.

69. The Florida Vacation and Timesharing Act requires that purchasers of resale timeshare periods be given how many days to cancel the purchase contract?
   a. 3 calendar days
   b. 3 business days
   c. 7 business days
   d. 10 calendar days

70. A buyer offered $150,000 for a home. The seller countered at $160,000. The buyer did not accept the seller's counteroffer. The seller told her broker that she was revoking the counteroffer and accepting the buyer's original offer. Which statement is TRUE regarding this situation?
   a. The buyer and the seller have entered into a sale and purchase agreement for $150,000.
   b. The seller can revoke her counteroffer and accept the buyer's original offer up until the time the buyer rejects the counteroffer.
   c. The seller cannot accept the original offer because it was extinguished by the counteroffer.
   d. The seller can accept the original offer after making a counteroffer, if the original offer has not passed the expiration date and time.

71. Which Florida statute governs the executive branch of Florida government?
   a. Chapter 20, F.S.
   b. Chapter 120, F.S.
   c. Chapter 455, F.S.
   d. Chapter 475, F.S.

72. The purpose of recording documents relating to real property is to
   a. give actual notice of legal documents.
   b. give constructive notice to future purchasers and creditors.
   c. prevent loss by adverse possession.
   d. eliminate squatters' rights.

73. The interest that a buyer receives upon executing a contract for purchase and prior to the closing is
    a. equitable title.
    b. legal title.
    c. beneficiary interest.
    d. promissory interest.

74. The real taxable value of a Florida resident's home will NOT be known until the
    a. age of the homeowner is known.
    b. total tax millage is applied to the assessed value.
    c. total existing exemptions are subtracted from the current market value.
    d. total existing exemptions are subtracted from the current assessed value.

75. A Florida broker purchased some raw acreage and developed it into several hundred building lots. The Florida broker contacted a broker in Alabama and offered the Alabama broker $150 for every prospect he sent to Florida who bought a lot from the Florida broker. Which statement is correct?
    a. The Florida broker has violated Chapter 475, F.S.
    b. The Alabama broker cannot legally accept compensation from the Florida broker unless he is licensed as a broker in Florida.
    c. The Florida broker can be fined and imprisoned.
    d. The Florida broker may pay a referral fee to the Alabama broker.

76. A sales associate obtained an offer from an investor to buy an undeveloped apartment site. The investor refused to sign any sale agreement until she returned from a vacation in Alaska. While the investor was on vacation, the sales associate took a two-week vacation but still returned several days ahead of the investor. Within a few days after returning, the investor contacted the sales associate and purchased the apartment site. Neither the sales associate nor the investor was aware that, during their vacations, the zoning for the property had been changed from multifamily to single-family zoning, thereby prohibiting the use of the property the investor had intended. The investor brought suit against the sales associate and his broker, which resulted in collection of damages. What legal basis did the investor have for her suit?
    a. Conversion
    b. Concealment
    c. Culpable negligence
    d. Commingling of interests

77. To determine the correct amount of property tax for property, multiply the tax rate by the
    a. assessed value of the property.
    b. last recorded sale price.
    c. taxable value of the property.
    d. appraised value of the property.

78. Which description fulfills the experience requirement to become licensed as a real estate broker?
    a. Registered for 12 months as an active sales associate in the state of Florida.
    b. Provide proof of employment in a property appraiser's office during the previous three-year period.
    c. Registered for the last 24 months as an active New York sales associate.
    d. Registered from 2000 to 2005 as an active Florida real estate sales associate.

79. A buyer decided she would pay the asking price of a house if the seller agreed to accept $6,000 cash as the total down payment. The seller agreed to accept the offer on the condition that the buyer arrange her own financing and pay the balance of the purchase price at closing. The buyer accepted this condition with the stipulation that her $6,000 be returned to her in the event she was unsuccessful in obtaining adequate financing. The seller agreed to the financing contingency and instructed her broker to prepare a contract incorporating the agreed conditions and contingencies.

    The buyer was unable to obtain financing and therefore had to revoke the sale contract under the provisions of the financing contingency. The buyer requested the return of her $6,000. The seller agreed with the buyer's request and notified the broker to return the deposit. To the surprise of both the buyer and the seller, the broker pointed out a clause in the small print of the sale contract giving the broker the deposit in the event the transaction did not close. Who is entitled to the $6,000?
    a. The $6,000 must be turned over to the broker.
    b. The $6,000 must be returned to the buyer.
    c. The $6,000 must be split between the seller and the broker.
    d. The $6,000 must be split between the buyer and the seller.

80. A broker, representing a newly formed syndicate of investors, arranged the purchase of 1,800 acres of ranch land for $1,650,000 from a citizen of Venezuela. The seller demanded all cash, with the buyers to arrange their own financing. The broker helped the investors arrange the financing. Further, the broker recommended that the buyers withhold what percent of the selling price in order to comply with an IRS regulation?
    a. 15%
    b. 45%
    c. 65%
    d. 85%

81. A real estate broker followed the instructions of an escrow disbursement order. The seller sued the broker and obtained a judgment against the broker for $15,000 in damages plus $10,000 in attorney's fees and court costs. The broker incurred $3,000 in attorney's fees. The Commission is authorized to pay
    a. $15,000.
    b. $18,000.
    c. $25,000.
    d. $28,000.

82. A broker manages a residential rental property. The owner wants another real estate office to manage the property and asks the broker to transfer the security deposits to the new rental agent. Which statement applies to this situation?
    a. The broker must first secure the tenants' permission to transfer the deposits.
    b. The broker must close the bank accounts and return the funds directly to the owner.
    c. The broker must transfer the funds to the new agent along with an accounting.
    d. The deposits must be reimbursed to the tenants.

83. In the cost-depreciation approach to estimating value, land value is commonly estimated by
   a. comparable sales analysis.
   b. development cost analysis.
   c. residual value subtraction analysis.
   d. subtracting building value from total property value.

84. The VA total monthly obligations ratio is determined by dividing the total monthly
   a. housing expenses (PITI) by the net monthly income.
   b. obligations by the gross monthly income.
   c. housing expenses (PITI) by the gross monthly income.
   d. obligations by the net monthly income.

85. Where the government survey system is used to describe real property, the primary north-south line and the primary east-west line that form the basic reference point for the system are correctly called the
   a. principal meridian and base line.
   b. primary meridian and primary base line.
   c. principal meridian and primary base line.
   d. primary meridian and principal base line.

86. An up-front fee paid to the lender in exchange for a reduced interest rate is referred to as
   a. commitment fees.
   b. origination fees.
   c. the discount rate.
   d. discount points.

87. For income tax purposes, the term *adjusted sale price* means the sale price of a home
   a. less the original cost.
   b. less allowable fix-up and selling expenses.
   c. less the down payment when seller financing is involved.
   d. adjusted to reflect the negotiation and acceptance of a counteroffer.

88. The real estate term *situs* refers to
   a. commercial properties designated on a site plan.
   b. properties listed in the historic properties register.
   c. scenic rural or farm areas.
   d. value derived from preferred property locations.

89. The master plan developed by planning commissions to manage local growth and preserve living conditions is called the
   a. growth management plan.
   b. comprehensive plan.
   c. development plan.
   d. environmental impact plan.

90. An investor purchased two adjoining lots, each measuring 150' across the front and 180' in depth. He paid $7,500 for each lot. The investor divided the property into three equal lots and sold each one for $125 per front foot. What percent of profit did the investor make on the original investment?
    a. 25%
    b. 60%
    c. 67%
    d. 150%

91. A homebuyer has arranged a conventional mortgage of $135,000 at 5% interest for 30 years. By agreement, the first three monthly payments are to consist of interest only with payment on principal to begin with payment number four. How much total interest will the homebuyer pay during the first three months?
    a. $1,687.50
    b. $1,700.75
    c. $1,900.00
    d. $2,250.00

92. The closing date is September 10. Day of closing belongs to the seller. Property taxes for the year are $1,700. Calculate the proration using the 365-day method.
    a. $1,178.36 debit seller, credit buyer
    b. $1,173.70 debit seller, credit buyer
    c. $521.64 credit seller, debit buyer
    d. $516.99 debit seller, credit buyer

93. The sale price of a home is $165,000. A savings association has agreed to lend 80% of the sale price. The prospective buyer has made a binder deposit of $12,200. How much more cash must the buyer produce at closing?
    a. $12,200
    b. $20,800
    c. $28,000
    d. $33,000

94. A developer purchased a tract measuring 1,452 feet by 1,200 feet for $3,000 per acre. The sale contract provided for the developer to pay the seller 29% of the purchase price in cash, the developer to assume a $50,000 existing first mortgage, and the seller to take back a new second mortgage for the remainder of the purchase price. How much must the seller pay for doc stamps on the deed?
    a. $596.40
    b. $660.00
    c. $720.00
    d. $840.00

95. A buyer bought a new home for $230,000. The lender agreed to loan the buyer $200,000 at 3½% interest with six points discount. What approximate yield will this provide the lender?
    a. 3.75%
    b. 4.00%
    c. 4.25%
    d. 4.50%

96. Which parcel contains 2½ acres of land?
    a. W½ of the NE¼ of the NW¼
    b. S½ of the NW¼ of the N½ of the NE¼
    c. SE¼ of the SW¼ of the SW¼
    d. SW¼ of the NE¼ of the NW¼ of the NE¼

97. A homesteaded property is located in Duval County, Florida. The city tax rate is 8.2 mills, the county tax rate is 9.0 mills, and the school tax rate is 7.3 mills. The homeowner has qualified for homestead exemption. The home has an assessed value of $230,000. What does the homeowner owe for property taxes?
    a. $3,096.00
    b. $4,410.00
    c. $4,592.50
    d. $5,022.50

98. A property owner asks a licensee to estimate the value of his office building prior to listing it for sale. The building is seven years old, and it would cost $90,000 to reproduce the structure new. The economic life of the structure is estimated at 40 years. The land is valued at $20,000. The owner paid $70,000 for the building and the land five years ago. What is the estimated value of the property?
    a. $98,750
    b. $94,250
    c. $90,750
    d. $81,250

99. Sales Associate A listed a parcel of undeveloped commercial property for $215,000. The agreed sale commission is 10% on the first $50,000, 5% on the next $100,000, and 3% on any balance. Sales Associate B sold the property for $210,000, and the owner paid the sale commission per the listing agreement. The broker paid the listing sales associate 10% of the total commission and split the remaining commission 65% to Sales Associate B and 35% to himself. What was Sales Associate B's commission?
    a. $7,670
    b. $6,903
    c. $4,130
    d. $3,717

100. On March 1, an investor bought a 10-unit apartment building for $360,000. The investor paid $72,000 in cash and obtained a 30-year mortgage in the amount of $288,000. A review of the accounts over the preceding two years revealed that vacancy and collection losses were stable at 4%. Potential gross income for the property is $70,400 and the operating expenses are $12,770, including reserve for replacements of $2,812. Mortgage payments are $2,742.71. Calculate the net operating income.
    a. $49,259
    b. $52,002
    c. $54,814
    d. $67,584

100 MULTIPLE-CHOICE QUESTION EXAM 2

Instructions. This second practice examination is designed to give you additional help in preparing for your state license examination. Mark your answer choices on the Answer Sheet provided on page 219. Explanations of the correct answers are provided in the Practice 2 Answer Key at the end of the book.

1. A grandmother decided she wanted to leave her summer cottage to her granddaughter, so she executed a general warranty deed to the property and gave it to her granddaughter. The grandmother died a few weeks later, prior to the recording of the deed. Which statement applies to this situation?
   a. The cottage is part of the grandmother's estate and must be probated.
   b. Title to the property was conveyed to the granddaughter when the grandmother executed and delivered the deed to her granddaughter.
   c. The deed must be recorded in order to convey title to the granddaughter.
   d. The granddaughter will have to pay inheritance taxes on the taxable value of the home prior to recording the deed.

2. An unlicensed personal assistant may perform which activity?
   a. Conduct listing presentations
   b. Show a listed home to a buyer
   c. Hand out objective, written information on a rental property
   d. Present an offer to the seller

3. A sales associate has not completed his continuing education prior to the expiration of his license. In a previous renewal cycle, the sales associate completed his post-licensing requirement. What should the sales associate do?
   a. Mail in his renewal card and fee prior to the expiration of his license and then do his continuing education requirement at the earliest opportunity.
   b. Complete his education requirement and send in the renewal fee, renewal application, late fee, and the appropriate DBPR form to reactivate his license.
   c. Complete 21 hours of in-class instruction.
   d. Retake the 45-hour post-licensing course.

4. A buyer is considering making an offer to purchase a 50-unit beachfront time-share development from the seller. The buyer and seller have requested that a licensed real estate sales associate act as a single agent representative for each of them. Which statement applies to this situation?
   a. The buyer and the seller must each have assets in excess of $1 million.
   b. The sales associate must give the buyer and seller the single agent disclosure.
   c. This arrangement is a violation of Chapter 475, F.S.
   d. Because this is residential property, it does not qualify for designated sales associate representation.

5. Which task is NOT required when implementing designated sales associates?
   a. The buyer and seller must each sign a disclosure notice stating that their assets meet the $1 million threshold.
   b. The designated sales associate disclosure notice must include language regarding how confidential information will be handled.
   c. The designated sales associate disclosure notice must include the duties of a single agent.
   d. The broker must retain the brokerage relationship disclosure documents for 10 years for all nonresidential transactions that close.

6. A sales associate regularly does cold calling for potential listings. The sales associate called a party who informed the associate that he was on the national do-not-call list and did not want to be disturbed. Which statement applies to this situation?
   a. The sales associate can be fined for calling a person who is listed on the do-not-call list.
   b. The sales associate made an honest mistake and should jot down the phone number so that she won't disturb the man again.
   c. Real estate licensees are not bound by the national do-not-call restrictions.
   d. As long as the sales associate initially identified herself and the name of the brokerage company for which she works, she has acted properly.

7. A sales associate decides to mail personalized notepads to the residents of a neighborhood. The notepads include the associate's photo, name, phone number, and email address. The sales associate paid the cost of printing and mailing the notepads. Which statement applies to this situation?
   a. The notepads are a form of real estate advertisement and, therefore, must include the name of the brokerage firm.
   b. The name of the brokerage firm is required in newspaper advertisements and For Sale signs only.
   c. Because the sales associate paid for the printing and mailing of the notepads, the associate can choose the wording and content.
   d. The sales associate needs to add the license status to the information printed on the notepads.

8. The seller accepted an offer on a home. The contract was contingent on several inspections. Several weeks prior to the closing, the sale fell through due to one of the inspections. Which statement is true regarding the retention of documents?
   a. The broker is not obligated to retain a copy of the property file because the transaction did not close.
   b. The broker is required to keep a copy of the property file for five years.
   c. The broker may dispose of the "dead files" after two years.
   d. The broker is only obligated to retain documentation regarding disbursement of the earnest money deposit.

9. A sales associate has become frustrated with buyers who use his time and expertise and then make an offer to purchase through another real estate company. To help "tie" prospective buyers to the sales associate, he requires prospective buyers to deposit $500 with the real estate company to show intent to deal through the sales associate's broker. If the buyer makes a purchase, the $500 is applied to the earnest money deposit. However, if the prospective buyer does not make a purchase, the deposit is forfeited. Which statement is true regarding this arrangement?
   a. This is a constructive way to prevent buyers from jumping from one sales associate to another.
   b. The $500 is an illegal kickback.
   c. The $500 is a trust fund and must be paid to his broker.
   d. The $500 is a referral fee.

10. A licensed real estate sales associate conducted an appraisal for a fee. The FREC found the licensee to be in violation of the *Uniform Standards of Professional Practice*. Which statement is TRUE?
   a. Real estate licensees are not required to abide by the *USPAP*.
   b. The licensee is subject to FREC discipline.
   c. Only the Appraisal Board can impose a penalty in this case—the FREC does not have authority over appraisal matters.
   d. Real estate sales associates may not conduct appraisals for a fee unless they are also certified or licensed real estate appraisers.

11. A sales associate and his former broker have a dispute over a commission. What recourse does the sales associate have to resolve the commission dispute?
   a. The sales associate can request the FREC to issue an escrow disbursement order.
   b. The sales associate can sue the principal named in the listing contract that is in dispute.
   c. The sales associate can sue his former broker and request the civil courts to resolve the matter.
   d. The sales associate can seek relief from the Real Estate Recovery Fund.

12. A broker purchased a list of FHA foreclosure properties from an employee of the FHA. The broker has promised to pay the FHA employee a percentage of all commissions earned by the brokerage company resulting from FHA foreclosure sales on the list.
   a. The broker has violated Chapter 475, F.S., by compensating an unlicensed person for performing services that require a real estate license.
   b. The broker may compensate a salaried employee of a government agency.
   c. FHA foreclosure properties are exempt from the Florida Real Estate License Law.
   d. The broker is allowed to compensate the FHA employee as long as the FHA employee does not provide real estate services to the buyer and seller.

13. Which requirement does NOT apply regarding dwellings built prior to 1978?
   a. Sellers and lessors must disclose the presence of known lead-based paint in residential dwellings.
   b. Sale contracts and leases must include specific lead-based paint warning and disclosure language.
   c. Buyers and tenants must acknowledge that they have received the warning and disclosure.
   d. Buyers must have the property inspected for lead-based paint.

14. A Florida broker is an active broker for Brokerage Company One as well as Brokerage Company Two. A sales associate for Brokerage Company One has procured a listing as a single agent to sell a condo. A sales associate for Brokerage Company Two is a single agent of a buyer who has entered into a contract to purchase the condo. Which applies?
    a. Because the Florida broker is the broker of both brokerage companies, this is an illegal dual agency relationship.
    b. This is a legal arrangement because two separate real estate firms are involved.
    c. The buyer and seller must agree to allow the Florida broker to transition to a transaction broker to complete this sale.
    d. The Florida broker has violated Chapter 475, F.S.

15. Broker Ellen Sammis of Newcomer Realty, Inc., is opening a real estate office. What information is NOT required on the exterior entrance sign?
    a. Ellen Sammis
    b. Licensed Real Estate Broker
    c. REALTOR®
    d. Newcomer Realty, Inc.

16. Buyer and seller have entered into a real estate contract. The broker neglected to include a closing date on the contract. Which statement is correct?
    a. This is a valid and enforceable contract.
    b. This is an unenforceable contract.
    c. The contract is void.
    d. The broker can be disciplined for fraud and misrepresentation.

17. A licensed real estate sales associate recently purchased a condo and moved out of the former apartment. Is the sales associate required to notify the DBPR?
    a. As long as the sales associate continues to work under the same broker, there is no need to notify the DBPR.
    b. The sales associate must notify the DBPR of the change in current mailing address within 10 days after the change.
    c. The sales associate must notify the Commission within 60 days of a change in residency.
    d. If the sales associate's license is inactive, the licensee is not required to notify the DBPR.

18. Two close friends own a nursery as joint tenants with right of survivorship. One owner died unexpectedly. Who now owns the nursery?
    a. If the deceased owner was married at the time of death, the deceased's interest in the nursery will descend to the surviving spouse.
    b. The surviving owner will have to wait until the deceased owner's estate is probated before taking sole ownership of the property.
    c. If the deceased owner has minor children, the children will receive a remainder estate for the deceased owner's interest in the nursery, and the surviving owner will take a life estate.
    d. The surviving owner becomes sole owner of the nursery by operation of law.

19. A broker wants to relocate a branch office's location. What is required?
    a. The broker must send a letter to the DBPR notifying it that the broker is transferring a branch office registration from one location to another.
    b. The broker must fill out a change of address form only.
    c. The broker must register the new location and pay the appropriate fee.
    d. The broker must register the new location without paying an additional fee.

20. A landlord owns a duplex that she rents to college students. The landlord has an inactive real estate license and collects the rent on her own behalf. Which statement is TRUE regarding this situation?
    a. The landlord is required to maintain deposit money and advance rents in compliance with the Florida Residential Landlord and Tenant Act.
    b. Because there are only two dwelling units, the landlord does not have to set aside rental deposits and advance rent.
    c. Because the landlord has a real estate license, she must secure the rental deposits in an escrow account.
    d. Owners are exempt from rental deposit requirements stipulated in the Florida Residential Landlord and Tenant Act.

21. A broker may NOT establish an escrow account in a Florida
    a. credit union.
    b. commercial bank.
    c. savings association.
    d. stock brokerage account.

22. A broker chooses not to maintain an escrow account. Which statement is TRUE regarding this situation?
    a. Brokers are required to maintain an escrow account.
    b. If the title company is handling the closing, the title company may hold the earnest money deposit in escrow.
    c. If an attorney is conducting the closing, the attorney may hold the deposit in escrow provided the broker is a signatory on the account.
    d. The broker is subject to disciplinary action by the FREC.

23. Discount points are
    a. a charge to financial lenders for borrowing from the Federal Reserve Bank.
    b. an up-front charge, usually paid by the developer to lower the buyer's mortgage interest rate for the first one to three years.
    c. up-front charges to the FHA for mortgage insurance.
    d. a charge by a lender to increase the interest yield on a mortgage.

24. A prospective tenant wants to install a ramp to the front door and handrails in the bathroom of a bungalow cottage. Which statement is TRUE?
    a. If the landlord is the property owner (no management company is involved), the owner does not have to allow the tenant to make modifications to the property.
    b. The owner is responsible for the cost of modifying the dwelling, provided the tenant agrees to sign a one-year (or longer) lease agreement.
    c. The tenant may make the modification at the tenant's expense.
    d. Owners of less than four units do not have to allow a tenant to make modifications to a residential dwelling.

25. The township located due East of T1N, R1E is
    a. T1N, R2E.
    b. T1N, R1W.
    c. T2N, R1E.
    d. T1S, R2E.

26. An applicant responded "No" to the question on the real estate application regarding whether the applicant had ever been found guilty of a crime. Four years ago, the applicant was divorced and became unemployed. He found another job a short time later but went ahead and cashed two unemployment checks totaling $700. The applicant went to court for illegally cashing the unemployment checks. The applicant repaid the $700 and adjudication of guilt was withheld. What action, if any, will the FREC likely take?
    a. Because the incident took place four years ago, the FREC will probably take no action.
    b. Because adjudication of guilt was withheld, the Commission will not have any information concerning the case.
    c. The Commission will likely consider this to be a case of obtaining a license by fraud, misrepresentation, or concealment and discipline the license, or deny a license if not yet issued.
    d. The FREC will likely issue a notice of noncompliance.

27. The subject property is a three-bedroom, two-bath home. A comparable property is a three-bedroom, two and one-half-bath home. An appraiser has determined that the extra half bath is worth about $2,200. What adjustment should the appraiser make?
    a. Subtract $2,200 from the estimated value of the subject property.
    b. Subtract $2,200 from the comparable's transaction price.
    c. Add $2,200 to the comparable's transaction price.
    d. Add $2,200 to the estimated value of the subject property.

28. At age 19, an applicant was charged with one count of petty theft. The 19-year old paid a fine during a 10-minute court proceeding and was not sentenced to probation or any other penalty. Nine years later, the applicant is completing the sales associate application. How should the applicant respond to the question on the application concerning whether the applicant has ever been convicted of a crime, found guilty, or entered a plea of guilty or no contest even if adjudication was withheld?
    a. The applicant was a minor when the incident occurred, so it was expunged at age 21.
    b. Because the applicant was not sentenced, there is no record of the petty theft, and therefore, the applicant does not need to disclose the incident on the application.
    c. The applicant must disclose the petty theft incident on the application.
    d. The crime will most likely not be discovered in the fingerprint check, so the applicant can simply answer "No" to the question on the application.

29. What is the maximum allowable homestead exemption for a 65-year-old widower who is legally blind?
    a. $25,500
    b. $30,500
    c. $50,500
    d. $51,000

30. A landlord has become frustrated that one of her tenants has not paid his rent, so while the tenant is away, the landlord has a locksmith change the locks on the apartment.
    a. The landlord is within her rights as a property owner-landlord to regain possession of the property.
    b. The landlord's actions are a violation of Florida's Landlord and Tenant Act.
    c. As long as the landlord posted a three-day notice and the three days have passed, she may legally change the locks.
    d. Only the sheriff may legally change the locks.

31. If a real estate sales associate fails to complete the 45-hour post-licensing course prior to the expiration of the initial license, what happens to the license?
    a. The license automatically reverts to an involuntary inactive license.
    b. The license remains inactive until the licensee completes the education requirement and pays a late fee.
    c. The license reverts to inactive status and the licensee is issued a notice of noncompliance.
    d. The license becomes null and void by operation of law.

32. Under the Truth in Lending Act, certain words trigger disclosures of the amount or percentage of down payment, the terms of repayment, and the annual percentage rate. Which statement is NOT a "triggering term"?
    a. The amount of down payment in a credit sale transaction
    b. The amount of any payment
    c. The number of payments
    d. The name of the lender

33. A commercial tenant pays a pro-rata share of the property taxes, hazard insurance, and utilities. The tenant has what type of lease?
    a. Net lease
    b. Expense lease
    c. Prorated lease
    d. Percentage lease

34. A prospective tenant was previously evicted for failure to pay rent. The prospective tenant has inspected another rental property and wishes to enter into a lease agreement with the landlord. May the landlord refuse to rent to this tenant?
    a. No, this would be a violation of the Fair Housing Act.
    b. Yes, provided the tenant is not disabled.
    c. Yes, based on the tenant's poor credit history.
    d. No, this would be a violation of the Fair Credit Act.

35. Which statement is TRUE regarding townships?
    a. A township is a parcel containing 36 square miles.
    b. A township contains 640 acres.
    c. Townships are a part of the metes-and-bounds method of legal description.
    d. Checks are smaller units that make up a township.

36. A customer obtained a judgment against a real estate licensee for negligent conduct involving a real estate brokerage transaction. The licensee had an inactive license at the time that the negligence occurred. If the customer is unable to collect on the judgment, can the customer be reimbursed from the Real Estate Recovery Fund?
    a. Yes, it is irrelevant that the real estate license was inactive.
    b. Yes, provided the amount of the claim does not exceed $50,000.
    c. No, the license must have been active when the incident occurred.
    d. No, because of negligence on the part of the licensee.

37. The Commission's authority to adopt administrative rules is an exercise of which power?
    a. Executive
    b. Administrative
    c. Quasi-judicial
    d. Quasi-legislative

38. A broker obtained a judgment from a Florida court against the seller for an unpaid commission. May the broker record the judgment?
    a. Real estate licensees are prohibited from doing anything that would create a lien on an owner's property.
    b. The broker is prohibited from recording a judgment against a principal.
    c. The broker's only recourse is to seek relief from the Real Estate Recovery Fund.
    d. The broker may record the judgment in the county where the debtor owns property.

39. The market value of a site is determined by its
    a. current use.
    b. zoning.
    c. highest and best use.
    d. physical characteristics.

40. The income approach to value requires collection of data pertaining to
    a. reproduction costs of improvements.
    b. expected future expenses.
    c. market evidence of depreciation.
    d. recent land sales.

41. Which survey method is used when developed subdivisions have been recorded?
    a. Survey method
    b. Lot and block method
    c. Subdivision method
    d. Metes-and-bounds method

42. If probable cause is found to exist, the probable-cause panel will direct the DBPR to file a formal complaint against the subject of the investigation. Which statement is TRUE?
    a. At this point the licensee will be scheduled to attend an informal hearing before the FREC.
    b. At this point the findings of the probable-cause panel are reduced to a stipulation and mailed to the licensee.
    c. The licensee is entitled to either a formal or informal hearing, or the licensee may agree to a stipulation.
    d. The FREC makes a determination regarding whether to dismiss the case.

43. A real estate licensee indicates on his business cards that he is a REALTOR®. However, the sales associate has not paid dues to the Florida Realtors® for two years and has allowed his membership to lapse. Can the FREC discipline this licensee for using the REALTOR® logo on his business cards?
    a. No, the FREC has no jurisdiction over the use of the term REALTOR®.
    b. Yes, the FREC can fine the licensee $300 for misrepresenting that he is a REALTOR®.
    c. No, only the Florida Realtors® can discipline this licensee.
    d. No, the term REALTOR® is used interchangeably with the term sales associate.

44. A court awarded a judgment against a broker for $30,000 actual damages and for $45,000 punitive damages regarding a real estate brokerage transaction. What is the claim available from the Real Estate Recovery Fund?
    a. $30,000
    b. $50,000
    c. $75,000
    d. $150,000

45. A sales associate finds a buyer for another brokerage firm's listing. The buyer gives the sales associate an earnest money deposit check made payable to the sales associate personally. What should the sales associate do?
    a. Deposit the check in her own account and then immediately write a check payable to the listing company.
    b. Put a limited endorsement on the back of the check to the listing broker's escrow account.
    c. Return the check to the buyer and request that the buyer make out a new check payable to the escrow account of the sales associate's broker.
    d. Cash the check and then turn the money over to the sales associate's employing broker.

46. Which parties constitute an arm's length transaction?
    a. Medallion Financial Services, Inc., to Medallion Taxi Enterprises, Inc.
    b. Mrs. Sammis, mother, to Dean Sammis, son
    c. Mr. Perez to Miss Root (not related)
    d. Microfirm, Inc., to Net, Inc. (Microfirm is a shareholder of Net, Inc.)

47. A property owner purchased a weather vane. The owner bolted the weather vane to the roof ridge. The weather vane is
    a. personal property.
    b. a fixture.
    c. constructive property.
    d. considered air rights.

48. A sales associate works for ABC Realty Company in Naples, Florida. While the sales associate is visiting a friend in St. Petersburg, she sees a waterfront lot listed by XYZ Realty. The sales associate sells the lot to her friend, and XYZ Realty pays the sales associate a 10% commission.
    a. As long as the sales associate's real estate license is active, it is legal for XYZ Realty to pay the sales associate a commission.
    b. The sales associate may be compensated by XYZ Realty because it is the listing company.
    c. For this transaction to be legal, the 10% commission must be classified as a finder's fee.
    d. Both the sales associate and the broker of XYZ have violated Florida's Real Estate License Law.

49. The process by which private property is acquired through judicial process to build a police station is called
    a. condemnation.
    b. escheat.
    c. foreclosure.
    d. hypothecation.

50. A property owner falls behind in paying his debts. He owns homesteaded property. The homesteaded property is protected from which debt?
    a. The tax collector's office for delinquent property taxes on the principal residence
    b. A pool company for an in-ground swimming pool at the owner's principal residence, which he charged on his credit card
    c. Delinquent mortgage payments on his principal residence
    d. An overdue installment loan to purchase furniture for his principal residence

51. A company pays the property owner rent in the amount of $500 per month plus 3% of gross sales revenue. The company has entered into what type of lease agreement?
    a. Gross lease
    b. Percentage lease
    c. Indexed lease
    d. Step-up lease

52. A buyer makes a written offer on a seller's property. The seller makes a counteroffer, which the buyer accepts. The listing broker conveys the buyer's written acceptance to the seller. At this point, the offer becomes
    a. an express contract.
    b. a parol contract.
    c. a ratified offer.
    d. a contingent contract.

53. Which expense associated with a principal residence is deductible for income tax purposes?
    a. Depreciation
    b. Operating expenses
    c. Maintenance costs
    d. Property taxes

54. A broker had an exclusive listing to sell a small apartment complex. The owner canceled the listing agreement before an offer was presented and then entered into a lease-management agreement with a third party. Is the broker entitled to a commission?
    a. Yes, because the seller has entered into an agreement with another broker
    b. Yes, if the broker can find a buyer for the property prior to the expiration date specified in the original listing agreement
    c. No, because the broker did not meet the conditions for payment of commission prior to the cancellation of the agreement
    d. No, because the broker did not have an exclusive right to lease agreement with the owner

55. Which business structure is designed to protect personal assets?
    a. General partnership
    b. Sole proprietorship
    c. Corporation
    d. Joint venture

56. A broker was served a citation. The broker wants to dispute the citation. Which statement applies to this situation?
    a. The broker may dispute the citation within 30 days of its being served.
    b. The broker must pay the fine and then petition for a reconsideration.
    c. The broker must pay the citation without challenge or risk further disciplinary action.
    d. The broker may dispute the citation by attending the next scheduled Commission meeting.

57. A sales associate applicant failed the state license exam. If the applicant desires to review the exam, the request must be received by the Division of Real Estate within what period of time?
    a. 15 days
    b. 21 days
    c. 30 days
    d. 45 days

58. A buyer made an offer to purchase and paid a $500 earnest money deposit. The seller accepted the offer. A few weeks later, the transaction fell through. Neither the buyer nor the seller has made a claim on the escrowed deposit. Attempts to contact the buyer and seller have been unsuccessful. What should the broker do with the earnest money deposit?
    a. The broker should give the buyer and seller at least one month to make a claim for the deposit.
    b. The broker should notify the FREC that the broker is holding abandoned funds.
    c. The broker should refund the deposit to the buyer because that is who paid the earnest money deposit.
    d. The broker must notify the FREC within 15 business days that the broker has a good-faith doubt.

59. A Florida-licensed broker wants to register an office located in New York City as her principal real estate office. May she do so?
   a. No, the brokerage office must be located within the State of Florida.
   b. Yes, a broker's principal office may be located outside the State of Florida as long as the broker's escrow account is maintained in a Florida institution.
   c. No, only a branch office may be located outside the State of Florida.
   d. Yes, a broker's registered principal office may be located outside the State of Florida. However, the broker must have all escrow funds held in trust by a Florida-based title company.

60. A property owner has two mortgage liens on his property. One lien was recorded on January 15, and the second lien was recorded on February 1 of the same year. What document would give the February 1 lien a higher priority?
   a. A deed-in-lieu of foreclosure
   b. An estoppel certificate
   c. A lis pendens
   d. A subordination agreement

61. The purpose of the Real Estate Settlement Procedures Act is to ensure
   a. uniform credit costs.
   b. that elderly applicants have an opportunity to secure long-term financing.
   c. that buyers are informed regarding the amount and type of charges they can expect at closing.
   d. that the annual percentage of interest is disclosed.

62. Can a real estate licensee working in a nonrepresentative role with a seller provide the seller a CMA?
   a. No, providing a CMA for a seller can only be done in a transaction broker or single agent capacity.
   b. No, providing a CMA would constitute a fiduciary relationship with the seller.
   c. Yes, provided the seller signs a notice that states that the seller will not construe the CMA to create an agency relationship.
   d. Yes, there is no restriction in Chapter 475, F.S., to prevent a licensee from preparing a CMA for a buyer or seller.

63. A married couple own homesteaded property in both their names. One spouse owns investment real estate in severalty. That spouse dies testate. Which statement is TRUE?
   a. Both the homestead and the investment property will be devised according to the will.
   b. The surviving spouse owns the principal residence and the investment property through right of survivorship.
   c. The surviving spouse owns the principal residence through right of survivorship, and the investment property will be devised according to the will.
   d. Both the principal residence and the investment property will be disbursed according to probate law.

64. A railroad track easement is which type of easement?
   a. Appurtenant
   b. Necessity
   c. Prescription
   d. In gross

65. An acknowledgment is a
   a. notary seal.
   b. recorded document.
   c. declaration by the signer that the signing is of her own free will.
   d. constructive notice.

66. A couple have been married for 40 years. One spouse is planning on retiring at age 60, and so the couple has decided to sell their spacious family home and buy a smaller condo. How does the current tax law affect their capital gains on the sale of their family home?
   a. The couple can take their one-time tax exclusion on the gain from the sale of their home.
   b. As long as the couple meets the two-year principal-residence test, they may exclude up to $500,000 of gain when they sell the home, if filing jointly.
   c. The couple must pay all of the deferred gain on the previous homes. However, any gain on their current residence is excluded up to $500,000, if filing jointly.
   d. The couple must pay a reduced long-term capital gain on the rollover only.

67. A mortgage must include
   a. a due-on-sale clause.
   b. a legal description.
   c. a granting clause.
   d. the mortgagee's signature.

68. A broker receives a $100 referral fee from a title company for every transaction that closes through the title company. Because of this, the broker has inserted a sentence into his standard contract for sale and purchase requiring the buyer to use that particular title company. Which statement(s) applies to this situation?
   a. This is a legal referral fee because the title company is disclosed to the buyer and seller in the sale and purchase agreement.
   b. The broker has violated the Florida Fair Housing Act.
   c. The title company has violated the Truth in Lending Act.
   d. Both the broker and the title company have violated the Real Estate Settlement Procedures Act.

69. The statement that there must be at least a two-hour fire wall rating between attached common walls would most likely appear in the
   a. zoning code.
   b. building code.
   c. condominium documents.
   d. deed restrictions.

70. Which statement is FALSE regarding Florida Real Estate Commissioners?
   a. One of the Commissioners must be a consumer (unlicensed or lay) member who has never held a Florida real estate license.
   b. At least one of the Commissioners must be 60 years of age or older.
   c. One Commissioner must be either a Florida real estate broker or sales associate who has held an active license during the two years preceding appointment.
   d. Commissioners may not serve more than two consecutive four-year terms.

71. Variables that influence demand do NOT include
    a. availability of mortgage credit.
    b. population size and household composition.
    c. availability of skilled labor.
    d. consumer tastes or preferences.

72. Which valuation product MUST be prepared by a licensed or certified appraiser?
    a. Broker's price opinion
    b. Appraisal to originate a federally related loan
    c. Valuation for an estate sale
    d. Comparative market analysis for a listing presentation

73. Which individual is required to have a real estate license?
    a. A mortgage broker working for a lender in the loan processing department
    b. A property manager who is paid an annual salary
    c. A broker who exclusively markets business opportunities
    d. A person who sells cemetery lots

74. A written disclosure form is NOT required regarding which brokerage relationship?
    a. Create a transaction broker relationship
    b. Transition from single agent to transaction broker
    c. Appoint designated sales associates in a qualifying nonresidential transaction
    d. Written disclosures are required for all of the brokerage relationships described above

75. A transaction broker does NOT have which duty?
    a. Accounting for all funds
    b. Disclosing all known facts that materially affect the value of residential real property and are not readily observable to the buyer
    c. Using skill, care, and diligence in the transaction
    d. Loyalty

76. If a broker receives conflicting demands on escrowed property, the broker must notify the FREC, in writing, within 15 business days of the last demand and institute one of four settlement procedures *unless* the transaction
    a. concerns a time-share unit.
    b. concerns a residential sale contract on HUD-owned property.
    c. involves commercial real estate.
    d. concerns the sale of a business opportunity on leased land.

77. The broker of record for a real estate company is working with a buyer as a buyer's single agent. The buyer has become interested in a property listed by the brokerage as a transaction broker. Which statement applies to this situation?
    a. The real estate company may serve as a transaction broker with the seller and as a single agent for the buyer to complete this transaction.
    b. The broker must appoint a designated sales associate to represent the buyer before completing the transaction.
    c. The real estate company cannot be a transaction broker for one party and a single agent for the other party.
    d. The broker may complete the transaction but he can only collect a commission from the buyer.

78. Which action will NOT terminate a real estate contract?
    a. Assignment
    b. Performance
    c. Breach
    d. Lapse of time

79. A Presbyterian church owns a nursing home for its members. The church admits only church members to the nursing facility. Is this legal?
    a. No, this is a violation of the Fair Housing Act.
    b. Yes, the church is exempt under the Fair Housing Act and may restrict the use of the facility to its members.
    c. The church has violated the Civil Rights Act of 1866.
    d. The church may only exclude others if they paid cash for the facility and did not finance the purchase of the nursing home facility.

80. An individual is eligible to seek recovery from the Real Estate Recovery Fund if
    a. the seller was an active licensed sales associate selling the home for-sale-by-owner.
    b. at the time the real estate contract was executed, the sales associate's license was in inactive status.
    c. the claim is based on a final judgment against the active licensee involved in a real estate brokerage transaction.
    d. the individual wishes to avoid a court process.

81. A tenant rents a college apartment and pays rent on the tenth of every month. The tenant has a written agreement with the property owner; however, there is no specified termination date. Which statement is TRUE?
    a. The tenant is a tenant at sufferance.
    b. The tenant must be given at least 15 days' notice to vacate prior to the end of the monthly period.
    c. The tenant is a holdover tenant.
    d. The tenant must be given 30 days' notice to vacate if the owner wants to end the lease.

82. A previous owner has stipulated that future owners of a tract of land may not operate any type of business on the property that produces a toxic substance of any kind and might potentially harm a natural spring on the property. Where would a real estate licensee interested in listing this property find this information?
    a. EPA property report
    b. Local zoning code
    c. Deed restrictions
    d. Survey of the property

83. When using the metes-and-bounds method of legal description, the fixed objects used to identify the corners of a parcel are called
    a. point of beginning (POB).
    b. monuments.
    c. the primary reference line.
    d. datum.

84. The following are paired relationships EXCEPT
 a. 36 sections—1 township.
 b. 24 miles square—check.
 c. range—north-south.
 d. meridian—east-west.

85. Two friends discuss the purchase and sale of a tract of land over a beer one Friday night. They jot down the sale price and other terms and conditions on a bar napkin and they put their signatures on the napkin. This is
 a. an unenforceable contract.
 b. a valid contract.
 c. a parol contract.
 d. an offer.

86. A buyer makes an offer to purchase a home built in the early 1970s that is listed by a real estate company. Prior to signing the contract for purchase and sale, what MUST occur?
 a. The buyer must give an earnest money deposit to the broker.
 b. The seller must disclose any known presence of lead-based paint in the home.
 c. The buyer must sign a release waiving the right to a paint inspection.
 d. The buyer must have the home inspected for lead-based paint.

87. If a prospective buyer suspects that there is an encroachment on a property the buyer is considering purchasing, to which document should the buyer refer?
 a. A recent survey
 b. Seller's deed
 c. Title insurance policy
 d. Blueprints

88. Which entity may NOT register as a real estate broker?
 a. Nonprofit corporation
 b. Sole proprietorship
 c. Corporation sole
 d. Limited liability partnership

89. If the Fed wants to stimulate a sluggish economy, it may choose to
 a. raise the reserve requirement.
 b. sell securities in the open market.
 c. decrease the prime rate.
 d. lower the discount rate.

90. Three individuals purchase a property with no right of survivorship. Their estate is referred to as a
 a. joint tenancy.
 b. leasehold estate.
 c. tenancy in common.
 d. tenancy by the entireties.

91. Annual property taxes are $1,460. Closing is June 1. Use the 365-day method of proration. Charge day of closing to the buyer. How is the proration entered on the closing disclosure?
   a. Debit seller $608, credit buyer $608
   b. Debit buyer $856, credit seller $604
   c. Debit buyer $856, credit seller $856
   d. Debit seller $604, credit buyer $604

92. A property sold two years ago for $120,000. An appraiser estimates that properties in the market area where the parcel is located have appreciated 5% annually. How much is the property worth today, assuming no other factors?
   a. $126,000
   b. $132,000
   c. $132,300
   d. $144,000

93. The adjusted sale prices of three comparables are $87,900, $88,500, and $82,750. The appraiser applies weights of 30%, 50%, and 20%, respectively. Calculate the indicated value of the subject property.
   a. $86,383
   b. $87,170
   c. $87,950
   d. $88,100

94. An investor owns a 30-unit apartment complex that produces a net monthly rental income of $9,200. This monthly income represents a 9.5% annual return for the owner during the first year of ownership. What did the investor pay for the building? (Round to the nearest dollar.)
   a. $96,842
   b. $116,211
   c. $1,042,100
   d. $1,162,105

95. The N½ of the NE¼ of the SW¼ and the S½ of the SE¼ of a section contains
   a. 2.5 acres.
   b. 20 acres.
   c. 80 acres.
   d. 100 acres.

96. A 130-unit apartment complex contains 80 one-bedroom apartments that rent for $750 per month and 50 two-bedroom apartments that rent for $950 per month. The one-bedroom units are 10% vacant, and the two-bedroom units are 5% vacant. Calculate the projected annual effective gross income for this investment property.
   a. $107,500
   b. $1,189,500
   c. $1,290,000
   d. $1,344,000

97. A sales associate sells a property for $98,500. The listing broker has agreed to pay the sales associate's broker 40% of the total sale commission of 8%. The sales associate receives 55% of all commissions the sales associate earns. How much commission did the sales associate receive?
    a. $1,418.40
    b. $1,733.60
    c. $2,127.60
    d. $2,600.40

98. The city is proposing to pave the streets in your neighborhood at a cost of $47 per foot. The city will absorb 30% of the cost. Your lot has a front footage of 110 feet. Assuming there are homes on both sides of the street, calculate the amount of your paving assessment.
    a. $1,551.50
    b. $1,809.50
    c. $3,619
    d. $5,170

99. The loan-to-value ratio offered by a local financial institution is 75%. If a buyer wishes to acquire a property selling for $129,500, the buyer will need to make a down payment of
    a. $1,727.
    b. $5,180.
    c. $32,375.
    d. $97,125.

100. The monthly payment for principal and interest on a $92,000 loan at 7½% for 30 years is $643.28. What amount of the second month's payment will be applied to principal?
    a. $68.28
    b. $68.71
    c. $574.57
    d. $575

ANSWER SHEET

PRACTICE EXAM 1

Score: ____________________

Wrong Ways to mark answers:

✔ Ⓧ ⊙ O

RIGHT WAY to mark answers:

●

1 Ⓐ Ⓑ Ⓒ Ⓓ	21 Ⓐ Ⓑ Ⓒ Ⓓ	41 Ⓐ Ⓑ Ⓒ Ⓓ	61 Ⓐ Ⓑ Ⓒ Ⓓ	81 Ⓐ Ⓑ Ⓒ Ⓓ
2 Ⓐ Ⓑ Ⓒ Ⓓ	22 Ⓐ Ⓑ Ⓒ Ⓓ	42 Ⓐ Ⓑ Ⓒ Ⓓ	62 Ⓐ Ⓑ Ⓒ Ⓓ	82 Ⓐ Ⓑ Ⓒ Ⓓ
3 Ⓐ Ⓑ Ⓒ Ⓓ	23 Ⓐ Ⓑ Ⓒ Ⓓ	43 Ⓐ Ⓑ Ⓒ Ⓓ	63 Ⓐ Ⓑ Ⓒ Ⓓ	83 Ⓐ Ⓑ Ⓒ Ⓓ
4 Ⓐ Ⓑ Ⓒ Ⓓ	24 Ⓐ Ⓑ Ⓒ Ⓓ	44 Ⓐ Ⓑ Ⓒ Ⓓ	64 Ⓐ Ⓑ Ⓒ Ⓓ	84 Ⓐ Ⓑ Ⓒ Ⓓ
5 Ⓐ Ⓑ Ⓒ Ⓓ	25 Ⓐ Ⓑ Ⓒ Ⓓ	45 Ⓐ Ⓑ Ⓒ Ⓓ	65 Ⓐ Ⓑ Ⓒ Ⓓ	85 Ⓐ Ⓑ Ⓒ Ⓓ
6 Ⓐ Ⓑ Ⓒ Ⓓ	26 Ⓐ Ⓑ Ⓒ Ⓓ	46 Ⓐ Ⓑ Ⓒ Ⓓ	66 Ⓐ Ⓑ Ⓒ Ⓓ	86 Ⓐ Ⓑ Ⓒ Ⓓ
7 Ⓐ Ⓑ Ⓒ Ⓓ	27 Ⓐ Ⓑ Ⓒ Ⓓ	47 Ⓐ Ⓑ Ⓒ Ⓓ	67 Ⓐ Ⓑ Ⓒ Ⓓ	87 Ⓐ Ⓑ Ⓒ Ⓓ
8 Ⓐ Ⓑ Ⓒ Ⓓ	28 Ⓐ Ⓑ Ⓒ Ⓓ	48 Ⓐ Ⓑ Ⓒ Ⓓ	68 Ⓐ Ⓑ Ⓒ Ⓓ	88 Ⓐ Ⓑ Ⓒ Ⓓ
9 Ⓐ Ⓑ Ⓒ Ⓓ	29 Ⓐ Ⓑ Ⓒ Ⓓ	49 Ⓐ Ⓑ Ⓒ Ⓓ	69 Ⓐ Ⓑ Ⓒ Ⓓ	89 Ⓐ Ⓑ Ⓒ Ⓓ
10 Ⓐ Ⓑ Ⓒ Ⓓ	30 Ⓐ Ⓑ Ⓒ Ⓓ	50 Ⓐ Ⓑ Ⓒ Ⓓ	70 Ⓐ Ⓑ Ⓒ Ⓓ	90 Ⓐ Ⓑ Ⓒ Ⓓ
11 Ⓐ Ⓑ Ⓒ Ⓓ	31 Ⓐ Ⓑ Ⓒ Ⓓ	51 Ⓐ Ⓑ Ⓒ Ⓓ	71 Ⓐ Ⓑ Ⓒ Ⓓ	91 Ⓐ Ⓑ Ⓒ Ⓓ
12 Ⓐ Ⓑ Ⓒ Ⓓ	32 Ⓐ Ⓑ Ⓒ Ⓓ	52 Ⓐ Ⓑ Ⓒ Ⓓ	72 Ⓐ Ⓑ Ⓒ Ⓓ	92 Ⓐ Ⓑ Ⓒ Ⓓ
13 Ⓐ Ⓑ Ⓒ Ⓓ	33 Ⓐ Ⓑ Ⓒ Ⓓ	53 Ⓐ Ⓑ Ⓒ Ⓓ	73 Ⓐ Ⓑ Ⓒ Ⓓ	93 Ⓐ Ⓑ Ⓒ Ⓓ
14 Ⓐ Ⓑ Ⓒ Ⓓ	34 Ⓐ Ⓑ Ⓒ Ⓓ	54 Ⓐ Ⓑ Ⓒ Ⓓ	74 Ⓐ Ⓑ Ⓒ Ⓓ	94 Ⓐ Ⓑ Ⓒ Ⓓ
15 Ⓐ Ⓑ Ⓒ Ⓓ	35 Ⓐ Ⓑ Ⓒ Ⓓ	55 Ⓐ Ⓑ Ⓒ Ⓓ	75 Ⓐ Ⓑ Ⓒ Ⓓ	95 Ⓐ Ⓑ Ⓒ Ⓓ
16 Ⓐ Ⓑ Ⓒ Ⓓ	36 Ⓐ Ⓑ Ⓒ Ⓓ	56 Ⓐ Ⓑ Ⓒ Ⓓ	76 Ⓐ Ⓑ Ⓒ Ⓓ	96 Ⓐ Ⓑ Ⓒ Ⓓ
17 Ⓐ Ⓑ Ⓒ Ⓓ	37 Ⓐ Ⓑ Ⓒ Ⓓ	57 Ⓐ Ⓑ Ⓒ Ⓓ	77 Ⓐ Ⓑ Ⓒ Ⓓ	97 Ⓐ Ⓑ Ⓒ Ⓓ
18 Ⓐ Ⓑ Ⓒ Ⓓ	38 Ⓐ Ⓑ Ⓒ Ⓓ	58 Ⓐ Ⓑ Ⓒ Ⓓ	78 Ⓐ Ⓑ Ⓒ Ⓓ	98 Ⓐ Ⓑ Ⓒ Ⓓ
19 Ⓐ Ⓑ Ⓒ Ⓓ	39 Ⓐ Ⓑ Ⓒ Ⓓ	59 Ⓐ Ⓑ Ⓒ Ⓓ	79 Ⓐ Ⓑ Ⓒ Ⓓ	99 Ⓐ Ⓑ Ⓒ Ⓓ
20 Ⓐ Ⓑ Ⓒ Ⓓ	40 Ⓐ Ⓑ Ⓒ Ⓓ	60 Ⓐ Ⓑ Ⓒ Ⓓ	80 Ⓐ Ⓑ Ⓒ Ⓓ	100 Ⓐ Ⓑ Ⓒ Ⓓ

ANSWER SHEET

PRACTICE EXAM 2

Score: ____________________

Wrong Ways to mark answers:

✔ Ⓧ ⊙ Ⓞ

RIGHT WAY to mark answers:

1 Ⓐ Ⓑ Ⓒ Ⓓ	21 Ⓐ Ⓑ Ⓒ Ⓓ	41 Ⓐ Ⓑ Ⓒ Ⓓ	61 Ⓐ Ⓑ Ⓒ Ⓓ	81 Ⓐ Ⓑ Ⓒ Ⓓ
2 Ⓐ Ⓑ Ⓒ Ⓓ	22 Ⓐ Ⓑ Ⓒ Ⓓ	42 Ⓐ Ⓑ Ⓒ Ⓓ	62 Ⓐ Ⓑ Ⓒ Ⓓ	82 Ⓐ Ⓑ Ⓒ Ⓓ
3 Ⓐ Ⓑ Ⓒ Ⓓ	23 Ⓐ Ⓑ Ⓒ Ⓓ	43 Ⓐ Ⓑ Ⓒ Ⓓ	63 Ⓐ Ⓑ Ⓒ Ⓓ	83 Ⓐ Ⓑ Ⓒ Ⓓ
4 Ⓐ Ⓑ Ⓒ Ⓓ	24 Ⓐ Ⓑ Ⓒ Ⓓ	44 Ⓐ Ⓑ Ⓒ Ⓓ	64 Ⓐ Ⓑ Ⓒ Ⓓ	84 Ⓐ Ⓑ Ⓒ Ⓓ
5 Ⓐ Ⓑ Ⓒ Ⓓ	25 Ⓐ Ⓑ Ⓒ Ⓓ	45 Ⓐ Ⓑ Ⓒ Ⓓ	65 Ⓐ Ⓑ Ⓒ Ⓓ	85 Ⓐ Ⓑ Ⓒ Ⓓ
6 Ⓐ Ⓑ Ⓒ Ⓓ	26 Ⓐ Ⓑ Ⓒ Ⓓ	46 Ⓐ Ⓑ Ⓒ Ⓓ	66 Ⓐ Ⓑ Ⓒ Ⓓ	86 Ⓐ Ⓑ Ⓒ Ⓓ
7 Ⓐ Ⓑ Ⓒ Ⓓ	27 Ⓐ Ⓑ Ⓒ Ⓓ	47 Ⓐ Ⓑ Ⓒ Ⓓ	67 Ⓐ Ⓑ Ⓒ Ⓓ	87 Ⓐ Ⓑ Ⓒ Ⓓ
8 Ⓐ Ⓑ Ⓒ Ⓓ	28 Ⓐ Ⓑ Ⓒ Ⓓ	48 Ⓐ Ⓑ Ⓒ Ⓓ	68 Ⓐ Ⓑ Ⓒ Ⓓ	88 Ⓐ Ⓑ Ⓒ Ⓓ
9 Ⓐ Ⓑ Ⓒ Ⓓ	29 Ⓐ Ⓑ Ⓒ Ⓓ	49 Ⓐ Ⓑ Ⓒ Ⓓ	69 Ⓐ Ⓑ Ⓒ Ⓓ	89 Ⓐ Ⓑ Ⓒ Ⓓ
10 Ⓐ Ⓑ Ⓒ Ⓓ	30 Ⓐ Ⓑ Ⓒ Ⓓ	50 Ⓐ Ⓑ Ⓒ Ⓓ	70 Ⓐ Ⓑ Ⓒ Ⓓ	90 Ⓐ Ⓑ Ⓒ Ⓓ
11 Ⓐ Ⓑ Ⓒ Ⓓ	31 Ⓐ Ⓑ Ⓒ Ⓓ	51 Ⓐ Ⓑ Ⓒ Ⓓ	71 Ⓐ Ⓑ Ⓒ Ⓓ	91 Ⓐ Ⓑ Ⓒ Ⓓ
12 Ⓐ Ⓑ Ⓒ Ⓓ	32 Ⓐ Ⓑ Ⓒ Ⓓ	52 Ⓐ Ⓑ Ⓒ Ⓓ	72 Ⓐ Ⓑ Ⓒ Ⓓ	92 Ⓐ Ⓑ Ⓒ Ⓓ
13 Ⓐ Ⓑ Ⓒ Ⓓ	33 Ⓐ Ⓑ Ⓒ Ⓓ	53 Ⓐ Ⓑ Ⓒ Ⓓ	73 Ⓐ Ⓑ Ⓒ Ⓓ	93 Ⓐ Ⓑ Ⓒ Ⓓ
14 Ⓐ Ⓑ Ⓒ Ⓓ	34 Ⓐ Ⓑ Ⓒ Ⓓ	54 Ⓐ Ⓑ Ⓒ Ⓓ	74 Ⓐ Ⓑ Ⓒ Ⓓ	94 Ⓐ Ⓑ Ⓒ Ⓓ
15 Ⓐ Ⓑ Ⓒ Ⓓ	35 Ⓐ Ⓑ Ⓒ Ⓓ	55 Ⓐ Ⓑ Ⓒ Ⓓ	75 Ⓐ Ⓑ Ⓒ Ⓓ	95 Ⓐ Ⓑ Ⓒ Ⓓ
16 Ⓐ Ⓑ Ⓒ Ⓓ	36 Ⓐ Ⓑ Ⓒ Ⓓ	56 Ⓐ Ⓑ Ⓒ Ⓓ	76 Ⓐ Ⓑ Ⓒ Ⓓ	96 Ⓐ Ⓑ Ⓒ Ⓓ
17 Ⓐ Ⓑ Ⓒ Ⓓ	37 Ⓐ Ⓑ Ⓒ Ⓓ	57 Ⓐ Ⓑ Ⓒ Ⓓ	77 Ⓐ Ⓑ Ⓒ Ⓓ	97 Ⓐ Ⓑ Ⓒ Ⓓ
18 Ⓐ Ⓑ Ⓒ Ⓓ	38 Ⓐ Ⓑ Ⓒ Ⓓ	58 Ⓐ Ⓑ Ⓒ Ⓓ	78 Ⓐ Ⓑ Ⓒ Ⓓ	98 Ⓐ Ⓑ Ⓒ Ⓓ
19 Ⓐ Ⓑ Ⓒ Ⓓ	39 Ⓐ Ⓑ Ⓒ Ⓓ	59 Ⓐ Ⓑ Ⓒ Ⓓ	79 Ⓐ Ⓑ Ⓒ Ⓓ	99 Ⓐ Ⓑ Ⓒ Ⓓ
20 Ⓐ Ⓑ Ⓒ Ⓓ	40 Ⓐ Ⓑ Ⓒ Ⓓ	60 Ⓐ Ⓑ Ⓒ Ⓓ	80 Ⓐ Ⓑ Ⓒ Ⓓ	100 Ⓐ Ⓑ Ⓒ Ⓓ

SAMPLE EXAM QUESTIONS

Answers to 511 multiple-choice sample exam questions are grouped in the sequence license law, general law, principles and practices, and math. The unit number (in parentheses) indicates where the question topics can be found in the textbooks *Florida Real Estate Principles, Practices & Law* and *Florida Real Estate Broker's Guide*. The correct letter answer is followed by a brief explanation of the correct answer.

REAL ESTATE LAW, FLORIDA REAL ESTATE LICENSE LAW SECTIONS

Real Estate License Law and Qualifications for Licensure: Florida Real Estate Principles, Practices & Law (Unit 2); Florida Real Estate Broker's Guide (Unit 1)

1. c An individual who does not intend to engage actively in the real estate business, such as an officer of a real estate corporation, simply registers this information with the DBPR so that the information can be entered into the DRE's records.
2. d Section 475.01, F.S., defines a broker associate as, "a person who is qualified to be issued a license as a broker but who operates as a sales associate in the employ of another."
3. c A spouse or a surviving spouse who holds a valid real estate license from another state or foreign jurisdiction, upon application, must be issued a Florida license.
4. b Nonresident applicants and licensees must comply with all F.S. 475 requirements and FREC rules.
5. b An individual who has earned a four-year or higher real estate degree is exempt from the sales associate and broker prelicense courses and post-license education requirements; however, the individual is required each renewal period to complete the continuing education requirement.
6. a There are eight real estate services (A BAR SALE): advertise, buy, appraise, rent or provide rental lists (information), sell, auction, lease, and exchange.
7. c Pursuant to 61J2-26.001, F.A.C., mutual recognition agreements apply exclusively to nonresidents licensed in other jurisdictions.
8. b A sales associate or broker associate may have only one registered employer at any time.
9. a Proof of U.S. citizenship is not required to hold a Florida real estate license.
10. c Pursuant to Section 475.011, F.S., persons acting within the limitations of their duties as designated by a will, proper court, or statutory authority to serve as a personal representative or trustee are specifically exempted from licensure.
11. c There is no legislative authority to extend the post-license requirement beyond six months.
12. b Section 475.181, F.S., states that if an applicant does not pass the licensing examination within two years after the successful course completion date, the applicant's successful course completion is invalid for licensure.
13. a Prima facie evidence is a legal term used to refer to evidence that is good and sufficient on its face to establish a given fact or prove a case.
14. b Florida Statute 455 governs the DBPR and the professions regulated by the DBPR.
15. d An owner-developer is an unlicensed entity that sells, leases, or exchanges its own property.

Real Estate License Law and Commission Rules: Florida Real Estate Principles, Practices & Law (Unit 3); Florida Real Estate Broker's Guide (Unit 1)

16. c The governor, subject to confirmation by the state Senate, appoints FREC members to four-year terms. Florida statutes prohibit Commission members from serving more than two consecutive terms.
17. d The FREC's quasi-legislative responsibilities include the power to enact administrative rules and regulations.

18. c The director of the DRE is appointed by the secretary of the DBPR, subject to approval by majority vote of the FREC.

19. a The Commission is obligated to report any criminal violation of Chapter 475, when knowledgeable of such violations, to the state's attorney having jurisdiction.

20. d The powers of the FREC are limited to administrative matters and do not extend to criminal actions. The FREC cannot impose imprisonment as a penalty.

21. c Individuals who previously qualified for current license status but who do not renew their licenses before they expire are placed on involuntary inactive status.

22. d A member of the U.S. Armed Forces who, at the time of entry to active duty, was a Florida licensee in good standing, is exempt from all renewal requirements while on active duty and for two years thereafter. When the military duty is out of state, the exemption also applies to a licensed spouse.

23. c Licensees who have been involuntary inactive for more than 12 months but less than 24 months are required to complete 28 hours of a Commission-prescribed education course.

24. c A sales associate's license is placed in involuntary inactive status when an employer's license is suspended or revoked. The sales associate is, however, registered under another broker as soon as new employment is secured.

25. d A Florida broker may be issued, on request, additional Florida broker licenses whenever it is shown that the additional licenses are necessary to the conduct of business. A broker who holds more than one Florida broker license is said to hold multiple licenses.

26. c FREC's quasi-judicial responsibilities include the power to grant or deny license applications, to determine license law violations, and to administer penalties.

27. b The owner-developer does not have to hold a real estate license to sell the owner-developer's lots, but if the owner-developer employs licensed sales associates, the owner-developer must register with the DBPR. This creates a "pseudo number" under which the sales associates can register.

28. b When a broker changes business address, the brokerage firm permit holder must file with the DBPR a notice of the change of address, along with the names of any sales associates who are no longer employed by the brokerage. Sales associates who are no longer employed with the broker of record are placed in involuntary inactive status.

Authorized Relationships, Duties, and Disclosure: Florida Real Estate Principles, Practices & Law (Unit 4); Florida Real Estate Broker's Guide (Unit 10)

29. d Personal medical information must not be disclosed without the seller's prior authorization. Florida statute mandates the fact that a property was, or was at any time suspected to have been, the site of a homicide, suicide, or death is not a material fact in a real estate transaction.

30. b A special agent is authorized by the buyer or seller to handle only a specific business transaction or to perform only a specific act. A real estate broker, in a single agent relationship, typically is authorized by the buyer or seller to act as a special agent.

31. a The broker must retain one legible copy of the contract and any brokerage relationship disclosures required by Chapter 475, F.S., for five years. This requirement applies to any written contract to purchase and sell real property, even if the contract fails to close.

32. b The broker and the broker's sales associates are obligated to follow the lawful instructions of the owner.

33. c An agency relationship exists between a broker and a sales associate (agent) who is either an employee of or an independent contractor of the broker (principal). The sales associate is obligated to act in conformity with the broker's instructions as long as they are legal and relevant to the contractual relationship. Otherwise, the sales associate should withdraw from the relationship.

34. d The broker must provide the single agent notice to the seller before, or at the time of, entering into a listing agreement.

35. b A sales associate or broker associate owes the same fiduciary obligations to the principal as does the broker, regardless of whether the associate, for tax purposes, is an employee or an independent contractor.

36. c The licensee must secure the written consent and approval of the seller (or buyer, if the licensee is a buyer's agent) before transitioning to another relationship.

37. b The disclosures do not apply to the rental or leasing of real property, unless an option to purchase all or a portion of the property improved with four or fewer residential units is involved.

38. d Dual agency is prohibited under 475.272(1), F.S.

39. c Transaction brokers have a duty of limited confidentiality, unless waived in writing. This limited confidentiality will prevent disclosure that the seller will accept a price less than the asking or listing price, the motivation of any party for buying or selling property, or any other information requested by a party to remain confidential. The licensee should inform the seller that to use race as a basis for making a decision whether or not to accept an offer is a violation of Fair Housing Laws.

40. c Undivided loyalty, full disclosure, and obedience are single agent duties. Transaction brokers have a duty to disclose all known facts that materially affect the value of real property and are not readily observable to the buyer (latent defects).

41. a In nonresidential transactions involving a buyer and seller who each have assets of $1 million or more, the broker at the request of the buyer and seller may designate sales associates to act as single agents for different customers in the same transaction. Such designated sales associates have the duties of a single agent, including disclosure requirements.

42. b A broker in a no brokerage relationship has a duty to account for all funds entrusted to the broker with regard to a real estate transaction. Loyalty, obedience, and confidentiality are single agent duties.

43. c Common law is law based on usage, general acceptance, and custom.

44. c *Caveat emptor* is a Latin term meaning "let the buyer beware."

Real Estate Brokerage Activities and Procedures: Florida Real Estate Principles, Practices & Law (Unit 5); Florida Real Estate Broker's Guide (Units 2 and 4)

45. d Yard signs and classified ads must include the registered name of the brokerage firm.

46. a Antitrust laws prohibit brokers from splitting up market areas so they do not compete with each other. This illegal activity is known as market allocation.

47. c A "broker associate" is a person who is qualified to be licensed as a broker, but who operates as a sales associate. Therefore, the licensee must use the full title, "broker associate" on her business card.

48. d Because a licensee has superior knowledge and expertise in real estate, the "by owner" licensee-seller, to reduce liability, should disclose at the first point of meaningful negotiation that the seller is a real estate licensee.

49. a Commingling of funds is the illegal practice of mixing a buyer's or seller's funds with the broker's own money or of mixing escrow money with the broker's personal funds or business funds.

50. c In the case of a corporation, brokerage entrance signs must contain the name of the corporation, the name of at least one of the active brokers, and the words "Licensed Real Estate Broker" or "Lic. Real Estate Broker."

51. c The broker must deposit the funds by the end of business on the third business day. The three-day period begins on Tuesday.

52. b If a broker receives conflicting demands on escrowed property, the broker must notify the FREC, in writing, within 15 business days of the party's last demand.

53. d Acceptable depositories for escrow accounts are Florida-based title companies having trust powers, Florida commercial banks, credit unions, and savings associations, or, if designated in the sale contract, a Florida attorney.

54. b Real estate licensees are prohibited from sharing commission with an unlicensed person. However, Florida law does allow the sharing of part of the commission with the buyer or seller in a real estate transaction.

55. c Florida's Telemarketing Act and the Telephone Consumer Protection Act restrict solicitation calls to the hours of 8:00 am to 9:00 pm.

56. a The FREC may choose not to issue an escrow disbursement order (EDO). If the broker is informed in writing by the Commission that an EDO will not be issued, the broker must use another settlement procedure: mediation, arbitration, or litigation.

57. d According to Rule 61J2-14.0110(1), Florida Administrative Code (FAC), at least one broker of a brokerage firm must be a signatory on the escrow account. The broker may hire someone else to prepare the monthly reconciliation statements; however, the broker must review, sign, and date the statements.

58. d It is illegal for a licensee to pay an unlicensed person any sum of money for the referral of real estate business.

59. b There are three exceptions to the notice requirements: (1) escrow deposits concerning a residential sale contract utilized by HUD in the sale of HUD-owned property; (2) buyers of residential condominium units who timely deliver written notice of their intent to cancel the contract as authorized by the Condominium Act; and (3) buyers who in good faith fail to satisfy the terms specified in the financing clause of a contract for sale and purchase.

60. b If a prospective tenant does not obtain a rental, the prospect is entitled to a refund of 75% of the fee paid if requested within 30 days of the contract/receipt date. The demand for a refund may be verbal or in writing.

61. c The Commercial Real Estate Sales Commission Lien Act, Part III of F.S. 475, gives the broker the right to place a lien for commission owed against the seller's net proceeds from the sale of a commercial property. The effective date of the lien is the date the lien is recorded.

62. c Sales associates may employ licensed personal assistants and pay the assistant for any administrative work. However, the licensed assistant must register with the sales associate's broker to perform any service of real estate and can only be paid for those services by the employing broker.

63. d A broker may be disciplined by the FREC for failure to secure the written permission of all interested parties prior to placing trust (escrow) funds in an interest-bearing escrow account.

64. c All monies earned by a sales associate as a result of any real estate service must be paid to the sales associate by the associate's employer and not directly by the buyer or seller.

65. b Chapter 673, F.S., provides for checks and other negotiable instruments to be postdated; however, extreme caution should be taken in handling such deposits. In all cases, the seller's approval must be obtained before accepting the postdated check.

66. b Broker associates and sales associates may form a professional association so that the broker can pay commission to the professional association rather than to the individual licensee. A licensed sales associate may register with the Department of State (DOS) a professional corporation (PA), limited liability company (LLC), or a professional limited liability (PLLC) company in his legal name only.

67. a Rule 61J2-14.008 states that the licensee who prepared the sale contract shall indicate the name, address, and telephone number of the title company.

68. a Brokers are allowed to place in a sales escrow account an amount up to $1,000 in order to open and maintain the account and to cover monthly service charges. Additionally, brokers may keep up to $5,000 of their own monies in a property management escrow account.

69. a In a general partnership, each of the partners is responsible for all the debts incurred in conducting the business.

70. a A quasi-partnership exists where there is not a real partnership but the parties act, or do business, in such a manner that the public, having no knowledge of the private relations of the parties, would reasonably be deceived into believing that a partnership exists.

71. d A sales associate or broker associate may not be a general partner in a partnership registered as a real estate broker.

72. c Broker associates and sales associates must have their licenses issued in their legal names. They may not be licensed or registered under a trade name.

73. b A joint venture is a temporary form of business arrangement. The joint venture structure is normally used when two or more parties combine their efforts to complete a single business transaction or a fixed number of business transactions.

74. c The broker must institute one of the settlement procedures within 30 business days from the time the broker received the conflicting demands. Because 12 business days have already passed, the broker has 18 business days remaining to implement one of the settlement procedures.

75. b The Junk Fax Prevention Act regulates unsolicited advertisements to residential and business fax machines. It is unlawful to send unsolicited advertisements to a residential or business fax machine without the recipient's prior express invitation or permission.

76. c Listing presentations must be conducted by a real estate licensee.

Violations of License Law, Penalties, and Procedures: Florida Real Estate Principles, Practices & Law (Unit 6); Florida Real Estate Broker's Guide (Unit 5)

77. a Pursuant to Section 475.25(2), F.S., a license may be revoked or canceled if it was issued through a mistake or inadvertence of the Commission. Such revocation or cancellation will not prejudice any future application for licensure filed by the person against whom action was taken.

78. d Anyone may file a complaint against a licensee, an applicant, or an unlicensed person for actions believed to be in violation of Chapter 475, F.S.

79. c Once a case has been investigated and found valid, the probable-cause panel determines whether probable cause exists.

80. b A person may not disseminate or cause to be disseminated by any means any false or misleading information for the purpose of offering for sale, or for the purpose of causing or inducing any other person to purchase; lease; or rent, real estate located in the state or for the purpose of causing or inducing any other person to acquire an interest in the title to real estate located in the state. To do so is a misdemeanor of the second degree.

81. c Misrepresentation is an untrue statement of fact and an incorrect or false misrepresentation of the facts.

82. a A licensee has 30 days from receipt of a citation to accept or reject the alleged violation(s), as specified in the citation. Failure to pay the fine in a timely manner will give rise to the filing of an administrative complaint.

83. b Florida Statute requires licensees to inform the Commission, in writing, within 30 days of being convicted or found guilty of a crime.

84. c If a licensee disputes the alleged facts that are made in an administrative complaint (also known as a formal complaint), the case must be heard by an administrative law judge in a formal hearing.

85. b Pursuant to Rule 61J2-24.003, the Commission sets forth a list of minor violations for which the DBPR must issue a notice of noncompliance as a first response to a minor violation by a licensee.

86. d Conversion is a licensee's personal use or misuse of client (or customer) monies.

87. a The FREC is authorized to order reimbursement to any licensee who is required by a court of law to pay money damages as a result of the licensee's compliance with an escrow disbursement order. If the licensee had previously requested an EDO and complied with it, no action will be taken against the licensee.

88. b The spouse of the offending licensee (judgment debtor) is not eligible for reimbursement from the recovery fund.

89. a The recovery fund will reimburse the claimant for actual monetary damages only. The judgment was for $15,000 of actual monetary damages.

90. b One of the probable-cause panel members may be a former Commissioner. However, if a former professional board member serves on the panel, the former Commissioner must currently hold an active real estate license.

91. a The licensee-respondent must be given at least 14 days' notice of a hearing. The notice of hearing informs the licensee-respondent of the time, place, nature of the hearing, and includes a statement regarding the legal authority and jurisdiction under which the hearing is being held.

92. c A stipulation is an agreement as to the facts of the case and the penalty reached between the attorneys for the DRE and the licensee or licensee's attorney.

93. c Falsifying a license application and unlicensed practice of real estate are third-degree felonies. Theft or reproduction of a license exam are third-degree felonies.

94. a Payments for claims arising out of the same transaction are limited, in total, to $50,000 or the unsatisfied portion of a judgement claim, whichever is less.

95. d In a claim resulting from an EDO, the fund will reimburse compensatory damages, attorney's fees, court costs, but not punitive damages, treble (triple) damages, or interest.

GENERAL REAL ESTATE LAW SECTIONS

Federal and State Laws Pertaining to Real Estate: Florida Real Estate Principles, Practices & Law (Unit 7); Florida Real Estate Broker's Guide (Units 2, 12, 17, and 18)

96. a In 1968, the U.S. Supreme Court, in the case of *Jones v. Mayer*, upheld the Civil Rights Act of 1866, which prohibits discrimination on the basis of race.

97. a The Civil Rights Act of 1968 made discrimination illegal in sales, leasing, advertising sales or rentals, financing, or brokerage services if such discrimination is based on race, color, religion, sex, national origin, handicap, or familial status.

98. d The Fair Housing Act is part of the Civil Rights Act of 1968.

99. b The Civil Rights Act of 1964 ended racial segregation in public schools, in the workplace, and in public accommodations.

100. c Protected classes under the Fair Housing Act include race, color, religion, sex, handicap status, familial status, and national origin.

101. a Blockbusting refers to using the entry, or rumor of the entry, of a protected class into a neighborhood to persuade owners to sell.

102. b Denying loans or insurance coverage or other restrictive practices by a lending institution or insurer that represents different terms or conditions for homes in certain neighborhoods is known as redlining.

103. c Channeling protected-class homeseekers away from areas that are not mixed with that class into areas that are is known as steering.

104. d The Interstate Land Sales Full Disclosure Act is designed to protect consumers from misrepresentation by land developers. Purchasers must be furnished a Property Report before signing a purchase contract or lease.

105. b Brokers must obey the lawful instructions of the owner. It is not a violation of the Fair Housing Act to inform the member of the protected class that the property cannot be shown while the owner is out of town *provided* the statement is the truth and the refusal to show the property in the owner's absence applies to *all* prospective buyers.

106. b The landlord is obligated to account for security deposits and advance rents in one of three ways. One of the three methods is to post a surety bond with the clerk of the circuit court in the total amount of the security deposits and advance rents or $50,000, whichever is less, and pay the tenant 5% per year simple interest. If a licensed broker performs property management services for a landlord, the broker must place security deposits and advance rents into an escrow account.

107. a The Florida Residential Landlord and Tenant Act requires that the landlord inform tenants in writing, within 30 days from the receipt of advance rent or security deposit, of the manner in which the tenant's funds are being held.

108. d If a tenant vacates rented premises at the end of a lease, the landlord is required to notify the tenant within 30 days if the landlord intends to claim a part or all of the tenant's security deposit.

109. a The Interstate Land Sales Full Disclosure Act requires developers of subdivisions of 100 or more lots to register with the Consumer Financial Protection Bureau.

110. a Any right or duty stated in Chapter 83, Part II, F.S., is enforceable by civil action, which means that all legal remedies sought by either tenant or landlord are pursued through the civil courts.

111. d Real estate brokers must abide by Chapter 475 with regard to handling deposits and advance rent. The deposits and advance rents are trust funds and, as such, must be deposited into the broker's escrow account by the end of the third business day after receipt of the trust funds.

Property Rights: Estates and Tenancies, Condominiums, Cooperatives, and Time Sharing:
Florida Real Estate Principles, Practices & Law (Unit 8); Florida Real Estate Broker's Guide (Units 11, 12, and 18)

112. c Riparian rights are associated with land abutting the banks of a river, stream, or other watercourse.

113. a Real property includes the land and anything permanently attached to it.

114. a Real property can become personal property by the act of severance. For example, timber is real property but when cut becomes personal property by the act of severance.

115. b A trade fixture is an item of personal property attached to real property that is owned by a tenant and is used in a business. It is legally removable by the tenant.

116. c Pursuant to Chapter 83, F.S., a notice of fifteen days is required to terminate a month-to-month tenancy at will.

117. c A freehold estate is a tenancy in real property with no set termination date; it can be measured by the lifetime of an individual or can be inherited.

118. c A joint tenancy is an estate owned by two or more persons, each having equal rights of possession and ownership, and right of survivorship.

119. c A freehold estate is an ownership interest for an indefinite period that can be inherited. A proprietary lease is associated with cooperatives. A tenancy by the entireties is a joint tenancy between spouses.

120. a A tenancy in common is a form of ownership by two or more persons each having an equal or unequal interest and passing the interest to heirs, not to surviving tenants.

121. b A joint tenancy features right of survivorship. If a co-owner dies, that owner's interest goes to the surviving co-owners, not to the deceased owner's heirs.

122. b A tenancy in common provides the best protection for each owner's families because each tenant in common's legal interest will descend to the legal heirs.

123. b The right of disposition allows the owner to sell, mortgage, dedicate, give away, or otherwise dispose of all or any portion of the property.

124. b A tenancy in common is the most frequently used form of co-ownership, except for husband-and-wife ownership.

125. c If removing the item in question results in damage to real property, the article is classified as a fixture. This test is the method or degree of attachment.

126. d The rescission period is 15 calendar days for residential cooperative apartments sold by a developer.

127. b As joint tenants die, their shares are divided among the surviving tenants until only one owner is left. The sole survivor then has a fee simple estate in severalty.

128. d Two documents are required exclusively for more than 20 residential units sold by a developer—the prospectus and the estimated operating budget. The rules of the association, governance form, and the most recent year-end financial report are disclosures required for resale units sold by a previous owner.

129. b An estate for years is a tenancy with a definite termination date. An estate for years is a leasehold estate that must be created by a properly executed lease agreement.

130. b Right to use ownership is a leasehold interest in a time-share unit based on the limited time (one or more weeks) specified in the agreement.

131. d When a life estate ends, the property reverts (returns) to the original grantor or goes to a third party, called a remainderman. If the life estate reverts to the original grantor, an estate in reversion is created.

132. b If an individual is a salaried employee of an owner-developer whose primary business is the development and sale of time-share units, the salesperson is not required to hold a real estate license, provided the salesperson is not paid a commission or otherwise compensated on a transactional basis, such as with bonuses based on sales quotas. The salaried employees receive bonuses based on sales production, so they must be licensed.

133. a The bylaws of a condominium association govern the administration of the association and include the rules and regulations.

134. b The contract for resale of a residential condominium unit must include a clause that states that the buyer acknowledges receipt of the condo documents and that the buyer may cancel the contract within three business days after the execution of the contract and receipt of the condo documents.

135. b A tenant at sufferance has no estate or title but only "naked" possession.

136. d Homesteaded property is protected from forced sale for debts resulting from personal loans, credit cards, and so forth. However, the protection does not prevent foreclosure for nonpayment of property taxes, special assessments, mortgages, vendors' liens, or construction liens secured with the homesteaded property.

137. c The bundle of rights under the allodial system includes (DEEP "C"): disposition, enjoyment, exclusion, possession, and control (or use).

138. c Common elements include all portions of the condominium property not included in the individual units.

139. c A tenancy at will is a leasehold in which the tenant holds possession of the premises with the owner's permission but without a fixed term.

140. a A condominium is created by recording a declaration in the public records of the county where the land is located, executed, and acknowledged with the requirements of a deed.

141. b Purchase of stock in the corporation entitles the purchaser to a proprietary lease and the right to occupy a particular unit in the cooperative.

142. c Condominium documents that define the rights and obligations of condominium owners include the declaration, bylaws, and articles of incorporation.

143. a Accretion is the process of land buildup from water-borne rock, sand, and soil.

144. d Developers of 20 or more new residential units must prepare a prospectus in addition to the other condominium documents. A copy of the prospectus must be given to prospective purchasers.

Title, Deeds, and Ownership Restrictions: Florida Real Estate Principles, Practices & Law (Unit 9); Florida Real Estate Broker's Guide (Units 15 and 18)

145. b Voluntary alienation can be by deed or by will.

146. b Adverse possession must continue for seven or more consecutive years without the consent of the owner.

147. b A gift of real property in a will is known as a devise, and the recipient of the gift is the devisee.

148. d Adverse possession must continue for seven or more consecutive years without the consent of the owner.

149. b Constructive notice refers to information that has been made public by recording the information in the public records.

150. d A deed or other conveyance instrument will not be effective in transferring title to property until it is delivered to and accepted by the grantee.

151. c Acknowledgment is the formal declaration before a notary public by the grantor that the grantor's signing is a free act.

152. d Legal title can be conveyed by descent (inheritance), quitclaim deed, or eminent domain. *Novation* is the term used for the substitution of a new party and/or new terms to an existing obligation.

153. d The grantee is the person who received the deed (buyer). The grantor is the person conveying title (seller).

154. d "The policy is issued for an amount equal to the unpaid balance of the mortgage loan" describes the lender's title insurance policy.

155. a Because the seller delivered the deed to the couple and the couple accepted the deed, the couple now owns the property. When the couple took physical possession of the property, they gave actual notice of legal title.

156. b Essential elements of a deed include consideration, execution (signed) by a competent grantor and two witnesses, and voluntary delivery and acceptance. Seal refers to a mark, emblem, or impression on a document used to authenticate a signature. A seal is not required to make a deed valid.

157. a The granting clause contains the necessary words used to convey property, such as "grants, bargains, and sells" or similar words.

158. c The habendum clause is a provision in a deed to real property that stipulates the estate or interest the grantee is to receive and the type of title conveyed.

159. c Only attorneys may draft leases on someone else's behalf. Property owners may draft leases for their own property, but owners may not delegate that authority to nonattorneys.

160. a The seisin clause is a covenant in a deed that warrants that the grantor (seller) holds the property by virtue of a fee simple title and has a complete right to dispose of the property.

161. b Instead of the usual wording "grants, bargains, and sells," the quitclaim deed uses the words "remise, release, and quitclaim." This allows the grantor to sign a deed transferring any and all interests, if any, without claiming ownership of any right of title whatsoever.

162. b Police powers, eminent domain, and escheat are all governmental restrictions on ownership. Deed restrictions are among the broadest restrictions in the private category.

163. a The covenant of further assurance is a provision in a deed containing a covenant of warranty to perform any further acts the buyer might require to perfect title to the property.

164. c Upon the death of an owner, the probate court appoints a personal representative to handle the affairs of the deceased. If the estate includes real property to be sold, the personal representative will sign the deed for the decedent.

165. b Escheat is the reversion of property to the state when an owner dies without leaving a will (intestate) or any known heirs.

166. b Under police power, the use of real property may be regulated. Eminent domain is the taking for just compensation.

167. b The constitutions of the federal government and state governments grant eminent domain power to take private property for a public use.

168. b Appurtenances to real property pass with the real property to which they are appurtenant. A typical appurtenance is condominium parking stalls.

169. a Escheat is the reversion of property to the state when an owner dies without leaving a will or any known heirs.

170. c An easement by necessity is created by court order to allow property owners to enter and exit their landlocked property.

171. c The requirements of a valid lease include names of the lessor and lessee, legal capacity, consideration, the term of the lease, and the property identification.

172. b The Florida Residential Landlord and Tenant Act requires landlords to approve or deny the rental application of an active service member within seven days.

173. d A sublease is effected when the lessee assigns less than the entire property or assigns all of the property for less than the full remaining period. Subleasing is also called subrogation or subordination of space.

174. a A quitclaim deed is a conveyance by which the grantor transfers whatever interest in the real estate, without making any warranties or obligations. Quitclaim deeds are often used to clear clouds on title.

175. c An encroachment is the unauthorized use of another's property. It is an infringement or intrusion on property without the owner's consent.

176. b When the use of property such as a roadway has continued openly without interruption for more than 20 years, an easement by prescription is created.

177. d A lease is an interest in, but not title to, real property.

178. c The person who leaves a will, if female, is the testatrix.

179. b A leasehold is an estate in real property held under a lease arrangement that may be any length of time from less than a year to a period of many years.

180. d The terms eviction, assignment, and subrogation apply to leasing real property.

181. b Police power is the government's right to impose laws, statutes, and ordinances to protect the public health, safety, and welfare. Police power represents the broadest power of the government to limit the rights of property owners.

182. a A lien is an encumbrance on the title to real property; however, not all encumbrances on property are liens. Specific liens affect only a certain property (not all property of a debtor). A property tax lien is an example of a specific (not a general) lien.

183. c Lenders will typically use a special warranty deed because the lender only assumes title responsibility for the period the title was in the lender's name, thus avoiding title liability for the period prior to foreclosure.

184. b Property tax liens, special assessment liens, and federal estate tax liens are superior to all other liens regardless of recording date.

185. d An assignment of a lease occurs when a lessee assigns to another party all of the leased property for the full remaining period.

186. b A sublease is affected when the lessee assigns less than the entire property or assigns all of the property for less than the full remaining period.

187. d An income tax lien is a general lien meaning that it is not restricted to one property but may affect all properties of a debtor.

188. c Eminent domain is the right of a government or a municipal quasi-public body (a railroad) to acquire property for a public use through a court action known as condemnation.

189. d A mortgage is a lien voluntarily placed on real property by a borrower who pledges the property as security to the lender.

190. a The date the mortgage is filed and recorded with the clerk of the circuit court establishes the priority of the lien against other claims on the property.

191. b The date of recordation establishes the priority.

192. b A specific lien is a claim that affects only the property designated in the lien instrument. Property taxes are involuntary because they become liens as soon as the assessment is complete.

193. c An attachment is a legal writ obtained to prevent removal of property that is expected to be used to satisfy a judgment.

194. b A vendor's lien is a claim against property giving the seller the right to hold the property as security for any unpaid purchase money.

195. b Equitable title is a beneficial interest in real estate that implies that an individual will receive legal title at a future date.

Real Estate Contracts:
Florida Real Estate Principles, Practices & Law (Unit 11); Florida Real Estate Broker's Guide (Unit 11)

196. b Pursuant to the statute of frauds, certain contracts, including those pertaining to the transfer of interests in real property, must be in writing to be enforceable.

197. d A real estate contract typically is not recorded.

198. b An essential element of a valid real estate contract is an offer and acceptance (or a meeting of the minds).

199. d To be enforceable, a contract must have a lawful purpose; one that is not prohibited by law or contrary to public policy.

200. a Contracts covered by the statute of frauds include purchase and sale contracts, option contracts, deed and mortgage instruments, lease agreements for a term longer than one year, and listing agreements for a term longer than one year.

201. d The signatures of the buyer and seller indicate that they agree to the terms of the contract.

202. a A unilateral contract is one that obligates only one party to an agreement without any obligation on the part of the other party involved. The broker is obligated to pay the bonus if the sales associate sells 20 homes; however, the sales associate is not obligated to sell 20 homes.

203. b The licensee must give a valuable consideration (substantial and not nominal) for the option contract.

204. c Sellers cannot use "as is" wording in a contract to shield themselves from possible fraud charges brought on by neglecting to disclose known material defects in the property.

205. d An informal contract is an oral (or parol) contract.

206. c When a prospective buyer submits a real estate contract accompanied by an earnest money deposit, an offer is considered to have been made. It does not become a contract for sale and purchase until the seller acknowledges acceptance of the price and terms by signing the sale and purchase agreement.

207. a A counteroffer indicates a willingness to contract, but on terms or conditions different from those contained in the offer. The original offer is dead forever and cannot be accepted later.

208. c Pursuant to Section 720.401, F.S., a buyer, who does not receive a mandatory homeowners association disclosure prior to signing the sale contract, has the right to cancel the contract within three days of receiving the disclosure. Any waiver of the right to cancel will have no effect.

209. b An offeror may revoke an offer at any time until notice of the offeree's acceptance is received by the offeror or the offeror's designated agent.

210. b A licensee can be charged with fraudulent or dishonest dealing by trick, scheme, or device by offering for sale lottery chances where the property price will depend on chance or the amount of sales made.

211. c "Time is of the essence" is a phrase in a contract making failure to perform by a specified date a breach or violation of the agreement.

212. a A wronged party may sue for specific performance to have the courts force the other party to perform as the contract specifically states.

213. d If required to effect a sale, the buyer must close on the property for the broker to earn a commission.

214. b The statute of limitations designates the period of time during which the terms of a contract may be enforced and protects people from being compelled to perform or otherwise be sued after a specific period of time has expired.

215. d Power of attorney is the designation of another person to act for a principal.

216. a An attorney-in-fact can bargain and sign for the person who granted power of attorney, provided that power is specifically granted.

217. c Real estate licensees may not draw lease agreements. However, licensees may fill in the blanks on Florida Supreme Court preapproved lease instruments for lease periods that do not exceed one year. Real estate licensees are allowed to assist buyers and sellers with the drawing of four types of contracts: listing, buyer-brokerage, sale, and option contracts.

218. d A net listing is created when a seller agrees to sell a property for a stated minimum amount.

219. a In an open listing, the owner gives a listing to a number of brokers and also reserves the right to sell the property himself. The seller is not obligated to pay a commission to any broker except the broker who first finds a buyer to purchase the property. In an open listing, the broker who is the procuring cause is the only broker entitled to compensation.

220. c Pursuant to Section 120.69, F.S., if a property has been cited as being in violation of building code, the seller must disclose the violation to the buyer and inform the buyer that the buyer will be responsible for the violation after closing. The disclosure does not require the seller to clear the violation before closing.

221. c An option contract is an agreement in which the seller grants the optionee the right (but not the obligation) to buy the property within a specified period for a certain price and terms.

222. c Any contract that obligates both parties to perform in accordance with the terms of the contract is a bilateral contract.

223. b Letters and telegraphic communications can be part of a valid sale contract.

224. d A minor's contract is voidable because the minor can choose to void the contract.

225. b An express contract is an agreement wherein the terms are specifically stated by the parties, either orally, in writing, or a combination of the two.

226. c The broker must give a copy of the written listing agreement to the seller within 24 hours after the seller signs the agreement. Failure to do so is a violation of Section 475.25(1)(r), F.S.

227. a The person to whom legal rights in a contract are transferred is the assignee.

228. b Frequently, a contract includes an amount of money (usually the earnest money deposit) to be paid to the seller in the event of default by the buyer.

229. b One remedy for breach of contract is a suit for damages. Usually, the party bringing suit seeks an amount of money equal to the extent of loss suffered, called compensatory damages.

230. d A contract can contain all of the essentials of a valid contract (competent parties, mutual assent, legal purpose, and consideration) and yet it is an unenforceable contract. A contract may be unenforceable because it is not in writing, as required by the statute of frauds, or because the statute of limitations has passed, or because the property is destroyed.

Planning, Zoning, and Environmental Hazards: Florida Real Estate Principles, Practices & Law (Unit 19); Florida Real Estate Broker's Guide (Unit 16)

231. c The concurrency provision in Florida's Growth Policy Act mandates that the infrastructure, such as roads and water and waste treatment facilities needed to support additional population, be in place before new development is allowed.

232. b A buffer zone is a strip of land separating one land use from another.

233. b City planning commissions are commonly delegated final authority for subdivision plat approval, site plan approval, and sign control.

234. c Zoning ordinances authorize segmentation of a community into districts or zones in keeping with the character of the land and structures. Each zone is assigned a specific land-use classification. "R" is usually reserved for residential classification.

235. b Building codes establish minimum standards for a building's design, construction, use and occupancy, and quality.

236. d A variance allows a property owner to vary from strict compliance with all or part of a zoning code (such as the minimum number of parking spaces) because to comply would force an undue hardship on the property owner.

237. a To be granted a variance, a property owner must show that a hardship related to land use exists or will be created by strict compliance with zoning.

238. a Nonconforming use properties usually are not allowed to be increased in size or to undergo structural changes. Most zoning authorities restrict repairs and maintenance to those needed for sanitation and safety purposes.

239. d Local government enforces building codes. The process begins by issuing a building permit. Municipal inspectors visit each job site to conduct periodic building inspections. A final certificate of occupancy is issued once construction is completed. A condemnation proceeding is associated with eminent domain *not* building code enforcement.

240. a A final certificate of occupancy is issued once construction is completed and the municipal building inspector agrees that the structure conforms to code.

241. a Both a legal and a development design concept, a planned unit development permits a mix of land uses along with a high density of residential units resulting from clustering homes together and the creation of open green spaces.

242. c Industrial zoning controls industry's by-products such as noise, odor, smoke congestion, and chemicals.

243. d The DBPR licenses mold assessors and remediators.

244. b Land located in a 100-year flood plain is called a special flood hazard area (SFHA).

REAL ESTATE PRINCIPLES AND PRACTICES SECTIONS

The Real Estate Business: Florida Real Estate Principles, Practices & Law (Unit 1)

245. a Business brokers are real estate licensees who engage in the sale, purchase, or lease of businesses. To do so, they must hold active real estate licenses.

246. b Dedication is the gift of land by an owner, typically a developer, to a government body for public use.

247. b Tract building involves building model homes in a new subdivision so that buyers can choose a floor plan and then have a home built on a lot in the new subdivision.

248. c Property management is devoted to the leasing, managing, marketing, and overall maintenance of property for others. The scope of a property manager's functions goes far beyond rent collection, maintenance, and repair. Absentee ownership has increased (not decreased) demand for property managers.

249. c Follow-up is what a sales associate does after the sale to maintain customer contact and goodwill.

250. d Federal law (FIRREA) mandates that appraisal reports involving a federally related transaction must be prepared by a state-certified or licensed appraiser.

251. b A subdivision plat map indicates the size and location of individual lots, streets, and public utilities, including water lines and arrangements for sewage disposal.

252. b An absentee owner is a property owner who does not reside on the property and who often relies on a professional property manager to manage the owner's investment.

253. a Target marketing involves developing a database of prospects to direct a specific message.

254. d A broker's price opinion (BPO) is a written opinion of value often requested by lenders involved in short sales.

Legal Descriptions
Florida Real Estate Principles, Practices & Law (Unit 10)

255. a A metes-and-bounds description begins with a starting reference point, called a point of beginning (POB). Metes refers to "distance" and bounds refers to "direction."

256. d Sections are numbered beginning in the northeast corner of a township with section number 1. The section numbers progress consecutively from east to west—from the upper right corner of the township across the top row of sections to number 6. Immediately to the west of section 6 a new township begins, numbered beginning in the northeast corner of the township with section number 1.

257. c North is 0 degrees on a compass. Therefore, the direction closest to 0 degrees is most northerly. Because 30 minutes is closer to 0 than 45 minutes, N 0° 30' W is the most northerly of the answer choices.

258. b Opposite of south is north. Opposite of east is west; therefore, N 45° W is a straight line opposite to S 45° E.

259. d Principal meridians and base lines intersect to form basic reference points in the government survey system. There are 36 sets of principal meridians and base lines. In Florida, the principal meridian and base line cross at a point in the city of Tallahassee.

260. c There are 640 acres in a section. There are 23,040 acres in a township (640 acres × 36 sections).

261. c 640 ÷ 4 ÷ 4 ÷ 4 = 10 acres

262. a Range lines are numbered consecutively from 1 both east and west of the principal meridian. Because the principal meridian runs north-south through the city of Tallahassee, a small numbered range (2) will be closest to Tallahassee.

263. b A check is a square 24 miles on each side created by intersecting guide meridians and correction lines. A check is used to adjust the grid pattern of squares because of the curvature of the earth. A check contains 16 townships.

264. b Range lines are numbered consecutively, from 1 both east and west of the principal meridian.

265. a Sections are numbered beginning in the northeast corner of the township with section 1 and progress consecutively from east to west through section 6. The second horizontal row begins directly under section 6 and progresses west to east from section 7 to section 12. Section 13 is directly under number 12. The row is numbered consecutively from east to west to section 18. Section 19 is directly under 18, and then the sections are numbered consecutively from west to east through section 24. Section 13 therefore is directly above (north) of section 24.

266. c The most common type of legal description used for single-family dwellings located in developed subdivisions is the lot and block method, which can be used only where plat maps of developed subdivisions have been recorded in the public records.

267. d 640 ÷ 4 ÷ 2 = 80 acres;
640 ÷ 4 ÷ 4 = 40 acres;
80 + 40 = 120 acres

Residential Mortgages:
Florida Real Estate Principles, Practices & Law (Unit 12); Florida Real Estate Broker's Guide (Unit 12)

268. b A deed in lieu of foreclosure is a way for the mortgagor (borrower) to avoid foreclosure. The borrower who is in default under the terms of the mortgage gives a deed to the lender.

269. b The promissory note is the legal instrument that represents the primary evidence of a debt.

270. a A defeasance clause included in mortgages in title theory states provides that the conveyance of title by the borrower to the lender is "defeated" when all of the terms and conditions of the mortgage have been met. It is the vehicle by which title is returned to the borrower when the debt has been repaid.

271. d The promissory note states the total amount of indebtedness, interest rate, repayment method, and term or time period to repay.

272. c The mortgagor is the borrower who signs the note.

273. d The holder of a first mortgage can voluntarily take a lower priority through a subordination agreement.

274. d The loan-to-value ratio is the loan amount divided by the purchase price (or value of the property). $360,000 loan ÷ $450,000 purchase price = .80 or 80% loan-to-value.

275. a The acceleration clause authorizes the lender to accelerate (advance) the due date of the entire unpaid balance should the mortgagor fail to fulfill any of the covenants contained in the mortgage.

276. a The right to reinstate is the mortgagor's right to reinstate the original repayment terms in the note after the lender initiated the acceleration clause.

277. b A receivership clause allows a receiver to be appointed to collect income from the property and use the income to make mortgage payments in the event of default.

278. d A takeout commitment is long-term permanent financing. In large construction projects, the developer obtains two types of financing. Interim financing is a short-term loan to cover construction costs. The interim lender typically requires a commitment by a permanent lender to agree to "take out" the interim lender. The lender pays off the construction loan and the developer gets a permanent long-term loan when construction is complete.

279. d A due-on-sale clause is a provision in the mortgage that states that the entire balance of the note is immediately due and payable if the mortgagor transfers (sells) the property. The due-on-sale clause prevents a third party from assuming the mortgage.

280. c Once a mortgagor has paid off a mortgage loan in full, Florida statute requires the mortgagee to cancel the mortgage and send the recorded satisfaction to the mortgagor within 60 days.

281. c An estoppel certificate is a legal instrument setting forth the exact unpaid balance of a mortgage, the current rate of interest, and the date to which interest has been paid.

282. a The loan-to-value ratio is the relationship between the amount borrowed and the appraised value (or sale price) of a property.

283. a The monthly mortgage payment paid by the borrower consists of principal and interest on the loan and the monthly reserve for property taxes and hazard insurance (PITI).

284. d When a buyer secures new financing, the seller pays off the old debt and a release of mortgage is recorded.

285. b In an assumption, the buyer signs a new promissory note.

286. d With a contract for deed, the buyer gets possession of the property while making payments to the seller and has equitable title to the property. However, the seller retains legal title until the buyer has made all the payments. A contract for deed is also called a land contract, agreement for deed, or installment sale contract.

287. b Hypothecation describes the pledging of property as collateral for a loan without giving up possession of the property.

288. c A novation makes the buyer solely responsible for a default.

289. d The larger the down payment of the borrower, the lower the risk for the lender (mortgagee).

290. a The process of transferring ownership of a mortgage from one individual to another is accomplished by executing an assignment of mortgage.

291. a When litigation is initiated involving a specific parcel of real property, a lis pendens (notice of pending legal action) usually is filed with the clerk of the county in which the property is located.

292. a When calculating the actual cost in dollars added by discount points, each point is equal to 1% of the loan amount (1 point = 1%).

293. b 1 ÷ 8 = .125 × 2 points = 0.25; 4% + .25 = 4.25% effective yield

294. b A loan origination fee is a charge by a lender for taking a mortgage in exchange for a loan.

Types of Mortgages and Sources of Financing: Florida Real Estate Principles, Practices & Law (Unit 13)

295. d The major federal agencies active in secondary market activities are Fannie Mae, Ginnie Mae, and Freddie Mac.

296. c Fannie Mae purchases conventional, FHA, and VA mortgage loans.

297. b When the Fed decides to sell securities through open-market bulk trading, all funds received are held by the Fed. This reduces the supply of money in circulation.

298. d Fannie Mae recycles capital by purchasing loans previously made by primary lenders. Fannie Mae does not originate new loans.

299. d A shorter loan term results in larger monthly payments but the loan is paid off earlier, reducing the total amount of interest paid.

300. c The index is an economic indicator used to adjust the interest rate in an ARM.

301. c Freddie Mac provides a secondary market for loans originated by savings associations.

302. b The discount rate is the interest rate charged banks for borrowing money from the Fed.

303. b ARMs typically feature a lifetime cap that caps the total amount the interest rate may increase over the life of the loan.

304. c National banks are members of the Federal Reserve System.

305. c Mortgage loan originators (MLOs) who are not employed by a federal agency-regulated lender must be licensed by the state.

306. c Nonconventional loans are insured or guaranteed by a government agency.

307. a The Equal Credit Opportunity Act ensures that financial institutions and firms engaged in extending credit will make credit available with fairness and without discrimination on the basis of race, color, religion, national origin, sex, marital status, age, or receipt of income from public assistance programs.

308. a The Truth in Lending Act is implemented by Federal Reserve Regulation Z and requires that lenders disclose the annual percentage rate of interest and finance charges imposed by consumers.

309. c The Truth in Lending Act requires that lenders disclose the annual percentage rate (APR) of interest and finance charges imposed on consumers.

310. b Mortgage loans secured by a mobile home are exempt from the TILA-RESPA rule.

311. b Transactions exempt from TILA-RESPA include reverse mortgage loans.

312. d A prepayment penalty clause provides for the lender to charge a penalty for early payment. Both FHA and VA mortgages allow early payment of the debt without penalty.

313. b An applicant's credit history is the best indicator of a willingness to repay debt. Lenders use credit scores to determine applicants' willingness to repay debt. A credit score is a financial snapshot of a borrower's credit history and current credit usage at a given point in time.

314. c The Department of Veterans Affairs (VA) has the authority to partially guarantee mortgage loans made to veterans by private lenders.

315. a The VA establishes loan guarantee limits referred to as the "VA loan guarantee" or the "maximum entitlement."

316. b A borrower can obtain an FHA-insured mortgage loan with a minimum cash investment of 3.5%.

317. c FHA functions as an insurance company, insuring mortgage loans made by lending institutions.

318. b FHA requires borrowers to escrow property taxes and hazard insurance.

319. c A loan amortization schedule indicates payments of principal and interest required to pay off the loan based on loan amount, term, and interest rate.

320. b FHA loans feature a monthly mortgage insurance premium payment (MIP). Lenders require private mortgage insurance (PMI) on the amount of loan over 80% LTV ratio. VA charges borrowers a funding fee or user's fee. VA loans do *not* require a down payment (minimum cash investment).

321. c The flow of funds into deposits held by primary lenders, increasing the mortgage money supply is called intermediation.

322. d On a fully amortized fixed-rate loan, the same amount is paid each month. However, the portion used to pay interest decreases each month, while the portion used to repay principal increases each month.

323. c Term mortgages require payment of interest only, until the full term of the mortgage has expired.

324. b A partial release clause commonly used in blanket mortgages provides for the release of individual parcels from the blanket mortgage.

325. b A home equity conversion mortgage (HECM) is also called a reverse mortgage.

326. c FHA lenders use two qualifying ratios for loan applicants.

327. d With a partially amortized mortgage, the buyer makes regular payments smaller than what is required to completely pay off the loan. A final large balloon payment of accrued interest and unpaid principal is due on loan maturity.

Real Estate Appraisal:
Florida Real Estate Principles, Practices & Law (Unit 16); Florida Real Estate Broker's Guide (Units 6–8)

328. d Plottage is the added value as a result of combining two or more properties into one large parcel.

329. b Market value is defined as the most probable price that a property should bring in a competitive and open market under all conditions requisite to a fair sale, the buyer and seller each acting prudently and knowledgeably, and assuming the price is not affected by undue stimulus.

330. a Section 475.25, F.S., empowers the Commission to discipline brokers and sales associates who violate any of the standards of the USPAP; however, CMAs are exempted from compliance with the USPAP.

331. d If the capitalization rate is held constant and the NOI is increased, the result is an increase in value. For example, \$6,000 NOI ÷ .08 cap rate = \$75,000 value. However, \$8,000 NOI ÷ .08 cap rate = \$100,000.

332. b Cost is the total expenditure required to bring a new improvement into existence plus the cost of the land.

333. b The four characteristics of value are demand, utility, scarcity, and transferability.

334. a A vacant lot in a residential subdivision is not suitable to the income or cost approaches. A comparative market analysis is not a formal appraisal. The most suitable approach for

appraising a vacant lot is to consider the selling prices of comparable lots.

335. d Apartment buildings are best suited to the income approach. Hospitals are best suited to the cost approach. Single-family dwellings are best suited to the sales comparison approach. Raw land is best suited to the sales comparison approach.

336. c The cost approach is the most applicable approach for special purpose buildings.

337. b The objective of the income capitalization approach is to measure a flow of income projected into the future.

338. b If a comparable is superior on a given feature, a downward adjustment is made to the comparable property (subtract the value of the difference).

339. b The basis of the cost approach is to estimate the cost to acquire an equivalent site (land value) and to reproduce a structure as if new, and then subtract accrued depreciation.

340. d The gross income multiplier (GIM) is the ratio to convert annual income into market value.

341. c A gross rent multiplier (GRM) is the ratio between a property's gross monthly income and its selling price.

342. b Liquidation value is the value associated with a rapid sale.

343. b Exterior dimensions are used to calculate gross living area.

344. d Land is not depreciated in the cost-depreciation approach; only the buildings or other improvements to land are subject to depreciation.

345. d A property owner has least control over loss in value caused from factors in the surrounding area that are external to the subject property.

346. b Anything that is inferior due to operational inadequacies, poor design, or changing tastes and preferences is classified as functional obsolescence.

347. c Layout of the traffic pattern concerns poor design and is an example of functional obsolescence.

348. a Poor design is an example of functional obsolescence. An incurable defect is one in which the cost of curing the defect is greater than the value added by the cure.

349. b External obsolescence results from a loss in value due to influences originating outside the boundaries of the property.

350. c Anything that is inferior due to operational inadequacies (one-car garage) is classified as functional obsolescence.

351. a An incurable defect is one in which the cost of curing the defect is greater than the value added by the cure. The owners are unable to get their money back in added value, or in other words, the value added by the cure is less than the cost of the cure.

352. d Economic life is the period of time a property may be expected to be profitable or productive; its useful life.

353. a Progression is the principle that the value of an inferior property is enhanced by its association with superior properties.

354. c The first step in the income capitalization approach is to estimate potential gross income (PGI). Vacancy and collection losses are subtracted from PGI to arrive at effective gross income (EGI). Operating expenses are subtracted from EGI to arrive at net operating income.

355. c Appraisals associated with an FHA mortgage loan must conform to USPAP.

Real Estate Investments and Business Opportunity Brokerage:
Florida Real Estate Principles, Practices & Law (Unit 17); Florida Real Estate Broker's Guide (Units 9 and 15)

356. c Liquidity refers to the ability to sell an investment quickly without loss of one's capital.

357. b Leverage is the use of borrowed funds to finance the purchase of an asset; the use of another's money to make more money.

358. d Real estate investments receive certain tax benefits.

359. c The balance sheet shows the company's financial position at a stated moment in time, the close of business on the date of the balance sheet.

360. d Goodwill is the intangible asset attributed to a business's reputation and the expectation of continued customer loyalty.

361. c Going concern value is the value of an established business property, compared with the value of just the physical assets of a business that is not yet established.

362. a The use of leverage may increase or decrease equity return. If the equity leverage is positive, it means that the borrower's return on equity was positive; there is a positive return on the cash investment after taking into account the financing cost.

363. c The methods used to estimate a business's value are comparable sales analysis, cost approach, income analysis, and liquidation analysis.

364. c One disadvantage of real estate as an investment is the relatively high risk.

365. a Cash flow is the total amount of spendable income generated from an investment.

366. b A capital gain is the difference between the adjusted basis of property and its net selling price.

367. b Business risk is the probability that projected income will not be achieved.

368. d Business opportunities is the type of real estate investment that involves the sale or lease of a business.

369. d Real estate brokerage and business brokerage both typically involve the sale of real property or the assignment of a long-term lease.

Taxes Affecting Real Estate: Florida Real Estate Principles, Practices & Law (Unit 18); Florida Real Estate Broker's Guide (Unit 14)

370. d Although reserve for replacements is deducted when calculating NOI, it is not a cash expense and is not deductible when computing taxable income.

371. a The installment sale method relieves the seller of paying tax on gain not yet collected. Generally, it calls for the gain to be reported only as payments are actually received, with each payment treated as part profit and part recovery of investment.

372. a Property taxes become a lien on all real estate in Florida on January 1 each year.

373. a The Value Adjustment Board is made up of five members: two county commissioners, one county school board member, and two citizen members.

374. b Florida has a three-step protest procedure. The first step is to seek an adjustment by contacting the county property appraiser's office.

375. d The assessed value is greater than \$75,000; therefore, the homesteader is entitled to the \$25,000 base exemption and the \$25,000 additional exemption on property with an assessed value greater than \$75,000. \$50,000 homestead + \$500 surviving spouse + \$500 disability = \$51,000 cumulative tax exemption.

376. b Property owned by a church that is used for nonprofit purposes is exempt from property taxes. Property that once was part of the tax base, if changed to exempt property, will require higher taxes on taxable property.

377. d County hospitals and consolidated high schools are immune properties. Churches are exempt properties. Undeveloped farmland is subject to property taxation.

378. a Florida law authorizes county property appraisers to assess agricultural land by a more favorable method than that used for other properties. Florida's Green Belt law was designed to protect farmers from having taxes increased just because the land might be suited for development.

379. d Property taxes are payable to the county tax collector on or after November 1 each year.

380. c To calculate the dollar amount of property taxes owed, the taxable value is multiplied by the appropriate millage rate. A mill is one one-thousandth of a dollar (or one-tenth of a cent).

381. b The tax rate is calculated based on the following formula:

$$\frac{\text{approved budget} - \text{nonproperty tax revenue}}{\text{total assessed value} - \text{exemptions}}$$

382. a The city or county government is responsible for the cost of its day-to-day operation and must collect delinquent taxes. To accomplish this, property tax certificates in the amount of taxes owed are issued for each delinquent property.

383. a The Save Our Home amendment limits the allowable increase in assessed value of homesteaded property to the lesser of 3% or the CPI for the previous year.

384. b Homeowners who itemize their deductions may deduct the interest portion of their mortgage payment and their property taxes.

385. a Special assessments are a one-time tax levied on properties to help pay for some public improvement that benefits the property.

386. b Exclusion of gain from the sale of a principal residence is allowed only once every two years. However, homeowners who do not meet the two-year requirement due to change in health or place of employment may be eligible for a prorated exclusion of gain.

387. c The Taxpayer Relief Act of 1997 allows homeowners to exclude up to $250,000 ($500,000 for married couples filing a joint return) realized on the sale or exchange of a principal residence. The taxpayer is not required to reinvest the sale proceeds in a new residence to claim the exclusion.

388. b Depreciation allowance deductions are allowed on investment property only.

389. c The IRS has established the useful asset life of 39 years for nonresidential income-producing property.

390. c The TRIM notice reflects what the owner will likely be charged on the November property tax bill.

391. d Homestead property owners are able to transfer up to $500,000 of their Save Our Home tax benefit.

392. d A surviving spouse of a veteran who died while on active duty is entitled to a 100% tax exemption on the homesteaded property.

393. b A property owner is allowed 25 days after the TRIM notice is mailed to file an assessment appeal.

Real Estate Markets and Analysis: Florida Real Estate Principles, Practices & Law (Unit 15)

394. b Because real estate is immobile, location largely influences the value of real estate.

395. c No two tracts of land are identical. There is no standard product. The uniqueness of land is referred to as heterogeneity (or nonhomogeneous).

396. b The household is the basis for most population analysis.

397. c Variables that influence supply include the availability of skilled labor, construction loans and financing, land, and materials.

398. c Whenever the supply and demand equilibrium is upset by excess demand, a seller's market develops. This allows sellers to demand higher prices from buyers, who are forced to compete for available space.

399. d Situs refers to a buyer's preference for a certain location. Area preference and a property's location (situs) is considered the most important economic characteristics of real estate.

400. b When supply increases relative to demand, prices go down.

Real Estate–Related Computations and Closing of Transactions: Florida Real Estate Principles, Practices & Law (Unit 14); Florida Real Estate Broker's Guide (Unit 13)

401. c The only entries that are a credit to the seller are the purchase price and any items the seller prepaid.

402. d The buyer should make a decision regarding the insurance company early in the transaction.

403. b In some areas or by negotiation, the day of closing will be charged to the seller. In that situation, the seller is charged with an additional day.

404. a Mortgage interest is paid at the end of the period (in arrears). It is therefore charged to the seller up to the date of closing, and that amount is credited to the buyer in the offsetting double entries.

405. b Closing statement items credited to the buyer include the earnest money deposit, new and assumed mortgages, prorated taxes, interest, and prepaid rent.

406. d The seller is usually required to remove any encumbrances on the title.

407. a Any rental income collected in advance belongs to the new owner as of the date of closing. The buyer is credited for the rent from day of closing through the remainder of the month. The seller is debited the same amount.

MATH PROBLEMS

408. b (9, 14)
$546 doc stamps ÷ $.70 rate ×
100 increments = $78,000 sale price

409. b (18)
$117,500 assessed value – $50,000 homestead exemption = $67,500 taxable value for city and county taxes;
$67,500 × .020 mills = $1,350 taxes due for city and county taxes;
$117,500 assessed value – $25,000 homestead exemption = $92,500 taxable value for school board taxes;
$92,500 taxable value for school board taxes × .006 school board mills = $555 taxes due for school board;
$1,350 + $555 = $1,905 total taxes due

410. b (18)
$50,000 exemption for city and county × .020 mills = $1,000 savings;
$25,000 exemption for school board × .010 mills = $250 savings;
$1000 + $250 = $1,250 total savings

411. a (18)
$325,000 × .06 = $19,500 broker commission
$325,000 – $19,500 – $3,500 closing costs =
$302,000 amount realized from sale
$249,000 purchase price + $21,000 capital improvements = $270,000 adjusted basis
$302,000 – $270,000 = $32,000 capital gain

412. c (18)
180 ft. × $24 per foot =
$4,320 total paving cost;
180 ft. × .70 = $3,024 total private share;
$3,024 ÷ 2 = $1,512 owner's side of street

413. b (14)
$18,000 second mortgage × .002 rate =
$36 intangible tax;
$18,000 note ÷ $100 increments =
180 taxable increments;
180 × $.35 = $63 doc stamps on note;
$72,000 ÷ $100 increments =
720 taxable increments;
720 × $.35 = $252; $252 + $63 =
$315 doc stamps on note

414. b (12,14)
$287,500 × .75 LTV ratio = $215,625 mortgage loan;
$215,625 × .002 rate =
$431.25 intangible tax

415. c (14)
$825.30 doc stamps ÷ $.70 = $1,179;
$1,179 × $100 increments =
$117,900 purchase price

416. b (18)
$5,600,000 × .15 withholding =
$840,000 due IRS

417. c (10)
640 acres per section ÷ 2 = 320 acres

418. b (18)
$235,000 × .80 =
$188,000 depreciable basis;
$188,000 ÷ 27.5 years = $6,836.36, or $6,836 rounded annual depreciation deduction

419. c (10)
891 ft. × 440 ft. = 392,040 sq. ft.;
392,040 ÷ 43,560 sq. ft. per acre = 9 acres

420. c (10)
640 acres per section ÷ 4 ÷ 2 = 80 acres;
80 acres × $4,000 per acre =
$320,000 sale price

421. b (10)
4,000 ft. × 2,000 ft. = 8,000,000 sq. ft.;
8,000,000 sq. ft. ÷ 43,560 = 183.65 acres;
$1,306,800 sale price ÷ 183.65 acres =
$7,115.71 per acre, or approx. $7,116

422. d (10)
73 × 120 = 8,760 sq. ft.;
8,760 ÷ 43,560 = .20 or ⅕

423. a (14)
$248 ÷ .002 rate = $124,000 loan amount;
$124,000 note ÷ $100 increments =
1,240 taxable increments;
1,240 × $.35 = $434.00 documentary stamp taxes on note

424. b (12)
$140,000 loan ÷ $180,000 sale price =
.7778, or 78% LTV

425. d (12)
$129,500 sale price × .25 =
$32,375 down payment

426. b (13)
$325,000 unpaid balance × .05 rate = $16,250 interest ÷ 12 months = $1,354.17 first month's interest;
$1,744.67 monthly payment – $1,354.17 interest = $390.50 payment on principal in month one;
$325,000 – $390.50 principal paid first month = $324,609.50 new principal balance
$324,609.50 unpaid balance × .05 rate =
$16,230.475 interest ÷ 12 months =
$1,352.54 second month's interest;
$1,744.67 monthly payment – $1,352.54 interest = $392.13 payment on principal in month two

427. b (13)
$260,000 unpaid balance × .04 rate = $10,400 interest ÷ 12 months = $866.67 first month's interest;
$1,241.27 monthly payment – $866.67 interest = $374.60 payment on principal in month one;
$260,000 – $374.60 principal paid first month = $259,625.40 new principal balance;
$259,625.40 unpaid balance × .04 rate =
$10,385.016 ÷ 12 months = $865.42 second month's interest;
$1,241.27 month payment – $865.42 interest = $375.85 payment on principal in month two

428. a (13)
$696 monthly housing expenses ÷
$2,400 monthly gross income =
.29 FHA housing expense ratio

429. c (12)
$2,500 discount ÷ $50,000 loan =
.05 or 5 points

430. d (12)
$105,000 mortgage × .03 points =
$3,150 cost of points;
$105,000 mortgage × .01 =
$1,050 loan origination fee;
$3,150 + $1,050 =
$4,200 total loan charges

431. b (12)
$90,000 × .10 = $9,000 down payment;
$90,000 – $9,000 down payment =
$81,000 loan;
$81,000 loan × .01 =
$810 loan origination fee;
$9,000 + $810 = $9,810 total cash

432. d (10,14)
¼ = ⅖ + ⅛ = ⅜ for pond and road;
⁸⁄₈ – ⅜ = ⅝ usable area;
5 ÷ 8 = .625;
43,560 sq. ft. × .625 =
27,225 usable sq. ft.

433. d (11)
$100,000 net to seller + $5,000 closing costs = $105,000;
100% – commission rate = .94;
$105,000 ÷ .94 = $111,702.13
(round to $111,702) sale price

434. b (14)
$320,000 sale price × .07 rate =
$22,400 total commission;
100% – .45 sales associate split =
.55 broker's split;
$22,400 × .55 =
$12,320 broker's commission

435. d (14)
110 front feet × $325 per front foot =
$35,750 per lot;

$35,750 × 5 lots = $178,750 total cost;
8 lots × $28,000 sale price =
$224,000 total received;
$224,000 – $178,750 cost =
$45,250 made on sale;
$45,250 made ÷ $178,750 cost =
25.3 or approximately 25% profit.

436. a (14)
$98,400 × .07 = $6,888 total commission;
$6,888 ÷ 2 = $3,444 each broker's share

437. c (14)
$2\frac{3}{4} = 2\frac{9}{12}$; $3\frac{5}{12}$; $4\frac{5}{6} = 4\frac{10}{12}$;
$2\frac{9}{12} + 3\frac{5}{12} + 4\frac{10}{12} = 9\frac{24}{12} = 11$ acres

438. c (13)
15 years × 12 payments a year =
180 payments to date:
$450 × 180 = $81,000 total paid to date;
$45,000 mortgage × .50 paid =
$22,500 principal paid;
$81,000 – $22,500 =
$58,500 interest paid to date

439. a (16)
$200,000 lease income + $12,000 other income = $212,000 total income;
$1,395,000 ÷ $212,000 = 6.58 or 6.6 GIM

440. b (14)
$70,000 home × 2 = $140,000 home;
$30,000 lot × 300% = $90,000 amount of increase;
$70,000 + $90,000 = $160,000 profit;
$160,000 profit ÷ $100,000 cost = 1.6 or 160%

441. d (16)
$920 × 12 months = $11,040;
$940 × 12 months = $11,280;
$900 × 12 months × 3 apartments = $32,400;
$11,040 + $11,280 + $32,400 =
$54,720 annual gross income;
$54,720 × .55 = $30,096 operating expenses;
$54,720 – $30,096 = $24,624 net income

442. b (16)
$8,424 net income ÷ .105 rate =
$80,228.57 value

443. c (19)
43,560 square feet per acre × .75 land available for lots = 32,670 square feet available per acre;
32,670 ÷ 15,000 minimum square feet per lot = 2.178 lots per acre;
2.178 × 200 acres = 435.6 or 435 total subdivision lots

444. a (14)
$280,000 × .80 = $224,000 loan amount;
$224,000 × .03 = $6,720 points;
$280,000 + $6,720 = $286,720 total buyer debits;
$224,000 loan + $5,000 earnest money deposit + $2,734 tax credit = $231,734 total buyer credits;
$286,720 total debits – $231,734 total credits = $54,986 due at closing
Alternative solution:
$280,000 × .80 = $224,000 loan amount;
$224,000 × .03 = $6,720 points;
$280,000 – $224,000 = $56,000 down payment;
$56,000 + $6,720 = $65,720;
$65,720 – $5,000 earnest money deposit – $2,734 tax credit = $54,986 due at closing

445. d (14)
$289,000 × .06 rate = $17,340 total commission;
$17,340 × .50 = $8,670 selling office split;
$8,670 × .55 = $4,768.50 selling sales associate's commission

446. c (14)
100% cost – 10% loss = selling price;
90% = $36,000;
$36,000 sale price ÷ .90 = $40,000 cost

447. c (14)
100% + 20% more sales = 180 home sales;
120% = 180;
180 ÷ 1.20 = 150 home sales last year

448. d (14)
$5,600 × .20 =
$1,120 overage to the listing broker's office;
$1,120 ÷ 2 = $560 the listing broker's overage after split to sales associate

449. a (12)
$94,500 × .15 = $14,175 down payment;
$14,175 + $1,575 closing costs = $15,750;
$15,750 total buyer costs –
$10,150 earnest money =
$5,600 cash at closing

450. c (18)
$274,500 assessed value – $25,000 base exemption = $249,500 taxable value × .007 mills = $1,746.50 school taxes;
$274,500 assessed value – $50,000 total exemption = $224,500 taxable value × .018 mills = $4,041 non-school taxes;
$1,746.50 + $4,041 = $5,787.50 total property taxes due

451. d (10,14)
½ of a ¼ section = 640 ÷ 4 ÷ 2 = 80 acres;
80 acres × 43,560 sq. ft. per acre = 3,484,800 sq. ft.; 3,484,800 – 484,800 = 3,000,000 buildable sq. ft.;
3,000,000 ÷ 12,000 sq. foot lots = 250 lots;
$160,000 cost × 5 = $800,000 development cost;
$160,000 + $800,000 = $960,000 total cost;
$960,000 × 1.10 = $1,056,000 ÷ 250 lots = $4,224 average per lot

452. b (14)
$217,500 mortgage loan × .035 = $7,612.50 annual interest;
$7,612.50 ÷ 365 = $20.856164 daily rate of interest;
$20.856164 × 7 days = $145.99 debit seller; $145.99 credit buyer

453. b (16)
$334,500 × .45 = $150,525
$327,500 × .35 = $114,625
$317,900 × .20 = $63,580
$150,525 + $114,625 + $63,580 = $328,730

454. c (18)
$235,000 assessed value – $25,000 base homestead exemption – $500 survivor exemption – $500 blind exemption = $209,000 taxable value for school taxes
$235,000 assessed value – $50,000 base homestead exemption – $500 survivor exemption – $500 blind exemption = $184,000 taxable value for city and county taxes
$209,000 taxable value for school taxes × .005 = $1,045 school taxes
7.2 mills city + 8.1 mills county = 15.3 mills = .0153
$184,000 taxable value × .0153 = $2,815.20 city and county taxes
$1,045.00 + $2,815.20 = $3,860.20 total taxes due

455. a (14)
31 + 28 + 31 + 30 = 120 seller unpaid days;
$1,095 ÷ 365 days per year × 120 days = $360 debit

456. d (18)
$199,000 assessed value – $25,000 base homestead exemption – $500 survivor exemption – $500 blind exemption = $173,000 taxable value for school taxes;
$199,000 assessed value – $50,000 base homestead exemption – $500 survivor exemption – $500 blind exemption = $148,000 taxable value for city and county taxes;
$173,000 taxable value × .005 = $865 school taxes;
8.1 mills city + 8.9 mills county = 17 mills = .017;
$148,000 taxable value × .017 = $2,516 city and county taxes;
$865 + $2,516 = $3,381 total taxes due

457. b (16)
$140,000 sale price – $12,500 location + $8,000 size + $5,000 age = $140,500 adjusted sale price

458. b (16)
$89,500 cost ÷ 50-year useful life = $1,790 annual depreciation;
$1,790 × 4 years = $7,160 accumulated depreciation

459. c (14)
$600 × 2 units = $1,200 monthly rent;
$1,200 ÷ 30 days = $40 per day;
$40 × 16 days belong to buyer = $640;
Entered on closing statement;
$640 debit seller; $640 credit buyer

460. c (16)
Sale 1: $36,720 ÷ (100' × 120' = 12,000 sq. ft.) = $3.06 per sq. ft.;
Sale 2: $29,800 ÷ (100' × 100' = 10,000 sq. ft.) = $2.98 per sq. ft.;
Sale 3: $36,800 ÷ (110' × 110' = 12,100 sq. ft.) = $3.04 per sq. ft.;
Sale 4: $29,700 ÷ (90' × 110' = 9,900 sq. ft.) = $3 per sq. ft.;
$3.06 + $2.98 + $3.04 + $3 = $12.08 ÷ 4 = $3.02 average;
100' × 110' = 11,000 sq. ft. × $3.02 = $33,220 market value

461. b (16)
Sale 1: \$5,600 ÷ (100' × 130' = 13,000 sq. ft.) = \$.431 per sq. ft.;
Sale 2: \$5,800 ÷ (104' × 132' = 13,728 sq. ft.) = \$.422 per sq. ft.;
Sale 3: \$5,600 ÷ (102' × 130' = 13,260 sq. ft.) = \$.422 per sq. ft.;
Sale 4: \$5,600 ÷ (102' × 130' = 13,260 sq. ft.) = \$.422 per sq. ft.;
Sale 5: \$5,400 ÷ (100' × 132' = 13,200 sq. ft.) = \$.409 per sq. ft.;
\$.431 + \$.422 + \$.422 + \$.422 + \$.409 = \$2.106 ÷ 5 = \$.4212;
110' × 130' = 14,300 sq. ft. × \$.4212 = \$6,023 (rounded to the nearest dollar)

462. c (16)
\$144,000 ÷ 1,800 sq. ft. = \$80 per sq. foot

463. c (16)
\$113,750 ÷ \$875 monthly rent = 130 GRM

464. d (16)
1,800 sq. ft. × \$.70 = \$1,260 monthly rent;
\$1,260 rent × 120 GRM = \$151,200 market value

465. b (16)
\$480,000 reproduction cost ÷ 40 years = \$12,000 annual depreciation;
\$12,000 annual depreciation × 6 years = \$72,000 accrued;
\$480,000 – \$72,000 depreciation + \$100,000 site value = \$508,000 market value

466. c (16)
40' × 60' = 2,400 sq. ft.;
\$202,080 sale price ÷ 2,400 sq. ft. = \$84.20 cost per sq. foot

467. c (16)
100% ÷ 20 years = 5% loss per year

468. d (16)
20' × 40' = 800 sq. ft.;
\$840 monthly rent × 12 months = \$10,080 annual rent;
\$10,080 ÷ 800 sq. ft. = \$12.60 per sq. foot

469. b (16)
\$4,800 monthly net × 12 months = \$57,600 annual NOI;
\$57,600 NOI ÷ .12 rate = \$480,000 original cost

470. a (16)
\$475 rent × 8 units × 12 months = \$45,600 PGI;
\$45,600 × .10 = \$4,560 vacancy loss;
\$45,600 – \$4,560 = \$41,040 EGI;
\$41,040 EGI – (\$1,875 × 12 months = \$22,500 operating expense) = \$18,540 NOI;
\$18,540 NOI ÷ .12 cap rate = \$154,500 market value

471. c (16)
\$96,400 EGI – \$36,600 operating expense = \$59,800 NOI

472. d (19)
120' × 150' × 2 stories = 36,000 total sq. ft.;
36,000 × .90 = 32,400 sq. ft. available for bin storage;
10' × 12'= 120 sq. ft. per bin;
32,400 sq. ft. ÷ 120 sq. ft. = 270 bins

473. d (16)
\$185,000 × .08 cap rate = \$14,800 NOI;
\$14,800 NOI ÷ .40 = \$37,000 EGI

474. b (16)
Project 1: \$39,400 NOI ÷ \$345,000 sale price = .114;
Project 2: \$45,680 NOI ÷ \$464,000 sale price = .098;
Project 3: \$36,800 NOI ÷ \$386,000 sale price = .095;
Project 4: \$43,790 NOI ÷ \$424,000 sale price = .103;
.114 + .098 + .095 + .103 = .41 ÷ 4 = .1025 = 10.25%

475. c (12)
1 ÷ 8 = .125 × 3 points = 0.375
4% + .375 = 4.375% effective yield

476. c (12)
\$145,000 loan + \$55,000 down payment = \$200,000 sale price;
\$145,000 ÷ \$200,000 = .725 or 72.5% LTV

477. a (16)
\$26,750 EGI – \$8,350 operating expense = \$18,400 NOI

478. b (16)
\$26,750 PGI – (\$8,350 fixed expense + \$450 reserves);
\$26,750 PGI – \$8,800 operating expense = \$17,950 NOI

479. b (18)
(a) $49,500 value × 100% = $49,500
(b) $66,900 value × 75% = $50,175
(c) $81,400 value × 60% = $48,840
(d) $119,600 value × 40% = $47,840

480. b (14)
Seller owes 31 days in May + 15 days in June = 46 days; $105,500 mortgage balance × .08 = $8,440 ÷ 365 = $23.12 interest per day; $23.12 × 46 days = $1,063.52 debit

481. d (13)
FHA allows up to 31% for housing expense ratio (HER); FHA allows up to 43% for total obligations ratio (TOR); HER = $658 monthly housing expense ÷ $2,350 monthly gross income = 28%; $658 monthly housing expense + $282 other credit obligation = $940; TOR = $940 total monthly obligation ÷ $2,350 monthly gross income = 40%

482. c (16)
8 years effective age ÷ 55 years economic life = .145; .145 × $300,000 = $43,500 accrued depreciation

483. c (12)
$1,500,000 value – $1,250,000 mortgage = $250,000 equity

484. d (12)
$190,000 purchase price × .60 LTV = $114,000 loan amount; $190,000 – $114,000 = $76,000 buyer responsibility; $76,000 × .43 = $32,680 purchase money mortgage; $114,000 + $32,680 = $146,680 amount financed; $190,000 – $146,680 = $43,320 down payment

485. c (16)
$319,900 × .45 = $143,955
$312,500 × .35 = $109,375
$308,500 × .20 = $61,700
$143,955 + $109,375 + $61,700 = $315,030

486. b (16) $150,000 investor funds × .20 return = $30,000 income needed; $30,000 + $30,000 operating expenses = $60,000 total needed; $60,000 ÷ 12 months = $5,000 per month needed; $5,000 ÷ 4 units = $1,250 monthly rent per unit

487. d (16)
$220 rent × 10 units = $2,200 × 12 months = $26,400 income; $185 rent × 6 units = $1,110 × 12 months = $13,320 income; $35 × 4 units = $140 × 52 weeks = $7,280 income; $26,400 + $13,320 + $7,280 = $47,000 gross rental income

488. d (10)
140 feet × 160 feet = 22,400 square feet; 22,400 ÷ 43,560 square feet per acre = .514 acre
.514 acre × 100% = 51.4%

BROKER INVESTMENT PROBLEMS

489. c $650 rent × 12 units × 12 months = $93,600 PGI

490. b $93,600 PGI × .05 V&C rate = $4,680 V&C loss;
$93,600 – $4,680 = $88,920 effective gross income

491. c $88,920 EGI × .30 = $26,676 operating expenses

492. d $88,920 EGI – $26,676 operating expenses = $62,244 NOI

493. a $1,995.91 × 12 months = $23,950.92 rounded to $23,951 annual debt service

494. d $62,244 NOI ÷ $23,951 = 2.599 or 2.60 rounded

495. d $62,244 NOI – $23,951 annual debt service = $38,293 before-tax cash flow

496. c $26,676 operating expenses ÷ $88,920 EGI = .30

497. d $38,293 before-tax cash flow ÷ $50,000 down payment = .7658 or 76.6%

498. b $350,000 purchase price – $50,000 land = $300,000 depreciable basis;
$300,000 ÷ 27.5 years = $10,909 annual depreciation

499. a $26,676 operating expenses – $10,000 reserves + $23,951 annual debt service = $40,627; $40,627 ÷ $93,600 PGI = .434 or 43.4%

500. a $345,000 appraised value × .80 maximum loan/value ratio = $276,000 maximum loans allowed; $276,000 total loans allowed – $181,435 current 1st mortgage = $94,565 available for 2nd mortgage

501. d $995,000 total purchase price + $4,500 appraisal + $900 survey + $3,400 title insurance = $1,003,800 total acquisition cost; $1,003,800 × .80 allocated to the building = $803,040 depreciable basis

502. c $1,675,000 purchase price × .80 building allocation = $1,340,000 depreciable basis; $1,340,000 ÷ 39 years = $34,358.97 rounded to $34,359 typical depreciation

503. d $3,250 base rent × 12 months = $39,000 annual base rent; $39,000 ÷ .05 percentage rate = $780,000 annual sales before additional rent is due

CLOSING DISCLOSURE QUESTIONS FOR BROKER CANDIDATES

504. c $47,950 ÷ $100 = 479.5, round up to 480; 480 × $.35 = $168; $20,000 ÷ $100 = 200; 200 × $.35 = $70; $20,000 × $.002 = $40.00; $168 + $70 + $40 = $278.00. Government expenses of the sale appear on page two of the closing disclosure.

505. b 3 mills + 4.5 mills + 8.5 mills = 16 total mills (.016); $96,000 × .016 = $1,536 taxes for year; $1,536 ÷ 365 = $4.0208219 per day × 221 seller days = $930.02. Prorations are entered on page three of the closing disclosure.

506. b $20,000 × .09 (9%) = $1,800; $1,800 ÷ 365 = $4.931507 per day × 22 days = $108.49. Lender charges to be prepaid at closing are shown on page two of the closing disclosure.

507. a Buyer owns the property for 22 days of the rental period for apartment one; $475 ÷ 31 = $15.322258 per day × 22 days = $337.10; buyer owns the property for 5 days of the rental period for apartment two; $475 ÷ 31 = $15.322258 per day × 5 days = $76.61; $337.10 + $76.61 = $413.71 credit for the buyer. Prorations are entered on page three of the closing disclosure.

508. a The binder deposit is always shown on page three of the closing disclosure as a credit for the buyer.

509. c Documentary stamps on the deed: $115,650 purchase price ÷ $100 = 1156.5 round up to 1157; $1,157 × $.70 = $809.90. Commission: $115,650 × .075 (7½%) = $8,673.75. Government expenses of the sale and commission are entered on page two of the closing disclosure.

510. d Assumed loan balance of $47,950 × .01 (1%) = $479.50; discount points on new loan of $20,000 × .015 (1½%) = $300.00. Lender charges for the buyer are shown on page two of the closing disclosure.

511. b The seller owes the lender 10 days of interest for the month of August; $23,000 × .10 (10%) = $2,300 ÷ 12 = $191.67 interest for month of August; $191.67 ÷ 31 = $6.182903 per day × 10 days = $61.83; $61.83 + $23,000 loan balance = $23,061.83. Any loan the seller is required to pay off is shown on page three of the closing disclosure.

MATH CROSS-REFERENCE KEY

You will find each type of real estate math problem explained and worked out in the companion textbook, *Florida Real Estate Principles, Practices & Law.*

Textbook Unit	***Math Subject***
3	license fees
6	administrative fines
6	Real Estate Recovery Fund payments
14	state documentary stamp tax on deeds
10	legal descriptions; measurements
10, 19	lots per acre and lot prices
10, 16	building square footages and prices
14	state intangible tax on mortgages
14	state documentary stamp tax on notes
13	FHA mortgage insurance program (MIP)
13	FHA down payments and loan amounts
13	VA down payments and loan amounts
12	loan-to-value ratios (LTV)
13	private mortgage insurance (PMI)
13	adjustable-rate mortgage (ARM)
13	housing expense ratio; total obligations ratio
12	discount points
12	loan origination and service fees
14	fractions, decimals, and percentages
14	sale commissions
14	selling price, cost, and profit
13	mortgage amortization
13	mortgage interest
14	prorated expenses
14	prepaid rent
14, 18	property taxes
14	hazard insurance
14	state taxes—three
14	other charges at closings
16	estimating value comparable sales
16	comparable market analysis (CMA)

Textbook Unit	***Math Subject***
16	net adjustments
16	gross rent (income) multipliers (GRM, GIM)
16	estimating value cost approach
16	depreciation (straight-line)
16	economic (useful) life
16	estimating value income approach
16	potential gross income (PGI)
16	effective gross income (EGI)
16	net operating income (NOI)
16	overall capitalization rate (OAR)
16	return on investment
18	federal income taxes
18	homestead tax exemptions
18	property tax rates
18	special assessments
18	capital gains
18	sale of residence
19	density for zoning, land-use requirements

PRACTICE EXAM 1

Note: Correct letter answer is followed (in parenthesis) by *Florida Real Estate Principles, Practices & Law* unit number(s) and a brief explanation of the correct answer.

1. c (11) A community development district (CDD) is an independent district authorized by Florida law to service the long-term specific needs of its community.
2. c (5) Rule 61J2-10.028(2) provides that a licensee may share a commission with a party to a real estate transaction, which includes real estate sale and purchase agreements and lease agreements, provided the arrangement is disclosed to all interested parties.
3. a (17) Goodwill is the intangible asset attributed to a business's reputation and the expectation of continued customer loyalty. The value of goodwill may be approximated by subtracting the value of tangible assets from the value of the business.
4. c (8) An estate for years exists for a designated period, which may be any length of time from less than a year to many years, such as a 99-year lease.
5. b (10) A township is a square six miles on each side (6 miles square). There are 640 acres in a section (not a township).
6. c (15) A 90% occupancy means 10% or 43 units are vacant.
7. a (7) The landlord is required to provide exterminating service, garbage receptacles and pickup, and working equipment for heat, plus running water. The landlord is allowed to charge tenants for services provided, if the charges are a part of the rental agreement.
8. a (11) Section 475.25(1)(r), F.S. indicates that a listing agreement must include a definite expiration date, description of the property, price and terms, and fee or commission. However, there is no requirement that the listing be in written form.
9. b (16) The highest and best use of land as though vacant is the legal (permissible) use of the site that would produce the greatest value.
10. c (7) The Fair Housing Act only prohibits discrimination based on race, color, religion, national origin, gender, familial status, and disability. College students are not a protected class.
11. a (5) Brokers must deposit earnest money no later than the end of the third business day following receipt of a deposit by a sales associate or employee of the brokerage firm.
12. d (4) Chapter 475.78, F.S. requires real estate licensees to submit all offers up until title closing unless instructed otherwise by the seller.
13. c (3) If the military duty is out of state (not in Florida), the exemption also applies to a licensed spouse.
14. d (5) If the only active broker of a brokerage dies, resigns, or is unexpectedly unable to remain in the position as active broker, the vacancy must be filled within 14 calendar days.
15. c (6) The buyer can be reimbursed for the lost earnest money deposit up to a maximum of $50,000. Punitive damages cannot be recovered from the Recovery Fund.

16. d (6) Conversion is the unauthorized control or use of another's personal property, including misappropriation of an employed sales associate's commission.

17. d (1) Community association management is applicable to mobile home parks, planned unit developments, homeowners associations, cooperatives, timeshares, and condominiums. A CAM license is not required to manage apartment buildings, commercial property, or single-family dwellings.

18. d (13) The Real Estate Settlement Procedures Act (RESPA) prohibits a seller from requiring the homebuyer to use a particular title insurance company as a condition of sale.

19. d (8) A tenancy at sufferance is said to exist when the tenant, after rightfully being in possession of the rented premises, continues possession after the lease agreement has ended.

20. a (5) Rule 61J2-10.032(2)(c) requires brokers to notify the FREC within 10 business days if the dispute is settled or the matter goes to court before an EDO is issued.

21. b (18) The Save Our Home amendment of the Florida Constitution caps how much the assessed value of homesteaded property can increase in a given year.

22. d (2) Section 475.01, F.S. requires that anyone who performs real estate services for another for compensation of any type must be licensed. Compensation is defined as anything of value.

23. c (4) The appropriate type of brokerage relationship is determined by the broker. Some brokerage firms choose to operate as transaction brokers exclusively or only as single agents for buyers.

24. d (4) A licensee is obligated to disclose facts regarding a property's true worth.

25. d (18) The maximum allowable homestead exemption for this homestead is: $25,000 base exemption + $500 surviving spouse exemption + $5,000 exemption for disabled veterans + $25,000 additional homestead exemption on homesteaded properties with an assessed value of $75,000 or more = $55,500.

26. a (5) The court procedure used if the broker does not have a financial claim to the disputed escrow funds is known as interpleader.

27. a (4) One situation that does not create a brokerage relationship is at a bona fide open house or model home showing that does not involve eliciting confidential information; the execution of a contractual offer or an agreement for representation; or negotiations concerning price, terms, or conditions of potential sale. When a licensee encounters a prospective buyer in this situation, the licensee is not required to give the buyer a disclosure notice.

28. b (12) The defeasance clause is a provision in a mortgage that specifies the terms and conditions to be met in order to avoid default and thereby defeat the mortgage.

29. a (6) If probable cause is found to exist, the probable-cause panel will direct the Department to file a formal complaint against the subject of the complaint.

30. d (2) It is a violation of Chapter 475 to pay an unlicensed person for performing the services of real estate. Compensation is anything paid or expected to be paid associated with performing real estate services.

31. c (4) Full disclosure is a single agent duty. Limited confidentiality is a transaction broker duty. Dealing honestly and fairly, and accounting for all funds are duties of transaction brokers and single agents.

32. d (5) Rule 61J2-10.023(2) states that a mere temporary shelter on a subdivision being sold by the broker, for the protection of the sales staff and customers, and where transactions are not closed, is not considered to be a branch office.

33. c (8) Reliction is the process of gradual receding of water that uncovers land that previously was covered by water.

34. b (3) A sales associate who is employed by an owner-developer may be issued a group license according to Rule 61J2-6.006.

35. c (5) The broker must deposit the earnest money in his escrow account by the end of the third business day following receipt of the funds.

36. a (5) If a buyer of a residential condominium unit timely delivers to a licensee written notice of the buyer's intent to cancel the contract as authorized by the Condominium Act, the licensee may return the escrowed property to the purchaser without notifying the Commission or initiating any of the settlement procedures.

37. d (6) A Florida broker may pay a referral fee to a broker licensed in another state so long as the foreign broker does not violate Florida law. It is a violation of Section 475.25, F.S. for a licensee to share a commission or pay a fee to a person not properly licensed under Chapter 475, F.S. and to practice without a valid and current Florida license. In this case the Florida broker shared a commission with a broker who was not licensed in Florida and who came to Florida and performed real estate services in Florida.

38. b (5) All general partners who expect to deal with the public on behalf of the limited partnership must be licensed as active brokers, with at least one of the general partners personally qualified and licensed as an active broker at all times.

39. b (5) A broker who receives conflicting demands regarding escrowed funds must notify the FREC, in writing, within 15 business days.

40. c (9) In a quitclaim deed, the grantor makes no warranties about the quality or extent of the title being conveyed. The grantor does not warrant to defend the title interest conveyed.

41. b (7) Blockbusting is the illegal practice of inducing homeowners to sell their property by making misrepresentations regarding the entry of certain groups of people in order to cause a turnover of properties in the neighborhood.

42. d (19) Setbacks are restrictions established by zoning or deed on the space required between lot lines and building lines.

43. b (17) When the interest paid for borrowed money is higher than the overall return from an investment, the result is negative leverage.

44. b (2) Certified public accountants (CPAs) are exempt from real estate licensure when performing accounting duties within the scope of their professional duties. However, in this situation, the CPA is performing real estate services and therefore has violated Chapter 475, F.S. Additionally, the owner-developers have paid an unlicensed person for performing real estate services. Therefore, all three individuals have violated Chapter 475, F.S.

45. a (8) The Florida Vacation Plan and Timesharing Act applies to all time-share plans consisting of more than seven time-share periods over a span of at least three years.

46. a (7) Section 83.62(2), F.S., states that the landlord or the landlord's agent may remove any personal property found on the premises to or near the property line.

47. b (12) The doctrine of caveat emptor has been held to apply in foreclosure sales. The purchaser is presumed to know that he is purchasing subject to any prior liens of record or interests for which there is constructive notice.

48. d (13) A purchase money mortgage is any new mortgage taken as part of the purchase price of real property by the seller. Technically speaking, any mortgage on real property executed to secure the purchase money by a purchaser simultaneously with acquiring legal title is a purchase money mortgage. In a contract for deed, the purchaser does not get legal title until all payments have been made.

49. d (16) Active real estate licensees are allowed to perform a comparative market analysis (CMA) for the purpose of obtaining a listing.

50. d (2) Persons who work on site in a leasing capacity and are paid a salary are exempt from licensure. If they are paid a commission or bonuses based on numbers of transactions, they must be licensed.

51. b (11) The elements of a valid real estate contract are competent buyer and seller; offer and acceptance; legal purpose; consideration; and that the contract be in writing and signed.

52. c (12) In a subject to the mortgage arrangement, the buyer makes regular periodic payments on the mortgage but does not assume responsibility for the mortgage.

53. a (8) An estate for years is a leasehold or nonfreehold estate.

54. c (8) Any property acquired during the marriage, whether by one spouse or both spouses, is considered a marital asset and will be distributed equitably.

55. d (2) An unlicensed individual may not perform real estate services for compensation. Compensation is defined as anything of value or a valuable consideration, directly or indirectly paid, promised, or expected to be paid or received.

56. c (2, 6) The promise or expectation of compensation for performing real estate services without a license is illegal. The unlicensed practice of real estate is a third-degree felony.

57. c (16) If correction of a defect results in greater added value than the cost to correct, the defect is curable.

58. c (4) A listing that is not reasonably priced will attract very few prospects in relation to the carry costs, including MLS fees, advertising, and so forth.

59. d (4) Expiration of the terms of the listing agreement will terminate a brokerage relationship.

60. d (6) False advertising and culpable negligence are misdemeanors of the second degree. Unlicensed practice of real estate is a felony of the third degree. Failing to provide accurate and current rental information for a fee is a first-degree misdemeanor.

61. d (1) Dedication is the gift of land by a developer to a governmental body for a public use.

62. b (12) A note is a promise to repay that makes the borrower personally liable for the obligation. The mortgage note serves as evidence of the debt for which the mortgage on the property is the security. If the security is insufficient to cover the indebtedness, the holder of the note can obtain a deficiency judgment against the debtor.

63. a (6) A broker who purchases property from the listing seller and subsequently sells it at a higher price and keeps the profit may be considered to be guilty of fraud, misrepresentation, concealment, and/or dishonest dealing and could expose the broker to liability for the full amount of the secret profit and disciplinary action.

64. d (16) The principle of substitution is the basis for all three approaches to market value. It means that a prudent buyer or investor will pay no more for a property than the cost of acquiring, through purchase or construction, an equally desirable alternative property.

65. d (8) A condominium is created by recording a declaration in the public records. Buyers own an undivided fractional share of the buildings and land known as common elements. Condominium owners are responsible for mortgage payments on their units. Shares of stock are associated with cooperatives.

66. c (12) Novation is the substitution of a new party and/or new terms to an existing obligation.

67. d (14) Interest on an assumed mortgage is entered as a debit to the seller and as a credit to the buyer.

68. d (17) Financial risk, also called operating financial risk, is associated with the ability of a property to cover operating expenses from funds provided from operations, borrowing, and equity sources.

69. d (11) The Florida Vacation and Timesharing Act requires that purchasers of a time-share period may cancel the purchase agreement within 10 calendar days of contract signing or receipt of the public offering statement, whichever is later. The 10-calendar-day rescission period applies to time-share periods sold by the developer and resale.

70. c (11) Once a counteroffer is made, the buyer's original offer is no longer available for acceptance.

71. a (2) Chapter 20, Florida statutes, establishes the structure of the executive branch of Florida's government.

72. b (9) Recording a properly executed and acknowledged instrument of conveyance puts the world on notice regarding an owner's interests in real property.

73. a (9) Equitable title is a beneficial interest in real property implying that an individual will receive legal title at a future date.

74. d (18) Taxable value is the assessed value less allowable exemptions resulting in an amount to which the tax rate is applied to determine property taxes due.

75. d (2) It is legal to pay an out-of-state broker a referral fee, provided the out-of-state broker does not come to Florida and practice real estate services in this state.

76. c (6) Culpable negligence is the inadequate attention to duties and obligations by one who knows, or should know, what is required.

77. c (18) To calculate the dollar amount of property taxes owed, the taxable value of the property is multiplied by the appropriate tax rate.

78. c (2) A broker applicant must hold an active real estate license for at least 24 months during the five-year period preceding application to become a Florida real estate broker.

79. b (5) The amount of commission to be paid is negotiable, and it is arrived at by agreement between the broker and the buyer or the seller. A provision providing for the broker to retain the deposit would need to be disclosed and agreed to by all parties.

80. a (18) To prevent foreign sellers from avoiding the payment of taxes due on the sale of real property, the IRS requires that buyers withhold 15% of the gross sale price (including cash paid and any debt assumed by the buyer). The buyer must report the purchase and pay the IRS the amount withheld.

81. d (6) If a broker requested an EDO and complied with it, the Commission is authorized to pay the broker's reasonable attorney's fees and court costs. The Commission is also authorized to pay the plaintiff's reasonable attorney fees and court costs.

82. c (11) The Florida Landlord and Tenant Act provides that, upon a change in the designated rental agent, the security deposits and advance rents being held for the benefit of the tenants must be transferred to the new agent with an accounting statement showing the amounts to be credited to each tenant's account.

83. a (16) The sales comparison approach is typically used for vacant lots or for valuing a site as though vacant.

84. b (13) The VA uses a total monthly obligations ratio of 41%. The VA total obligations ratio is determined by dividing total PITI and other monthly payments by the total monthly gross income.

85. a (10) In the government survey system, certain north-south longitudes were designated principal meridians and certain east-west latitudes were designated base lines.

86. d (12) If a borrower wants to get a lower interest rate, the lender will often agree to a lower rate if the borrower agrees to pay the lender discount points at closing.

87. b (18) The amount realized (or adjusted sale price) is the selling price minus selling expenses.

88. d (16) Situs refers to relationships and influences created by location of a property that affect value, such as accessibility and personal preference.

89. b (19) To plan efficiently beyond local community boundaries, a comprehensive plan (or master plan) is developed for the purpose of guiding future growth.

90. d (14) Amount made on sale divided by total cost equals percent profit
$125 per foot × 300 feet =
$37,500 sale price;
$37,500 sale price – $15,000 orig cost =
$22,500 ÷ 15,000 = 1.5 or 150% profit

91. a (14) $135,000 loan × .05 interest =
$6,750 annual interest;
$6,750 ÷ 12 months =
$562.50 interest month 1;
$562.50 × 3 months = $1,687.50

92. a (14) The exact number of days owed by the seller are January 31 + February 28 + March 31 + April 30 + May 31 + June 30 + July 31 + August 31 + September 10 = 253 days;
$1,700 ÷ 365 = 4.6575342 per day;
$4.6575342 per day × 253 days = $1,178.3562 rounded to $1,178.36 (debit seller; credit buyer)

93. b (12) $165,000 sale price × .20 =
$33,000 down payment;
$33,000 – $12,200 deposit =
$20,800 cash at closing

94. d (14)
1,452 × 1,200 = 1,742,400 sq. ft.; 1,742,400 ÷ 43,560 = 40 acres;
40 × $3,000 = $120,000 sale price;
$120,000 ÷ 100 × .70 =
$840 doc stamps on deed

95. c (12)
6 × ⅛ = 6/8 = ¾;
3½ + ¾ = 4¼% or 4.25% yield

96. d (10)
640 ÷ 4 ÷ 4 ÷ 4 ÷ 4 = 2.5 acres

97. c (18)
$230,000 assessed value – $25,000 =
$205,000 taxable value for schools
$230,000 – $50,000 = $180,000 taxable value for city and county taxes
$205,000 × .0073 = $1,496.50 school taxes
8.2 mills city + 9.0 mills county = 17.2 mills city and county
$180,000 × .0172 = $3,096.00
$1,496.50 + $3,096.00 = $4,592.50

98. b (16)
$90,000 ÷ 40 total economic life × 7 years =
$15,750 accrued depreciation;
$90,000 – $15,750 + $20,000 land value =
$94,250

99. b (14)
$50,000 × .10 = $5,000;
$100,000 × .05 = $5,000;
$60,000 × .03 = $1,800;
$5,000 + $5,000 + $1,800 =
$11,800 total commission;
$11,800 × .90 = $10,620 remaining after listing commissions paid;
$10,620 × .65 =
$6,903 Sales Associate B's commission

100. c (16)
$70,400 PGI × .04 = $2,816 V&C;
$70,400 PGI – $2,816 V&C = $67,584 EGI;
$67,584 EGI – $12,770 op. exp. =
$54,814 NOI

PRACTICE EXAM 2

Note: Correct letter answer is followed (in parenthesis) by *Florida Real Estate Principles, Practices & Law* unit number(s) and a brief explanation of the correct answer.

1. b (9) A completed and signed deed transfers title to the grantee when the grantor voluntarily delivers it to the grantee and the grantee willingly accepts it.

2. c (5) The FREC created a list of activities that may be conducted by an unlicensed personal assistant. One of the permissible activities is to hand out objective—written information on a listing or a rental. Conducting listing presentations, showing property to a buyer, and presenting offers are real estate services that require a real estate license.

3. b (3) The sales associate completed his post-licensing education in a previous renewal cycle. If the sales associate completes his 14-hour continuing education requirement and renews within 12 months following the expiration of his license, he will be charged a late fee.

4. c (4) In nonresidential transactions where both the buyer and seller have assets of at least $1 million each, the buyer and seller may request that the broker designate one licensee in the firm to be a single agent representative of the buyer and *another* licensee to be a single agent representative of the seller. For an individual to represent both the buyer and the seller as a single agent representative is a dual agency relationship, which is a violation of Section 475.272(1).

5. d (4) Brokers must retain brokerage relationship disclosure documents for five years for all nonresidential transactions (even for contracts that fail to close) that use designated sales associates.

6. a (5) A real estate licensee must verify that a telephone number is not listed on the National Do Not Call Registry before cold calling for potential listings. Violators can be fined up to $16,000 for each illegal call.

7. a (5) If sales associates create promotional materials, such as refrigerator magnets and notepads, they must include the licensed name of the brokerage firm.

8. b (4) Section 475.5015, F.S. requires the broker to retain, for at least five years, brokerage relationship disclosure documents in all transactions that result in a written contract to purchase and sell real property. The law does *not* stipulate only "closed" transactions.

9. c (5) Buyer paid fees must be placed in the broker's escrow (trust) account.

10. b (16) Section 475.25(1)(t) requires real estate licensees to abide by the USPAP. Rule 61J2-24.001(3)(t) sets forth the usual disciplinary guidelines for violating the USPAP.

11. c (5) Sales associates are prohibited from initiating a suit or action for compensation in connection with a real estate transaction against anyone except the person registered as their employer.

12. a (2) The broker could have paid a flat fee for the HUD list. However, to tie the compensation to transactions that close is a violation of Chapter 475, F.S.

13. d (11) Buyers of homes built prior to 1978 are required to sign a "Lead Disclosure" form before signing the sale contract. Sellers are required to disclose the presence of any known lead-based paint in the home, and buyers and renters must be given an EPA pamphlet regarding lead-based paint. Buyers have a right to have the home inspected for lead-based paint but are not required to have the home inspected.

14. b (4) Brokerage relationships extend throughout the business entity and include any branch offices of the firm. However, they do not extend to other real estate brokerage entities.

15. c (5) Entrance signs must include the name of the broker, trade name (if applicable), and the words "Licensed Real Estate Broker." In the case of a corporation, the sign must include the name of the corporation.

16. a (11) Although it is desirable to have a closing date on the contract, it is not a required element to make a real estate contract enforceable. If necessary, the courts interpret the closing to be accomplished in "a reasonable period of time."

17. b (3) Rule 61J2-10.038 states that real estate licensees must notify the DBPR in writing of a change in mailing address within 10 days after the change.

18. d (8) An important characteristic of joint tenancies with right of survivorship is that the property automatically belongs to the surviving joint tenant on the death of the other joint tenant.

19. c (5) If a broker desires to conduct business from additional locations, the broker must register each additional location as a branch office and pay the appropriate registration fees.

20. a (7) When money is given to a landlord as a security deposit or advance rent, the landlord, without regard to the total number of dwelling units, is obligated to account for the funds in one of three ways: (1) hold the funds in a separate non-interest-bearing Florida bank for the benefit of the tenant; (2) hold the money in a separate interest-bearing Florida bank account for the benefit of the tenant (and pay the tenant at least 75% of the annualized average interest or 5% per year); or (3) post a bond.

21. d (5) Escrow accounts may be established in a Florida-based title company having trust powers, Florida commercial banks, credit unions, savings associations, or, if designated in the sale contract, a Florida attorney.

22. b (5) A broker is not required to maintain an escrow account. However, without one, the broker cannot hold funds belonging to others.

23. d (12) Discount points are an extra, up-front fee to increase the real yield, or annual percentage rate, to the lender.

24. c (7) Section 760.23(9)(a), F.S. prohibits landlords from refusing to allow a tenant with a disability to make reasonable modifications to a residential dwelling at the tenant's own expense.

25. a (10) Ranges are numbered east and west of the principal meridian. The range due east of R1E is R2E, so the township due east of T1N, R1E would be T1N, R2E.

26. c (2) The question on the application for licensure requires the applicant to disclose the crime regarding the unemployment checks even if adjudication was withheld. See Section 475.25(1)(m), F.S. and 61J2-24.001(n), F.A.C.

27. b (16) The comparable property is superior to the subject regarding number of bathrooms. The value of the extra half bath is subtracted from the comparable's transaction price.

28. c (2) The question requires applicants to disclose if they have ever been convicted of a crime, found guilty, or entered a plea of guilty or nolo contendere, even if adjudication was withheld. The question applies to violation of laws without regard to whether an individual was placed on probation or had adjudication withheld, or was paroled or pardoned. Failure to answer truthfully could result in denial of licensure.

29. d (18) The maximum allowable homestead exemption for this homestead is: $25,000 base exemption + $500 surviving spouse exemption + $500 legally blind exemption + $25,000 additional homestead exemption on homesteaded properties with an assessed value of $75,000 or more = $51,000.

30. b (7) Section 83.67(2), F.S. of the Florida Landlord and Tenant Act prohibits a landlord from preventing a tenant reasonable access to the dwelling unit. The landlord must seek legal remedy through eviction procedures.

31. d (2) The post-licensing education requirement has the effect of placing initial licenses in a probationary status because failure to complete the post-licensing education will cause the license to become null and void.

32. d (13) Regulation Z of the Truth in Lending Act requires certain disclosures when triggering terms are included in advertisements. Triggering terms include the amount or percentage of the down payment, the amount of any payment, the number of payments, the period of repayment, and the amount of any finance charge.

33. a (9) A net lease requires the tenant to pay property expenses, including property taxes, hazard insurance, and utilities.

34. c (7) The tenant's financial status is not a protected classification. The landlord, however, is obligated to use uniform criteria and screening practices with all prospective tenants.

35. a (10) A township is a square six miles on each side (6 miles square) containing 36 square miles (36 sections).

36. c (6) Section 475.48(2)(d), F.S. mandates that a claim cannot be made against the Real Estate Recovery Fund if the license was not a valid, current, and active one at the time of the transaction.

37. d (3) Quasi-legislative responsibilities of the Commission include the power to enact administrative rules and regulations and to interpret questions regarding the practice of real estate.

38. d (5) Florida law does not prohibit licensees from recording judgments.

39. c (16) The potential highest and best use of a site determines the site's value.

40. b (16) Reproduction costs of improvements and market evidence of depreciation apply to the cost-depreciation approach. Recent land sales applies to the sales comparison approach. The income approach is based on present value of expected income. Information regarding expenses is necessary to calculate projected net operating income.

41. b (10) The most common type of legal description used for single-family dwellings located in developed subdivisions is the lot and block method of land description, which can be used only where plat maps have been recorded in the public records.

42. c (6) The licensee is entitled to an informal or formal hearing. A licensee may choose an informal hearing only if there is no disagreement regarding the material facts of the case. A stipulation is a voluntary agreement between the petitioner (DBPR, DRE) and the respondent (licensee).

43. b (5) Licensees can be issued a $300 citation for misrepresenting themselves as REALTORS® when they are not current members of the Florida Realtors®.

44. a (6) Punitive damages may not be reimbursed from the Real Estate Recovery Fund. The claimant may seek reimbursement of $30,000 in actual damages.

45. c (5) The best advice is to request the buyer to write a check payable to the broker's escrow account.

46. c (4) An arm's length transaction is one in which the parties are dealing from equal bargaining positions. Medallion Financial Services, Inc., to Medallion Taxi Enterprises, Inc. and Microfirm, Inc., to Net, Inc. (Microfirm is a shareholder of Net, Inc.) involve transactions where there is a business relationship of some sort. Mrs. Sammis, mother, to Dean Sammis, son is a transaction between relatives.

47. b (8) Fixtures are objects that were personal property permanently attached to or made part of real property and thus are now real property.

48. d (5) The sales associate can be compensated only by the employing broker, ABC Realty Company. XYZ must pay the selling portion of the commission to XYZ Realty.

49. a (9) Condemnation is the taking of private real property for a public purpose under the right of eminent domain for a fair price.

50. d (8) Homesteading the principal residence protects the property from personal debts, such as lawsuits, credit card debt, medical expenses, and so on. It does not protect against expenses associated with the principal residence, such as property taxes, mortgage payments, and improvements made to the property. (See Chapter 222.10, F.S.)

51. b (9) A percentage lease is a proportional sharing of the monthly or annual gross sales made on leased premises.

52. a (11) An express contract is an actual written agreement of the parties in which the terms have been stated clearly.

53. d (18) Homeowners may deduct property taxes and interest paid on a mortgage on a principal residence.

54. c (11) No commission is due because it has not been earned under the terms of the listing agreement. The broker is entitled to damages for out-of-pocket expenses incurred while marketing the property prior to the seller's cancellation of the contract.

55. c (5) A corporation is an artificial or fictitious person formed to conduct business activities. A major advantage of a corporation structure is protection of personal assets.

56. a (6) Section 455.224, F.S. provides that a licensee has 30 days from the day a citation is served to dispute it. After that, the citation becomes a final order and constitutes discipline.

57. b (2) Requests to review the license exam must be received within 21 days after the date of the examination (release date on the original exam report).

58. d (5) When one or more of the parties has expressed intention not to close and the broker has not received identical instructions from all parties concerning disbursement of escrowed funds, good-faith doubt exists.

59. b (5) A broker may have an office(s) in another state, provided the broker agrees in writing to cooperate with any investigation initiated under Chapter 475, F.S. The broker must maintain an escrow account with a title company, bank, credit union, or savings association located and doing business in Florida.

60. d (12) A subordination agreement signed by the first mortgage lienholder will permit the junior mortgage to have priority over the first mortgage.

61. c (13) The Real Estate Settlement Procedures Act (RESPA) was enacted to ensure that buyers are informed regarding the amount and type of charges they will pay at closing.

62. d (4) The licensee working in a nonrepresentative capacity may provide a CMA to a buyer or seller. However, "the licensee should refrain from making recommendations or consulting with the buyer or seller when in a nonrepresentative role and may not represent the CMA as an appraisal."

63. c (8, 9) The surviving spouse gets the homestead through right of survivorship, but the investment property will be devised according to the will.

64. d (9) An easement in gross is a type of easement that is not related to a specific adjacent parcel. Utility easements and railroad easements are easements in gross.

65. c (9) An acknowledgment is a formal declaration before an authorized official, by the person who executed the instrument, that it is a free act.

66. b (18) The current tax law allows gain up to $500,000 to be excluded when filing a joint return ($250,000 when filing a single tax return). Any gain in excess of the exclusion is taxable.

67. b (12) The due-on-sale clause and granting clause apply to deed instruments. The mortgagor (not mortgagee) signs the mortgage

instrument. A legal description is included in all mortgage instruments.

68. d (13) The Real Estate Settlement Procedures Act (RESPA) prohibits both the payment and receipt of referral fees for any service needed to close a real estate transaction.

69. b (19) Building codes are enacted by local governments to protect the public health and safety from inferior construction practices. They establish minimum standards for a building's design, construction, use and occupancy, and quality.

70. a (3) Two Commissioners are consumer (unlicensed or lay) members who have never been real estate brokers or sales associates.

71. c (15) Availability of skilled labor is a variable that influences supply.

72. b (1) Only a state-certified or licensed appraiser can prepare an appraisal that involves a federally related transaction.

73. c (2) The definition of real estate includes business opportunities; therefore, individuals who market business opportunities must hold real estate licenses.

74. a (4) There is no requirement to give a written transaction broker disclosure notice to the buyer and/or the seller.

75. d (4) Loyalty is a duty associated with single agency.

76. b (5) Brokers handling the sale of HUD-owned properties are exempted from the notice and settlement procedures in Chapter 475, F.S. However, the broker is required to follow HUD's Agreement to Abide, Broker Participation Requirements.

77. c (4) The buyer must agree to transition to a transaction broker relationship in order for the buyer to be shown the property listed by the brokerage company.

78. a (11) A contract is terminated by performance, mutual rescission, impossibility of performance, lapse of time, and breach. An assignment of a contract transfers a person's rights and duties under a contract to another person.

79. b (7) Religious organizations may restrict dwelling units they own or operate to members of their religion if the organization does not otherwise discriminate in accepting its membership.

80. c (6) Chapters 475.482 and 475.483, F.S., specify who is eligible to seek reimbursement from the Real Estate Recovery Fund.

81. b (8) The required notice for a month-to-month tenancy at will is not less than 15 days prior to the end of the monthly period.

82. c (9) A property owner, such as a developer, can restrict the future use of a property by recording deed restrictions.

83. b (10) The surveyor identifies each corner of the parcel with a visible marker called a monument.

84. d (10) Meridians run north and south.

85. b (11) The contract for sale and purchase of real estate must be in writing. However, a specific form is not required.

86. b (11) In homes built prior to 1978, the buyer must sign a lead disclosure form prior to signing the sale contract. Sellers are required to disclose the presence of known lead-based paint hazards, and the buyer must be given a copy of an EPA pamphlet regarding lead-based paint.

87. a (9) An encroachment occurs when a building or other improvement, such as a fence, extends beyond the land of the owner and illegally intrudes on land of an adjoining owner. A survey will reveal if there is an encroachment.

88. c (5) A corporation sole is an artificial or fictitious person formed by an ecclesiastical body and as such may not register as a broker. Chapter 475 does not restrict a not-for-profit corporation from registering as a broker. However, to do so may create other issues with the Florida Department of Revenue and the IRS.

89. d (13) The discount rate is the interest rate charged member banks for borrowing money from the Fed. If the discount rate is lowered, member banks pay less for borrowing money from the system.

90. c (8) To have a joint tenancy, the words "with right of survivorship" are required. Without right of survivorship, a tenancy in common exists.

91. d (14) Jan 31 + Feb 28 + Mar 31 + April 30 + May 31 = 151 days;
$1,460 ÷ 365 = $4.00 per day;
$4.00 × 151 days =
$604 debit to seller and credit to buyer

92. c (14) $120,000 × 1.05 = $126,000 year 1;
$126,000 × 1.05 = $132,300 year 2

93. b (16) $87,900 × .30 = $26,370;
$88,500 × .50 = $44,250;
$82,750 × .20 = $16,550;
$26,370 + $44,250 + $16,550 =
$87,170 indicated value

94. d (16) $9,200 × 12 months = $110,400 NOI;
$110,400 ÷ .095 = $1,162,105

95. d (10)
640 ÷ 4 ÷ 4 ÷ 2 = 20 acres;
640 ÷ 4 ÷ 2 = 80 acres;
20 acres + 80 acres = 100 total acres

96. b (16) 80 × $750 × 12 months =
$720,000 × .90 = $648,000;
50 × $950 × 12 months =
$570,000 × .95 = $541,500;
$648,000 + $541,500 = $1,189,500

97. b (14) $98,500 sale price × .08 =
$7,880 total commission;
$7,880 × .40 to sales associate's broker =
$3,152;
$3,152 × .55 = $1,733.60 sales associate's commission

98. b (18) $47.00 × .70 homeowner's share =
$32.90;
$32.90 × 110' = $3,619;
$3,619 ÷ 2 sides of street = $1,809.50

99. c (12) $129,500 sale price × .75 =
$97,125 loan amount;
$129,500 – $97,125 =
$32,375 down payment

100. b (13) $92,000 × .075 = $6,900 ÷ 12 months = $575.00 interest, month 1;
$643.28 – $575.00 =
$68.28 principal, month 1;
$92,000 – $68.28 =
$91,931.72 remaining loan balance;
$91,931.72 × .075 = $6,894.879 ÷ 12 months = $574.57 interest, month 2;
$643.28 – $574.57 =
$68.71 principal, month 2

INDEX

A

answer key with explanations
- broker investment problems, 244
- closing disclosure questions for broker candidates, 245
- general real estate law sections, 224
- math problems, 239
- practice exams, 249
- real estate law, Florida real estate license law sections, 219
- real estate principles and practices sections, 231
- sample exam questions, 219

answer sheets, 215, 217

B

broker investment problems, 175

Broker's Guide, Florida Real Estate, answer key with explanations
- broker investment problems, 244
- closing disclosure questions for broker candidates, 245
- Unit 1, 219
- Unit 2, 221, 224
- Unit 4, 221
- Unit 5, 223
- Unit 6, 235
- Unit 7, 235
- Unit 8, 235
- Unit 9, 236
- Unit 10, 220
- Unit 11, 225, 229
- Unit 12, 224, 225, 233
- Unit 13, 238
- Unit 14, 237
- Unit 15, 227, 236
- Unit 16, 231
- Unit 17, 224
- Unit 18, 224, 225, 227

Broker's Guide, Florida Real Estate, important dates and time periods to remember
- Unit 1, 7, 13
- Unit 2, 32, 43
- Unit 4, 32
- Unit 5, 38
- Unit 10, 19
- Unit 11, 50, 64
- Unit 12, 43, 50
- Unit 14, 112
- Unit 15, 57
- Unit 17, 43
- Unit 18, 43, 50, 57

Broker's Guide, Florida Real Estate, important formulas to remember
- Unit 6, 100
- Unit 7, 100
- Unit 8, 100
- Unit 9, 106
- Unit 12, 83
- Unit 13, 119
- Unit 14, 112
- Unit 15, 57, 106
- Unit 16, 69
- Unit 18, 57

Broker's Guide, Florida Real Estate, key concepts
- Unit 1, 2, 10
- Unit 2, 22, 39
- Unit 4, 22
- Unit 5, 34
- Unit 6, 97
- Unit 7, 97
- Unit 8, 97
- Unit 9, 104
- Unit 10, 16
- Unit 11, 46, 60
- Unit 12, 39, 46, 81
- Unit 13, 117
- Unit 14, 110
- Unit 15, 53, 104
- Unit 16, 66
- Unit 17, 39
- Unit 18, 39, 46, 53

Broker's Guide, Florida Real Estate, key point review
- general real estate law, 39, 45, 51, 59, 65
- real estate law, Florida real estate license law, 1, 9, 15, 21, 33
- real estate principles and practices, 71, 75, 79, 85, 95, 103, 109, 115, 117

Broker's Guide, Florida Real Estate, key term review
- Unit 1, 1, 9
- Unit 2, 21, 39
- Unit 4, 21
- Unit 5, 33
- Unit 6, 95
- Unit 7, 95
- Unit 8, 95
- Unit 9, 103
- Unit 10, 15
- Unit 11, 45, 59
- Unit 12, 39, 45, 79
- Unit 13, 117
- Unit 14, 109
- Unit 15, 51, 103
- Unit 16, 65
- Unit 17, 39
- Unit 18, 39, 45, 51

Broker's Guide, Florida Real Estate, sample exam questions
- broker investment problems, 175
- closing disclosure questions for broker candidates, 177
- Unit 1, 123, 125
- Unit 2, 128, 135
- Unit 4, 128
- Unit 5, 132
- Unit 6, 156
- Unit 7, 156
- Unit 8, 156
- Unit 9, 158
- Unit 10, 126
- Unit 11, 137, 143
- Unit 12, 135, 137, 151
- Unit 13, 162
- Unit 14, 159
- Unit 15, 139, 158
- Unit 16, 147
- Unit 17, 135
- Unit 18, 135, 137, 139

C

closing disclosure questions for broker candidates, 177

E

exam, practice 1, 179
exam, practice 2, 197
exam-taking strategies, successful, xi

G

general real estate law sample exam questions, 135

H

how to use this manual, vii

M

math cross-reference key, 247
math problems, 165

P

practice exams, 179, 197
Principles, Practices & Law, Florida Real Estate, answer key with explanations
- Unit 1, 231
- Unit 2, 219
- Unit 3, 219
- Unit 4, 220
- Unit 5, 221
- Unit 6, 223
- Unit 7, 224
- Unit 8, 225
- Unit 9, 227
- Unit 10, 232
- Unit 11, 229
- Unit 12, 233
- Unit 13, 234
- Unit 14, 238
- Unit 15, 238
- Unit 16, 235
- Unit 17, 236
- Unit 18, 237
- Unit 19, 231

Principles, Practices & Law, Florida Real Estate, important dates and time periods to remember
- Unit 2, 7
- Unit 3, 13
- Unit 4, 19
- Unit 5, 32
- Unit 6, 38
- Unit 7, 43
- Unit 8, 50
- Unit 9, 57
- Unit 11, 64
- Unit 13, 92
- Unit 18, 112

Principles, Practices & Law, Florida Real Estate, important formulas to remember
- Unit 9, 57
- Unit 10, 78
- Unit 12, 83
- Unit 13, 92
- Unit 14, 119
- Unit 15, 116
- Unit 17, 106
- Unit 18, 112
- Unit 19, 69

Principles, Practices & Law, Florida Real Estate, key concepts
- Unit 1, 72
- Unit 2, 2
- Unit 3, 10
- Unit 4, 16
- Unit 5, 22
- Unit 6, 34
- Unit 7, 39
- Unit 8, 46
- Unit 9, 53
- Unit 10, 76
- Unit 11, 60
- Unit 12, 81
- Unit 13, 87
- Unit 14, 117
- Unit 15, 115
- Unit 16, 97
- Unit 17, 104
- Unit 18, 110
- Unit 19, 66

Principles, Practices & Law, Florida Real Estate, key point review
- general real estate law, 39, 45, 51, 59, 65
- real estate law, Florida real estate license law, 1, 9, 15, 21, 33
- real estate principles and practices, 71, 75, 79, 85, 95, 103, 109, 115, 117

Principles, Practices & Law, Florida Real Estate, key term review
- Unit 1, 71
- Unit 2, 1
- Unit 3, 9
- Unit 4, 15
- Unit 5, 21
- Unit 6, 33
- Unit 7, 39
- Unit 8, 45
- Unit 9, 51
- Unit 10, 75
- Unit 11, 59
- Unit 12, 79
- Unit 13, 85
- Unit 14, 117
- Unit 15, 115
- Unit 16, 95
- Unit 17, 103
- Unit 18, 109
- Unit 19, 65

Principles, Practices & Law, Florida Real Estate, sample exam questions
- Unit 1, 149
- Unit 2, 123
- Unit 4, 126
- Unit 5, 128
- Unit 6, 132
- Unit 7, 135
- Unit 8, 137
- Unit 9, 139
- Unit 10, 150
- Unit 11, 143
- Unit 12, 151
- Unit 13, 153
- Unit 14, 162
- Unit 15, 161
- Unit 16, 156
- Unit 17, 158
- Unit 18, 159
- Unit 19, 147

R

real estate law, Florida real estate license law questions, 123
real estate principles and practices sample exam questions, 149

S

sample exam, 123
sample exam questions
- broker investment problems, 175
- closing disclosure questions for broker candidates, 177
- general real estate law, 135
- math problems, 165
- practice exams, 179, 197
- real estate law, Florida real estate license law, 123
- real estate principles and practices, 149

strategies, successful exam-taking, xi

Broker	Broker associate	Compensation	Expungement
Florida resident	License	Mutual recognition agreement	Nolo contendere/no contest
Owner-developer	Prima facie evidence	Real estate services	Reciprocity

A process by which the record of a criminal conviction is destroyed or sealed after expiration of time.

(Unit 2 in *Florida Real Estate Principles, Practices & Law* and Unit 1 in *Florida Real Estate Broker's Guide*)

Anything of value or a valuable consideration, directly or indirectly paid, promised, or expected to be paid or received.

(Unit 2 in *Florida Real Estate Principles, Practices & Law* and Unit 1 in *Florida Real Estate Broker's Guide*)

An individual who meets the requirements of a broker but who chooses to work in real estate under the direction (employ) of another broker.

(Unit 2 in *Florida Real Estate Principles, Practices & Law* and Unit 1 in *Florida Real Estate Broker's Guide*)

A licensee who, for another and for compensation or other consideration, performs real estate services.

(Unit 2 in *Florida Real Estate Principles, Practices & Law* and Unit 1 in *Florida Real Estate Broker's Guide*)

A plea of no contest entered in a criminal court of law. The defendant does not admit or deny the charges.

(Unit 2 in *Florida Real Estate Principles, Practices & Law* and Unit 1 in *Florida Real Estate Broker's Guide*)

A transactional agreement between Florida and another state that provides for the two states to recognize each other's real estate license education.

(Unit 2 in *Florida Real Estate Principles, Practices & Law* and Unit 1 in *Florida Real Estate Broker's Guide*)

A written document issued by the Department of Business and Professional Regulation (DBPR) that serves as prima facie evidence that the person is licensed on the date shown.

(Unit 2 in *Florida Real Estate Principles, Practices & Law* and Unit 1 in *Florida Real Estate Broker's Guide*)

A Florida resident, for application and licensing purposes, is a person who has resided in Florida continuously for a period of four calendar months or more within the preceding year, regardless of whether the person resided in a recreational vehicle, hotel, rental unit, or other temporary or permanent location.

(Unit 2 in *Florida Real Estate Principles, Practices & Law* and Unit 1 in *Florida Real Estate Broker's Guide*)

The practice of mutual exchanges of privileges. Some states have reciprocal arrangements for recognizing and granting licenses to licensed real estate professionals from other states.

(Unit 2 in *Florida Real Estate Principles, Practices & Law* and Unit 1 in *Florida Real Estate Broker's Guide*)

Real estate activities involving compensation for performing the activities for another.

(Unit 2 in *Florida Real Estate Principles, Practices & Law* and Unit 1 in *Florida Real Estate Broker's Guide*)

A legal term used to refer to evidence that is good and sufficient on its face to establish a given fact or prove a case.

(Unit 2 in *Florida Real Estate Principles, Practices & Law* and Unit 1 in *Florida Real Estate Broker's Guide*)

An unlicensed entity that sells, exchanges, or leases its own property.

(Unit 2 in *Florida Real Estate Principles, Practices & Law* and Unit 1 in *Florida Real Estate Broker's Guide*)

Registration	Sales associate	Sealed	Withhold adjudication
Active license	Cancel	Cease to be in force	Current mailing address
Current status	Executive powers	Group license	Involuntary inactive

When the court determines that a defendant is not likely to again engage in a criminal act and that the ends of justice and the welfare of society do not require that the defendant suffer the penalty imposed by law, the court may withhold adjudication of guilt, stay (stop) the imposition of the sentence, and place the defendant on probation.
(Unit 2 in *Florida Real Estate Principles, Practices & Law* and Unit 1 in *Florida Real Estate Broker's Guide*)

Records that cannot be examined except by order of the court or by designated officials.

(Unit 2 in *Florida Real Estate Principles, Practices & Law* and Unit 1 in *Florida Real Estate Broker's Guide*)

A licensed individual who performs real estate services for compensation under the direction, control, and management of an active broker or an owner-developer.

(Unit 2 in *Florida Real Estate Principles, Practices & Law* and Unit 1 in *Florida Real Estate Broker's Guide*)

The official placement of a real estate business or individual into the records of the DBPR.

(Unit 2 in *Florida Real Estate Principles, Practices & Law* and Unit 1 in *Florida Real Estate Broker's Guide*)

The current residential address a licensee uses to receive mail through the U.S. Postal Service®.

(Unit 3 in *Florida Real Estate Principles, Practices & Law* and Unit 1 in *Florida Real Estate Broker's Guide*)

When certain events occur, such as a broker changes business address, the licensee cannot conduct business until the DBPR receives notification of the change.

(Unit 3 in *Florida Real Estate Principles, Practices & Law* and Unit 1 in *Florida Real Estate Broker's Guide*)

When a license becomes void, effective as of the date approved by the Commission, and does not involve disciplinary action.

(Unit 3 in *Florida Real Estate Principles, Practices & Law* and Unit 1 in *Florida Real Estate Broker's Guide*)

A current, valid license registered with the DBPR. The status required to actively engage in the real estate business.

(Unit 3 in *Florida Real Estate Principles, Practices & Law* and Unit 1 in *Florida Real Estate Broker's Guide*)

The license status that results when a license is not renewed at the end of the license period.

(Unit 3 in *Florida Real Estate Principles, Practices & Law* and Unit 1 in *Florida Real Estate Broker's Guide*)

A sales associate or broker associate employed by an owner-developer (real estate developer) who owns properties in the name of various entities can be issued a group license that entitles the licensee to work for the separate sales projects owned by the owner-developer.

(Unit 3 in *Florida Real Estate Principles, Practices & Law* and Unit 1 in *Florida Real Estate Broker's Guide*)

The Florida Real Estate Commission (FREC) includes the power to regulate and enforce license law.

(Unit 3 in *Florida Real Estate Principles, Practices & Law* and Unit 1 in *Florida Real Estate Broker's Guide*)

Indicates whether the licensee is up to date with respect to the DBPR's licensure requirements.

(Unit 3 in *Florida Real Estate Principles, Practices & Law* and Unit 1 in *Florida Real Estate Broker's Guide*)

Ministerial duties	Multiple licenses	Null and void	Probation
Promulgate	Quasi-judicial	Quasi-legislative	Voluntary inactive
Voluntary relinquish	Administrative law	Agent	At arm's length

The licensee is allowed to continue to practice real estate under the guidance of the FREC for a period of time while completing conditions specified by the FREC.

(Unit 3 in *Florida Real Estate Principles, Practices & Law* and Unit 1 in *Florida Real Estate Broker's Guide*)

Means to no longer exist.

(Unit 3 in *Florida Real Estate Principles, Practices & Law* and Unit 1 in *Florida Real Estate Broker's Guide*)

When a broker holds more than one broker's license at one time, the broker is said to hold multiple licenses.

(Unit 3 in *Florida Real Estate Principles, Practices & Law* and Unit 1 in *Florida Real Estate Broker's Guide*)

Ministerial duties of the Division of Real Estate (DRE) involve recordkeeping.

(Unit 3 in *Florida Real Estate Principles, Practices & Law* and Unit 1 in *Florida Real Estate Broker's Guide*)

The license status that results when a licensee has met all the requirements for licensure, yet the licensee chooses not to engage in the real estate business and has requested that the license be placed in this status.

(Unit 3 in *Florida Real Estate Principles, Practices & Law* and Unit 1 in *Florida Real Estate Broker's Guide*)

Powers delegated to the FREC to enact rules and regulations and to decide questions of practice.

(Unit 3 in *Florida Real Estate Principles, Practices & Law* and Unit 1 in *Florida Real Estate Broker's Guide*)

Powers delegated to the FREC include the power to grant or deny applications, to determine license law violations, and to administer penalties.

(Unit 3 in *Florida Real Estate Principles, Practices & Law* and Unit 1 in *Florida Real Estate Broker's Guide*)

The formal act of enacting a statute or an administrative rule; to publish and officially announce a new or amended rule or statute. The FREC may promulgate rules and regulations.

(Unit 3 in *Florida Real Estate Principles, Practices & Law* and Unit 1 in *Florida Real Estate Broker's Guide*)

People dealing at arm's length conduct negotiations on their own behalf without trusting the other's fairness or integrity and without being subject to the other's control or influence.

(Unit 4 in *Florida Real Estate Principles, Practices & Law* and Unit 10 in *Florida Real Estate Broker's Guide*)

A person entrusted with another person's business. An agent is authorized by the principal to act on the principal's behalf.

(Unit 4 in *Florida Real Estate Principles, Practices & Law* and Unit 10 in *Florida Real Estate Broker's Guide*)

A body of law created by administrative agencies in the form of rules, regulations, orders, and decisions.

(Unit 4 in *Florida Real Estate Principles, Practices & Law* and Unit 10 in *Florida Real Estate Broker's Guide*)

When a person no longer wants to engage in the real estate business, provided there is no investigation or discipline pending against the licensee.

(Unit 3 in *Florida Real Estate Principles, Practices & Law* and Unit 1 in *Florida Real Estate Broker's Guide*)

Caveat emptor	Common law	Consent to transition	Customer
Designated sales associates	Dual agency	Fiduciary	General agent
Limited representation	No brokerage relationship	Nonrepresentation	Principal

A member of the public who is or may be a buyer or a seller of real property and may or may not be represented by a real estate licensee in an authorized brokerage relationship.

(Unit 4 in *Florida Real Estate Principles, Practices & Law* and Unit 10 in *Florida Real Estate Broker's Guide*)

A written agreement to gain the principal's written permission to a change in brokerage relationship.

(Unit 4 in *Florida Real Estate Principles, Practices & Law* and Unit 10 in *Florida Real Estate Broker's Guide*)

Judge-made law manifested in decrees and judgments of the courts (case law) as opposed to statutory law.

(Unit 4 in *Florida Real Estate Principles, Practices & Law* and Unit 10 in *Florida Real Estate Broker's Guide*)

A policy of let the buyer beware (buyer is responsible for own knowledge in real estate transactions.

(Unit 4 in *Florida Real Estate Principles, Practices & Law* and Unit 10 in *Florida Real Estate Broker's Guide*)

A general agent is authorized by the principal to perform acts associated with the continued operations of a particular job or a certain business of the principal.

(Unit 4 in *Florida Real Estate Principles, Practices & Law* and Unit 10 in *Florida Real Estate Broker's Guide*)

A relationship of trust and confidence with the broker as agent and the seller or the buyer as principal.

(Unit 4 in *Florida Real Estate Principles, Practices & Law* and Unit 10 in *Florida Real Estate Broker's Guide*)

A broker who is representing as a fiduciary both the buyer and the seller in a residential real estate transaction; dual agency is illegal in Florida.

(Unit 4 in *Florida Real Estate Principles, Practices & Law* and Unit 10 in *Florida Real Estate Broker's Guide*)

Two real estate licensees designated to represent the buyer and the seller as single agents in a nonresidential transaction. The buyer and the seller must have assets of $1 million or more and sign disclosures stating that their assets meet the required threshold.

(Unit 4 in *Florida Real Estate Principles, Practices & Law* and Unit 10 in *Florida Real Estate Broker's Guide*)

The seller or the buyer (but not both) in a single agent relationship. The principal authorizes the agent to act on the principal's behalf; the principal is responsible for the actions of the agent.

(Unit 4 in *Florida Real Estate Principles, Practices & Law* and Unit 10 in *Florida Real Estate Broker's Guide*)

A no brokerage relationship.

(Unit 4 in *Florida Real Estate Principles, Practices & Law* and Unit 10 in *Florida Real Estate Broker's Guide*)

An arrangement in which the broker does not represent either the buyer or the seller but in which the broker instead works to facilitate the transaction.

(Unit 4 in *Florida Real Estate Principles, Practices & Law* and Unit 10 in *Florida Real Estate Broker's Guide*)

A non-fiduciary representation to a buyer, a seller, or both in a real estate transaction.

(Unit 4 in *Florida Real Estate Principles, Practices & Law* and Unit 10 in *Florida Real Estate Broker's Guide*)

Residential sale	Single agent	Special agent	Statutory laws
Subagent	Transaction broker	Antitrust laws	Arbitration
Blind advertisement	Commingle	Conflicting demands	Corporation

Written statutes and rules enacted by the legislature.

(Unit 4 in *Florida Real Estate Principles, Practices & Law* and Unit 10 in *Florida Real Estate Broker's Guide*)

One authorized by a principal to perform a particular act or transaction without contemplation of continuity of service as with a general agent.

(Unit 4 in *Florida Real Estate Principles, Practices & Law* and Unit 10 in *Florida Real Estate Broker's Guide*)

A broker who represents either the buyer or the seller (but not both) and has a fiduciary relationship with the party represented.

(Unit 4 in *Florida Real Estate Principles, Practices & Law* and Unit 10 in *Florida Real Estate Broker's Guide*)

The sale of improved residential property of four or fewer units, the sale of unimproved residential property intended for use as four or fewer units, or the sale of agricultural property of 10 or fewer acres.

(Unit 4 in *Florida Real Estate Principles, Practices & Law* and Unit 10 in *Florida Real Estate Broker's Guide*)

A process whereby, with the prior written consent of all parties to the dispute, the matter is submitted to a disinterested third party who makes a binding judgment.

(Unit 5 in *Florida Real Estate Principles, Practices & Law* and Units 2 and 4 in *Florida Real Estate Broker's Guide*)

State and federal laws designed to maintain and preserve business competition.

(Unit 5 in *Florida Real Estate Principles, Practices & Law* and Units 2 and 4 in *Florida Real Estate Broker's Guide*)

A broker who provides limited representation to a buyer, a seller, or both in a real estate transaction but does not represent either in a fiduciary capacity or as a single agent.

(Unit 4 in *Florida Real Estate Principles, Practices & Law* and Unit 10 in *Florida Real Estate Broker's Guide*)

A person authorized to assist and represent the agent. A subagent has the same duties as the agent.

(Unit 4 in *Florida Real Estate Principles, Practices & Law* and Unit 10 in *Florida Real Estate Broker's Guide*)

An artificial person or legal entity created by law and consisting of one or more persons that is formed by filing articles of incorporation.

(Unit 5 in *Florida Real Estate Principles, Practices & Law* and Units 2 and 4 in *Florida Real Estate Broker's Guide*)

When the buyer and the seller make demands regarding the disbursing of escrowed property that are inconsistent and cannot be resolved.

(Unit 5 in *Florida Real Estate Principles, Practices & Law* and Units 2 and 4 in *Florida Real Estate Broker's Guide*)

The mixing of a buyer's, seller's, tenant's, or landlord's funds with the broker's own money or mixing escrow money with the broker's personal funds or brokerage funds.

(Unit 5 in *Florida Real Estate Principles, Practices & Law* and Units 2 and 4 in *Florida Real Estate Broker's Guide*)

An advertisement of a listed property that provides only a telephone number, a post office box, and/or an address without the licensed name of the brokerage firm.

(Unit 5 in *Florida Real Estate Principles, Practices & Law* and Units 2 and 4 in *Florida Real Estate Broker's Guide*)

Declaratory judgment	Deposit	Earnest money deposit	Escrow account
Escrow disbursement order (EDO)	General partnership	Good faith doubt	Immediately
Interpleader	Kickback	Limited liability company (LLC)	Limited liability partnership (LLP)

An account for the deposit of money held by a third party in trust for another for safekeeping.

(Unit 5 in *Florida Real Estate Principles, Practices & Law* and Units 2 and 4 in *Florida Real Estate Broker's Guide*)

Money given as good faith to accompany an offer to purchase or lease real property; also called a good-faith deposit or binder deposit.

(Unit 5 in *Florida Real Estate Principles, Practices & Law* and Units 2 and 4 in *Florida Real Estate Broker's Guide*)

A sum of money, or its equivalent, delivered to a real estate licensee as earnest money, payment, or partial payment in connection with a real estate transaction.

(Unit 5 in *Florida Real Estate Principles, Practices & Law* and Units 2 and 4 in *Florida Real Estate Broker's Guide*)

Filed with the judge in a court of law by brokers who believe they are entitled to a portion of disputed escrow funds.

(Unit 5 in *Florida Real Estate Principles, Practices & Law* and Units 2 and 4 in *Florida Real Estate Broker's Guide*)

The time frame when trust funds must be deposited into an escrow account, according to Chapter 475, F.S.

(Unit 5 in *Florida Real Estate Principles, Practices & Law* and Units 2 and 4 in *Florida Real Estate Broker's Guide*)

A party's honest intent to transact business, free from any intent to defraud the other party; each party's faithfulness to one's duty or obligations set forth by contract.

(Unit 5 in *Florida Real Estate Principles, Practices & Law* and Units 2 and 4 in *Florida Real Estate Broker's Guide*)

An association of two or more persons for the purpose of jointly conducting a business, each being responsible for all the debts incurred in the conducting of that business.

(Unit 5 in *Florida Real Estate Principles, Practices & Law* and Units 2 and 4 in *Florida Real Estate Broker's Guide*)

A determination by the FREC of who is entitled to disputed funds.

(Unit 5 in *Florida Real Estate Principles, Practices & Law* and Units 2 and 4 in *Florida Real Estate Broker's Guide*)

A business entity that features protection from personal liability in much the same way as limited partners in a limited partnership.

(Unit 5 in *Florida Real Estate Principles, Practices & Law* and Units 2 and 4 in *Florida Real Estate Broker's Guide*)

A form of business organization that offers the best features of a corporation and a partnership; members of an LLC are protected from personal liability, as in a corporate form of ownership, and enjoy the tax advantages of a partnership.

(Unit 5 in *Florida Real Estate Principles, Practices & Law* and Units 2 and 4 in *Florida Real Estate Broker's Guide*)

When a broker receives money from someone other than the buyer or the seller, such as for referring a buyer or a seller to a particular vendor for services.

(Unit 5 in *Florida Real Estate Principles, Practices & Law* and Units 2 and 4 in *Florida Real Estate Broker's Guide*)

A legal proceeding whereby the broker, having no financial interest in the disputed funds, deposits with the court the disputed escrow deposit so that the court can determine the rightful claimant.

(Unit 5 in *Florida Real Estate Principles, Practices & Law* and Units 2 and 4 in *Florida Real Estate Broker's Guide*)

Limited partnership	Litigation	Market allocation	Mediation
Ostensible partnership	Personal assistants	Point of contact information	Price-fixing
Professional association (PA)	Sole proprietorship	Telephone solicitation	Trade name

An informal, nonadversarial process intended to reach a negotiated settlement that is not binding.

(Unit 5 in *Florida Real Estate Principles, Practices & Law* and Units 2 and 4 in *Florida Real Estate Broker's Guide*)

An agreement between brokers to split up competitive market areas among themselves and not compete in each other's areas.

(Unit 5 in *Florida Real Estate Principles, Practices & Law* and Units 2 and 4 in *Florida Real Estate Broker's Guide*)

One of the settlement (escape) procedures that provides for the matter to be resolved in a court of law when there are disputing parties regarding escrow funds.

(Unit 5 in *Florida Real Estate Principles, Practices & Law* and Units 2 and 4 in *Florida Real Estate Broker's Guide*)

A business entity consisting of one or more general partners and one or more limited partners.

(Unit 5 in *Florida Real Estate Principles, Practices & Law* and Units 2 and 4 in *Florida Real Estate Broker's Guide*)

Competing brokers conspire to establish a standard commission rate rather than let the rate be set by the open market.

(Unit 5 in *Florida Real Estate Principles, Practices & Law* and Units 2 and 4 in *Florida Real Estate Broker's Guide*)

Any means by which to contact the brokerage firm or individual licensee, including mailing address(es), physical street address(es), email address(es), telephone number(s), or facsimile telephone number(s); the brokerage firm's name must be above, below, or adjacent to the point of contact information.

(Unit 5 in *Florida Real Estate Principles, Practices & Law* and Units 2 and 4 in *Florida Real Estate Broker's Guide*)

Individuals hired by a licensee to perform administrative tasks associated with real estate transactions. The tasks performed by a personal assistant determine whether the assistant must be a real estate licensee.

(Unit 5 in *Florida Real Estate Principles, Practices & Law* and Units 2 and 4 in *Florida Real Estate Broker's Guide*)

Exists where the parties do not form a real partnership but act or do business in such a manner that the public, having no knowledge of the private relations of the parties, would reasonably be deceived into believing that a partnership exists.

(Unit 5 in *Florida Real Estate Principles, Practices & Law* and Units 2 and 4 in *Florida Real Estate Broker's Guide*)

A business name other than the legal name of the person doing business.

(Unit 5 in *Florida Real Estate Principles, Practices & Law* and Units 2 and 4 in *Florida Real Estate Broker's Guide*)

The initiation of a telephone call for the purpose of encouraging the purchase of, or investment in, property, goods, or services.

(Unit 5 in *Florida Real Estate Principles, Practices & Law* and Units 2 and 4 in *Florida Real Estate Broker's Guide*)

A business owned by one person with no legal separation between the owner and the business.

(Unit 5 in *Florida Real Estate Principles, Practices & Law* and Units 2 and 4 in *Florida Real Estate Broker's Guide*)

A business corporation consisting of one or more individuals engaged in a primary business that provides a professional service.

(Unit 5 in *Florida Real Estate Principles, Practices & Law* and Units 2 and 4 in *Florida Real Estate Broker's Guide*)

Trust funds	Trust liability	Breach of trust	Citations
Commingle	Complaint	Concealment	Conversion
Culpable negligence	Division of Administrative Hearings (DOAH)	Failure to account for and deliver	Final orders

Fines for violations that have been specified in the citation rule for which there is no substantial threat to the public health, safety, and welfare.

(Unit 6 in *Florida Real Estate Principles, Practices & Law* and Unit 5 in *Florida Real Estate Broker's Guide*)

The breaking of a promise or obligation.

(Unit 6 in *Florida Real Estate Principles, Practices & Law* and Unit 5 in *Florida Real Estate Broker's Guide*)

The sum total of all deposits received, pending, and being held by the broker at a point in time.

(Unit 5 in Florida Real Estate Principles, Practices & Law and Units 2 and 4 in *Florida Real Estate Broker's Guide*)

Cash, checks, money orders, or other items that can be converted to cash, which are held by a third party in connection with a real estate transaction.

(Unit 5 in Florida Real Estate Principles, Practices & Law and Units 2 and 4 in *Florida Real Estate Broker's Guide*)

A licensee's personal use or misuse of client (or customer) monies.

(Unit 6 in *Florida Real Estate Principles, Practices & Law* and Unit 5 in *Florida Real Estate Broker's Guide*)

The withholding of information.

(Unit 6 in *Florida Real Estate Principles, Practices & Law* and Unit 5 in *Florida Real Estate Broker's Guide*)

An alleged violation of a law or rule.

(Unit 6 in *Florida Real Estate Principles, Practices & Law* and Unit 5 in *Florida Real Estate Broker's Guide*)

To mix the money of a buyer or a seller with a broker's own money.

(Unit 6 in *Florida Real Estate Principles, Practices & Law* and Unit 5 in *Florida Real Estate Broker's Guide*)

The Commission's final decisions as to innocence or guilt and the determination of the appropriate penalty.

(Unit 6 in *Florida Real Estate Principles, Practices & Law* and Unit 5 in *Florida Real Estate Broker's Guide*)

The act of failing to pay money to a person entitled to receive it.

(Unit 6 in *Florida Real Estate Principles, Practices & Law* and Unit 5 in *Florida Real Estate Broker's Guide*)

The entity that employs administrative law judges (ALJs) to conduct formal hearings of administrative complaints against licensees.

(Unit 6 in *Florida Real Estate Principles, Practices & Law* and Unit 5 in *Florida Real Estate Broker's Guide*)

Negligent conduct that, while not intentional, involves a disregard for the consequences likely to result for one's actions.

(Unit 6 in *Florida Real Estate Principles, Practices & Law* and Unit 5 in *Florida Real Estate Broker's Guide*)

Formal (administrative) complaint	Formal hearings	Fraud	Informal hearings
Legally sufficient	Material fact	Misrepresentation	Moral turpitude
Notice of noncompliance	Probable cause	Recommended order	Stipulation

Disciplinary hearings that are an expedited way of resolving a disciplinary case provided that the licensee does not dispute the alleged facts stated in the complaint.

(Unit 6 in *Florida Real Estate Principles, Practices & Law* and Unit 5 in *Florida Real Estate Broker's Guide*)

The intentional deceit and reliance on the deception for the purpose of inducing another person to rely on the deceitful information and as a consequence be harmed by the deceit.

(Unit 6 in *Florida Real Estate Principles, Practices & Law* and Unit 5 in *Florida Real Estate Broker's Guide*)

Disciplinary hearings heard by an administrative law judge if the licensee-respondent either requests a formal hearing or if the licensee-respondent disputes the allegations.

(Unit 6 in *Florida Real Estate Principles, Practices & Law* and Unit 5 in *Florida Real Estate Broker's Guide*)

An outline of the charges against a licensee that must be answered within the statutory time limit; also referred to as an administrative complaint.

(Unit 6 in *Florida Real Estate Principles, Practices & Law* and Unit 5 in *Florida Real Estate Broker's Guide*)

Conduct contrary to honesty, good morals, justice, and accepted custom.

(Unit 6 in *Florida Real Estate Principles, Practices & Law* and Unit 5 in *Florida Real Estate Broker's Guide*)

An untrue statement of fact or an incorrect or false representation of the facts.

(Unit 6 in *Florida Real Estate Principles, Practices & Law* and Unit 5 in *Florida Real Estate Broker's Guide*)

A piece of information that is relevant to a person making a decision and that affects the value of the real property.

(Unit 6 in *Florida Real Estate Principles, Practices & Law* and Unit 5 in *Florida Real Estate Broker's Guide*)

A complaint that contains facts indicating that a violation of a Florida statute, a DBPR rule, or a FREC rule has occurred.

(Unit 6 in *Florida Real Estate Principles, Practices & Law* and Unit 5 in *Florida Real Estate Broker's Guide*)

An agreement as to the penalty reached between the attorneys for the DRE and the licensee or licensee's attorney.

(Unit 6 in *Florida Real Estate Principles, Practices & Law* and Unit 5 in *Florida Real Estate Broker's Guide*)

An administrative law judge's findings, conclusions, and recommended penalty.

(Unit 6 in *Florida Real Estate Principles, Practices & Law* and Unit 5 in *Florida Real Estate Broker's Guide*)

Reasonable grounds (sufficient facts and evidence) to warrant prosecution.

(Unit 6 in *Florida Real Estate Principles, Practices & Law* and Unit 5 in *Florida Real Estate Broker's Guide*)

Issued by the DBPR for a first-time, minor rule violation that does not endanger the public health, safety, and welfare.

(Unit 6 in *Florida Real Estate Principles, Practices & Law* and Unit 5 in *Florida Real Estate Broker's Guide*)

Subpoena	Summary (emergency) suspension	Voluntary relinquishment for permanent revocation	Blockbusting
Civil Rights Act of 1866	Fair Housing Act	Familial status	Handicap status
Property reports	Public accommodations	Redlining	Steering

To use entry, or rumor of entry, of a protected class into a neighborhood to persuade owners to sell.

(Unit 7 in *Florida Real Estate Principles, Practices & Law* and Units 2, 12, 17, and 18 in *Florida Real Estate Broker's Guide*)

Occurs when a licensee-respondent chooses to avoid a disciplinary hearing by relinquishing the real estate license, permanently putting the licensee out of the real estate business.

(Unit 6 in *Florida Real Estate Principles, Practices & Law* and Unit 5 in *Florida Real Estate Broker's Guide*)

An order that must be issued by the DBPR secretary or the secretary's designee.

(Unit 6 in *Florida Real Estate Principles, Practices & Law* and Unit 5 in *Florida Real Estate Broker's Guide*)

A command to appear at a certain time and place to give testimony.

(Unit 6 in *Florida Real Estate Principles, Practices & Law* and Unit 5 in *Florida Real Estate Broker's Guide*)

A protected class of people, under the Fair Housing Act, who have a physical or mental impairment that interferes with normal life functions.

(Unit 7 in *Florida Real Estate Principles, Practices & Law* and Units 2, 12, 17, and 18 in *Florida Real Estate Broker's Guide*)

A protected class of people, under the Fair Housing Act, consisting of families with children younger than 18 and pregnant women.

(Unit 7 in *Florida Real Estate Principles, Practices & Law* and Units 2, 12, 17, and 18 in *Florida Real Estate Broker's Guide*)

Act that creates protected classes of people and prohibits discrimination when selling or renting certain residential property.

(Unit 7 in *Florida Real Estate Principles, Practices & Law* and Units 2, 12, 17, and 18 in *Florida Real Estate Broker's Guide*)

A federal act that prohibits any type of discrimination based on race in any real estate transaction (sale or rental) without exception.

(Unit 7 in *Florida Real Estate Principles, Practices & Law* and Units 2, 12, 17, and 18 in *Florida Real Estate Broker's Guide*)

Channeling protected-class homeseekers away from areas that are not mixed with that class into areas that are.

(Unit 7 in *Florida Real Estate Principles, Practices & Law* and Units 2, 12, 17, and 18 in *Florida Real Estate Broker's Guide*)

To deny loans or insurance coverage by a lender or insurer or presenting different terms or conditions for homes in certain neighborhoods.

(Unit 7 in *Florida Real Estate Principles, Practices & Law* and Units 2, 12, 17, and 18 in *Florida Real Estate Broker's Guide*)

Public accommodations are facilities open to the public, including sales and rental establishments, hotels, and shopping centers.

(Unit 7 in *Florida Real Estate Principles, Practices & Law* and Units 2, 12, 17, and 18 in *Florida Real Estate Broker's Guide*)

Disclosure documents required under the federal Interstate Land Sales Full Disclosure Act.

(Unit 7 in *Florida Real Estate Principles, Practices & Law* and Units 2, 12, 17, and 18 in *Florida Real Estate Broker's Guide*)

Bundle of legal rights	Common elements	Concurrent ownership	Condominium documents
Condominiums	Cooperative	Declaration of Condominium	Estate for years
Estate in severalty	Fee simple estate	Fixtures	Freehold estate

A set of papers describing the condominium and the association.

(Unit 8 in *Florida Real Estate Principles, Practices & Law* and Units 11, 12, and 18 in *Florida Real Estate Broker's Guide*)

Ownership by two or more persons at the same time, such as joint tenants, tenants by the entirety, or tenants in common.

(Unit 8 in *Florida Real Estate Principles, Practices & Law* and Units 11, 12, and 18 in *Florida Real Estate Broker's Guide*)

Elements such as roofs, elevators, and recreational facilities that are legally attached to condominium units and are transferred with the units when they are sold.

(Unit 8 in *Florida Real Estate Principles, Practices & Law* and Units 11, 12, and 18 in *Florida Real Estate Broker's Guide*)

Real property ownership rights consisting of the rights of disposition, enjoyment, exclusion, possession, and control.

(Unit 8 in *Florida Real Estate Principles, Practices & Law* and Units 11, 12, and 18 in *Florida Real Estate Broker's Guide*)

A written lease with a definite termination date.

(Unit 8 in *Florida Real Estate Principles, Practices & Law* and Units 11, 12, and 18 in *Florida Real Estate Broker's Guide*)

A recorded document that creates the condominium.

(Unit 8 in *Florida Real Estate Principles, Practices & Law* and Units 11, 12, and 18 in *Florida Real Estate Broker's Guide*)

A multiunit project consisting of individual dwelling units owned by the corporation. Owners purchase shares in the corporation and receive a proprietary lease.

(Unit 8 in *Florida Real Estate Principles, Practices & Law* and Units 11, 12, and 18 in *Florida Real Estate Broker's Guide*)

Multiunit projects consisting of individual ownership of a dwelling unit and undivided ownership of common areas.

(Unit 8 in *Florida Real Estate Principles, Practices & Law* and Units 11, 12, and 18 in *Florida Real Estate Broker's Guide*)

An ownership interest for an indefinite period.

(Unit 8 in *Florida Real Estate Principles, Practices & Law* and Units 11, 12, and 18 in *Florida Real Estate Broker's Guide*)

Objects that were once considered to be personal property but have become real property because of attachment to, or use in, improvements to real property.

(Unit 8 in *Florida Real Estate Principles, Practices & Law* and Units 11, 12, and 18 in *Florida Real Estate Broker's Guide*)

The most common type of ownership; it is the most comprehensive collection of property rights and may be inherited.

(Unit 8 in *Florida Real Estate Principles, Practices & Law* and Units 11, 12, and 18 in *Florida Real Estate Broker's Guide*)

When title to property is held by one person.

(Unit 8 in *Florida Real Estate Principles, Practices & Law* and Units 11, 12, and 18 in *Florida Real Estate Broker's Guide*)

Homestead	Joint tenancy	Land	Leasehold estate (tenancy)
Life estate	Littoral rights	Nonfreehold estate	Personal property
Proprietary lease	Prospectus	Real estate	Real property

An interest in real property that a tenant possesses (measured in calendar time).

(Unit 8 in *Florida Real Estate Principles, Practices & Law* and Units 11, 12, and 18 in *Florida Real Estate Broker's Guide*)

The surface of the earth and everything attached to it by nature.

(Unit 8 in *Florida Real Estate Principles, Practices & Law* and Units 11, 12, and 18 in *Florida Real Estate Broker's Guide*)

An ownership interest between two or more persons with right of survivorship.

(Unit 8 in *Florida Real Estate Principles, Practices & Law* and Units 11, 12, and 18 in *Florida Real Estate Broker's Guide*)

Florida law provides certain types of protection and benefits to homeowners regarding their permanent residence.

(Unit 8 in *Florida Real Estate Principles, Practices & Law* and Units 11, 12, and 18 in *Florida Real Estate Broker's Guide*)

Also known as chattel, it is any tangible item that is not real property and is movable.

(Unit 8 in *Florida Real Estate Principles, Practices & Law* and Units 11, 12, and 18 in *Florida Real Estate Broker's Guide*)

An estate in real property that has a known duration and does not involve an ownership interest.

(Unit 8 in *Florida Real Estate Principles, Practices & Law* and Units 11, 12, and 18 in *Florida Real Estate Broker's Guide*)

Legal rights associated with land abutting bodies of water such as an ocean, sea, or lake.

(Unit 8 in *Florida Real Estate Principles, Practices & Law* and Units 11, 12, and 18 in *Florida Real Estate Broker's Guide*)

A freehold estate that ends with the death of a named person; ownership for an individual's natural life span.

(Unit 8 in *Florida Real Estate Principles, Practices & Law* and Units 11, 12, and 18 in *Florida Real Estate Broker's Guide*)

All real estate plus the legal bundle of rights inherent in the ownership of real estate.

(Unit 8 in *Florida Real Estate Principles, Practices & Law* and Units 11, 12, and 18 in *Florida Real Estate Broker's Guide*)

Land and all improvements permanently attached to land.

(Unit 8 in *Florida Real Estate Principles, Practices & Law* and Units 11, 12, and 18 in *Florida Real Estate Broker's Guide*)

A developer is required to provide purchasers a prospectus if the condominium consists of more than 20 residential units or is part of a group of residential condominiums that will be served by property to be used in common by unit owners of more than 20 units. The prospectus summarizes some of the major points detailed in the condominium documents.

(Unit 8 in *Florida Real Estate Principles, Practices & Law* and Units 11, 12, and 18 in *Florida Real Estate Broker's Guide*)

The document that entitles a shareholder in a cooperative to possession of a unit.

(Unit 8 in *Florida Real Estate Principles, Practices & Law* and Units 11, 12, and 18 in *Florida Real Estate Broker's Guide*)

Remainderman	Right of survivorship	Riparian rights	Separate property
Tenancy at sufferance	Tenancy at will	Tenancy by the entireties	Tenants in common
Time-share	Trade fixture	Undivided interest	Abstract of title

Nonmarital assets.

(Unit 8 in *Florida Real Estate Principles, Practices & Law* and Units 11, 12, and 18 in *Florida Real Estate Broker's Guide*)

Rights associated with land abutting the banks of a river, stream, or other watercourse.

(Unit 8 in *Florida Real Estate Principles, Practices & Law* and Units 11, 12, and 18 in *Florida Real Estate Broker's Guide*)

When one co-owner dies, that co-owner's share goes to the surviving co-owner(s) and not to the deceased tenant's heirs.

(Unit 8 in *Florida Real Estate Principles, Practices & Law* and Units 11, 12, and 18 in *Florida Real Estate Broker's Guide*)

The third party to whom property is transferred at the end of a life estate.

(Unit 8 in *Florida Real Estate Principles, Practices & Law* and Units 11, 12, and 18 in *Florida Real Estate Broker's Guide*)

The most frequently used form of co-ownership except for ownership by a married couple.

(Unit 8 in *Florida Real Estate Principles, Practices & Law* and Units 11, 12, and 18 in *Florida Real Estate Broker's Guide*)

An estate created by a married couple who take title together at the same time.

(Unit 8 in *Florida Real Estate Principles, Practices & Law* and Units 11, 12, and 18 in *Florida Real Estate Broker's Guide*)

A leasehold in which the tenant holds possession of the premises with the owner's permission but without a fixed term.

(Unit 8 in *Florida Real Estate Principles, Practices & Law* and Units 11, 12, and 18 in *Florida Real Estate Broker's Guide*)

Exists when the tenant, after rightfully being in possession of the rented property, continues possession after the tenant's right has ended (a holdover tenant).

(Unit 8 in *Florida Real Estate Principles, Practices & Law* and Units 11, 12, and 18 in *Florida Real Estate Broker's Guide*)

A summary report of what a title search found in the public record.

(Unit 9 in *Florida Real Estate Principles, Practices & Law* and Units 15 and 18 in *Florida Real Estate Broker's Guide*)

An interest in the entire property rather than ownership of a particular part of the property.

(Unit 8 in *Florida Real Estate Principles, Practices & Law* and Units 11, 12, and 18 in *Florida Real Estate Broker's Guide*)

An item of personal property attached to real property that is owned by the tenant and used in a business that is legally removable by the tenant.

(Unit 8 in *Florida Real Estate Principles, Practices & Law* and Units 11, 12, and 18 in *Florida Real Estate Broker's Guide*)

Ownership that involves an undivided interest in a living unit according to the number of weeks purchased.

(Unit 8 in *Florida Real Estate Principles, Practices & Law* and Units 11, 12, and 18 in *Florida Real Estate Broker's Guide*)

Acknowledgment	Actual notice	Adverse possession	Alienation
Appurtenance	Assignment	Chain of title	Condemnation
Construction lien	Constructive notice	Deed	Deed restrictions

The act of transferring ownership, title, or an interest or estate in real property.

(Unit 9 in *Florida Real Estate Principles, Practices & Law* and Units 15 and 18 in *Florida Real Estate Broker's Guide*)

When the true owner of record fails to maintain possession, and the property is seized by another.

(Unit 9 in *Florida Real Estate Principles, Practices & Law* and Units 15 and 18 in *Florida Real Estate Broker's Guide*)

Direct knowledge acquired in the course of a transaction, such as having actually seen the deed instrument or heard that there is a lien on the property.

(Unit 9 in *Florida Real Estate Principles, Practices & Law* and Units 15 and 18 in *Florida Real Estate Broker's Guide*)

The formal declaration before a notary public by the grantor that the grantor's signing is a free act.

(Unit 9 in *Florida Real Estate Principles, Practices & Law* and Units 15 and 18 in *Florida Real Estate Broker's Guide*)

A judicial proceeding to exercise the power of eminent domain.

(Unit 9 in *Florida Real Estate Principles, Practices & Law* and Units 15 and 18 in *Florida Real Estate Broker's Guide*)

The complete successive record of a property's ownership.

(Unit 9 in *Florida Real Estate Principles, Practices & Law* and Units 15 and 18 in *Florida Real Estate Broker's Guide*)

Assignment of a lease occurs when a lessee (tenant) assigns to another person all the leased property for the remainder of the lease.

(Unit 9 in *Florida Real Estate Principles, Practices & Law* and Units 15 and 18 in *Florida Real Estate Broker's Guide*)

A right or privilege associated with the property, such as a parking space in a multiunit building.

(Unit 9 in *Florida Real Estate Principles, Practices & Law* and Units 15 and 18 in *Florida Real Estate Broker's Guide*)

Part of the deed and affect a particular property's future use.

(Unit 9 in *Florida Real Estate Principles, Practices & Law* and Units 15 and 18 in *Florida Real Estate Broker's Guide*)

A written instrument used to convey title to real property through sale or gift that must be in writing, signed by a competent grantor and two witnesses, and voluntarily accepted by the grantee.

(Unit 9 in *Florida Real Estate Principles, Practices & Law* and Units 15 and 18 in *Florida Real Estate Broker's Guide*)

The recording of a document or an instrument in the public records designed to give adequate notice to all.

(Unit 9 in *Florida Real Estate Principles, Practices & Law* and Units 15 and 18 in *Florida Real Estate Broker's Guide*)

A statutory right of material suppliers or laborers to place a lien on property that has been improved by their supplies and/or labor.

(Unit 9 in *Florida Real Estate Principles, Practices & Law* and Units 15 and 18 in *Florida Real Estate Broker's Guide*)

Easement	Easement appurtenant	Easement by necessity	Easement by prescription
Easement in gross	Eminent domain	Encroachment	Equitable title
Escheat	Further assurance	General lien	General warranty deed

Created through a court of law after longtime, uninterrupted use.

(Unit 9 in *Florida Real Estate Principles, Practices & Law* and Units 15 and 18 in *Florida Real Estate Broker's Guide*)

An easement created by a court of law in cases where justice and necessity dictate it, such as when property is landlocked.

(Unit 9 in *Florida Real Estate Principles, Practices & Law* and Units 15 and 18 in *Florida Real Estate Broker's Guide*)

An easement that benefits an adjacent parcel of land.

(Unit 9 in *Florida Real Estate Principles, Practices & Law* and Units 15 and 18 in *Florida Real Estate Broker's Guide*)

The right to enter and use a portion of an owner's land for a specific use.

(Unit 9 in *Florida Real Estate Principles, Practices & Law* and Units 15 and 18 in *Florida Real Estate Broker's Guide*)

The beneficial interest in real estate that implies an individual will receive legal title at a future date.

(Unit 9 in *Florida Real Estate Principles, Practices & Law* and Units 15 and 18 in *Florida Real Estate Broker's Guide*)

Unauthorized use of another person's property created when an improvement crosses over a boundary line.

(Unit 9 in *Florida Real Estate Principles, Practices & Law* and Units 15 and 18 in *Florida Real Estate Broker's Guide*)

Gives government the power to take land for a public use from an owner through a legal process known as condemnation.

(Unit 9 in *Florida Real Estate Principles, Practices & Law* and Units 15 and 18 in *Florida Real Estate Broker's Guide*)

A type of easement that benefits an individual or business entity and is not related to a specific adjacent parcel (e.g., utility easements).

(Unit 9 in *Florida Real Estate Principles, Practices & Law* and Units 15 and 18 in *Florida Real Estate Broker's Guide*)

The most common type of deed for conveying real estate. It contains all the covenants and warranties available to give the most complete protection.

(Unit 9 in *Florida Real Estate Principles, Practices & Law* and Units 15 and 18 in *Florida Real Estate Broker's Guide*)

A claim that is not restricted to one property and may affect all the properties of a debtor.

(Unit 9 in *Florida Real Estate Principles, Practices & Law* and Units 15 and 18 in *Florida Real Estate Broker's Guide*)

A promise in a general warranty deed that guarantees the grantor will sign and deliver any legal instrument that might be required.

(Unit 9 in *Florida Real Estate Principles, Practices & Law* and Units 15 and 18 in *Florida Real Estate Broker's Guide*)

Provides for the State of Florida to take the property of an owner who dies intestate and without any known heirs.

(Unit 9 in *Florida Real Estate Principles, Practices & Law* and Units 15 and 18 in *Florida Real Estate Broker's Guide*)

Grantee	**Granting clause**	**Grantor**	**Gross lease**
Ground lease	**Habendum clause**	**Intestate**	**Involuntary alienation**
Junior liens	**Legal title**	**Lender's policy**	**Lien**

An agreement for the tenant to pay a fixed (base) rent with the landlord paying all the expenses associated with the property.

(Unit 9 in *Florida Real Estate Principles, Practices & Law* and Units 15 and 18 in *Florida Real Estate Broker's Guide*)

The person giving title to property in a deed.

(Unit 9 in *Florida Real Estate Principles, Practices & Law* and Units 15 and 18 in *Florida Real Estate Broker's Guide*)

A clause in a deed that contains the premises or the words of conveyance.

(Unit 9 in *Florida Real Estate Principles, Practices & Law* and Units 15 and 18 in *Florida Real Estate Broker's Guide*)

The person receiving title to property in a deed.

(Unit 9 in *Florida Real Estate Principles, Practices & Law* and Units 15 and 18 in *Florida Real Estate Broker's Guide*)

When a person dies intestate and the property either descends to the descendant's heirs or the property transfers to the state through escheat.

(Unit 9 in *Florida Real Estate Principles, Practices & Law* and Units 15 and 18 in *Florida Real Estate Broker's Guide*)

To die without leaving a will.

(Unit 9 in *Florida Real Estate Principles, Practices & Law* and Units 15 and 18 in *Florida Real Estate Broker's Guide*)

A clause in a deed that describes the type of estate being conveyed and starts with the words "to have and to hold."

(Unit 9 in *Florida Real Estate Principles, Practices & Law* and Units 15 and 18 in *Florida Real Estate Broker's Guide*)

An agreement for the tenant to lease the land only and erect a building on the land.

(Unit 9 in *Florida Real Estate Principles, Practices & Law* and Units 15 and 18 in *Florida Real Estate Broker's Guide*)

A written document that states that a person is owed money and establishes that the party may foreclose on the property if the debt is not satisfied; the right to have property sold to satisfy the debt.

(Unit 9 in *Florida Real Estate Principles, Practices & Law* and Units 15 and 18 in *Florida Real Estate Broker's Guide*)

Title insurance issued for the amount of mortgage debt to protect the lender (mortgagee) against title defects.

(Unit 9 in *Florida Real Estate Principles, Practices & Law* and Units 15 and 18 in *Florida Real Estate Broker's Guide*)

Ownership of a freehold estate.

(Unit 9 in *Florida Real Estate Principles, Practices & Law* and Units 15 and 18 in *Florida Real Estate Broker's Guide*)

Characterized by priority based on the date of recording in the public records.

(Unit 9 in *Florida Real Estate Principles, Practices & Law* and Units 15 and 18 in *Florida Real Estate Broker's Guide*)

Mechanics' liens	Net lease	Opinion of title	Owner's policy
Percentage lease	Police power	Quiet enjoyment	Quitclaim deed
Restrictive covenants	Seisin (seizin)	Specific liens	Sublease

Title insurance issued for the total purchase price of the property to protect the new owner against unexpected title risks.

(Unit 9 in *Florida Real Estate Principles, Practices & Law* and Units 15 and 18 in *Florida Real Estate Broker's Guide*)

A formal statement executed by an attorney after studying the abstract of title.

(Unit 9 in *Florida Real Estate Principles, Practices & Law* and Units 15 and 18 in *Florida Real Estate Broker's Guide*)

An agreement for the tenant to pay fixed rent plus property costs such as taxes, insurance, and utilities.

(Unit 9 in *Florida Real Estate Principles, Practices & Law* and Units 15 and 18 in *Florida Real Estate Broker's Guide*)

Statutory liens created in favor of materialmen and mechanics to secure payment for materials, supplies, and services rendered in the improvement, repair, or maintenance of real property. Also known as a construction lien.

(Unit 9 in *Florida Real Estate Principles, Practices & Law* and Units 15 and 18 in *Florida Real Estate Broker's Guide*)

A type of deed that releases the grantor of any rights in the property the grantor may have and is used to clear clouds on the title and to cure title defects.

(Unit 9 in *Florida Real Estate Principles, Practices & Law* and Units 15 and 18 in *Florida Real Estate Broker's Guide*)

A promise in a general warranty deed that guarantees peaceful possession undisturbed by claim of title.

(Unit 9 in *Florida Real Estate Principles, Practices & Law* and Units 15 and 18 in *Florida Real Estate Broker's Guide*)

The broadest power of government to limit or regulate the rights of property owners in order to protect the health, safety, and welfare of the public.

(Unit 9 in *Florida Real Estate Principles, Practices & Law* and Units 15 and 18 in *Florida Real Estate Broker's Guide*)

An agreement for the tenant to pay rent based on the gross sales received by doing business on the leased property.

(Unit 9 in *Florida Real Estate Principles, Practices & Law* and Units 15 and 18 in *Florida Real Estate Broker's Guide*)

A lease given by the lessee for a portion of the leasehold interest, while the lessee retains some reversionary interest. The sublease may be for all or part of the premises, for the whole term or part of it, as long as the lessor retains some interest in the property.

(Unit 9 in *Florida Real Estate Principles, Practices & Law* and Units 15 and 18 in *Florida Real Estate Broker's Guide*)

Liens that apply only to a certain specified property.

(Unit 9 in *Florida Real Estate Principles, Practices & Law* and Units 15 and 18 in *Florida Real Estate Broker's Guide*)

The clause in a deed that is a promise that the grantor has the right to convey title (a statement of ownership).

(Unit 9 in *Florida Real Estate Principles, Practices & Law* and Units 15 and 18 in *Florida Real Estate Broker's Guide*)

Recorded by the developer along with the subdivision plat to maintain specific standards in the subdivision, such as requiring certain architectural specifications.

(Unit 9 in *Florida Real Estate Principles, Practices & Law* and Units 15 and 18 in *Florida Real Estate Broker's Guide*)

Superior liens	Testate	Title	Title insurance
Variable lease	Voluntary alienation	Warranty forever	Assignment
Attorney-in-fact	Bilateral contract	Buyer brokerage agreement	Community development district (CDD)

A contract that protects the policyholder from losses resulting from defects in the title.

(Unit 9 in *Florida Real Estate Principles, Practices & Law* and Units 15 and 18 in *Florida Real Estate Broker's Guide*)

A legal concept signifying ownership of a collection of rights to real property.

(Unit 9 in *Florida Real Estate Principles, Practices & Law* and Units 15 and 18 in *Florida Real Estate Broker's Guide*)

To die with a will.

(Unit 9 in *Florida Real Estate Principles, Practices & Law* and Units 15 and 18 in *Florida Real Estate Broker's Guide*)

Liens that take priority over all other liens are superior liens. There are three superior liens: (1) real estate tax liens, (2) special assessment liens, and (3) Federal estate tax liens.

(Unit 9 in *Florida Real Estate Principles, Practices & Law* and Units 15 and 18 in *Florida Real Estate Broker's Guide*)

A transfer of rights and duties under a contract.

(Unit 11 in *Florida Real Estate Principles, Practices & Law* and Unit 11 in *Florida Real Estate Broker's Guide*)

A promise in a general warranty deed guaranteeing that the grantor will forever warrant and defend the grantee's title against all unlawful claims.

(Unit 9 in *Florida Real Estate Principles, Practices & Law* and Units 15 and 18 in *Florida Real Estate Broker's Guide*)

A legal term used to indicate the transfer of title is accomplished with the owner's control and consent.

(Unit 9 in *Florida Real Estate Principles, Practices & Law* and Units 15 and 18 in *Florida Real Estate Broker's Guide*)

An agreement for the tenant to pay specified rent increases based on a predetermined index (CPI) at set future dates.

(Unit 9 in *Florida Real Estate Principles, Practices & Law* and Units 15 and 18 in *Florida Real Estate Broker's Guide*)

An independent special district created by law to service the long-term needs of its community.

(Unit 11 in *Florida Real Estate Principles, Practices & Law* and Unit 11 in *Florida Real Estate Broker's Guide*)

An employment contract with a purchaser.

(Unit 11 in *Florida Real Estate Principles, Practices & Law* and Unit 11 in *Florida Real Estate Broker's Guide*)

An agreement that obligates both parties to perform in accordance with the terms of the contract.

(Unit 11 in *Florida Real Estate Principles, Practices & Law* and Unit 11 in *Florida Real Estate Broker's Guide*)

A person who is authorized to perform certain acts for another under a power of attorney.

(Unit 11 in *Florida Real Estate Principles, Practices & Law* and Unit 11 in *Florida Real Estate Broker's Guide*)

Competent	Contract	Enforceable contract	Exclusive-agency listing
Exclusive right-of-sale listing	Fraud	Good consideration	Homeowners associations
Liquidated damages	Meeting of the minds	Misrepresentation	Net listing

Employment contract given to one real estate broker, but the seller reserves the right to sell the property without paying a commission.

(Unit 11 in *Florida Real Estate Principles, Practices & Law* and Unit 11 in *Florida Real Estate Broker's Guide*)

A legally binding contract that the law will recognize.

(Unit 11 in *Florida Real Estate Principles, Practices & Law* and Unit 11 in *Florida Real Estate Broker's Guide*)

An agreement between two or more competent parties to perform, or not perform, some legal act for a legal consideration.

(Unit 11 in *Florida Real Estate Principles, Practices & Law* and Unit 11 in *Florida Real Estate Broker's Guide*)

A party to a contract who possesses the legal capacity to enter into a binding contract (i.e., no mental defects and of legal age to enter into contracts).

(Unit 11 in *Florida Real Estate Principles, Practices & Law* and Unit 11 in *Florida Real Estate Broker's Guide*)

Responsible for the operation of a community in which the voting membership is made up of parcel owners, membership is a mandatory condition of parcel ownership, and the association is authorized to impose assessments that, if unpaid, may become a lien on the parcel.

(Unit 11 in *Florida Real Estate Principles, Practices & Law* and Unit 11 in *Florida Real Estate Broker's Guide*)

A promise that cannot be measured in terms of money, such as love and affection.

(Unit 11 in *Florida Real Estate Principles, Practices & Law* and Unit 11 in *Florida Real Estate Broker's Guide*)

The intent to misrepresent a material fact or to deceive in order to gain an unfair advantage or to harm another person.

(Unit 11 in *Florida Real Estate Principles, Practices & Law* and Unit 11 in *Florida Real Estate Broker's Guide*)

A listing given to one broker who is assured of a commission no matter who sells the property.

(Unit 11 in *Florida Real Estate Principles, Practices & Law* and Unit 11 in *Florida Real Estate Broker's Guide*)

A listing created when a seller agrees to sell a property for a stated acceptable minimum amount.

(Unit 11 in *Florida Real Estate Principles, Practices & Law* and Unit 11 in *Florida Real Estate Broker's Guide*)

An untrue statement of fact or the concealment of a material fact.

(Unit 11 in *Florida Real Estate Principles, Practices & Law* and Unit 11 in *Florida Real Estate Broker's Guide*)

To reach an agreement on all terms in a contract.

(Unit 11 in *Florida Real Estate Principles, Practices & Law* and Unit 11 in *Florida Real Estate Broker's Guide*)

The amount of valuable consideration specified in an agreement as a penalty for default.

(Unit 11 in *Florida Real Estate Principles, Practices & Law* and Unit 11 in *Florida Real Estate Broker's Guide*)

Novation	Open listing	Option contract	Parol contract
Procuring cause	Statute of frauds	Statute of limitations	Unenforceable contract
Unilateral contract	Valid Contract	Valuable consideration	Vendee

An oral agreement.

(Unit 11 in *Florida Real Estate Principles, Practices & Law* and Unit 11 in *Florida Real Estate Broker's Guide*)

A unilateral contract to keep an offer to sell or lease real property open for a specified period.

(Unit 11 in *Florida Real Estate Principles, Practices & Law* and Unit 11 in *Florida Real Estate Broker's Guide*)

An employment contract given to any number of brokers who work simultaneously to sell the owner's property.

(Unit 11 in *Florida Real Estate Principles, Practices & Law* and Unit 11 in *Florida Real Estate Broker's Guide*)

The substitution of a new party and/or new terms to an existing obligation.

(Unit 11 in *Florida Real Estate Principles, Practices & Law* and Unit 11 in *Florida Real Estate Broker's Guide*)

A contract that would not stand up in a court of law because it does not meet the requirements of the statute of frauds or because it runs beyond the statute of limitations.

(Unit 11 in *Florida Real Estate Principles, Practices & Law* and Unit 11 in *Florida Real Estate Broker's Guide*)

An act that designates the period during which the terms of a contract may be enforced.

(Unit 11 in *Florida Real Estate Principles, Practices & Law* and Unit 11 in *Florida Real Estate Broker's Guide*)

An act that requires that certain real estate instruments and contracts affecting title to real property be in writing in order to be enforceable.

(Unit 11 in *Florida Real Estate Principles, Practices & Law* and Unit 11 in *Florida Real Estate Broker's Guide*)

The chain of events that results in a sale.

(Unit 11 in *Florida Real Estate Principles, Practices & Law* and Unit 11 in *Florida Real Estate Broker's Guide*)

The buyer or purchaser of real property under an agreement of sale.

(Unit 11 in *Florida Real Estate Principles, Practices & Law* and Unit 11 in *Florida Real Estate Broker's Guide*)

The money or a promise of something that can be measured in terms of money.

(Unit 11 in *Florida Real Estate Principles, Practices & Law* and Unit 11 in *Florida Real Estate Broker's Guide*)

Binding on both parties and is legally enforceable.

(Unit 11 in *Florida Real Estate Principles, Practices & Law* and Unit 11 in *Florida Real Estate Broker's Guide*)

An agreement that obligates only one party to perform.

(Unit 11 in *Florida Real Estate Principles, Practices & Law* and Unit 11 in *Florida Real Estate Broker's Guide*)

Vendor	Void Contract	Voidable Contract	Asbestos
Buffer zone	Building codes	Building inspections	Building permit
Certificate of occupancy	Comprehensive plans	Concurrency	Density

A mineral fiber used until 1978 in a variety of building construction materials for insulation and as a fire retardant.

(Unit 19 in *Florida Real Estate Principles, Practices & Law* and Unit 16 in *Florida Real Estate Broker's Guide*)

Allows one of the parties to avoid contractual duties (e.g., when one party is a minor or when a party is mentally incompetent).

(Unit 11 in *Florida Real Estate Principles, Practices & Law* and Unit 11 in *Florida Real Estate Broker's Guide*)

Does not meet all the required elements of a valid contract and has no legal effect.

(Unit 11 in *Florida Real Estate Principles, Practices & Law* and Unit 11 in *Florida Real Estate Broker's Guide*)

The seller of real property in an agreement of sale.

(Unit 11 in *Florida Real Estate Principles, Practices & Law* and Unit 11 in *Florida Real Estate Broker's Guide*)

A document issued after local government has review of the architectural and engineering drawings and the energy calculations.

(Unit 19 in *Florida Real Estate Principles, Practices & Law* and Unit 16 in *Florida Real Estate Broker's Guide*)

Conducted by county officials during construction to confirm that the workmanship conforms to the building code.

(Unit 19 in *Florida Real Estate Principles, Practices & Law* and Unit 16 in *Florida Real Estate Broker's Guide*)

Government ordinances regulating construction practices and materials.

(Unit 19 in *Florida Real Estate Principles, Practices & Law* and Unit 16 in *Florida Real Estate Broker's Guide*)

A strip of land separating one land use from another.

(Unit 19 in *Florida Real Estate Principles, Practices & Law* and Unit 16 in *Florida Real Estate Broker's Guide*)

The number of homes or lots per acre.

(Unit 19 in *Florida Real Estate Principles, Practices & Law* and Unit 16 in *Florida Real Estate Broker's Guide*)

A provision in Florida's Growth Policy Act that requires water and waste treatment facilities needed to support additional population be in place before new development is allowed.

(Unit 19 in *Florida Real Estate Principles, Practices & Law* and Unit 16 in *Florida Real Estate Broker's Guide*)

Master plans for the future physical development of a city, county, or region.

(Unit 19 in *Florida Real Estate Principles, Practices & Law* and Unit 16 in *Florida Real Estate Broker's Guide*)

An occupancy permit issued by the local government after construction is completed and the final inspection is approved.

(Unit 19 in *Florida Real Estate Principles, Practices & Law* and Unit 16 in *Florida Real Estate Broker's Guide*)

Developments of regional impact (DRI)	Environmental due dilligence	Environmental impact statements	Health ordinances
Impact fees	Intensity	Laissez-faire	Mixed land use
Nonconforming use	Planned unit development (PUD)	Potentially responsible persons (PRP)	R-value

Local codes that regulate maintenance and sanitation of public spaces.

(Unit 19 in *Florida Real Estate Principles, Practices & Law* and Unit 16 in *Florida Real Estate Broker's Guide*)

Statements that summarize the effect that proposed development will have on the surroundings.

(Unit 19 in *Florida Real Estate Principles, Practices & Law* and Unit 16 in *Florida Real Estate Broker's Guide*)

The process by which a purchaser evaluates the likelihood of site contamination. It is normally accomplished by employing an environmental consultant to conduct an environmental site assessment.

(Unit 19 in *Florida Real Estate Principles, Practices & Law* and Unit 16 in *Florida Real Estate Broker's Guide*)

Any development that because of its character, magnitude, or location could have a substantial effect on the health, safety, and welfare of citizens of more than one county.

(Unit 19 in *Florida Real Estate Principles, Practices & Law* and Unit 16 in *Florida Real Estate Broker's Guide*)

More than one type of zoning, such as a condominium that has residential and commercial units.

(Unit 19 in *Florida Real Estate Principles, Practices & Law* and Unit 16 in *Florida Real Estate Broker's Guide*)

Noninterference by government in trade, industry and individual action.

(Unit 19 in *Florida Real Estate Principles, Practices & Law* and Unit 16 in *Florida Real Estate Broker's Guide*)

The concentration of pedestrian traffic and vehicular traffic used as a means of designating land for commercial zones.

(Unit 19 in *Florida Real Estate Principles, Practices & Law* and Unit 16 in *Florida Real Estate Broker's Guide*)

Charges by local governments to fund major off-site improvements.

(Unit 19 in *Florida Real Estate Principles, Practices & Law* and Unit 16 in *Florida Real Estate Broker's Guide*)

Refers to the effectiveness of insulation and is measured by its resistance to heat flow.

(Unit 19 in *Florida Real Estate Principles, Practices & Law* and Unit 16 in *Florida Real Estate Broker's Guide*)

Individuals who are liable for the cost to clean up a contaminated site, including past and present owners and operators of the site, creators of the hazardous material, and transporters of the hazardous material to the site.

(Unit 19 in *Florida Real Estate Principles, Practices & Law* and Unit 16 in *Florida Real Estate Broker's Guide*)

A self-contained development planned under special zoning ordinances that allow maximum use of open space by reducing lot sizes and street sizes.

(Unit 19 in *Florida Real Estate Principles, Practices & Law* and Unit 16 in *Florida Real Estate Broker's Guide*)

Continuing land use that is not in compliance with newly enacted zoning ordinances.

(Unit 19 in *Florida Real Estate Principles, Practices & Law* and Unit 16 in *Florida Real Estate Broker's Guide*)

Special exception	Special flood hazard areas (SFHAs)	Special purpose property	Subdivision regulations
Variance	Wetlands	Zoning ordinances	Absentee owner
Appraisal	Appraiser	Broker's price opinion (BPO)	Business brokers

Local regulations that control the size and location of streets, sidewalks, water and sewer lines, mandated drainage facilities, and the location of parks and open spaces.

(Unit 19 in *Florida Real Estate Principles, Practices & Law* and Unit 16 in *Florida Real Estate Broker's Guide*)

A combination of land and improvements with only one economically feasible use because of some special design.

(Unit 19 in *Florida Real Estate Principles, Practices & Law* and Unit 16 in *Florida Real Estate Broker's Guide*)

Special flood hazard areas (SFHAs) are located in a 100-year flood plain.

(Unit 19 in *Florida Real Estate Principles, Practices & Law* and Unit 16 in *Florida Real Estate Broker's Guide*)

Permission to build or use property in apparent conflict with existing zoning ordinances.

(Unit 19 in *Florida Real Estate Principles, Practices & Law* and Unit 16 in *Florida Real Estate Broker's Guide*)

A property owner who does not reside on the property and who usually relies on a property manager to supervise the investment.

(Unit 1 in *Florida Real Estate Principles, Practices & Law*)

Authorize the segmentation (dividing) of a community into districts or zones in keeping with the character of the land and structures, and with their suitability for particular uses to protect the property owners from undesirable land uses on neighboring property.

(Unit 19 in *Florida Real Estate Principles, Practices & Law* and Unit 16 in *Florida Real Estate Broker's Guide*)

Areas with groundwater levels at or near the surface for much of the year or areas that have aquatic vegetation.

(Unit 19 in *Florida Real Estate Principles, Practices & Law* and Unit 16 in *Florida Real Estate Broker's Guide*)

Allows property owners to vary from strict compliance with all or part of a zoning code because to comply would force an undue hardship on the property owner.

(Unit 19 in *Florida Real Estate Principles, Practices & Law* and Unit 16 in *Florida Real Estate Broker's Guide*)

Real estate licensees who engage in the sale, purchase, or lease of businesses.

(Unit 1 in *Florida Real Estate Principles, Practices & Law*)

A written opinion of the value of real property that may not be referred to as an appraisal.

(Unit 1 in *Florida Real Estate Principles, Practices & Law*)

A person who is registered, licensed, or certified by the DBPR and provides an estimate of value.

(Unit 1 in *Florida Real Estate Principles, Practices & Law*)

Professional service provided by a registered, licensed, or certified appraiser or real estate licensee to produce an estimate of value as of a specific date.

(Unit 1 in *Florida Real Estate Principles, Practices & Law*)

Business opportunity	Community Association Manager (CAM)	Comparative market analysis (CMA)	Dedication
Farm area	Follow-up	Multiple listing service (MLS)	Property management
Property manager	Real estate brokerage	REALTOR®	Rental agent

An offer of private land for some public use, by an owner, together with acceptance by or on behalf of the public.

(Unit 1 in *Florida Real Estate Principles, Practices & Law*)

An informal estimate of market value performed by a real estate licensee for the seller to assist in arriving at an appropriate listing price or, if working with the buyer, an informal estimate of market value to assist the buyer in arriving at an appropriate offering price.

(Unit 1 in *Florida Real Estate Principles, Practices & Law*)

A person who holds a CAM license and manages community associations of more than 10 units or associations with an annual budget in excess of $100,000.

(Unit 1 in *Florida Real Estate Principles, Practices & Law*)

The real estate activity dealing in the sale, purchase, or lease of businesses as going-concern operations.

(Unit 1 in *Florida Real Estate Principles, Practices & Law*)

The leasing, managing, marketing, and overall maintenance of property for others.

(Unit 1 in *Florida Real Estate Principles, Practices & Law*)

The MLS is a database that allows real estate brokers representing sellers under a listing contract to share information about properties with brokers who may represent potential buyers.

(Unit 1 in *Florida Real Estate Principles, Practices & Law*)

What a sales associate does after a sale to maintain customer contact and goodwill.

(Unit 1 in *Florida Real Estate Principles, Practices & Law*)

A selected geographical area or a group of people from which licensees solicit real estate business and devote special attention and study.

(Unit 1 in *Florida Real Estate Principles, Practices & Law*)

Someone who typically finds a tenant for property and collects a fee.

(Unit 1 in *Florida Real Estate Principles, Practices & Law*)

A REALTOR® is a real estate professional who is a member of a local board (or association) of REALTORS® and is affiliated with the Florida Realtors® and the NAR.

(Unit 1 in *Florida Real Estate Principles, Practices & Law*)

The part of the real estate business that is concerned with completing a real estate transaction and bringing buyers, sellers, owners, and renters together.

(Unit 1 in *Florida Real Estate Principles, Practices & Law*)

The local representative of the owner.

(Unit 1 in *Florida Real Estate Principles, Practices & Law*)

Subdivision plat map	Target market	Acre	Assessor's parcel number
Base lines	Check	Government survey system	Legal description
Lot and block	Metes-and-bounds description	Monument	Point of beginning (POB)

A number assigned to each parcel of land in a tax district that is used to prepare tax maps.

(Unit 10 in *Florida Real Estate Principles, Practices & Law*)

A measure of land area equal to 43,560 square feet.

(Unit 10 in *Florida Real Estate Principles, Practices & Law*)

A specific group of prospects chosen because of its demographic, financial, and lifestyle characteristics.

(Unit 1 in *Florida Real Estate Principles, Practices & Law*)

A plan of a tract of land subdivided into lots and showing required or planned amenities, streets, and utilities that is submitted to a local government agency.

(Unit 1 in *Florida Real Estate Principles, Practices & Law*)

A series of boundary lines on the earth's surface to identify the boundaries of a land parcel.

(Unit 10 in *Florida Real Estate Principles, Practices & Law*)

A type of land description developed by the federal government for subdividing lands utilizing surveying lines.

(Unit 10 in *Florida Real Estate Principles, Practices & Law*)

Formed when two guide meridians and two correction lines intersect to form a 24-by-24-mile square.

(Unit 10 in *Florida Real Estate Principles, Practices & Law*)

Imaginary lines running east and west and crossing a principal meridian at a definite point; used by surveyors for reference in locating and describing land under the government survey system.

(Unit 10 in *Florida Real Estate Principles, Practices & Law*)

The starting reference point in the metes-and-bounds method of property description.

(Unit 10 in *Florida Real Estate Principles, Practices & Law*)

A fixed object (marker) used to identify the point of beginning (POB) and the corners of a parcel.

(Unit 10 in *Florida Real Estate Principles, Practices & Law*)

The most accurate method of land description that is used to describe both regular- and irregular-shaped parcels.

(Unit 10 in *Florida Real Estate Principles, Practices & Law*)

A type of legal description used to identify lots within a recorded subdivision plat map.

(Unit 10 in *Florida Real Estate Principles, Practices & Law*)

Principal meridians	Range	Section	Survey
Tier	Township (or tier)	Township lines	Acceleration clause
Assignment of mortgage	Assumption	Blanket mortgages	Buydown

A drawing of a parcel of land showing the boundary lines that includes a legal description of the property.

(Unit 10 in *Florida Real Estate Principles, Practices & Law*)

A section is one mile square and contains 640 acres.

(Unit 10 in *Florida Real Estate Principles, Practices & Law*)

A six-mile-wide vertical (north/south) strip of land enclosed between two range lines.

(Unit 10 in *Florida Real Estate Principles, Practices & Law*)

Imaginary lines running north and south and crossing a base line at a definite point; used by surveyors for reference in locating and describing land under the government survey system.

(Unit 10 in *Florida Real Estate Principles, Practices & Law*)

Authorizes the mortgagee to accelerate or advance the due date of the entire unpaid balance and call the entire debt due and payable if the mortgagor defaults.

(Unit 12 in *Florida Real Estate Principles, Practices & Law* and Unit 12 in *Florida Real Estate Broker's Guide*)

Township lines are six miles apart, run east and west, and are parallel to the base line.

(Unit 10 in *Florida Real Estate Principles, Practices & Law*)

An east/west strip of land on either side of a base line (think of a tiered wedding cake); township also refers to the square formed by the intersection of two range lines and two township lines.

(Unit 10 in *Florida Real Estate Principles, Practices & Law*)

The east/west row of townships in the government survey system.

(Unit 10 in *Florida Real Estate Principles, Practices & Law*)

A way to temporarily lower the interest rate on a mortgage.

(Unit 12 in *Florida Real Estate Principles, Practices & Law* and Unit 12 in *Florida Real Estate Broker's Guide*)

Pledge a number of parcels, usually building lots as security for the loan.

(Unit 12 in *Florida Real Estate Principles, Practices & Law* and Unit 12 in *Florida Real Estate Broker's Guide*)

The taking over of an existing mortgage obligating the buyer to assume liability for the debt.

(Unit 12 in *Florida Real Estate Principles, Practices & Law* and Unit 12 in *Florida Real Estate Broker's Guide*)

A legal instrument that states that the mortgagee assigns (transfers) the mortgage and promissory note to the purchaser.

(Unit 12 in *Florida Real Estate Principles, Practices & Law* and Unit 12 in *Florida Real Estate Broker's Guide*)

Contract for deed (land contract)	Deed in lieu of foreclosure	Default	Defeasance clause
Discount points	Due-on-sale clause	Equity	Equity of redemption
Escrow (impound) accounts	Estoppel certificate	First mortgage	Foreclosure

In title theory states, the clause requires the lender to convey legal title to the borrower once the debt is repaid; in lien theory states, the clause requires the lender to release the mortgage lien when the debt is repaid.

(Unit 12 in *Florida Real Estate Principles, Practices & Law* and Unit 12 in *Florida Real Estate Broker's Guide*)

When a borrow fails to fulfill certain obligations agreed to in the promissory note.

(Unit 12 in *Florida Real Estate Principles, Practices & Law* and Unit 12 in *Florida Real Estate Broker's Guide*)

A friendly foreclosure (nonjudicial procedure) in which the mortgagor gives title to the mortgagee.

(Unit 12 in *Florida Real Estate Principles, Practices & Law* and Unit 12 in *Florida Real Estate Broker's Guide*)

A financing method in which the title to the real property remains with the seller until the loan is repaid.

(Unit 12 in *Florida Real Estate Principles, Practices & Law* and Unit 12 in *Florida Real Estate Broker's Guide*)

Allows the mortgagor to prevent foreclosure from occurring by paying to the mortgagee the principal and interest due plus any expenses the lender has incurred in attempting to collect the debt.

(Unit 12 in *Florida Real Estate Principles, Practices & Law* and Unit 12 in *Florida Real Estate Broker's Guide*)

The monetary interest the owner has in property over and above the mortgage indebtedness.

(Unit 12 in *Florida Real Estate Principles, Practices & Law* and Unit 12 in *Florida Real Estate Broker's Guide*)

A provision in a conventional mortgage that allows the mortgagee to call due the outstanding loan balance plus accrued interest, thereby preventing the loan assumption.

(Unit 12 in *Florida Real Estate Principles, Practices & Law* and Unit 12 in *Florida Real Estate Broker's Guide*)

An extra up-front fee charged by lenders to increase the real yield or the APR.

(Unit 12 in *Florida Real Estate Principles, Practices & Law* and Unit 12 in *Florida Real Estate Broker's Guide*)

A legal procedure whereby property used as security for a debt is sold to satisfy the debt owing to default in payment of the mortgage note or default of other terms in the mortgage document.

(Unit 12 in *Florida Real Estate Principles, Practices & Law* and Unit 12 in *Florida Real Estate Broker's Guide*)

The first mortgage loan to be executed and recorded.

(Unit 12 in *Florida Real Estate Principles, Practices & Law* and Unit 12 in *Florida Real Estate Broker's Guide*)

A written statement signed by the borrower verifying the amount of the unpaid balance, the rate of interest, and the date to which the interest has been paid prior to assignment; also, often requested by a closing agent to verify the payoff amount for the seller prior to conveying a property.

(Unit 12 in *Florida Real Estate Principles, Practices & Law* and Unit 12 in *Florida Real Estate Broker's Guide*)

Required by most lenders to set aside funds to cover future payments for taxes, assessments, private mortgage insurance, and hazard insurance.

(Unit 12 in *Florida Real Estate Principles, Practices & Law* and Unit 12 in *Florida Real Estate Broker's Guide*)

Hypothecation	Interest	Junior mortgage	Land development loan
Lien theory	Lis pendens	Loan origination fee	Loan servicing
Loan-to-value (LTV) ratio	Mortgage	Mortgagee	Mortgagor

Finances the installation of the on-site and off-site improvements.

(Unit 12 in *Florida Real Estate Principles, Practices & Law* and Unit 12 in *Florida Real Estate Broker's Guide*)

A mortgage that is behind (in priority) to the first mortgage.

(Unit 12 in *Florida Real Estate Principles, Practices & Law* and Unit 12 in *Florida Real Estate Broker's Guide*)

The cost for the use of borrowed funds.

(Unit 12 in *Florida Real Estate Principles, Practices & Law* and Unit 12 in *Florida Real Estate Broker's Guide*)

To pledge real or personal property as security for a debt or obligation without giving up possession of the property.

(Unit 12 in *Florida Real Estate Principles, Practices & Law* and Unit 12 in *Florida Real Estate Broker's Guide*)

An extra source of income for lenders earned by handling the loan payment collection and recordkeeping for the mortgages it originates.

(Unit 12 in *Florida Real Estate Principles, Practices & Law* and Unit 12 in *Florida Real Estate Broker's Guide*)

A finance fee charged by a lender for making a mortgage.

(Unit 12 in *Florida Real Estate Principles, Practices & Law* and Unit 12 in *Florida Real Estate Broker's Guide*)

Notice of pending legal action; it is filed before initiating a lawsuit.

(Unit 12 in *Florida Real Estate Principles, Practices & Law* and Unit 12 in *Florida Real Estate Broker's Guide*)

States treat a mortgage solely as a security interest in the secured real property with title retained by the mortgagor.

(Unit 12 in *Florida Real Estate Principles, Practices & Law* and Unit 12 in *Florida Real Estate Broker's Guide*)

A borrower who gives a mortgage on the property in order to obtain a loan from a lender.

(Unit 12 in *Florida Real Estate Principles, Practices & Law* and Unit 12 in *Florida Real Estate Broker's Guide*)

A lender who holds a mortgage on specific property as security for the money loaned to the borrower.

(Unit 12 in *Florida Real Estate Principles, Practices & Law* and Unit 12 in *Florida Real Estate Broker's Guide*)

A written agreement signed by the mortgagor to voluntarily pledge the property as collateral for the debt.

(Unit 12 in *Florida Real Estate Principles, Practices & Law* and Unit 12 in *Florida Real Estate Broker's Guide*)

Relationship between amount borrowed and appraised value (or sale price) of a property.

(Unit 12 in *Florida Real Estate Principles, Practices & Law* and Unit 12 in *Florida Real Estate Broker's Guide*)

Note	Novation	Partial release clauses	PITI
Prepayment clause	Prepayment penalty	Receivership clause	Right to reinstate
Satisfaction of mortgage	Short sale	Subject to the mortgage	Subordination agreement

The monthly principal, interest, taxes, and insurance payment charged on a mortgage loan.

(Unit 12 in *Florida Real Estate Principles, Practices & Law* and Unit 12 in *Florida Real Estate Broker's Guide*)

Commonly used in blanket mortgages and provide for the release of individual parcels from the blanket mortgage upon payment of a specified amount.

(Unit 12 in *Florida Real Estate Principles, Practices & Law* and Unit 12 in *Florida Real Estate Broker's Guide*)

The substitution of a new debtor (buyer) and release of a former debtor (seller) for an existing debt by mutual agreement and with approval of the mortgagee.

(Unit 12 in *Florida Real Estate Principles, Practices & Law* and Unit 12 in *Florida Real Estate Broker's Guide*)

The legal instrument that represents the evidence of a debt and a promise to repay the debt.

(Unit 12 in *Florida Real Estate Principles, Practices & Law* and Unit 12 in *Florida Real Estate Broker's Guide*)

The mortgagor's right to reinstate the original repayment terms in the note after the lender initiated the acceleration clause.

(Unit 12 in *Florida Real Estate Principles, Practices & Law* and Unit 12 in *Florida Real Estate Broker's Guide*)

Allows a receiver to be appointed to collect income from a property and use the income to make mortgage payments.

(Unit 12 in *Florida Real Estate Principles, Practices & Law* and Unit 12 in *Florida Real Estate Broker's Guide*)

Allows an extra charge if any amount of the loan is paid off early.

(Unit 12 in *Florida Real Estate Principles, Practices & Law* and Unit 12 in *Florida Real Estate Broker's Guide*)

A provision in a mortgage that allows the mortgagor to pay off part or all of the mortgage debt, without penalty or other fees, prior to maturity.

(Unit 12 in *Florida Real Estate Principles, Practices & Law* and Unit 12 in *Florida Real Estate Broker's Guide*)

A provision in a mortgage stipulating that the lender will voluntarily allow a subsequent mortgage to take priority over the lender's otherwise superior mortgage; the act of yielding priority.

(Unit 12 in *Florida Real Estate Principles, Practices & Law* and Unit 12 in *Florida Real Estate Broker's Guide*)

A buyer makes regular, periodic payments on the mortgage but does not assume responsibility for the mortgage note.

(Unit 12 in *Florida Real Estate Principles, Practices & Law* and Unit 12 in *Florida Real Estate Broker's Guide*)

A real estate transaction where the net proceeds at closing will not satisfy the payoff amount of mortgages and other liens on the property.

(Unit 12 in *Florida Real Estate Principles, Practices & Law* and Unit 12 in *Florida Real Estate Broker's Guide*)

A recordable instrument provided by the lender within 60 days of payoff as evidence the mortgage debt is paid in full.

(Unit 12 in *Florida Real Estate Principles, Practices & Law* and Unit 12 in *Florida Real Estate Broker's Guide*)

Takeout commitment	Title theory	Adjustable-rate mortgage (ARM)	Amortized mortgage
Annual percentage rate (APR)	Balloon payment	Biweekly mortgage	Closing Disclosure
Conforming loans	Conventional loan	Discount rate	Disintermediation

A loan in which the debt is gradually and systematically killed or extinguished by equal regular period payments; the entire loan is paid off at the end of the loan term.

(Unit 13 in *Florida Real Estate Principles, Practices & Law*)

A financing technique in which the lender can raise or lower the interest rate according to a predetermined index.

(Unit 13 in *Florida Real Estate Principles, Practices & Law*)

States consider the mortgagee to have legal title to the mortgaged property, and the mortgagor has equitable title until the debt is repaid.

(Unit 12 in *Florida Real Estate Principles, Practices & Law* and Unit 12 in *Florida Real Estate Broker's Guide*)

A commitment by a permanent lender to "take out" the interim lender by paying off the construction loan, leaving the developer with a permanent long-term loan once the project is complete.

(Unit 12 in *Florida Real Estate Principles, Practices & Law* and Unit 12 in *Florida Real Estate Broker's Guide*)

A form that must be provided to the borrower at least three business days prior to closing that replaced the HUD-1 statement.

(Unit 13 in *Florida Real Estate Principles, Practices & Law*)

A mortgage loan amortized the same way as other loans with monthly payments except that the borrower makes a payment every two weeks.

(Unit 13 in *Florida Real Estate Principles, Practices & Law*)

A single, large, final payment, including accrued interest and all unpaid principal due at maturity of a partially amortized mortgage.

(Unit 13 in *Florida Real Estate Principles, Practices & Law*)

The interest rate and other loan costs; represents the true yearly cost of credit.

(Unit 13 in *Florida Real Estate Principles, Practices & Law*)

The removal of intermediaries; buyers bypass the middlemen.

(Unit 13 in *Florida Real Estate Principles, Practices & Law*)

The interest rate charged banks for borrowing from the Fed.

(Unit 13 in *Florida Real Estate Principles, Practices & Law*)

A conventional loan is one that is not insured or guaranteed by a government agency.

(Unit 13 in *Florida Real Estate Principles, Practices & Law*)

Loans that meet Fannie Mae guidelines regarding size and type of loan.

(Unit 13 in *Florida Real Estate Principles, Practices & Law*)

Entitlement	Fannie Mae	Freddie Mac	Ginnie Mae
Home equity loan	Index	Intermediation	Level-payment plan
Lifetime cap	Loan estimate	Margin	Monetary policy

A federal agency that is part of the Department of Housing and Urban Development.

(Unit 13 in *Florida Real Estate Principles, Practices & Law*)

A secondary mortgage market institution that buys and sells conventional, FHA, and VA loans.

(Unit 13 in *Florida Real Estate Principles, Practices & Law*)

An institution in the secondary mortgage market that buys and sells mortgages.

(Unit 13 in *Florida Real Estate Principles, Practices & Law*)

The maximum amount for an individual veteran that the government will guarantee for a VA loan.

(Unit 13 in *Florida Real Estate Principles, Practices & Law*)

A mortgage in which the monthly payments are a fixed amount (payment does not change), but the amount applied to principal increases each month and the amount applied to interest decreases each month.

(Unit 13 in *Florida Real Estate Principles, Practices & Law*)

Financial institutions serve as intermediaries between depositors and borrowers.

(Unit 13 in *Florida Real Estate Principles, Practices & Law*)

The rate to which an adjustable-rate loan is tied; at set adjustment periods, the borrower's interest rate moves up or down as the index rate changes.

(Unit 13 in *Florida Real Estate Principles, Practices & Law*)

A mortgage secured by a personal residence. It provides a line of credit available for draws when needed by the homeowner. It is sometimes used as a home improvement loan.

(Unit 13 in *Florida Real Estate Principles, Practices & Law*)

The actions undertaken by the Fed to influence the availability and cost of money and credit.

(Unit 13 in *Florida Real Estate Principles, Practices & Law*)

The percentage that is added to the index to calculate each interest rate change in an adjustable-rate mortgage. It covers the lender's expenses plus profit.

(Unit 13 in *Florida Real Estate Principles, Practices & Law*)

A form that contains information about the lender, property, loan terms, projected payments, and total estimated cost at closing.

(Unit 13 in *Florida Real Estate Principles, Practices & Law*)

Limits the total amount the interest rate can increase over life of the loan.

(Unit 13 in *Florida Real Estate Principles, Practices & Law*)

Mortgage broker	Mortgage fraud	Mortgage insurance premium (MIP)	Mortgage lender
Mortgage loan originator (MLO)	Negative amortization	Nonconforming loans	Open market operations
Package mortgage	Partially amortized mortgage	Payment caps	Periodic caps

A business entity that originates, sells, and then services mortgage loans. Mortgage lenders are not depository institutions. They originate loans and then package the loans together and sell the entire package.

(Unit 13 in *Florida Real Estate Principles, Practices & Law*)

A premium for mortgage insurance on FHA mortgages to protect the lender from loss in the event of a default.

(Unit 13 in *Florida Real Estate Principles, Practices & Law*)

The intent to materially misrepresent or omit information on a mortgage loan application to obtain a loan or to obtain a larger loan than would have been obtained if the lender or the borrower had the true facts.

(Unit 13 in *Florida Real Estate Principles, Practices & Law*)

A person or business entity who conducts loan originator activities through one or more licensed mortgage loan originators.

(Unit 13 in *Florida Real Estate Principles, Practices & Law*)

Purchase and sale of U.S. Treasury and federal agency securities.

(Unit 13 in *Florida Real Estate Principles, Practices & Law*)

Exceed the Fannie Mae loan amount.

(Unit 13 in *Florida Real Estate Principles, Practices & Law*)

The mortgage payments are not large enough to cover the interest expense.

(Unit 13 in *Florida Real Estate Principles, Practices & Law*)

A person who solicits mortgage loans, accepts mortgage loan applications, negotiates the terms of new and existing mortgage loans on behalf of a borrower or lender, processes mortgage loan applications, or negotiates the sale of existing mortgage loans to noninstitutional investors for compensation.

(Unit 13 in *Florida Real Estate Principles, Practices & Law*)

Limit the amount the interest rate may increase at any one time, usually a year.

(Unit 13 in *Florida Real Estate Principles, Practices & Law*)

Limit the amount the monthly payments can increase during any adjustment.

(Unit 13 in *Florida Real Estate Principles, Practices & Law*)

The buyer is required to make regular payments smaller than what is required to completely pay off the loan. On the loan's maturity date, a balloon payment is due.

(Unit 13 in *Florida Real Estate Principles, Practices & Law*)

A loan including both real and personal property as security for the debt.

(Unit 13 in *Florida Real Estate Principles, Practices & Law*)

Primary market	Principal	Purchase money mortgage (PMM)	Receivership clause
Reserve requirements	Reverse mortgage	Secondary mortgage market	Special information booklet
Teaser rate	Triggering terms	Truth in Lending Act (TILA)	Up-front mortgage insurance premium (UFMIP)

Allows a receiver to be appointed to collect income from the property to ensure that it is used to make mortgage payments in the event of default.

(Unit 13 in *Florida Real Estate Principles, Practices & Law*)

Any new mortgage accepted by the seller as part of the purchase price.

(Unit 13 in *Florida Real Estate Principles, Practices & Law*)

The unpaid balance of the debt.

(Unit 13 in *Florida Real Estate Principles, Practices & Law*)

A market where securities are created.

(Unit 13 in *Florida Real Estate Principles, Practices & Law*)

A booklet containing consumer information regarding closing costs the borrower may be charged at closing.

(Unit 13 in *Florida Real Estate Principles, Practices & Law*)

An investor market that buys and sells already existing securities.

(Unit 13 in *Florida Real Estate Principles, Practices & Law*)

A type of mortgage that enables elderly homeowners to borrow against the equity in their homes so they can receive monthly payments needed to help meet living expenses.

(Unit 13 in *Florida Real Estate Principles, Practices & Law*)

The amount of funds that an institution must hold in reserve against deposit liabilities.

(Unit 13 in *Florida Real Estate Principles, Practices & Law*)

A one-time mortgage insurance fee paid at closing on FHA mortgage loans.

(Unit 13 in *Florida Real Estate Principles, Practices & Law*)

A federal law that is part of the Consumer Credit Protection Act and implemented by the Federal Reserve Board's Regulation Z. The act ensures that borrowers and customers of consumer credit are given information regarding the cost of credit so that consumers can compare credit terms available.

(Unit 13 in *Florida Real Estate Principles, Practices & Law*)

Certain credit terms or specific financing information included in an advertisement. Triggering terms include the amount or percentage of down payment, number of payments, period (term) of repayment, amount of any payment, and the amount of any finance charges.

(Unit 13 in *Florida Real Estate Principles, Practices & Law*)

A below-market interest rate usually offered for the first year on some adjustable-rate mortgages.

(Unit 13 in *Florida Real Estate Principles, Practices & Law*)

Appraisal	Assemblage	Automated valuation models (AVMs)	Cost
Cost approach	Curable depreciation	Depreciation	Economic life
Effective age	Effective gross income (EGI)	Federally related transaction	Gross income multiplier (GIM)

The amount to produce or acquire something.

(Unit 16 in *Florida Real Estate Principles, Practices & Law* and Units 6–8 in *Florida Real Estate Broker's Guide*)

Data analyses compiled using a computer database of closed sales.

(Unit 16 in *Florida Real Estate Principles, Practices & Law* and Units 6–8 in *Florida Real Estate Broker's Guide*)

The combining of two or more adjoining properties into one tract; the process of consolidating properties.

(Unit 16 in *Florida Real Estate Principles, Practices & Law* and Units 6–8 in *Florida Real Estate Broker's Guide*)

An opinion of value based on supportable evidence and approved methods.

(Unit 16 in *Florida Real Estate Principles, Practices & Law* and Units 6–8 in *Florida Real Estate Broker's Guide*)

The total estimated time in years that an improvement will add value; useful life.

(Unit 16 in *Florida Real Estate Principles, Practices & Law* and Units 6–8 in *Florida Real Estate Broker's Guide*)

Loss in value caused by things such as wear and tear, poor design, or the structure's surroundings (proximity).

(Unit 16 in *Florida Real Estate Principles, Practices & Law* and Units 6–8 in *Florida Real Estate Broker's Guide*)

When a building component has been added or repaired and the owners are able to get their money back in added value.

(Unit 16 in *Florida Real Estate Principles, Practices & Law* and Units 6–8 in *Florida Real Estate Broker's Guide*)

A method for estimating the market value of a property based on the cost to buy the site and to construct a new building on the site, less depreciation.

(Unit 16 in *Florida Real Estate Principles, Practices & Law* and Units 6–8 in *Florida Real Estate Broker's Guide*)

The ratio between a property's gross annual income and its selling price.

(Unit 16 in *Florida Real Estate Principles, Practices & Law* and Units 6–8 in *Florida Real Estate Broker's Guide*)

Any real estate–related financial transaction that a federal financial institution regulatory agency has either contracted for, or regulates, and requires the services of an appraiser.

(Unit 16 in *Florida Real Estate Principles, Practices & Law* and Units 6–8 in *Florida Real Estate Broker's Guide*)

The resulting amount when vacancy and collection losses are subtracted from potential gross income.

(Unit 16 in *Florida Real Estate Principles, Practices & Law* and Units 6–8 in *Florida Real Estate Broker's Guide*)

The age indicated by a structure's condition and utility.

(Unit 16 in *Florida Real Estate Principles, Practices & Law* and Units 6–8 in *Florida Real Estate Broker's Guide*)

Gross living area (GLA)	Gross rent multiplier (GRM)	Highest and best use	Income approach
Incurable depreciation	Investment value	Market value	Net operating income (NOI)
Overimprovement	Plottage	Potential gross income (PGI)	Price

A method for estimating the market value of a property based on the present worth of future income that the property can be expected to generate.

(Unit 16 in *Florida Real Estate Principles, Practices & Law* and Units 6–8 in *Florida Real Estate Broker's Guide*)

The most profitable, legal way that a property can be utilized.

(Unit 16 in *Florida Real Estate Principles, Practices & Law* and Units 6–8 in *Florida Real Estate Broker's Guide*)

The ratio between a property's gross monthly rental income and its selling price.

(Unit 16 in *Florida Real Estate Principles, Practices & Law* and Units 6–8 in *Florida Real Estate Broker's Guide*)

The square footage calculated by taking the exterior dimensions of a house and then subtracting the garage square footage and any other square footage that is not heated.

(Unit 16 in *Florida Real Estate Principles, Practices & Law* and Units 6–8 in *Florida Real Estate Broker's Guide*)

The resulting amount when all operating expenses are subtracted from effective gross income.

(Unit 16 in *Florida Real Estate Principles, Practices & Law* and Units 6–8 in *Florida Real Estate Broker's Guide*)

The most probable price a property will bring in a competitive and open market with the buyer and the seller each acting prudently and knowledgeably, assuming the price is not affected by undue stimulus.

(Unit 16 in *Florida Real Estate Principles, Practices & Law* and Units 6–8 in *Florida Real Estate Broker's Guide*)

The worth of a property to a particular investor based on the investor's desired rate of return and risk tolerance.

(Unit 16 in *Florida Real Estate Principles, Practices & Law* and Units 6–8 in *Florida Real Estate Broker's Guide*)

When a building component has been added or repaired but the owners are unable to get their money back in added value.

(Unit 16 in *Florida Real Estate Principles, Practices & Law* and Units 6–8 in *Florida Real Estate Broker's Guide*)

The amount paid for something.

(Unit 16 in *Florida Real Estate Principles, Practices & Law* and Units 6–8 in *Florida Real Estate Broker's Guide*)

The total annual income a property would produce with 100% occupancy and no collection or vacancy losses.

(Unit 16 in *Florida Real Estate Principles, Practices & Law* and Units 6–8 in *Florida Real Estate Broker's Guide*)

The added value as a result of combining two or more properties into one large parcel.

(Unit 16 in *Florida Real Estate Principles, Practices & Law* and Units 6–8 in *Florida Real Estate Broker's Guide*)

When an owner invests more money in a structure than the owner may reasonably expect to recapture.

(Unit 16 in *Florida Real Estate Principles, Practices & Law* and Units 6–8 in *Florida Real Estate Broker's Guide*)

Principle of substitution	Progression	Purpose of appraisals	Reconciliation
Regression	Replacement cost	Reproduction cost	Sales comparison approach
Subject property	Uniform Standards of Professional Appraisal Practice (USPAP)	Vacancy and collection losses	Value

The process of weighting the estimates of value derived from the sales comparison, cost, and income approaches to arrive at a final estimate of market value; also the process of weighted averaging used in the sales comparison approach to bring the adjusted values of several comparable properties into a single estimate of value.

(Unit 16 in *Florida Real Estate Principles, Practices & Law* and Units 6–8 in *Florida Real Estate Broker's Guide*)

To determine the problem to be solved and the type of value to be estimated.

(Unit 16 in *Florida Real Estate Principles, Practices & Law* and Units 6–8 in *Florida Real Estate Broker's Guide*)

Principle that states the value of an inferior property is enhanced by its association with superior properties of the same type.

(Unit 16 in *Florida Real Estate Principles, Practices & Law* and Units 6–8 in *Florida Real Estate Broker's Guide*)

Principle that states a prudent buyer or investor will pay no more for a property than the cost of acquiring an equally desirable substitute property.

(Unit 16 in *Florida Real Estate Principles, Practices & Law* and Units 6–8 in *Florida Real Estate Broker's Guide*)

A method for estimating the market value of a property by comparing similar properties to the subject property.

(Unit 16 in *Florida Real Estate Principles, Practices & Law* and Units 6–8 in *Florida Real Estate Broker's Guide*)

Amount required to duplicate the property exactly.

(Unit 16 in *Florida Real Estate Principles, Practices & Law* and Units 6–8 in *Florida Real Estate Broker's Guide*)

The amount of money required to replace a structure having the same use and functional utility as the subject property, using modern, available, or updated materials.

(Unit 16 in *Florida Real Estate Principles, Practices & Law* and Units 6–8 in *Florida Real Estate Broker's Guide*)

Principle stating that the value of a superior property is adversely affected by its association with an inferior property of the same type.

(Unit 16 in *Florida Real Estate Principles, Practices & Law* and Units 6–8 in *Florida Real Estate Broker's Guide*)

The worth of something.

(Unit 16 in *Florida Real Estate Principles, Practices & Law* and Units 6–8 in *Florida Real Estate Broker's Guide*)

The expected income loss that will result from occasional turnover of tenants and periodic vacancies as well as the likelihood that not all the rental income will be collected.

(Unit 16 in *Florida Real Estate Principles, Practices & Law* and Units 6–8 in *Florida Real Estate Broker's Guide*)

A set of guidelines (standards of practice) to follow when conducting appraisal services.

(Unit 16 in *Florida Real Estate Principles, Practices & Law* and Units 6–8 in *Florida Real Estate Broker's Guide*)

The property being appraised.

(Unit 16 in *Florida Real Estate Principles, Practices & Law* and Units 6–8 in *Florida Real Estate Broker's Guide*)

Appreciation	Asset	Balance sheet	Basis
Capital gain (loss)	Cash flow (after-tax cash flow)	Current ratio	Discounted cash flow analysis
Equity	Going concern value	Goodwill	Internal rate of return

An investor's initial cost of a property.

(Unit 17 in *Florida Real Estate Principles, Practices & Law* and Units 9 and 15 in *Florida Real Estate Broker's Guide*)

A financial report that shows the company's financial position at a stated moment in time.

(Unit 17 in *Florida Real Estate Principles, Practices & Law* and Units 9 and 15 in *Florida Real Estate Broker's Guide*)

Anything of value.

(Unit 17 in *Florida Real Estate Principles, Practices & Law* and Units 9 and 15 in *Florida Real Estate Broker's Guide*)

An increase in the worth or value of property.

(Unit 17 in *Florida Real Estate Principles, Practices & Law* and Units 9 and 15 in *Florida Real Estate Broker's Guide*)

An investment valuation technique that considers anticipated changes in cash flows over years, projects the current value of net proceeds from the sale of the property in the future, and accounts for the time value of money.

(Unit 17 in *Florida Real Estate Principles, Practices & Law* and Units 9 and 15 in *Florida Real Estate Broker's Guide*)

The measure of the business's ability to meet short-term obligations and is calculated by dividing the business's current assets by its current liabilities.

(Unit 17 in *Florida Real Estate Principles, Practices & Law* and Units 9 and 15 in *Florida Real Estate Broker's Guide*)

The total amount of money generated from an investment after expenses have been paid.

(Unit 17 in *Florida Real Estate Principles, Practices & Law* and Units 9 and 15 in *Florida Real Estate Broker's Guide*)

The difference between the adjusted basis of property and its net selling price.

(Unit 17 in *Florida Real Estate Principles, Practices & Law* and Units 9 and 15 in *Florida Real Estate Broker's Guide*)

The discount rate at which present values of future cash flows equal the down payment.

(Unit 17 in *Florida Real Estate Principles, Practices & Law* and Units 9 and 15 in *Florida Real Estate Broker's Guide*)

The intangible asset attributed to a business's reputation and the expectation of continued customer loyalty.

(Unit 17 in *Florida Real Estate Principles, Practices & Law* and Units 9 and 15 in *Florida Real Estate Broker's Guide*)

The value of an established business property compared with the value of just the physical assets of a business not yet established.

(Unit 17 in *Florida Real Estate Principles, Practices & Law* and Units 9 and 15 in *Florida Real Estate Broker's Guide*)

The property's value minus debt.

(Unit 17 in *Florida Real Estate Principles, Practices & Law* and Units 9 and 15 in *Florida Real Estate Broker's Guide*)

Inventory turnover ratio	Leverage	Liquidation analysis	Liquidity
Net present value (NPV)	Quick ratio	Real estate investment trust (REIT)	Risk
Tax Shelter	Adjusted basis	Ad valorem	Assessed value

The ability to sell an investment quickly, without loss of one's investment.

(Unit 17 in *Florida Real Estate Principles, Practices & Law* and Units 9 and 15 in *Florida Real Estate Broker's Guide*)

The valuation method used for a business that is going out of business.

(Unit 17 in *Florida Real Estate Principles, Practices & Law* and Units 9 and 15 in *Florida Real Estate Broker's Guide*)

The use of borrowed funds to finance the purchase of an asset; the use of another's money to make more money.

(Unit 17 in *Florida Real Estate Principles, Practices & Law* and Units 9 and 15 in *Florida Real Estate Broker's Guide*)

An analysis of a business's management of inventory and is calculated by dividing the cost of goods sold by the ending inventory.

(Unit 17 in *Florida Real Estate Principles, Practices & Law* and Units 9 and 15 in *Florida Real Estate Broker's Guide*)

The chance of losing all or part of an investment.

(Unit 17 in *Florida Real Estate Principles, Practices & Law* and Units 9 and 15 in *Florida Real Estate Broker's Guide*)

Offers investors the opportunity to invest in a pool of income-producing properties under professional management.

(Unit 17 in *Florida Real Estate Principles, Practices & Law* and Units 9 and 15 in *Florida Real Estate Broker's Guide*)

A more conservative measure compared with the current ratio, of the business's ability to meet short-term obligations because it does not include inventory in current assets. Divide current assets (minus inventory) by current liabilities.

Unit 17 in *Florida Real Estate Principles, Practices & Law* and Units 9 and 15 in *Florida Real Estate Broker's Guide*)

The present value of future cash flows (at a discount rate) minus the investor's down payment.

(Unit 17 in *Florida Real Estate Principles, Practices & Law* and Units 9 and 15 in *Florida Real Estate Broker's Guide*)

The value of a property for tax purposes.

(Unit 18 in *Florida Real Estate Principles, Practices & Law* and Unit 14 in *Florida Real Estate Broker's Guide*)

According to the value; in proportion to worth.

(Unit 18 in *Florida Real Estate Principles, Practices & Law* and Unit 14 in *Florida Real Estate Broker's Guide*)

The owner's original cost plus buying expenses and capital improvements.

(Unit 18 in *Florida Real Estate Principles, Practices & Law* and Unit 14 in *Florida Real Estate Broker's Guide*)

An investment that shields income from payment of income taxes.

(Unit 17 in *Florida Real Estate Principles, Practices & Law* and Units 9 and 15 in *Florida Real Estate Broker's Guide*)

Assessment limitation (SOH benefit)	Boot	Capital gain	Debt service
Depreciation	Exempt property	Green Belt Law	Home acquisition loan
Home equity loan	Immune property	Installment sale method	Just value

The amount of money needed to meet the periodic payments of principal and interest on a loan that is being amortized.

(Unit 18 in *Florida Real Estate Principles, Practices & Law* and Unit 14 in *Florida Real Estate Broker's Guide*)

Profit from the sale of property.

(Unit 18 in *Florida Real Estate Principles, Practices & Law* and Unit 14 in *Florida Real Estate Broker's Guide*)

Additional capital or personal property included in a like-kind exchange.

(Unit 18 in *Florida Real Estate Principles, Practices & Law* and Unit 14 in *Florida Real Estate Broker's Guide*)

The accumulated difference between the assessed value and the market value of a homesteaded property due to the annual limit on increases in assessed value.

(Unit 18 in *Florida Real Estate Principles, Practices & Law* and Unit 14 in *Florida Real Estate Broker's Guide*)

A loan used to buy, construct, or improve a residence.

(Unit 18 in *Florida Real Estate Principles, Practices & Law* and Unit 14 in *Florida Real Estate Broker's Guide*)

Legislation designed to protect farmers from having taxes increased just because the land might be in the path of urban growth.

(Unit 18 in *Florida Real Estate Principles, Practices & Law* and Unit 14 in *Florida Real Estate Broker's Guide*)

Property that is excluded from taxation, including property belonging to churches and nonprofit organizations.

(Unit 18 in *Florida Real Estate Principles, Practices & Law* and Unit 14 in *Florida Real Estate Broker's Guide*)

A key deduction when calculating taxable income from investment property because it reduces taxable income without requiring a cash outlay.

(Unit 18 in *Florida Real Estate Principles, Practices & Law* and Unit 14 in *Florida Real Estate Broker's Guide*)

The fair and reasonable value based on objective valuation methods for property tax purposes.

(Unit 18 in *Florida Real Estate Principles, Practices & Law* and Unit 14 in *Florida Real Estate Broker's Guide*)

A way to report gain for income tax purposes as the gain is from the sale of investment property.

(Unit 18 in *Florida Real Estate Principles, Practices & Law* and Unit 14 in *Florida Real Estate Broker's Guide*)

Real property that is owned by a unit of government and is not subject to taxation.

(Unit 18 in *Florida Real Estate Principles, Practices & Law* and Unit 14 in *Florida Real Estate Broker's Guide*)

A second mortgage, allows the borrower to take out a lump sum or to access a line of credit.

(Unit 18 in *Florida Real Estate Principles, Practices & Law* and Unit 14 in *Florida Real Estate Broker's Guide*)

Like-kind exchanges	Long-term capital gain	Mill	Passive income
Short-term capital gain	Special assessments	Taxable income	Taxable value
Tax rate	Buyer's market	Demand	Household

Income derived from rental properties or other trades or businesses in which a taxpayer does not materially participate.

(Unit 18 in *Florida Real Estate Principles, Practices & Law* and Unit 14 in *Florida Real Estate Broker's Guide*)

One one-thousandth of a dollar or one-tenth of a cent.

(Unit 18 in *Florida Real Estate Principles, Practices & Law* and Unit 14 in *Florida Real Estate Broker's Guide*)

A gain on a capital asset that has been held for more than one year, resulting in a more favorable capital gains tax rate.

(Unit 18 in *Florida Real Estate Principles, Practices & Law* and Unit 14 in *Florida Real Estate Broker's Guide*)

Allows investors to defer paying taxes by exchanging real property.

(Unit 18 in *Florida Real Estate Principles, Practices & Law* and Unit 14 in *Florida Real Estate Broker's Guide*)

The nonexempt assessed value that is determined by subtracting the applicable exemptions from the assessed value.

(Unit 18 in *Florida Real Estate Principles, Practices & Law* and Unit 14 in *Florida Real Estate Broker's Guide*)

The amount of income that remains after all applicable deductions and adjustments are applied.

(Unit 18 in *Florida Real Estate Principles, Practices & Law* and Unit 14 in *Florida Real Estate Broker's Guide*)

One-time taxes levied on properties to help pay for a public improvement that benefit the property.

(Unit 18 in *Florida Real Estate Principles, Practices & Law* and Unit 14 in *Florida Real Estate Broker's Guide*)

Profit from the sale of a property that is owned for 12 months or less taxed at the owner's marginal tax rate.

(Unit 18 in *Florida Real Estate Principles, Practices & Law* and Unit 14 in *Florida Real Estate Broker's Guide*)

Any person or group of persons occupying a separate housing space.

(Unit 15 in *Florida Real Estate Principles, Practices & Law*)

The desire and ability to purchase or rent goods and services.

(Unit 15 in *Florida Real Estate Principles, Practices & Law*)

When the supply of available properties exceeds the demand.

(Unit 15 in *Florida Real Estate Principles, Practices & Law*)

The millage rate multiplied by taxable value to determine the annual property taxes due.

(Unit 18 in *Florida Real Estate Principles, Practices & Law* and Unit 14 in *Florida Real Estate Broker's Guide*)

Seller's market	Situs	Supply	Vacancy rate
Arrears	Credit	Debit	Preclosing inspection
Profit	Proration	Title closing	

The percentage of rental units that are not occupied.

(Unit 15 in *Florida Real Estate Principles, Practices & Law*)

The quantity of goods or services offered for sale to consumers.

(Unit 15 in *Florida Real Estate Principles, Practices & Law*)

The relationship and influence created by location of a property that affect value.

(Unit 15 in *Florida Real Estate Principles, Practices & Law*)

When the demand for available properties exceeds the supply.

(Unit 15 in *Florida Real Estate Principles, Practices & Law*)

A final walk-through with the sales associate to verify that repairs have been completed and that the property is left in good condition.

(Unit 14 in *Florida Real Estate Principles, Practices & Law* and Unit 13 in *Florida Real Estate Broker's Guide*)

To be charged for an expense.

(Unit 14 in *Florida Real Estate Principles, Practices & Law* and Unit 13 in *Florida Real Estate Broker's Guide*)

To be reimbursed for an expense.

(Unit 14 in *Florida Real Estate Principles, Practices & Law* and Unit 13 in *Florida Real Estate Broker's Guide*)

Paid at the end of the period for which payment is due.

(Unit 14 in *Florida Real Estate Principles, Practices & Law* and Unit 13 in *Florida Real Estate Broker's Guide*)

The consummation of a real estate transaction, when the seller delivers title to the buyer in exchange for payment from the buyer of the purchase price.

(Unit 14 in *Florida Real Estate Principles, Practices & Law* and Unit 13 in *Florida Real Estate Broker's Guide*)

To divide various debts (charges) and credits between buyer and seller; a proration is a shared expense between the buyer and the seller.

(Unit 14 in *Florida Real Estate Principles, Practices & Law* and Unit 13 in *Florida Real Estate Broker's Guide*)

The amount one makes over and above one's cost.

(Unit 14 in *Florida Real Estate Principles, Practices & Law* and Unit 13 in *Florida Real Estate Broker's Guide*)

Notes

Notes

Notes

Notes

Notes

Notes